The

Revelation

of

Jesus

Scriptural references are taken from the New International Version unless otherwise noted.

ISBN 0-945383-36-3

Wake Up America Seminars, Inc.
P.O. Box 273
Bellbrook, Ohio 45305
(513) 848-3322

Larry Wilson

Second Edition

Printed By

TEACH Services
Donivan Road
Route 1, Box 182
Brushton, New York 12916

The Revelation of Jesus
26 Bible Studies On Coming Events

Acknowledgements

To those preparing for the immediate return of Jesus, this book is dedicated.

Deepest appreciation is due my faithful wife of 22 years who took full time employment so I could write this book, and after it was completed, she sacrificed a very secure position so that she might help promote this wonderful message.

Special thanks is also due to many precious friends who make this ministry a reality. I must mention a few: Jan and Shelley Betts have been faithful companions in this ministry for several years. No job has been too hard, nor any trip too long. If I could bestow sainthood, I'd start with them. Marty Purvis, CPA, has unselfishly spent many hours keeping our business matters in proper order. Were it not for Marty's efforts and wisdom, the business end of our operation would suffer. If I could bestow golden crowns, I'd start with him. Suzy Gray gave many hours to correcting my typing in this volume. If you find a typo, it is because I added a few more words here and there after she fixed everything. If I could bestow harps, I'd start with her, for she always radiates a sweet spirit and encouragement. I could go on and on for many have generously given this ministry a very high priority in their daily activities and prayers. I have this joyful consolation: Jesus knows who did what and He will soon reward accordingly.

Preface

Wake Up America Seminars, Inc. is a non-profit, non-denominational organization dedicated to the purpose of spreading the wonderful gospel of Jesus Christ. Because the apocalyptic prophecies of Daniel and Revelation are about to be fulfilled, the words of the Apostle Paul particularly apply to our generation. He said, **"...The hour has come for you to wake up from your slumber, because our salvation is nearer now than when we first believed. The night is nearly over; the day is almost here. So let us put aside the deeds of darkness and put on the armor of light."** (Romans 13:11,12)

Is it possible to tell if the present generation will be the last generation to live on earth? Can rational people assert that the coming of Jesus is near when people have been repeating this message for almost 2,000 years? What evidence proves that Jesus will soon return?

These are fair and reasonable questions. And there are two good answers. First, the apocalyptic prophecies of Daniel and Revelation and certain historical events combine to provide reasonable evidence that Jesus is about to return. Unlike other types of prophecies, apocalyptic sequences have a beginning point and an ending point. Apocalyptic sequences also contain events that allow us to mark the passage of time as they are fulfilled. By understanding the sequences and identifying those parts that have been fulfilled, we can reasonably determine our chronological position within God's great time clock.

Secondly, the very number of people currently living on our planet indicates horrific troubles are ahead. And, at the current rate of growth, another five billion people will swell the human race within 30 years! Will there be enough food, shelter and resources for everyone? Can earth's limited ecosystem sustain life for 10+ billion people?

Preparation for the second coming is all important. It is not enough to believe that Jesus is returning to earth, for the devil knows this to be true. It is not enough to understand the prophecies, for the devil understands the prophecies too. It is not enough to belong to some church, for the devil has infiltrated all the religious systems in the world. Preparation for the second coming is only obtained by receiving Jesus Christ as Lord of your life. This means following the teachings of Jesus, and this requires a lot of faith. Study your Bible, pray for understanding, share the things Jesus reveals to you, love the Lord with all your heart, mind and soul and your neighbor as yourself and you will grow in grace – **"attaining to the whole measure of the fullness of Christ."** (Ephesians 4:13)

This second edition contains many updates and corrections because my understanding of the gospel continues to unfold! Indeed, truth is eternal and everlasting. It is my comprehension of it that continues to grow. So, if this volume brings hope and salvation to just one person, my joy will be great.

Larry Wilson

July 1992

Chapter 1

New Truth in an Old Book?

The Bible contains many prophecies. What do you think this one means? **"For you know very well that the day of the Lord will come like a thief in the night. While people are saying, 'Peace and safety,' destruction will come on them suddenly, as labor pains on a pregnant woman, and they will not escape."** (1 Thessalonians 5:2,3) What is the Apostle Paul talking about? When does this destruction happen? Who receives this destruction? How wide-spread is this destruction? What causes this destruction?

This prophecy is not isolated from other prophecies in the Bible. In fact, other prophecies of the Bible collaborate with this statement by Paul to reveal the answer! The Bible not only predicts coming events, it also provides the means to understand how the prophecies will be fulfilled. A new mechanism has been discovered that allows us to see how all end-time prophecies fit together in a harmonious way. Thus, the prophecy of Paul compliments other end-time prophecies found throughout the Bible.

No book in the Bible holds more information about last day events than the book of Revelation. This book contains an extraordinary story that will involve all 5.4 billion people on earth in just a few months. Even though most people don't understand what the Bible has to say about the imminent future, this is about to change. God has decreed that the gospel will go to every person before the end shall come. See Matthew 24:14.

Most scholars recognize that Revelation has an Old Testament partner in the book of Daniel. These two books combine together to produce some very shocking predictions. Consider these:

1. Four *global* earthquakes are going to happen. It appears that the first of these will happen sometime around 1994. These earthquakes have no historical comparison — such will be their magnitude and coverage of earth.
2. The first earthquake will be followed by a series of enormous wild-fires around the world. These fires will be ignited by meteoric showers of burning hail. This may be caused as a result of earth passing through a dense region of an asteroid belt.
3. After the showers of burning hail, a great asteroid is going to impact one of earth's oceans. The resulting

tidal wave will sink many ships and destroy a large number of people who live in cities along the coasts of that body of water.

4. Then, a great asteroid is going to impact the land mass of one of earth's continents. The ground waves that follow the impact will sheer water-wells and septic systems. Even worse, buried waste will leach into underground streams. As a result, some of the aquifers deep in the earth will become contaminated and a large number of people will die as a result of drinking the water.

5. Then, darkness is going to cover a large portion of the earth. Perhaps the darkness will come from a chain of powerful volcanic eruptions on the Pacific rim. Millions of tons of ejecta could be blown into the heavens, and as a result, the sun, moon and stars will not be visible over a third of the earth. The darkness will remain for some time. As a result, many crops will die and famine will come to all nations.

6. Rain will stop falling in some areas. Drinking water for man and beast will simply disappear.

7. In response to these calamities, democratic constitutions will be set aside and martial law will be implemented. A great spiritual awakening will follow. The authority and wrath of Almighty God will become a household topic. Religious and political leaders will unite to seek ways of stopping the judgments of God.

As a result of these calamities, each nation will experience a serious revolution. Laws regarding the establishment of religion will be implemented in every nation, for the consuming issue in every land will be, "How do we appease God so that His awful judgments will stop?"

8. More than 1.4 billion people are going to die in these horrific judgments.

9. Economic chaos will accompany these global tragedies. As a result, rationing will be implemented overnight. Life as we now know it on our planet will change suddenly, and for most, these coming events are unexpected.

10. These horrific events will strangely unite people. The basis of the coming union will be shared grief: losses of family, friends and possessions. As the dust settles and day to day existence begins, all will ask, "Why have these things happened? Why has God done this?" Then the truth will be heard. People will widely agree that God's wrath has been exercised because His patience with our sinful ways has been exhausted.

11. Then comes the most amazing event that the world has ever witnessed. Out of nowhere, a glowing and radiant being will appear. He will appear in different cities and places around the world. He will claim to be "God Incarnate." He will perform wonderful miracles and to prove his divinity, he will even call fire down

out of heaven before large numbers of spellbound observers. He will claim that he has come to save the world. He will claim responsibility for sending the judgments upon earth because we reached an intolerable level of wickedness. And who can disagree?

His purpose, he will claim, is to establish a new world order of righteousness, a government of peace and light. However, he will insist, the prerequisites are global repentance and reformation. Many Jews will receive this glorious being as Messiah. Many Protestants and Catholics will unite, believing this is none less than Jesus Christ Himself. Many Moslems will receive this being as the "Promised One" who is to restore their sovereignty. Many atheists will, on the basis of undeniable miracles, confess that this is God. Eastern mystical religions will claim that this being is a true manifestation of God. And the heathen, who have no formal knowledge of God, will recognize the superiority of this being over all gods. In short, much of the world will receive this glorious being as God.

12. Capture the scene in your mind: In just a few months, the world's infrastructures will be destroyed by horrific judgments. The question of survival will be foremost in every mind. Grief, disease, famine, physical suffering and mental anguish will be everywhere. Billions of people will have no hope. Everyone will need a savior — and right before our eyes will be one claiming that he is God. And, he will have spectacular powers to perform miracles and do great wonders.

13. But the Bible says that this being is a fallen angel, the devil, the ancient adversary of God, who is allowed to impersonate God for a short time. Paul calls him the *man of sin*. (2 Thessalonians 2)

14. As the devil gains millions and millions of followers, he also gains control. His objective is to capture the world and force all of its inhabitants to worship at his feet as though he was God. The Bible predicts that the devil will be successful in his bid for world dominion. His conquest will far exceed the grasp of Hitler. And like Hitler, the Bible also predicts that the devil will lead many to eternal destruction.

New and improved?

These are just a few of the predictions that are soon to be fulfilled. But all of these predictions, and many more, can only be found in the Bible by using new technology. This new technology is very powerful and interesting to use. It is also quite simple if you correctly understand a few things first. The new technology is not an electronic gizmo, for technology is not limited to tangible inventions; rather, it is a new process of prophetic interpretation.

The new technology consistently builds upon events that qualify as prophetic fulfillments in the past as well as predictions about the future. Even more, this new technology allows people from all walks of life to reach *similar* prophetic conclusions without collaboration. This is not to say that every student of prophecy will reach identical conclusions; but they will reach similar conclusions if they follow these rules. This means that for the first time, people can now understand the essential prophecies of the Bible *for themselves.*

For the purpose of introduction, this new process of interpretation is revealed in three laws governing prophetic interpretation. Even though the reader may not understand the necessity and purpose of these laws, a brief introduction now will prove useful later on in this volume. The laws governing the interpretation of apocalyptic prophecies appear to be:

1. **All apocalyptic prophecies are identified by the presence of both, a beginning and ending point in time, and elements within each prophecy are given in chronological order.**

2. **A fulfillment of apocalyptic prophecy, or progression towards fulfillment, only occurs when all specifications of the prophecy or its element are met — including chronological order.**

3. **Symbols can only be interpreted with relevant scripture.**

A key word must be understood. These rules only apply to apocalyptic prophecy. The word *apocalyptic* comes from the word apocalypse which refers to prophecies in Revelation and Daniel. According to Webster, an apocalypse is a divine revelation of something very important. For this reason, the book of Revelation is often called, "The Apocalypse." Many people think it is a divine revelation of something important, but what does it say? How do we solve its mystery?

Whether the subject is mathematics, genetic research or Bible prophecy, rules are necessary to solve the unknown. In fact, the fundamental purpose of cancer research is to discover the rules by which cancer operates. The same is true in math. For example, we can only solve the problem, $3x = 6$, by using rules that allow us to manipulate the equation. In this case, x equals 2. The important point here is that the unknown can become known only by using rules.

A rule in Bible prophecy is like a rule in mathematics. A rule is something that is always true. The interesting thing about rules is that human beings cannot make them up. We can only discover rules. In other words, Sir Isaac Newton did not make up the rule of gravity. He discovered the rule and wrote down an equation expressing how the rule operates. The same is true of apocalyptic prophecy. We cannot make up the rules of interpretation. We can only discover the rules, and then we can express the result of applying the rules to the texts at hand. The end result is called an interpretation.

Rules of interpretation are indispensable to prophetic study. Here's why. If we have no consistent method of explaining prophecies from the past, we cannot consistently explain prophecies about the future. Therefore, we have to *first* demonstrate that the rules work on those portions of prophecy that have been historically fulfilled before we can apply the rules to those portions of prophecy that are yet future. More will be said about these matters later on.

Understand for yourself

Because we live at a time when knowledge is increasing so fast, it is almost impossible to keep up with discoveries in any single field. Some say that the half-life of knowledge today is approximately six years. This means that if you knew everything that is known today, in six years, you would only know half of what will be known.

Because the growth of knowledge has been so explosive this century, we have seen the rise of specialists in every field of study. Lawyers specialize in insurance claims, criminal law, constitutional law, corporate law and a host of other fields. Physicians specialize in cardiology, pulmonary functions, urology, pediatrics, endocrinology and many other specialties. When it comes to the study of the Bible, we also find a large number of specialists. To name a few,

there are Old Testament and New Testament scholars, Hebrew and Greek scholars, Pauline and Church history scholars. And yes, there are prophecy scholars too, for specializations never end.

Here is a pestiferous problem. It seems that no two scholars of prophecy agree. Everyone is saying something different. The biggest reason there is so much disagreement on prophecy is that few expositors consistently follow rules of interpretation. Because rules of interpretation are not written down in the Bible, they can only be discovered through careful Bible study. Understand that the study of prophecy is made up of two parts: one part history and one part future-solving. The history part requires matching historical events with predictions to demonstrate a fulfillment. The future-solving part refers to applying the rules of interpretation so that we might know what the next prophetic event will be.

Generally speaking, the public is dubious about prophecy scholars, and rightly so. Too many "prophecy experts" reveal their predictions as a scene of interest develops. If they truly were experts at prophecy, shouldn't they be able to predict *today* what newspapers will eventually print? After all, the Bible has been around for thousands of years!

For example, when the U.S. led coalition of 28 nations prepared for war on Iraq during 1990, a number of "prophecy experts" showed up on TV and radio talk shows. One radio commentator noticing this phenomenon said, "Every time there is a national emergency, apocalypse people crawl out of the woodwork." So, the question is valid: "If the Iraqi war of 1991 was a prophetic fulfillment, shouldn't prophecy scholars have predicted the war, the participants and its outcome a few years before it happened?"

Future telling always intrigues people. In 1991, a special TV show featured a 16th century French astrologer named Michel de Notredame (Nostradamus). The program attempted to verify that Nostradamus was a genuine future-teller by comparing some of his predictions with so-called fulfillments today. However, the more ambiguous the prediction, the weaker the veracity of fulfillment. Nostradamus was not a seer – no matter how convincingly TV may portray him. Like Nostradamus though, the future continues to play on our minds. What does the future hold? And, as economic circumstances grow more desperate, the question becomes more intense.

Become serious about Bible study

Most people dismiss the importance of prophetic Bible study for three reasons. First, the study of prophecy is complicated. And who has time for more complications these days? Secondly, we can't do anything about past fulfillments anyway. What happened in the past doesn't seem relevant right now. And lastly, the whole subject is slippery. No "future-teller" can prove that his conclusions about the future are true,

for it is impossible to prove something that hasn't happened. So, why get serious about studying Bible prophecy? Here is one reason:

Like a gold mine, the Bible contains very valuable, but hidden treasure. All down through the ages, the Holy Spirit has led men and women to discover precious truths hidden within the Bible. Each new discovery has lifted the saving power of Jesus Christ to a new height. The Bible tells us of our origin, our purpose and our destiny. The Bible tells us that man needs God – God does not need man. The Bible tells us that God loves man – and man rarely loves God. And lastly, the Bible tells us that this world and its problems are not going to last indefinitely. There is an end. Jesus is coming back to gather His people. And when every means of earthly support is taken away from mankind during the great tribulation, people will want some serious answers about God. And the answers will have to come from the Bible. This is why Bible study, especially prophetic study is so necessary at this time.

The new technology reveals that the end is almost here. When the world is turned upside down by calamities, and when the terrible predictions of Revelation commence, the opinions of scholars will avail us nothing. We must know for ourselves what the Bible says. This is why I've written this book. I want to help people understand the meaning of Bible prophecy for themselves. If salvation is a personal experience in trusting Jesus, then a study of His Word requires the same.

Chapter 2

The Purpose of Bible Prophecy

Introduction

Bible prophecy is a very broad and comprehensive subject. Those who study prophetic things study the deep things of God. Many people regard the Bible as "the Good Book" because the Bible promotes nobility, generosity and righteousness—all those good qualities that bring happiness and joy. But the Bible is much more than a "Good Book"! The Bible exists for the ultimate purpose of revealing what God is like! The Bible not only tells us what our Creator wants of us, but it also tells us what His plans are and why! If we know what He is like, and we know what He wants, then we can make an informed decision whether or not we want to love Him.

God gave prophecy so that we might trust in Him. He says, "...I am God, and there is no other; I am God, and there is none like me. I make known the end from the beginning, from ancient times, what is still to come.... What I have said, that will I bring about; what I have planned, that will I do." (Isaiah 46:9-11) Jesus told His disciples, "I am telling you now before it happens, so that when it does happen you will believe that I am He." (John 13:19)

Prophecy is a very important component in the plan of salvation. The Bible teaches that salvation comes by faith in Jesus — but how can we have faith in someone we haven't seen? How can we love someone we don't know? God does not ask us to place our faith in Him without first giving us reasonable evidence. Prophecy is a prediction of what God said He would do, and history is a confirmation of what He has done. Thus, prophecy is a light that shines into the dark uncertainty of tomorrow. When rightly understood, prophecy demonstrates and explains the character of God. Peter said, "And we have the word of the prophets made more certain, and you will do well to pay attention to it, as to a light shining in a dark place, until the day dawns and the morning star rises in your hearts. Above all, you must understand that no prophecy of Scripture came about by the prophet's own interpretation. For prophecy never had its origin in the will of man, but men spoke from God as they were carried along by the Holy Spirit." (2 Peter 1:19-21)

Prophecy also serves an important secondary purpose. It serves as a road map for students of the Bible. By understanding what God is going to do, students of God's Word know when and how to prepare! They know what to look for. For example, God told Noah to build an ark because He was going to destroy the world with a flood. Noah obeyed. He built an ark and saved his family.

Truth decay

Spirituality has decayed in America for the same reason it decayed in ancient Israel. We have forgotten God just as Israel did. Notice the parallels in modern America with Hosea's day. Hosea said, **"Hear the word of the Lord, you Israelites, because the Lord has a charge to bring against you who live in the land. 'There is no faithfulness, no love, no acknowledgement of God in the land. There is only cursing, lying and murder, stealing and adultery; they break all bounds, and bloodshed follows bloodshed'.... My people are destroyed from lack of knowledge... but they do not realize that I remember all their evil deeds. Their sins engulf them; they are always before me.... The days of punishment are coming, the days of reckoning are at hand. Let Israel know this. Because your sins are so many and your hostility so great, the prophet is considered a fool, the inspired man a maniac.... (My people) make many promises, take false oaths and make agreements; therefore lawsuits spring up like poisonous weeds in a plowed field."** Selections from Hosea, Chapters 4-10.

When people lose sight of God, the quality of life deteriorates quickly. The evidence is all about us. "...If I were called upon to identify the principal trait of the entire 20th century, I would be unable to find

anything more precise than to reflect once again on how we have lost touch with our Creator. Men have forgotten God." Aleksandr Solzhenitsyn, *Reader's Digest,* September, 1986.

Scoffers, famines, war and earthquakes

According to the Bible, what will be the signs of the end of the world?

"First of all, you must understand that in the last days scoffers will come, scoffing and following their own evil desires. They will say, 'Where is this coming he promised? Ever since our fathers died, everything goes on as it has since the beginning of creation.' " (2 Peter 3:3,4) These verses deal with a certain amount of justified skepticism. Christians have been saying for almost 2,000 years that Jesus is coming *soon* and He hasn't come yet. So, how can they go on saying such things and appear rational? What evidence proves that Jesus is *soon* to come? Doesn't the passage of millenniums indicate the continuation of millenniums?

"Jesus answered: 'Watch out that no one deceives you. For many will come in my name, claiming, 'I am the Christ,' and will deceive many. You will hear of wars and rumors of wars, but see to it that you are not alarmed. Such things must happen, but the end is still to come. Nation will rise against nation, and kingdom against kingdom. There will be famines and earthquakes in various places. All these are the beginning of birth pains.' " (Matthew 24:4-8) The careful reader will notice that wars, rumors of wars, famines and earthquakes must happen, but the end is still to come. So again we must ask ourselves, how can we know if we are living at the end of the world?

Horrible people

Paul told Timothy, "**But mark this: There will be terrible times in the last days. People will be lovers of themselves, lovers of money, boastful, proud, abusive, disobedient to their parents, ungrateful, unholy, without love, unforgiving, slanderous, without self-control, brutal, not lovers of the good, treacherous, rash, conceited, lovers of pleasure rather than lovers of God - having a form of godliness but denying its power. Have nothing to do with them.**" (2 Timothy 3:1-5) Sounds like Paul just read today's newspaper doesn't it? Are people becoming better or worse? What do you think?

Count on persecution

Those who believe in and hope for the imminent return of Jesus will receive some ridicule. Paul wisely warned Timothy saying, "**...everyone who wants to live a godly life in Christ Jesus will be persecuted.**" (2 Timothy 3:12)

Jesus warned His disciples that religious leaders are often hard-hearted. They can't deal with advancing truth. He predicted, "**They will put you out of the synagogue; in fact, a time is coming when anyone who kills you will think he is offering a service to God.**" (John 16:2) But, insists Jesus, "**Blessed are you when people insult you, persecute you and falsely say all kinds of evil against you because of me. Rejoice and be glad, because great is your reward**

in heaven, for in the same way they persecuted the prophets who were before you." (Matthew 5:11,12)

Because the most of the world does not know the Father, because the love of God is not widespread, we face perilous times. Paul draws a detailed picture of people living in the last days saying, "**They have become filled with every kind of wickedness, evil, greed and depravity. They are full of envy, murder, strife, deceit and malice. They are gossips, slanderers, God-haters, insolent, arrogant and boastful; they invent ways of doing evil; they disobey their parents; they are senseless, faithless, heartless, ruthless. Although they know God's righteous decree that those who do such things deserve death, they not only continue to do these very things but also approve of those who practice them.**" (Romans 1:29-32)

Having ears that hear

There is more to understanding prophecy than meets the eye. To the casual reader, the Bible can be made to appear inconsistent and contradictory. However, those who diligently search the Scriptures with an open mind will find great beauty and harmony within, for the Bible offers a harmonious message. It may have 40+ writers, but it has one Author. The biggest problem we face with Bible study is that some things have to be believed before they can be understood, and other things have to be understood before they can be believed. Every serious Bible student knows that some answers are a long time in coming. But, in the end, we know that faith and truth always meet. For this reason, we must be willing to do some possibility thinking in order to find right answers.

Jesus said to the Pharisees, **"He who belongs to God hears what God says. The reason you do not hear is that you do not belong to God."** (John 8:47) In Revelation 2 and 3, Jesus says seven times, **"He that has an ear to hear, let him hear what the Spirit says to the churches."** This phrase means that those who listen for the voice of God will hear and understand what the Holy Spirit says!

But, some people don't want to hear the Word of God. Jesus said, **"Everyone who does evil hates the light, and will not come into the light for fear that his deeds will be exposed. But whosoever lives by the truth comes into the light, so that it may be seen plainly that what he has done has been done through God."** (John 3:20,21)

The Apostle Paul said, **"The man without the Spirit does not accept the things that come from the Spirit of God, for they are foolishness to him, and he cannot understand them, because they are spiritually discerned."** (1 Corinthians 2:14) Even more, Daniel says of the last days, **"Many will be purified, made spotless and refined, but the wicked will continue to be wicked. None of the wicked will understand, but those who are wise will understand."** (Daniel 12:10)

The point here is that there is complete harmony between the operation of the Holy Spirit and truth as contained in the Bible. If there is some part of the Bible you do not understand, you are part of a great host of honorable men and women. No person can know everything in the Bible. Like God's love, the Bible is too broad, too deep and too large to fully understand. But, God requires a willing attitude to understand His truth so that we can mature in spiritual matters. See Hebrews 5:11-6:1.

The gift of prophecy

The ability to prophesy is a spiritual gift that comes from the Holy Spirit (1 Corinthians 12:28). Prophetic understanding is also a gift we should eagerly desire. Paul wrote to the church in Corinth, **"Follow the way of love and eagerly desire spiritual gifts, especially the gift of prophecy."** Why should we desire the gift of prophecy? **"Everyone who prophesies speaks to men for their strengthening, encouragement and comfort."** (1 Corinthians 14:1,3) So, Prophecy is much more than future-telling. Think about it. Suppose you knew what the future held. What would that knowledge do for you? Would you be dedicated to encouraging others to prepare for coming events? Would you suffer the reproach of family and friends if need be to proclaim an unpopular message? If there is anything that Bible history teaches, it is this: the life of a prophet is usually difficult and spartan, and most often, it ends in an untimely death. See Matthew 23:37.

False prophets

The Bible indicates that every future-teller is not a true prophet. "**Dear friends, do not believe every spirit, but test the spirits to see whether they are from God, because many false prophets have gone out into the world.**" (1 John 4:1) Jesus warned His disciples, "**For false Christs and false prophets will appear and perform great signs and miracles to deceive even the elect - if that were possible.**" (Matthew 24:24) So, if a great sign or miracle is not proof of truth or a true prophet, what is? The bottom line has to do with obeying God's Word. If a prophet encourages you to disobey the plain commands of God, you can be sure that he is not of God. "**This is love for God: to obey his commands. And his commands are not burdensome.**" (1 John 5:3)

Test the prophets

How do we test the prophets to determine if they are true or false? Moses told the children of Israel, "**If a prophet or one who foretells by dreams, appears among you and announces to you a miraculous sign or wonder, and if the sign or wonder of which he has spoken takes place, and he says 'Let us follow other gods and let us worship them,' you must not listen to the words of that prophet or dreamer. The Lord your God is testing you to find out whether you love him with all your heart and with all your soul. It is the Lord your God that you must follow, and him you must revere. Keep his commands and obey him; serve him and hold fast to him. That prophet or dreamer must be put to death, because he preached rebellion against the Lord your God, who brought you out of Egypt and redeemed you from the land of slavery; he has tried to turn you from the way the Lord your God commanded you to follow.**" (Deuteronomy 13:1-5)

Wrong conclusions and sad consequences

If we use faulty methods or faulty rules of interpretation, we will produce faulty conclusions. Study the following prophecy given by Malachi and notice how it was interpreted by the experts in Jesus' day. Even more, observe the outcome.

Malachi predicted

"**See, I will send you the prophet Elijah before that great and dreadful day of the Lord comes. He will turn the hearts of the fathers to their children, and the hearts of the children to their fathers; or else I will come and strike the land with a curse.**" (Malachi 4:5,6)

Malachi's prophecy was given about 350 years before Jesus was born. The Jews interpreted this prophecy to mean that Elijah would *personally* come down from heaven and introduce the Messiah when He arrived! (Elijah was taken to heaven in a whirlwind some 500 years before Malachi wrote these words. See 2 Kings 2:11.) This prophecy demonstrates two interesting points:

First

According to Luke 3:1,15, the Jews anticipated the arrival of Messiah during the 15th year of Tiberius Caesar. The Jews were not alone! Even the Samaritans anticipated the coming of Messiah! See John 4:25. Israel was in expectation that year because Daniel had prophesied that Messiah would appear at the beginning of the 70th week! (This prophecy from Daniel will be studied later.)

Adding to the expectation of the people, there was a strange, but powerful man that many recognized as a prophet. In A.D. 27, John the Baptist was preaching and baptizing down by the Jordan River. People went out to hear him for he spoke with unusual power. His message cut through the facade of cultural religiosity and people were "pricked in the hearts" because of their sins. There was something different about John the Baptist, and as his popularity grew, so did the jealousy of the religious leaders in Jerusalem.

One day the *Religious Affairs Department* in Jerusalem sent priests out to the Jordan River to question this man that was causing such interest. Their first question to John was, "Are you Messiah?" John answered, "No." Then they asked if he was Elijah. Again, John answered, "No." Then they asked if he was the prophet that Moses had predicted. (See Deuteronomy 18:15.) John again said, "No." Then in desperation, they asked, "Who are you?" John answered by quoting from Isaiah 40:3, saying, **"I am the voice of one calling in the desert, 'Make straight the way for the Lord.' "** (John 1:23)

Satisfied that John the Baptist was neither the Messiah, Elijah nor the prophet predicted by Moses, the priests returned to Jerusalem with their report. The problem with this investigation of John is

that the Jewish leaders later refused to accept Jesus as the Messiah *because* Elijah had not descended from heaven to herald the arrival of Messiah as predicted by Malachi! In other words, prophecy did not unfold as the way they thought it should. Therefore, Jesus could not be the Messiah. Look again at the prophecy of Malachi. Would you have doubted that Jesus was indeed the Messiah if Elijah had not appeared?

Second

The second point is that accurate prophetic conclusions can only be reached through the combined harmony of the scriptures and the Holy Spirit. After Peter, James and John saw Jesus visit with Elijah and Moses on the Mount of Transfiguration, they came to Jesus and asked about the prophetic argument which the Pharisees used against Jesus. They asked, **"Why then do the teachers of the law say that Elijah must come first?"** (Matthew 17:10) Jesus responded, **" 'To be sure, Elijah comes and will restore all things. But I tell you, Elijah has already come, and they did not recognize him, but have done to him everything they wished. In the same way the Son of Man is going to suffer at their hands.' Then the disciples understood that he was talking to them about John the Baptist."** (Matthew 17:11-13)

Was John the Baptist the promised Elijah? The answer is both yes and no. No, John the Baptist was not the physical person of Elijah for John was born of Zechariah and Elizabeth. But yes, John the Baptist was a *type* of Elijah. Notice what the angel said to John's father, Zechariah, before John was born, **"And he will go before the Lord, in the spirit and power of Elijah, to turn the hearts of the fathers to their children and the disobedient to the wisdom of the righteous - to make ready a people prepared for the Lord."** (Luke 1:17)

Jesus applies the prophecy

Jesus clearly understood the importance of John's work. He said, **"Among those born of women there has not risen anyone greater than John the Baptist; yet he who is least in the kingdom of heaven is greater than he. ...And if you are willing to accept it, he is the Elijah who was to come. He who has ears, let him hear."** (Matthew 11:11,14)

There's that phrase again, "He who has ears, let him hear." Notice that Jesus said, "...if you are willing to accept it, he (John the Baptist) is the Elijah who was to come." In other words, the prophecy of Malachi was not fulfilled by John the Baptist. This is why Jesus said, "...if you are willing to accept it, he is the Elijah who was to come." In other words, the fulfillment of the prophecy is still to come. But, John the Baptist was a representative of those who will "prepare the way of the Lord" when the time of the great and dreadful day of the Lord arrives. God's messengers at the end-time will go forth in the spirit and power of Elijah to announce the coming of Messiah just like John the Baptist did! Understand that the prophecy of Malachi still awaits fulfillment. (Review rule 2 on page 4.)

The prophets speak

When is the "great and dreadful day of the Lord" spoken of by Malachi? Notice what a number of Bible writers say about that great and awesome day:

Amos says, **"Woe to you who long for the day of the Lord! Why do you long for the day of the Lord? That day will be darkness, not light. It will be as though a man fled from a lion only to meet a bear, as though he entered his house and rested his hand on the wall only to have a snake bite him?"** (Amos 5:18-19)

Isaiah says, **"See, the day of the Lord is coming - a cruel day, with wrath and fierce anger - to make the land desolate and destroy the sinners within it. The stars of heaven and their constellations will not show their light. The rising sun will be darkened and the moon will not give its light. I will punish the world for its evil, the wicked for their sins. I will put an end to the arrogance of the haughty and will humble the pride of the ruthless."** (Isaiah 13:9-11)

Ezekiel says, **"For the day is near, the day of the Lord is near - a day of clouds, a time of doom for the nations."** (Ezekiel 30:3)

Joel says, **"Alas for that day! For the day of the Lord is near; it will come like destruction from the Almighty. The Lord thunders at the head of his army; his forces are beyond number, and mighty are those who obey his command. The day of the Lord is great; it is dreadful. Who can endure it? The sun will be turned to darkness and the moon to blood before the coming of the great and dreadful day of the Lord."** (Joel 1:15, 2:11,31)

Obadiah says, "The day of the Lord is near for all nations. As you have done, it will be done to you; your deeds will return upon your own head." (Obadiah 1:15)

Zephaniah says, "The great day of the Lord is near - near and coming quickly. Listen! The cry on the day of the Lord will be bitter, the shouting of the warrior there." (Zephaniah 1:14)

Peter says, "But the day of the Lord will come like a thief. The heavens will disappear with a roar; the elements will be destroyed by fire, and the earth and everything in it will be laid bare." (2 Peter 3:10)

A number of scriptures clearly point to the second coming of Jesus as the predicted great and dreadful day of the Lord! Notice what John says of the great and dreadful day of our Lord's wrath. "I watched as he opened the sixth seal. There was a great earthquake. The sun turned black like sackcloth made of goat hair, the whole moon turned blood red, and the stars in the sky fell to earth, as late figs drop from a fig tree when shaken by a strong wind. The sky receded like a scroll, rolling up, and every mountain and island was removed from its place. Then the kings of the earth, the princes, the generals, the rich, the mighty and every slave and every free man hid in caves and among the rocks of the mountains. They called to the mountains and the rocks, 'Fall on us and hide us from the face of him who sits on the throne and from the wrath of the Lamb! For the great day of their wrath has come, and who can stand?' " (Revelation 6:12-17)

The weight of evidence clearly shows that the great day of the Lord is yet future and so is the promise of Elijah because the prophecy of Malachi has to do with the great day of the Lord. One more point must be made. Because Jesus described the work of John as that of Elijah, we can anticipate that those who fulfill this prophecy will be to the second advent what John was to the first.

Five types of prophecy

The Bible presents a minimum of five distinct types of prophecy. These include:

1. Messianic prophecies

These prophecies specifically relate to the person of Jesus in either His first or second coming. Two excellent examples of Messianic prophecy are found in Isaiah 53 and Psalm 22.

2. Judaic prophecies

These prophecies relate to promises of prosperity or destruction for Israel. These prophecies have conditional elements in them most of the time. A good example of this type of prophecy is found in Deuteronomy 28. Judaic prophecies contain important object lessons and principles for all generations of people, for God's beneficent relationship with man is clearly revealed in these prophecies.

3. Day of the Lord prophecies

These prophecies are scattered throughout Scripture and relate to the vindication of God and/or His people. Elements within these prophecies are often general enough that they can have parallel applications at different times. Ultimately, these prophecies predict the triumph of God and/or the vindication of His people in a contemporary setting. For example, Isaiah 24 and Ezekiel 7 contain parallels between the final days of Israel and the final days of earth's history. Sometimes, "Day of the Lord" prophecies have conditional elements embedded in them if they are given as a warning.

Matthew 24 is a "Day of the Lord" prophecy. The prophecy concerning the end of Jerusalem in A.D. 70 and the end of the world are mingled together because there are ominous parallels between them.

4. Local prophecies

Local prophecies apply to specific people, places and times. For example, the prophecy concerning Nineveh was a local prophecy. Local prophecies usually require a "local prophet" or messenger to explain or proclaim the prophecy. In the case of Nineveh, Jonah was the local prophet. John the Baptist was a local prophet. His message was directly connected to the first advent of Christ. However, it is also fair to say that certain principles of John's message are applicable today as we approach the second advent of Christ.

5. Apocalyptic prophecies

Apocalyptic prophecy is defined as structural prophecy; that is, prophecy that outlines a specific sequence of events. An apocalyptic sequence is identified by having a beginning and an ending point in time. Both the fulfillment and sequence of apocalyptic prophecy are unconditional. A clear example of this type prophecy can be found in Daniel 2. Nebuchadnezzar's vision outlines a sequence of kingdoms which must occur in the order in which they were given.

Sometimes, the sequence or structure of apocalyptic prophecy is defined by numeric order. For example, the second trumpet in Revelation 8 occurs *after* the first trumpet. The critical point here is that chronological order is always maintained in an apocalyptic prophecy otherwise we could not know the chronological order of events.

Apocalyptic prophecies sometimes have conditional elements within their structure relating to fulfillment. For example, the winds of destruction are held back in Revelation 7:3 until the servants of God are sealed. That the winds will blow is unconditional; *when* they blow is conditional.

Apocalyptic structure

Apocalyptic prophecy is defined in this volume as prophecy that deals with a sequence of events. This means that apocalyptic prophecy predicts a certain sequence or order in which things come to pass. By comparing history with fulfilled prophecies, we can find our chronological position in the sequence. Even more, by carefully following consistent rules of interpretation, we can determine certain processes or events that will take place in the future. The rules of interpretation have been introduced, but a little discussion about each rule might be helpful.

1.   The books of Daniel and Revelation contain 18 apocalyptic stories or

sequences. These sequences mark the passage of time so that we can tell where we are in God's timetable. Apocalyptic prophecies are identified by the presence of a beginning point and ending point in time. By knowing the beginning and ending points of a sequence, we can find our chronological relationship within the sequence. Because apocalyptic prophecies have a beginning and ending point in time, they cannot have multiple fulfillments. An apocalyptic sequence can only occur once.

2. All prophecies of the Bible are subordinate to apocalyptic structure. This means that apocalyptic prophecy holds greater weight in terms of chronology than non-apocalyptic prophecies. For example, we read earlier that Amos, Ezekiel, Joel, Obadiah and New Testament prophets believed the Great Day of the Lord was "near." There's no question that what they saw in vision led them to conclude that the "Day of the Lord" was near. In Revelation, John also indicates that the fulfillment of the things he saw were "near or soon." The problem is that the prophets did not understand how their visions fit into the overall chronology of apocalyptic structure because God had not finished revealing the truth about the great day of the Lord. No one prophet was shown *everything* that God intends to bring about. Paul sums up the process of prophetic revelations saying, **"In the past God spoke to our forefathers through the prophets at many times**

and in various ways.... For we know in part and we prophesy in part." (Hebrews 1:1, 1 Corinthians 13:9)

Each time God spoke to a prophet about the end of time, more detail was provided. If we first understand apocalyptic structures, then the details from various prophets can then be put in place! The second rule then follows: a prophecy is not fulfilled until all the specifications of the prophecy are met, and this includes the chronology of the prophecy.

3. Obscure language within the apocalyptic structures clears up about the time the prophecy becomes applicable. In other words, when the prophecy becomes applicable, the language of the prophecy becomes meaningful. For example, John begins Revelation by saying, **"The Revelation of Jesus Christ, which God gave him to show his servants what must soon take place...."** (Revelation 1:1) The words "must soon take place" cannot mean 2,000 years. John did not have 2,000 years in mind when he wrote this. Words must mean what they say or we will not be able to understand the prophetic story. The point here is that God impressed on John that Revelation's story was about to be fulfilled. Thus, the language of Revelation becomes primarily applicable when Revelation's story is about to be fulfilled!

This may sound confusing at first. But understand that God put the apocalyptic prophecies in mystical language to hide their meaning until the time for fulfillment should come. So, our third rule is this: If we declare language to mean something other than what it literally says, we must find applicable scripture to explain the meaning of the symbol. Students cannot makeup their own interpretations of symbols. The Bible must interpret itself. The significance and importance of these three rules will be seen as we apply them later.

Summary—Elijah is still coming

In closing, the point must be clearly made that the world will yet see the fulfillment of Malachi's prophecy since it involves the "Great Day of the Lord." Revelation predicts that 144,000 people, having the spirit and power of Elijah just like John the Baptist, will herald the "coming of the Lord." It's going to be interesting to see who God chooses for that work! Stay tuned.

Note: There is an important distinction between an application and a fulfillment. Jesus *applied* the "Day of the Lord" prophecy of Malachi to John the Baptist because John was a "type" of what the real fulfillment will be. In addition, the reader must also understand that Malachi's prophecy is not an apocalyptic prophecy because an apocalyptic prophecy lays out a sequence of events which must happen in chronological order. Because an apocalyptic prophecy can only happen once, a fulfillment can only occur when all the specifications of the prophecy are fully met.

Notes:

Notes

Chapter 3

Who is Jesus?

Introduction

The Bible begins, **"In the beginning God created the heavens and the earth."** (Genesis 1:1) The first verse in the Bible introduces our Creator, and in English, we call Him God. Who is God? What is He like?

The Bible reveals information about our Creator that cannot be found in any other place. But, the Bible is limited. An infinite and omnipotent God cannot be adequately described on paper. For this reason, God has commissioned the Holy Spirit to help us "connect the dots" so that we might know what God is like. Jesus said, **"But when he, the Spirit of truth, comes, he will guide you into all truth. He will not speak on his own; he will speak only what he hears, and he will tell you what is yet to come. He will bring glory to me by taking from what is mine and making it known to you."** (John 16:13-14)

It takes time to understand what a person is like. For this reason, God chose to reveal Himself over a long period of time—to various generation of people—and have His actions written down in the Bible. By doing this, those wanting to know God can become acquainted with Him by reconciling *all* His actions recorded in the Bible over a long period of time. Because we can only know God through His actions, it is important to know that God is ever consistent. **"I the Lord do not change."** (Malachi 3:6) Paul says, **"Jesus Christ is the same yesterday and today and forever."** (Hebrews 13:8)

Man learns about God

From time to time, and in various ways, God revealed Himself to men and women. Paul encouraged Timothy to take heed to the Scriptures saying, **"All Scripture is God-breathed and is useful for teaching, rebuking, correcting and training in righteousness, so that the man of God may be thoroughly equipped for every good work."** (2 Timothy 3:16,17) The term "God-breathed" is further explained by Peter. **"For prophecy never had its origin in the will of man, but men spoke from God as they were carried along by the Holy Spirit."** (2 Peter 1:21) The bottom line is this: The Bible offers us more than just human speculation about God. Bible writers received special information or revelations of God through the Holy Spirit. The Bible says, **"When a prophet of the Lord is among you, I reveal myself to him in visions, I speak to him in dreams."** (Numbers 12:6)

The library

The Bible is a library of 66 books. It was written by 40+ authors over a period of about 15 centuries. There are 39 Old Testament and 27 New Testament books. The Old Testament was completed with Malachi's book about 350 years before Christ, and the 27 books comprising the New Testament were collected and approved as the New Testament about 350 years after Christ.

Coming to terms with terms

We must understand some simple but important matters regarding the Bible. First, the terms "Old Testament" and "New Testament" are terms that we use today to identify two sections of the Bible. The Old Testament was written before Christ and the New Testament was written after Christ lived on earth. Obviously, these terms were not used during the days of Jesus for the New Testament did not exist as a collection of writings until A.D. 350.

When we hear the word "Bible," we usually think of one book. But, this is a modern concept. The 39 books we call the Old Testament today were not viewed as one book in days of Jesus. Rather, they were grouped like books in a library. The Jews referred to them as the Law, the Psalms [Songs] and the Prophets. Early Christians also followed in the same tradition. See Luke 24:44,45. As the Christian movement grew in size, a church council was called in Nicaea about A.D. 350 to collect and assemble the writings of the apostles (and others). Even though a number of books by various authors were considered, 27 were ultimately selected and this collection became known as the "New Testament." This title automatically identified the older existing Scriptures as the "Old Testament."

Many people misunderstand the importance of the Old Testament. They say the Old Testament has no value or meaning for the Christian Church today. This is unfortunate. Notice what Paul wrote to Timothy about 300 years before the New Testament was even assembled: **"All Scripture is God-breathed and is useful for teaching, rebuking, correcting and training in righteousness, so that the man of God may be thoroughly equipped for every good work."** (2 Timothy 3:16,17) What is Paul calling Scripture? The *only* Scripture that existed when Paul wrote to Timothy is what we today call the Old Testament!

In the days of Jesus, the Scriptures were divided into three parts: The Law (the books of Moses), the Psalms (Proverbs, Song of Solomon, etc) and the Prophets (Daniel, Isaiah, Jeremiah, etc.). When Jesus gave His famous sermon on the mount, He said, **"Do not think that I have come to abolish the Law or the Prophets; I have not come to abolish them but to fulfill them. I tell you the truth, until heaven and earth disappear, not the smallest letter, not the least stroke of a pen, will by any means disappear from the Law until everything is accomplished."** (Matthew 5:17) Notice that Jesus was referring to the Scriptures! He spoke of the Law and Prophets—a title for the Scriptures. Again, at the close of His ministry Jesus said to His disciples, **"This is what I told you while I was still with you: Everything must be fulfilled that is written about me in the Law of Moses, the Prophets and the Psalms. Then he opened their minds so they could understand the Scriptures."** (Luke 24:44,45)

Same God in Old as in New

The Old and New Testament are inspired by the same Holy Spirit, have the same authority and reveal the same God! John says, "{1}In the beginning was the Word, and the Word was with God, and the Word was God. {2} He was with God in the beginning. {3} Through him all things were made; without him nothing was made that has been made. {4} In him was life, and that life was the light of men.... {10} He was in the world, and though the world was made through him, the world did not recognize him. {11} He came to that which was his own, but his own did not receive him. {12} Yet to all who received him, to those who believed in his name, he gave the right to become children of God - {13} children born not of natural descent, nor of human decision or a husband's will, but born of God. {14} The Word became flesh and made his dwelling among us. We have seen his glory, the glory of the One and Only, who came from the Father, full of grace and truth."** Selections from John 1:1-14.

These verses contain some profound information about Jesus. Read, the verses in this order: 14, 10, 3 and 1 and notice what they reveal about Jesus! Many people get confused about the title, "God." It may help to think of "God" as a last name. There is Father God, Son God, and Holy Spirit God. These three have the same last name, are equal in every way but have different roles. See Matthew 28:19 and John 15:26; 16:5-11; 17:1-5.

If you study over these verses from John 1 carefully, you will discover they are packed with valuable information about Jesus who is the Son God. After reading verse 14, we can carefully exchange some words and reach a clearer understanding about Jesus. For example, wherever "Word" is used in John 1, replace it with "Jesus" and notice the clarity of meaning!

The God of the Old Testament is Jesus

The Bible is very clear that Jesus was in heaven before the world was created. Keep in mind He wasn't named Jesus until He was born of a woman. So, we can't refer to "Jesus" by His earthly name in the Old Testament. However, you might be surprised to learn that most references to God in the Old Testament are references to the person we now call Jesus! Here's the evidence:

In Gethsemane, Jesus asked for His previous glory: **"And now, Father, glorify me in your presence with the glory I had with you before the world began."** (John 17:5) Clearly, Jesus shared glory with the Father before the world was created.

Jesus told the Pharisees that the Scriptures focus on Him: **"And the Father who sent me has himself testified concerning me. (The Father spoke at the baptism of Jesus saying, 'This is my Son.') You have never heard his voice nor seen his form, nor does his word dwell in you, for you do not believe the one he sent. You diligently study the Scriptures because you think that by them you possess eternal life. These are the Scriptures that testify about me, yet you refuse to come to me to have life."** (John 5:37-40) The Old Testament Scriptures reveal Jesus!

Paul tells us that Jesus is the creative agent within the Godhead. He writes, **"In the past God spoke to our forefathers through the prophets at many times and in various ways, but in these last days he has spoken to us by his Son, whom he appointed heir of all things, and through whom he made the universe."** (Hebrews 1:1,2) Jesus is the "hands-on" Creator.

Notice this statement by Paul affirming that Jesus is the creative agent within the Godhead, **"For by Him (Christ) all things were created: things in heaven and on earth, visible and invisible, whether thrones or powers or rulers or authorities; all things were created by him and for him. He is before all things, and in him all things hold together."** (Colossians 1:16,17)

Jesus is God just like the Father.

Paul says, **"For in Christ all the fullness of the Deity lives in bodily form... who is the head over every power and authority."** (Colossians 2:9,10) In Revelation Jesus said to John, **"I am the Alpha and the Omega, says the Lord God, who is, and who was, and who is to come, the Almighty."** (Revelation 1:8)

John, as mentioned earlier says, **"In the beginning was the Word, and the Word was with God, and the Word was God. He was with God in the beginning. Through him all things were made; without him nothing was made that has been made."** (John 1:1-3)

Peter says, **"He (Jesus) was chosen before the creation of the world, but was revealed in these last times for your sake."** (1 Peter 1:20)

Isaiah quotes the Lord, saying, **"Listen to me, O Jacob, Israel, whom I have called: I am he; I am the first and I am the last. My own hand laid the foundations of the earth, and my right hand spread out the heavens; when I summon them, they all stand up together.... This is what the Lord says - your Redeemer, the Holy One of Israel: I am the Lord your God, who teaches you what is best for you, who directs you in the way you should go."** (Isaiah 48:12,13,16,17)

Philip, one of the first disciples of Jesus, told his brother, **"We have found the one Moses wrote about in the Law, and about whom the prophets also wrote - Jesus of Nazareth, the son of Joseph."** (John 1:45)

It was Jesus who said to Abraham, **"...I am God Almighty; walk before me and be blameless."** (Genesis 17:1) The Jews argued with Jesus because He claimed to be greater than Abraham but Jesus said, **"Your father Abraham rejoiced at the thought of seeing my day; he saw it and was glad."** The Jews sneered back, **"You are not yet fifty years old..., and you have seen Abraham! 'I tell you the truth', Jesus answered, 'before Abraham was born, I am!' "** (John 8:56-58)

One last point. Old Testament writers knew Christ. The writer of Hebrews says, **"(Moses) regarded disgrace for the sake of Christ as of greater value than the treasures of Egypt, because he was looking ahead to his reward."** (Hebrews 11:26) John knew that Isaiah saw the glory of Jesus. He says, **"Isaiah said this because**

he saw Jesus' glory and spoke about him."
(John 12:41) After Jesus was baptized,
Philip excitedly ran to Nathanael and said,
"...We have found the one Moses wrote
about in the Law, and about whom the
prophets also wrote—Jesus of Nazareth,
the son of Joseph." (John 1:45)

Critical point

The nature and identity of Jesus is a
subject of revelation. In other words, the
nature and identity of Jesus is something
that is only revealed in the Bible and it
has been revealed over time. Early
prophets did not know as much about
Jesus as we know today. Notice how this
progression works. "God also said to
Moses, 'I am the Lord. I appeared to
Abraham, to Isaac and to Jacob as God
Almighty, but by my name the Lord I did
not make myself known to them.' "
(Exodus 6:2-3) The truth about Jesus is
always unfolding. In fact, by the time we
get to the last book in the Bible, it is
appropriately called, "The Revelation of
Jesus Christ." Indeed, this is what
Revelation is all about—the unfolding or
revealing of Jesus Christ and what He is
all about.

Going back to our verse, notice that God
clearly says that He did not reveal His
name to Abraham, Isaac or Jacob. Why
do you suppose He did that?

So, who is Jesus?

- Jesus is God Almighty. (Exodus
  6:3)

- Jesus is the Lord God. (Isaiah 48)

- Jesus is King of Kings and Lord of
  Lords. (Revelation 19:16)

- Jesus is the Angel of the Lord.
  (Exodus 3:2-6)

- Jesus is our Creator. (John 1:10)

- Jesus is our Redeemer. (Isaiah
  48)

- Jesus is our Friend. (John 15:13-
  15)

Jesus said to His disciples, "Do not let
your hearts be troubled. Trust in God;
trust also in me. In my Father's house
are many rooms; if it were not so, I would
have told you. I am going there to prepare
a place for you. And if I go and prepare
a place for you, I will come back and
take you to be with me that you also may
be where I am. You know the way to the
place where I am going." (John 14:1-4)
Do you think trust in God is different than
trust in Jesus?

Very interesting point

The role and identity of Jesus has not only
been a mystery to human beings, but to
angels also! Before coming to earth as a
man, Jesus lived in heaven as an angel.
The angels called Him "Michael" which
means "One who is like God." On five
occasions the name "Michael" is used in
the Bible. In Jude 9, Michael is called
the archangel, and in 1 Thessalonians 4:16
the voice of the archangel calls the dead
to life. In Daniel 10:13, Michael is called
"one of the chief princes [of heaven]." In
Daniel 12:1, the great tribulation begins

when Michael (who is presently seated at the right hand of the Father) stands up. Daniel appropriately identifies Jesus as "Michael" and a "son of man" (Daniel 7:13), for he writes about 600 years before "Michael" takes the name of Jesus.

In Revelation 12:7 we find Michael and His angels fighting Satan and his angels. Both Michael and Satan were angel kings before the creation of the world. Michael was the archangel over the faithful angels, and Satan became ruler over his angel followers. Thus the great controversy between Christ and Satan began before the world was created. *Each time the name Michael is used in the Bible, there is a conflict between Satan and Jesus.*

The real beauty of knowing that Michael is Jesus is that one of the Godhead lives in the form as one of His own creation! In other words, Jesus lived for many, many years as an angel, and then, He even stooped lower to live as a man. What divine love!

Satan's problems with Michael stemmed from the fact that a time came when he would no longer bow to another "angel." Satan came to feel in his heart that he was equal, if not greater than Michael. (See Isaiah 14 and Ezekiel 28.) The same problem recurred when Jesus was upon earth. Many human beings saw Jesus as only a man and accused him of blasphemy when He said that He "was the Son of God."

Some people resist the idea that Michael is another name for Jesus. Often, support for this is given from Jude 9 where Michael says to the devil, **"The Lord rebuke you."** The idea here is that if Michael is Jesus,

He would not refer to "the Lord" as though He were another person. But this is not uncommon literary practice! Zechariah 3:2 says, **"The Lord said to Satan, 'The Lord rebuke you, Satan! The Lord who has chosen Jerusalem, rebuke you!' "** Here the Lord clearly uses identical language. Jesus asserts His authority over the devil from time to time by reminding the devil who He really is. For example, when Jesus was tempted by the devil in the wilderness, He quoted from the Old Testament saying, **"Do not put the Lord your God to the test."** Jesus clearly knew who He was and so did the devil. So, in the Jude 9 conversation between Jesus and Satan, Satan was reminded again that he was dealing with God.

The reader should notice that each time the term Michael is used in the Bible, a controversy with Satan is under way!

The beauty of knowing that Michael is Jesus, is that the Son of God identified Himself as one of the angels before coming to earth in the same way He now identifies Himself as a son of man! He is Michael, the archangel, to the angels, and to us, He is Jesus the incomparable Son of Man!

One last point should be emphasized. When Jesus returns in glory, He will call the dead to life. Notice how Paul describes the event: **"For the Lord himself will come down from heaven, with a loud command, with the voice of the archangel and with the trumpet call of God, and the dead in Christ will rise first."** (1 Thessalonians 4:16) Paul says that the Lord Himself will call the righteous dead back to life. In this text, Paul uses the phrase, "the voice of the archangel," to emphasize the role of Jesus, the archangel at the second coming. Notice what Jesus said about Himself, **"I tell you the truth, a time is coming and has now come when the dead will hear the voice of the Son of God and those who hear will live."** (John 5:25)

Personal opinion

It is the author's opinion that Michael, the archangel, closely identified with the angels before the fall of Lucifer; thus, they really didn't understand all that He was. Christ's identity in heaven as an angel, albeit the archangel, or one of the chief princes, was perhaps one of the reasons Lucifer became jealous of Christ. Lucifer, the highest of the created angels, came to think that he was equal to or better than Michael. Such thinking led Lucifer to controversy and eventually expulsion from heaven.

If this opinion is true, the phrase, "the Revelation of Jesus" really comes into sharp focus. The book of Revelation is actually the conclusion to a long process: the revelation of all that Jesus really is! This process is not only true in heaven but to human beings on earth! Everyone will know WHO JESUS REALLY IS when the seventh seal is finally opened! Every knee will bow. And at that time, Michael/Jesus will destroy Lucifer/Satan.

Jesus, the angel, the Lord, is God

Many people are surprised to learn that Jesus is often called or referred to as "the angel of the Lord" in the Old Testament. Two excellent examples of this are provided. When Abraham was about to offer up Isaac, the Bible says, **"But the angel of the Lord called out to him from heaven, 'Abraham! Abraham!... Do not lay a hand on the boy,' he said. The angel of the Lord called to Abraham from heaven a second time and said.... 'I swear by myself, declares the Lord, that because you have done this and have not withheld your son, your only son, I will surely bless you and make your descendants as numerous as the stars in the sky and as the sand on the seashore. Your descendants will take possession of the cities of their enemies, and through your offspring all nations on earth will be blessed, because you have obeyed me.' "** Selections from Genesis 22:11-18. Did you notice that the angel of the Lord is the Lord in these verses?

The second example is even more convincing that Jesus is sometimes called the "angel of the Lord." One day when Moses was tending his sheep he discovered a burning bush. The Bible says, **"There the angel of the Lord appeared to him in flames of fire from within the bush. Moses saw that though the bush was on fire it did not burn up. So Moses thought, 'I will go over and see this strange sight - why the bush does not burn up.' When the Lord saw that he had gone over to look, God called to him from within the bush, 'Moses! Moses!' And Moses said 'Here I am.' 'Do not come any closer,' God said. 'Take off your sandals, for the place where you are standing is holy ground.' Then he said, 'I am the God of your father, the God of Abraham, the God of Isaac and the God of Jacob.' "** (Exodus 3:2-6) Did you notice that the angel of the Lord is God?

The Bible leads us in small steps to understand all that Jesus really is. Did you know that it was Jesus who tenderly cared for the Israelites in the wilderness? He was with them day and night. He provided their water and their food. Notice what Paul says, **"They all ate the same spiritual food and drank the same spiritual drink; for they drank from the spiritual rock that accompanied them, and that rock was Christ."** (1 Corinthians 10:4)

When Jesus came to earth, He stooped lower in the order of creation. Paul asks, **"What is man that you are mindful of him, the son of man that you care for him? You made him a little lower than the angels; you crowned him with glory and honor and put everything under his feet.... But we see Jesus, who was made a little lower than the angels, now crowned with glory and honor because he suffered death, so that by the grace of God he might taste death for everyone."** (Hebrews 2:6-9)

The story of Revelation is devoted to the singular point of revealing all that Jesus is. This is why the book is called "The Revelation of Jesus." When the last of the seven seals has been broken, then all the angels in heaven, the evil angels on earth, the wicked of earth and the redeemed will behold the fullness of all that Jesus really is. At that time the revelation of Jesus will be complete!

But then the most amazing thing happens. At the end of the millennium—when Jesus is fully revealed, He does something beyond our comprehension. Paul says, **"Then the end will come, when he [Jesus] hands over the kingdom to God the Father after he has destroyed all dominion, authority and power.... When he has done this, then the Son himself will be made subject to him who put everything under him, so that God may be all in all."** (1 Corinthians 15:24,28)

What a wonderful Savior is Jesus! Think of it. Michael, the Son of God, was humble enough to live as an angel. Then, He stooped even lower to live as a man. Even more, He willingly died on Calvary to pay the penalty for our sins. Is it any wonder that Jesus said, **"...whoever wants to become great among you must be your servant, and whoever wants to be first must be your slave - just as the Son of Man did not come to be served, but to serve, and to give His life a ransom for many."** (Matthew 20:26-28)

Thought questions

One of the most touching verses in the Bible is found in John 1:11. John says, **"He came to that which was his own, but his own did not receive him."** Reflect for a moment that Jesus was literally the One who chose Israel, the One who delivered Israel from bondage, the One who fed Israel with manna from heaven, the One who cared for and blessed Israel, the One who sought the affections of Israel—and He was the One rejected and crucified by His own people. But, what have you done with Jesus? Are you willing to be His servant? Are you willing to do what He asks? Are you willing to become what He wants you to be? Are you willing to go where He commands? If not now—when? If you are willing now, you are on the way to heaven. Read John 14:1-17:26 from your Bible. You'll be glad you did.

Chapter 4

The Plan of Salvation
Part I

"What must I do to be saved?" No question has ever provoked so many different answers. A few years ago, a Gallup poll was conducted on the subject of salvation. Eighty-seven percent of the people questioned were convinced that they were going to heaven, and almost ninety percent of the people responding knew someone going to hell.

"What must I do to be saved?" is a universal question. People of every culture, language and nation ask this question. Have you noticed that every nation and tribe has a religion of some kind? Why is this? The problem with the question about salvation is the answer. Ask a Catholic, Baptist, Jew, Moslem, and a Hindu this question and you'll get five different answers! Even more confusing is the fact that factions within each religious group will give different answers! Is there one correct answer? Is there only one way to heaven?

From heaven's point of view

Consider the issue of salvation from heaven's point of view. There are 5.4+ billion people on this planet and according to the Bible, God is not willing that anyone should perish. (2 Peter 3:9) God foreknew that people on earth would speak different languages, have diverse customs, and think differently about religion. Therefore, God prepared a plan of salvation that would encompass every human being that would ever live *before* He created the world. Consequently, those who wish to understand the enormous scope of salvation must understand something about the powers of God.

The powers of God

God is omnipotent. This means that He can do anything He pleases with anything or anybody. He is not accountable to anyone, yet He is willing to be studied. He is the source of all authority and power, yet He gives His subjects the power of choice. He speaks and worlds exist. He could double the size of our infinite universe in a split second by simply commanding it. He could speak earth's solar system out of existence if He wanted to and we would cease to be the very moment the words left His lips.

Through Him everything exists. Without Him, there is nothing. He creates matter. He destroys matter. He sets limits and none can change them. God says, **"This is what the Lord says — your Redeemer, who formed you in the womb: I am the Lord, who has made all things, who alone stretched out the heavens, who spread out** the earth by myself, who foils the signs of false prophets and makes fools of diviners, who overthrows the learning of the wise and turns it into nonsense. Remember the former things, those of long ago; I am God, and there is no other; I am God, and there is none like me. I make known the end from the beginning, from ancient times, what is still to come. I say: My purpose will stand, and I will do all that I please. From the east I summon a bird of prey; from a far-off land, a man to fulfill my purpose. What I have said, that will I bring about; what I have planned, that will I do." (Isaiah 44:24-25, 46:9-11)

God is omniscient. This means that He knows everything about everything. He knows everything about the past. He knows everything about the future. God knew before the world was created the names of those who would choose eternal life and who would not. In other words, God knew before the world began who would be saved and who would be lost.

This fact bothers a lot of people because they don't understand the difference between God's foreknowledge and His ability to predestine something. According to Webster, predestination means, "to decree beforehand." Because the Godhead is omnipotent, they can predestine things. For example, Jesus was predestined to die on Calvary long before the event took place. The plan of salvation was predestined before the world was created. Predestination means that God decrees that certain things shall happen because He wants them to happen. Again, God says, "I say: My purpose will stand, and I will do all that I please. From the east

I summon a bird of prey; from a far-off land, a man to fulfill my purpose. What I have said, that will I bring about; what I have planned, that will I do." (Isaiah 46:10,11) So, predestination is a function of God's omnipotence. He can decree beforehand anything to happen and it will happen because He is omnipotent.

On the other hand, foreknowledge is a function of God's omniscience. Because He knows everything about everything, He has foreknowledge. He knows what is going to happen – not because He makes it happen, but because He knows it will happen! God did not predestine Adam and Eve to sin. However, He foreknew that they would sin. In the same way He knows who will choose to be saved and who will choose to be lost. God has not predestined some people to be lost and others to be saved. The Bible says, **"He predestined us to be adopted as his sons through Jesus Christ, in accordance with his pleasure and will.... He (God) is patient with you, not wanting anyone to perish, but everyone to come to repentance."** (Ephesians 1:5, 2 Peter 3:9)

Note: To say that God predestines eternal reward is a false and malicious charge against His plan of salvation. If God predestined the eternal reward of a man without recognizing man's actions or power of choice, the plan of salvation would be nothing more than a deceptive trick. If God predestined people to be saved and others to be lost, there would have been no need for the plan of salvation, for what effect could come from choosing Jesus as our Savior if you were predestined to be lost?

In simple terms, the difference between predestination and foreknowledge is the following: Predestination (decreeing beforehand) is setting the alarm clock to go off at 5 a.m. the next morning. Foreknowledge (knowing beforehand) is looking at a clock and observing that it will go off at 5 a.m. in the morning.

Essential differences

Here is the bottom line: there is an essential difference between God's foreknowledge and God's predestination. Predestination *causes* the outcome whereas foreknowledge *knows* the outcome. Perhaps another illustration will demonstrate this difference. Suppose a airplane pilot can see the twists and turns of a long river. In one glance, he can see the end *and* the beginning. Also imagine there are people traveling down the river — not knowing where the river leads, but they are determined to reach its end. The pilot can see where they will be when they reach the end of their journey, but the pilot has nothing to do with the travelers reaching that destination. Rather, he can only see where the boaters will be when they reach the end of the river. Knowing the end from the beginning without making it happen is foreknowledge. On the other hand, predestination causes the outcome such as setting an alarm clock to go off at a certain time.

In short, God predestines *events* to happen. He does not predestine the eternal destiny of people. God, because He has foreknowledge, knows what people are going to choose to do and He not only grants us the power of choice, He encourages our use of it!

God predestines events, not people

The Old Testament story of Israel clearly points out that Jesus does not use His foreknowledge to change the outcome of events even when they run contrary to His plans! Notice this prophecy, **"And the Lord said to Moses: 'You are going to rest with your fathers, and these people will soon prostitute themselves to the foreign gods of the land they are entering. They will forsake me and break the covenant I made with them. On that day I will become angry with them and forsake them; I will hide my face from them, and they will be destroyed. Many disasters and difficulties will come upon them, and on that day they will ask, 'Have not these disasters come upon us because our God is not with us?' And I will certainly hide my face on that day because of all their wickedness in turning to other gods.' "** (Deuteronomy 31:16-18)

Jesus knew what Israel would do in the future. He clearly told Moses. And 1,470 years of Jewish history confirms that Jesus was right. But the same 1,470 years of Jewish history confirms that Jesus did not use His foreknowledge to make Israel a stubborn and stiff-necked people. In fact, the Old Testament verifies that God did everything possible to redirect Israel from her terrible ways—time after time! (See Jeremiah 3.) But Israel chose to rebel against God. The point here is that Jesus knew that Israel would rebel before they rebelled! The point here is that God does not deal with His creatures on the basis of His foreknowledge. He deals with us on the basis of His love and our need. Carefully think this point through and you'll stand in awe at the love of God!

Back to the question

The question, "What must I do to be saved?", implies a condition of being "unsaved." So what is the human race "unsaved" from? It has been noticed that life lasts about 70 years and then man dies. What follows? Why must man die? The Psalmist wrote, **"The length of our days is seventy years - or eighty, if we have the strength; yet their span is but trouble and sorrow, for they quickly pass, and we fly away."** (Psalm 90:10) The Bible gives a very clear explanation of who man is, where he came from, why he dies, and all that follows.

Watch what you eat

God created man and placed him in the Garden of Eden where he had access to the tree of life. As long as man remained in the garden he could live forever because the fruit of the tree of life sustained life indefinitely. The point is made that Jesus created man as a mortal being. The word mortal means subject to death. Jesus plainly told Adam, **"...You are free to eat from any tree in the garden; but you must not eat from the tree of the knowledge of good and evil, for when you eat of it you will surely die."** (Genesis 2:16,17)

It is interesting to note that both the tree of life and the tree of knowledge of good and evil were in the middle of Eden. (Genesis 2:9) Even more, these two trees

shadow the plan of salvation. Upon the tree of the knowledge of good and evil, Jesus would die so that man might have access to the tree of life. When Adam and Eve were created, they had a natural attraction for righteousness and lawful living for they were holy. As children today possess biological traits from their parents, so Adam and Eve possessed the traits of their Creator – Jesus. The Bible says, **"So God created man in his own image, in the image of God he created him; male and female he created them."** (Genesis 1:27)

A test of loyalty

A test was placed in the Garden of Eden to see if Adam and Eve would choose to obey or disobey. They were clearly informed that they were not to eat of the fruit of one tree in the middle of the garden. One day, as Eve went grocery shopping to get fruit from the tree of life, a serpent startled her by calling to her from the forbidden tree. Now the serpent in the Garden of Eden was the most beautiful and intelligent of all creatures. (Some scholars believe the serpent could fly until he was cursed to crawl upon his belly. See Genesis 3:14.) Apparently, Satan entered into the body of one of the most beautiful creatures on earth to tempt Eve. Wouldn't you be curious if you heard a beautiful creature speak and carry on a remarkably intelligent conversation?

Satan engaged Eve in a conversation and then lied to her. He deceived her into eating the fruit of the tree of the knowledge of good and evil. Satan said, **"You will not surely die. For God knows that when** you eat of it your eyes will be opened, and you will be like God, knowing good and evil." (Genesis 3:4,5) Satan led Eve to believe that God didn't want her to experience the knowledge of evil. This part of Satan's comment was true for God did not want Adam and Eve to experience the knowledge of evil. In fact, the devil often mixes 99% truth with 1% lie to capture his subjects. God knew that the knowledge of good was enough! But Satan lied about the fatal consequence of evil. Notice the clever mixture of error with truth in the text above!

Eve ate the fruit. Then, she gave some of the forbidden fruit to Adam and he ate also. Now a very important distinction must be made between the sins of Adam and Eve. Eve was led to believe a lie and she sinned without deliberation. Adam, on the other hand, willfully chose to eat the forbidden fruit and suffer the consequences. Therefore, Adam's sin was greater than Eve's for God had directly spoken to Adam about this matter. **"And the Lord God commanded the man, 'You are free to eat from any tree in the garden; but you must not eat from the tree of the knowledge of good and evil, for when you eat of it you will surely die.' "** (Genesis 2:16,17) Adam's sin was calculated and deliberate.

Passing the blame

That evening, Adam and Eve were confronted with their sin. They ran and hid themselves as Jesus came to visit with them. They were ashamed, naked and defensive. When confronted with their deeds, they were strangely unrepentant!

Eve blamed her act on the serpent. She said, **"The serpent deceived me, and I ate."** (Genesis 3:13) Even worse, Adam blamed his act of rebellion on his Creator and then on Eve! Adam said, **"The woman you put here with me - she gave me some fruit from the tree and I ate it."** (Genesis 3:12)

Then Jesus turned to Adam and said, **"...because you listened to your wife and ate from the tree about which I commanded you, 'You must not eat of it,' Cursed is the ground because of you; through painful toil you will eat of it all the days of your life.... By the sweat of your brow you will eat your food until you return to the ground, since from it you were taken; for dust you are and to dust you will return."** (Genesis 3:17-19)

Access denied

Adam and Eve were driven from the Garden of Eden so they might not have access to the tree of life! The Bible says, **"The Lord God said, 'The man has now become like one of us, knowing good and evil. He must not be allowed to reach out his hand and take also from the tree of life and eat, and live forever.' So the Lord God banished him from the Garden of Eden to work the ground from which he had been taken. After he drove the man out, he placed on the east side of the Garden of Eden cherubim and a flaming sword flashing back and forth to guard the way to the tree of life."** (Genesis 3:22-24)

Because of their sins, Adam and Eve were "doomed" to eternal death. **"For the wages of sin is death."** (Romans 6:23) They had literally tasted sin and would forever be sinners. They were banished from the garden and denied access to the life sustaining fruit of the tree of life, for God mercifully prevents sinners from living forever. The trait of rebellion against God (just like a biological trait) was passed on to the offspring of Adam and Eve. In fact, their firstborn, Cain, became a murderer!

Adam's sin was greater than Eve's sin. Adam was not deceived. He willfully and intentionally disobeyed God. Therefore, his suffering would be greater than Eve's. The words of the Apostle Paul make a lot of sense. **"Therefore, just as sin entered the world through one man, and death through sin, and in this way death came to all men, because all have sinned."** (Romans 5:12)

Think of Adam's suffering. The Bible says that Adam lived 930 years. (Genesis 5:5) Imagine living that long and observing the terrible consequences of your own wrong doing! In every death, suffering and sadness, Adam beheld the extended consequences of his own deed. He saw the blight of sin upon nature. And for more than nine centuries Adam witnessed the degenerate effects of his willful wrong doing.

Jesus not caught by surprise

The sin of Adam and Eve did not catch heaven by surprise. In fact, the very day Adam and Eve sinned, Jesus stepped in. He stepped between the wrath of God and the guilty pair. Jesus came to earth and told Adam and Eve that there was a way back to Eden. And ever since that

day, the way back to Eden has been called the "Plan of Salvation."

Since all 5.4 billion inhabitants of earth are descendants of Adam and Eve, and God knew when He created the world that the world would someday be populated with billions of people holding to different languages, customs and religious beliefs, the plan of salvation has been inclusive of all people from its beginning. The plan must work for Chinese, Russians, Americans and all people in every country. How can billions of people holding diverse beliefs find their way back to Eden?

Because God is love, the answer is actually quite simple. When each person is born, God instills a set of rules we may call "basic law."

Basic law

Basic law allows a person to determine right and wrong. This indwelling law enables people to distinguish or recognize right from wrong at an early age. This age is often called the age of accountability. People mature in the process of accountability as long as they seek truth. This progression was eloquently noted by Thomas Jefferson in the introduction of our Bill of Rights. He wrote, "We hold certain truths to be self evident...." However, we all know if people don't want to see truth, they can't understand it nor can they see the evidence of it! In fact, those who would justify evil are first to deny what is right.

God created human beings with reasoning powers for He wants us to distinguish good from evil. If a person strives to do all that he believes is good and right, then he is doing all that God asks of him. Paul says, **"Indeed, when Gentiles, who do not have the law [the revealed will of God], do by nature things required by the law, they are a law for themselves, even though they do not have the law, since they show that the requirements of the law are written on their hearts, their consciences also bearing witness, and their thoughts now accusing, now even defending them. This [is how it] will take place on the day when God will judge men's secrets through Jesus Christ, as my gospel declares."** (Romans 2:14-16. Note: The word "law" as used in this text includes the larger meaning of the word, that is, all scripture.) James also supports the concept of basic law. He says, **"Anyone, then, who knows the good he ought to do and doesn't do it, sins."** (James 4:17)

Salvation includes full restoration

The plan of salvation does not stop with "basic law." On the contrary, basic law is where it all begins. Salvation consists of much more than the promise of eternal life because the human race lost more than eternal life!

God not only wants to restore eternal life to all people, but even more, He wants to restore the traits of holiness, righteousness and divine love within man! He wants us restored back in His image! To do this, God has patiently worked through the human race in various ways to inform man of what He is like — hoping that people would respond. In God's economy, it is not enough to save man *in*

his sins. God intends to save man *from* his sins.

So the plan of salvation has two parts. Theologians have termed these two elements as "Justification" and "Sanctification." Justification means that God has personally paid the price for the salvation of everyone living in the world. Sanctification means that God wants to restore His image (traits) in all human beings. Actually, sanctification works two ways. First, holiness brings fullness of life, happiness, and joys never ending. (What a contrast to the wages of evil.) Secondly, sanctification serves as public relations for the Kingdom of Heaven. Those who experience the joy and fullness of life that comes through sanctification become living examples of what heaven is all about. Thus, uninformed people are brought to a knowledge of the God of Heaven through sanctified examples of what God offers!

These two concepts of sanctification are wonderfully explained in the sermon on the mount. (Matthew 5:3-7:29) For example, Jesus said, **"You have heard that it was said, 'Love your neighbor and hate your enemy.' But I tell you: 'Love your enemies and pray for those who persecute you, that you may be sons of your Father in heaven. He causes his sun to rise on the evil and the good, and sends rain on the righteous and the unrighteous. If you love those who love you, what reward will you get? Are not even the tax collectors doing that? And if you greet only your brothers, what are you doing more than others? Do not even pagans do that? Be perfect, therefore, as your heavenly Father is perfect.' "** (Matthew 5:43-48)

How the pieces fit

As mentioned before, every normal person is born with reasoning powers sufficient for "basic law." This ability is granted by God so that we might understand the difference between right and wrong. God appeals to this basic ability to reveal more and more light about Himself. The more we know about our Maker, the more we become like our Creator!

But some people don't want more information about God and His ways. Jesus told Nicodemus, **"This is the verdict: Light has come into the world, but men loved darkness instead of light because their deeds were evil. Everyone who does evil hates the light, and will not come into the light for fear that his deeds will be exposed. But whoever lives by the truth comes into the light, so that it may be seen plainly that what he has done has been done through God."** (John 3:19-21)

The rejection of truth can be corporate too. Entire cities, states or nations can rebel against truth! Jesus denounced Capernaum saying, **"And you, Capernaum, will you be lifted up to the skies? No, you will go down to the depths. If the miracles that were performed in you had been performed in Sodom, it would have remained to this day. But I tell you that it will be more bearable for Sodom on the day of judgment than for you."** (Matthew 11:23,24) In other words, Sodom's evil was not as great as Capernaum's evil because Capernaum had greater evidence of truth!

The conclusion of the matter

Some people want to know more about God. Some people don't want to know anything about God. Jesus made it clear to Nicodemus that those who live up to all they know will find more light while those who do evil will not want anymore light for fear their deeds will be exposed as evil.

Salvation then comes to any person, in any culture, in any language and in any religious body when they are willing to follow all the light they have. It's that simple and that universal. From "basic law," God attempts to lead each person into greater and greater light so that every person may become more like Him.

The final exam

Revelation indicates that God has prepared a final exam for all the people of the world living at the end of time. In the next chapter we'll begin to see how this exam will work. In effect, God is going to send a powerful testimony of truth throughout the world during a very short time to see who will follow it. Those living up to all the light they have and looking for more light will quickly see the beauty of this simple but powerful testimony and many will accept it even at great peril to life itself.

This final exam is carefully designed so that all who are living up to the light they have now will be separated from these three classes of people:

1. Those refusing more light
2. Those professing to walk in the light
3. Those indifferent to greater light

Chapter 5

The Plan of Salvation Part II

Sin causes death

Adam and Eve lost much and gained very little as a result of sin. They lost the privilege of eating fruit from the tree of life. Because they were mortal and restricted from the tree, death overtook them. They lost their beautiful Eden home. They lost the natural traits of God's righteous character, and in exchange for these things, they gained the knowledge of evil, suffering and sorrow. But their greatest loss was holiness. After sinning, Adam and Eve became attracted to sin. What a sad exchange!

Adam and Eve passed their sinful natures on to their children and their firstborn became a murderer. Consequently, sin has damaged and contaminated every descendent of Adam and Eve. According to Paul, **"All have sinned and fall short of the glory of God!"** (Romans 3:23) This is the fallen and unsaved condition of man. We may be unsaved but we are wanted! God wants to redeem us back to Himself. **"For the wages of sin is death, but the gift of God is eternal life in Christ Jesus our Lord."** (Romans 6:23) The penalty for sin is everlasting death. Jesus, our Creator, personally paid this penalty so that whosoever will believe in Him might be saved. What does "believe in Him" mean? How does a person receive salvation?

Basic law

In the last chapter we briefly mentioned "basic law." This concept suggests that God has placed within each rational person the basic ability to distinguish right from wrong. People living up to the fullness of their heart's understanding of truth glorify their Creator! On the other hand, those refusing to learn more truth are not candidates for salvation.

Some people don't want to know the difference between right and wrong. Why is this? Paul says, **"The wrath of God is being revealed from heaven against all the godlessness and wickedness of men who suppress the truth by their wickedness, since what may be known about God is plain to them, because God has made it plain to them... so that men are without excuse. For although they knew God, they neither glorified him as God nor gave thanks to him, but their thinking became futile and their foolish hearts were darkened.... Therefore God gave them over in the sinful desires of their hearts to sexual impurity for the degrading of their bodies with one another.... Furthermore, since they did not think it worthwhile to retain the knowledge of God, he gave them over to a depraved mind, to do what ought not to be done."** (Romans 1:18-28)

Down through the ages, billions of people have lived and died who never knew the particulars about salvation. God foreknew the darkness of sin. Consequently, the plan of salvation can save a person who doesn't understand all of the details. This is somewhat like the law of gravity. You don't have to fully understand gravity to be affected by its operation.

But God is not content with basic law. He desires to restore His image within man. In order for this to happen, man needs to know his Creator. This calls for much more information and education on the subject of the plan of salvation. Jesus wants a close relationship with His children, and a close relationship is only possible when each party knows the other well.

Stage set for faith

Now the stage for understanding salvation has been set. Salvation has two parts: first, to restore man to Eden and second, to restore within man the image of God. The price for restoring man to Eden was paid in full at Calvary. Through God's grace or unmerited favor on the human race, the price was paid. That God could love the human race and pay such an extreme price for our salvation is grace beyond comprehension. It is also love beyond comprehension. Paul calls this "the mystery of God." He wrote, **"Although I am less than the least of all God's people, this grace was given me: to preach to the Gentiles the unsearchable riches of Christ, and to make plain to everyone the administration of this mystery, which for ages past was kept hidden in God, who created all things."** (Ephesians 3:8,9)

The process of restoring man into the image of God is exciting, rewarding and excruciating—all at the same time. Our natural inclination or tendency is to be hostile towards God. Paul wrote, **"Those who live according to the sinful nature have their minds set on what that nature desires; but those who live in accordance with the Spirit have their minds set on what the Spirit desires. The mind of sinful man is death, but the mind controlled by the Spirit is life and peace; because the sinful mind is hostile to God. It does not submit to God's law, nor can it do so. Those controlled by the sinful nature cannot please God."** (Romans 8:5-8)

How can a person live in accordance with the Spirit and find life and peace? Jesus told Nicodemus, **"...I tell you the truth, unless a man is born again, he cannot see the kingdom of God.... Unless a man is born of water and the Spirit, he cannot enter the kingdom of God."** (John 3:3,5) What does being born of water and the Spirit mean? Some people interpret the words of Jesus, "born of water," to mean that "unless you are baptized," you cannot go to heaven.

(**Note:** Controversy over baptism developed within the Christian church about the second century. The issue was whether baptism was required for salvation. The Church finally decided that baptism was compulsory. Since the majority of infants died before reaching one year of age in those days, the baptism of infants was implemented to insure that they met the "mandatory" requirements of getting to heaven.)

Being born of water, though, meant something different to Nicodemus than it typically means to us today. Being born of water was an expression that was associated with becoming a Jew. If a Gentile (a person not born of Jewish ancestry) wished to become a Jew, he or she had to submit to months of extended education on the rules and practices of Judaism. After indoctrination, the candidate denounced his past life and then was dunked beneath the water. This symbolic act was known as being "born of water." The Jews thought the act of baptism overcame the terrible tragedy of being born a Gentile. As far as the convert was concerned, life began at baptism. Nothing between Gentile birth and baptism was worth remembering. Thus, being born of water was an expression of denouncing natural birth as a Gentile.

Nicodemus was well acquainted with the baptism of John. Remember, John the Baptist was baptizing at the Jordan River where there was plenty of water. (John 3:23) John was led by the Holy Spirit to use the symbol of being "born of water" to call Israel to repentance. (John 1:33) God sent John the Baptist to Israel to plead with them to forsake their evil past and put away their hard hearts so that they might recognize and receive Messiah! John's baptism was regarded as an expression of denouncing the hardness of heart that belonged to Israel! John the Baptist proclaimed, **"I baptize you with water for repentance. But after me will come one who is more powerful than I, whose sandals I am not fit to carry. He will baptize you with the Holy Spirit and with fire."** (Matthew 3:11)

So, Jesus was saying, "Nicodemus, you must be 'born of water.' You, Nicodemus, a respected leader of Israel, need to start over! You need a new heart, a new life. You, Nicodemus, need to repent of your spiritual pride and religious self exaltation. You, Nicodemus, need to live a humble life, 'born and led of the Spirit,' for He will guide you into more truth and light! You, Nicodemus, can mark this new beginning by being born of water!"

The answer

So, the answer to the question, "What must I do to be saved?", *begins* with a simple and inclusive sentence. Start right now. *Give yourself completely to Jesus.* This means to be, to do and to go as He directs you in your life. Humbly live up to what you know to be true, and seek more truth! If you are willing to do what God asks you, willing to be what God asks you, and willing to go where God sends you—then you're living by faith and God grants you salvation full and free when you are willing to live by faith!

The biblical definition of faith means full surrender. Remember Noah? He did all that God asked him to do. Remember Abraham? He went where God asked him to go. Remember Moses? He became what God wanted him to become. These worthy examples yielded their hearts to the will of God and freely received His righteousness! If we allow Jesus to be the Lord of our life, we will want to obey Him. Jesus told His disciples, **"You are my friends if you do what I command.... Whoever has my commands and obeys them, he is the one who loves me. He**

who loves me will be loved by my Father, and I too will love him and show myself to him." (John 15:14, 14:21)

God reveals the future

Now that salvation has been looked at from the personal view, we must look at the corporate or global view of how God implements the plan of salvation.

God's purpose in choosing the descendants of Abraham as a special people was not to make them the exclusive object of His love and special blessings. Rather, He chose them to be ambassadors of His love. **"...I will also make you a light for the Gentiles, that you may bring my salvation to the ends of the earth."** (Isaiah 49:6) Israel was to be a channel through which the world would come to know and love the God of Heaven, the Creator of all the universe. However, Satan thwarted that glorious plan by leading the Jews into total rebellion against their Creator.

For almost 850 years after Israel was delivered from the bondage of Egypt, Jesus worked with Israel to make them the great nation He wanted them to be. Each time Israel reached a plateau of physical comfort and wealth, they promptly forgot God and turned to idolatry. The reason idolatry was so attractive to Israel is that pagan religious services were very different than the worship of Jesus.

True worship

The worship of Jesus is thoughtful and reflective. The worship of Jesus causes soul searching and brings the sinner to a greater or daily realization of his need of a Savior. True worship unmasks our deceitful hearts. In short, the worship of Jesus is like going to the dentist for a checkup thinking that everything is OK and discovering there are hidden cavities! The worship of Jesus penetrates the soul and reveals hidden thoughts and motives that are impure. This type of worship is obviously contrary to human nature and thus, Israel sought other "more exciting" gods to worship.

Pagan worship

Pagan worship comes in a thousand forms and ranges from the sublime to the ridiculous. Satan has devised a counterfeit worship for every type of lust. Some forms of false worship appear very close to true worship while other forms are excuses for the most degrading acts. Given the diverse range of false worship, the only general statement that can be made about false worship is that it neither glorifies our Creator nor brings the worshiper into harmony with His truth. There is a psychological law that says, "By beholding, we become changed." This means that we become like the object of our worship! In time, false worship leads men and women to behave like the creator of sin while true worship leads men and women to become like their holy Creator!

False worship appeals to the carnal or fallen nature. Those who worship in darkness hate truth because their deeds are exposed by the light! Jesus told His disciples, **"If the world hates you, keep in mind that it hated me first. If you belonged to the world, it would love you as its own. As it is, you do not belong** to the world, but I have chosen you out of the world. That is why the world hates you... No servant is greater than his master. If they persecuted me, they will persecute you also." (John 15:18-20) In Israel's day, pagan worship included entertainment of all kinds. History tells us that everything from infant sacrifice to gross sexual practices were performed on or for the benefit of worshipers. Worship in many ways became a spectator's delight. The interesting thing about such drama is that people can live out certain fantasies without actually participating in the act.

Today, television, radio, magazines and novels fulfill many of the sensual desires that pagan worship services provided for ancient Israel. Many of the Israelites would not actually commit the indecent acts they witnessed, but they enjoyed watching them nonetheless. How does this compare with the multitude of evil acts committed on TV each day? Are we becoming a more noble and God-like nation as a result of our reading and entertainment?

God's wrath on Israel

By 605 B.C., the Jews had become so totally resistant to God's plan and so degenerate in behavior that something drastic had to be done to get their attention. Therefore, God planned the destruction of Israel. He would not destroy all of it. He would save a remnant. With this remnant He would start over and try one last time to achieve His objective. So Jesus sent Babylonian monarch, King Nebuchadnezzar, to destroy Jerusalem. After three sieges, Nebuchadnezzar completely destroyed Jerusalem and carried off a remnant of Israel into captivity. Jesus did not destroy Jerusalem without warning. He sent several prophets to Israel so they might know what He was going to do and why. But Israel not only rejected the warning messages, they killed or destroyed most of the prophets who gave them!

Jeremiah was one such prophet. Jesus speaking through Jeremiah said, **"O house of Israel..., I am bringing a distant nation against you - an ancient and enduring nation, a people whose language you do not know, whose speech you do not understand. Their quivers are like an open grave; all of them are mighty warriors. They will devour your harvests and food, devour your sons and daughters; they will devour your flocks and herds, devour your vines and fig trees. With the sword they will destroy the fortified cities in which you trust. Yet even in those days... I will not destroy you completely. And when the people ask 'Why has the Lord our God done all this to us?' you will tell them, 'As you have forsaken me and served foreign gods in your own land, so now you will serve foreigners in a land not your own'.... This is what the Lord Almighty, the God of Israel, says: 'Listen! I am going to bring on this city and the villages around it every disaster I pronounced against them, because they were stiff-necked and would not listen to my words.... I will hand all Judah over to the king of Babylon, who will carry them away to Babylon or put them to the sword.' "** (Jeremiah 5:15-19, 19:15, 20:4)

One of the remnant taken into captivity was a young man named Daniel. This young man, unlike most young men of his time, loved the Lord with all his heart. The story of his life is quite remarkable for God used this humble young man to reach the proud heart of King Nebuchadnezzar, the emperor of the world.

Jesus revealed to Daniel a great prophetic chart or outline describing the future of Israel, and of the rest of the world. The visions recorded in the book of Daniel not only provide a wealth of information about the timing of the plan of salvation but they also tell us how God works. We will now investigate one of the apocalyptic visions of Daniel and see how close we are to that glorious day.

Daniel 2 opens the future

Stop! If you are not acquainted with the story in Daniel 2, please read Daniel 2 in your Bible before continuing with this study. Four important issues are presented from this chapter.

1.   First, we see the omniscience of God declared. Daniel said, **"...there is a God in heaven who reveals mysteries. He has shown King Nebuchadnezzar what will happen in days to come...."** (Daniel 2:28) After explaining the vision, Daniel said, **"...The great God has shown the king what will take place in the future. The dream is true and the interpretation is trustworthy."** (Daniel 2:45)

2.   Jesus revealed to the great monarch of Babylon that astrologers,

magicians, enchanters and soothsayers are not connected to God, nor do they have the ability to "predict" the future. Their works (then and now) are essentially a collection of clever lies. (Daniel 2:8-11)

3.   Daniel 2 reveals the omnipotence of Jesus. Omnipotence means "having all power." Daniel said, **"Praise be to the name of God for ever and ever; wisdom and power are his. He changes times and seasons; he sets up kings and deposes them. He gives wisdom to the wise and knowledge to the discerning. He reveals deep and hidden things; he knows what lies in darkness, and light dwells with him."** (Daniel 2:20-22) In a later vision Daniel again reminded the king, **"...the Most High is sovereign over the kingdoms of men and gives them to anyone he wishes."** (Daniel 4:25)

4.   The vision and interpretation given to King Nebuchadnezzar and Daniel contains a broad apocalyptic outline of the future. Apocalyptic prophecy refers to prophecy that deals with a structured or sequential series of events. Jesus revealed to king Nebuchadnezzar that subsequent kingdoms would rise and fall until the time came for the God of Heaven to set up His kingdom on earth.

The kingdoms of man were appropriately represented to King Nebuchadnezzar by the symbol of an image made of different metals. Babylon was represented by the head of gold and kingdoms that followed were represented by metals of lesser value.

King Nebuchadnezzar was told another kingdom would succeed Babylon. This kingdom was represented by the chest and arms of silver. Afterwards, another kingdom would arise represented by the thighs of brass. The fourth kingdom was represented by the legs of iron. The fifth kingdom was represented by the feet of iron and clay and the last kingdom of earth was represented by 10 toes which represents a brief reign of 10 kings (a global confederation) just before Jesus appears.

King Nebuchadnezzar was told that during the reign of these 10 kings that, **"In the time of those kings (the last 10 kings), the God of heaven will set up a kingdom that will never be destroyed, nor will it be left to another people. It will crush all those kingdoms and bring them to an end, but it will itself endure forever."** (Daniel 2:44)

So Nebuchadnezzar's dream may be seen as a very broad explanation of the destiny of mankind beginning with his day. Comparing prophecy with history, we discover the following progression of world

empires: Babylon, Medo-Persia, Greece, Rome, many kings, 10 last kings and finally, the kingdom of God. History and prophecy harmoniously combine so that we might understand the plans of God!

Just as Jesus predicted (remember, He is omniscient), the first four kingdoms have come and gone. As you can see from the diagram below, we are about to enter the time period of the "ten toes". Soon, we will see a brief confederation of 10 kings, and we will know that the return of Jesus is at the door! More will be said about the brief reign of these 10 kings when we study Revelation 17.

For now, it is important to recognize two things:

a.   When "The Rock Of Ages" sets up His kingdom, it fully and completely destroys all the kingdoms of man. Daniel told the king, **"...a rock was cut out, but not by human hands. It struck the statue on its feet of iron and clay and smashed them. Then the iron, the clay, the bronze, the silver and the gold were broken to pieces at the same time and became like chaff on a threshing floor in the summer. The wind swept them away without leaving a trace. But the**

Nebuchadnezzar's Dream

Daniel 2:31-35

rock that struck the statue became a huge mountain and filled the whole earth." (Daniel 2:34,35) In other words, the kingdom of Jesus will not co-exist with the sinful kingdoms of man. Jesus will not reign on a sinful earth. Jesus will reign upon earth after sin has been destroyed.

b.   Twenty-five hundred years ago Daniel told King Nebuchadnezzar, "...The great God has shown the king what will take place in the future. The dream is true and the interpretation is trustworthy." (Daniel 2:45) Today, we see the truthfulness of the dream. In an earlier lesson the point was made that prophecy is history written in advance and history is prophecy fulfilled in the past. From the dream given to Nebuchadnezzar, it is clear that we are close to the end of the kingdoms of man. How close are we?

Salvation and prophecy work together

We have studied the plan of salvation and its two components. First, the penalty of sin was paid in full by the death of Jesus on Calvary. (Justification) Secondly, our Creator wants to restore His image in those who choose salvation. (Sanctification) Prophecy is to the plan of salvation what the wedding date is to a couple planning for marriage. The Bible often compares the second coming of Jesus to a marriage feast or a wedding. "Let us rejoice and be glad and give him glory! For the wedding of the Lamb has come." (Revelation 19:7) Those who have received salvation are anxious for the return of Jesus and consequently, they are interested in prophecy! What would you say about a couple who were indifferent about the date of their wedding? What would you say of Christians who are indifferent about the time of Christ's coming?

When it comes to the fullness of salvation, many people are confused. If it's so simple, why is it so hard to understand? The answer might be summed up by saying the plan is simple, but not shallow. It is wonderful, but intricate. The plan of salvation is a deep and fascinating subject and those who love God find great joy learning about His plans to return man to Eden. In the next chapter, we will investigate some of the sobering issues that stand behind the scenes of Calvary.

Chapter 6

The Ministry of Jesus

Jesus told Moses, "...have them make a sanctuary for me, and I will dwell among them. Make this tabernacle and all its furnishings exactly like the pattern I will show you." (Exodus 25:8,9)

Moses built a sanctuary in the wilderness according to the blue-prints given to him by God. Every detail was carefully followed. The sanctuary complex constructed in the wilderness consisted of the following items. (See Exodus 25-40.) See if you can identify each item listed below in the diagram on the next page.

a. The courtyard
b. A small building with two rooms: holy place/ most holy place
c. The altar of burnt offering
d. The laver
e. The altar of incense
f. The table of shewbread
g. The candlesticks
h. The ark of the covenant

The sanctuary was built in such a manner that it could be disassembled and carried from place to place. Jewish history reveals that every piece of metal, cloth, wood and stone used in the construction of the sanctuary had a name on it—the name of the person responsible for carrying it. When the bearer died, the next of kin became responsible. Thus, the responsibility of carrying the sanctuary was passed down through generations until the sanctuary was given a permanent resting place.

Understand the sanctuary service

The sanctuary service is a vital study. The significance of how and why each event took place is as broad and comprehensive as God is. Most Christians do not understand the value or meaning of the sanctuary service because the New Testament is clear that the religious *services* conducted in the earthly sanctuary became obsolete at the death of Jesus. However, many Christians are surprised to learn that the religious *meaning* of what took place in the earthly sanctuary applies to prophetic events, some of which are soon to take place. This point will be demonstrated later in this volume.

Jesus gave the sanctuary service to Israel as a model of the plan of salvation. They were to study into the meaning of the sanctuary events and understand the scope of the plan of salvation. Through a careful study of the sanctuary service, they were to comprehend the love and compassion of God. They were to be drawn into deepest appreciation of who God is and what He offers to the human family. They

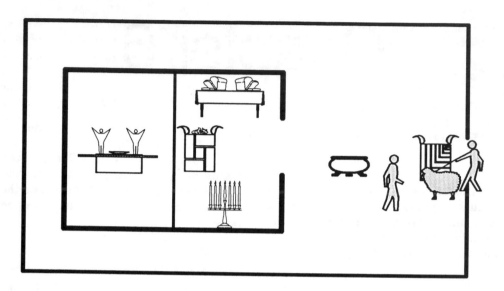

were to discover the love of God as they contemplated the price He would pay for salvation. And most of all, they were to share an understanding of God's love with the world! As receptors of God's blessings, they were to be the human agency through which the knowledge of God would be spread abroad.

Fundamental point about Israel

There is a lot of confusion among Christians about God's relationship with ancient Israel. Some believe that the covenant given to Abraham exclusively belonged to the Jews. While it is clear that God chose the people of Israel to accomplish His purpose, it is also important to understand that God was not excluding the rest of the people living upon earth at that time. Rather, it was God's intention that Israel demonstrate what He was like *to the rest of the world* and thus bring many to know and love the God of

Abraham. In this way, the entire world would be blessed through Abraham's descendants. Israel was to be an agent for distributing God's blessings and truth—not the exclusive object of His affection.

God's purpose for the Jews

Before Moses died, he reminded Israel of their calling. He said,

"...The Lord your God has chosen you out of all the peoples on the face of the earth to be his people, his treasured possession. The Lord did not set his affection on you and choose you because you were more numerous than other peoples, for you were the fewest of all peoples. But it was because the Lord loved you and kept the oath he swore to your forefathers that he brought you out with a mighty hand and redeemed you from the land of slavery, from the power of Pharaoh king of Egypt. Know therefore that the Lord your God is God; he is the faithful God, keeping his covenant of love to a thousand generations of those who love him and keep his commands. But those who hate him he will repay to their face by destruction; he will not be slow to repay to their face those who hate him. Therefore, take care to follow the commands, decrees and laws I give you today." (Deuteronomy 7:6-11)

History reveals that the Jews never caught the vision of God's plan for their nation. The Jews failed to become a model nation. They were to represent the God of Heaven in such a way that others would want to know their God. But Israel failed to grasp the concept. About 700 B.C., the Lord revealed through Isaiah that Israel was so far away from His plan, that He was going to destroy the nation and start over with a remnant. After His wrath passed, God promised that He would restore Israel and said, "...I will also make you a light for the Gentiles that you may bring my salvation to the ends of the earth." (Isaiah 49:6)

Seven hundred years later, Jesus Himself emphasized the intended purpose of the Jews saying, "You are the salt of the earth. But if the salt loses its saltiness, how can it be made salty again? It is no longer good for anything, except to be thrown out and trampled by men. You are the light of the world. A city on a hill cannot be hidden... let your light shine before men, that they may see your good deeds and praise your Father in heaven." (Matthew 5:13-16)

Now the Pharisees recognized the responsibility of winning converts to Judaism, but the reputation of the Jews among nations became so bad, that no one wanted to be a part of them! Jesus said to them, "Woe to you, teachers of the law and Pharisees, you hypocrites! You travel over land and sea to win a single convert, and when he becomes one, you make him twice as much a son of hell as you are." (Matthew 23:15)

If the Jews had not been so stiff-necked, they would have understood their glorious opportunity. They were the people through whom Messiah would come. But, in their self-centered nationalistic views, they vainly thought that the Messiah would come and elevate them above all other nations. They didn't realize that their role was to exalt the Messiah above all false gods.

It is ironic that many Samaritans, half-breeds whom the Jews hated, understood the purpose of the promised Messiah. They told the woman at the well, "We no longer believe just because of what you said: now we have heard for ourselves, and we know that this man really is the Savior of the world." (John 4:42)

Jesus tried to get Nicodemus to realize that Messiah's purpose was not the elevation of Israel. The scope was much larger. Jesus said, "For God so loved the *world* that He gave His one and only Son...." (John 3:16) King David recognized the sovereignty of the Lord over the whole world. He said, "Let all the earth fear the Lord; let all the people of the world revere him. For he spoke, and it came to be; he commanded, and it stood firm." (Psalm 33:8,9)

God chooses some poor people

Many people are confused about dispensationalism. The premise behind dispensationalism is that God changes the conditions for salvation from time to time. In other words, people are saved today in a different way than in times past. This doctrine is built upon a misunderstanding of God's covenant with man. God's offer of salvation to man has never changed. From Adam and Eve to this very day, salvation has *always* come by faith in God. The problem with salvation is that faith is often misunderstood. Faith is much more than an intellectual ascent or agreement with truth. The Bible's definition of faith is "complete surrender to the will of God." See Matthew 7:21. This is where ancient Israel failed. This is where most of us fail.

To understand why God selected Abraham and his descendants and gave them the rich treasures of His blessings, we have to review a little Bible history:

a.   About 400 years after the flood, while the population of earth was relatively small, God looked down upon the earth and found a descendent of Noah that was a good man. God introduced Himself to Abram, and eventually, He called Abram out of heathenism and chose him to be the person through which all people on earth would be blessed. God said to Abram, **"I will make you into a great nation and I will bless you.... I will bless those who bless you and whoever curses you I will curse; and all peoples on earth will be blessed through you."** (Genesis 12:2,3)

b.   One night God asked Abram to count the stars – if he could. Then God said, **"So shall your offspring be. Abraham believed the Lord, and He credited it to him as righteousness."** (Genesis 15:6) It is important to realize that both Noah and Abram were declared *righteous* because they believed what God said. Notice what Paul says about these two men, **"By faith Noah, when warned about things not yet seen, in holy fear built an ark to save his family. By his faith he condemned the world and became heir of the righteousness that comes by faith. By faith Abraham, when called to go to a place he would later receive as his inheritance, obeyed and went, even though he did not know where he was going.... And so from this one man... came descendants as numerous as the stars in the sky and as countless as the sand on the seashore."** (Hebrews 11:7,8,12)

Timeout for a thought question

Do you think God promised Abraham a great number of biological descendants or was God promising to make Abraham the spiritual forefather of millions who would live by faith just as he lived by faith?

Note: A spiritual relative is someone who walks the same way as Abraham or Noah lived, that is, by faith. Jesus said to the Jews, **"...If you were Abraham's children... then you would do the things Abraham did."** (John 8:39) Christians often use the term "brother" or "sister" to denote kinship in a spiritual sense. Notice how Jesus defines who His brothers and sisters and mother are: **"While Jesus was still**

talking to the crowd, his mother and brothers stood outside, wanting to speak to him. Someone told him, 'Your mother and brothers are standing outside, wanting to speak to you.' He replied to him, 'Who is my mother, and who are my brothers?' Pointing to his disciples, he said, 'Here are my mother and my brothers. For whoever does the will of my Father in heaven is my brother and sister and mother.' " (Matthew 12:46-50)

Before answering the question of whether Abraham's offspring was to be literal or spiritual, consider this question: Can the faith and righteousness of an ancestor save a descendent from eternal death? Can the evil deeds of an ancestor condemn a descendant to eternal death? The answer in both cases is no. See Ezekiel 14:12-23. The Bible is clear. *Your* eternal destiny comes from *your* choices. Jesus said, "Behold, I am coming soon! My reward is with me, and I will give to everyone according to what he has done." (Revelation 22:12) Then what spiritual advantage came with being a Jew?

Abram and Sarai, his wife, thought the promise of God referred to biological offspring. To solve their childless problem, Sarai suggested that Abram sleep with Hagar, her maidservant, and thus they could begin a family. Abraham and Hagar bore Ishmael, and Ishmael became the father of 12 tribes. It may come as a surprise to learn that Abraham is the biological father of a great multitude currently exceeding 1 billion people: the Arabs. For further study read Genesis 16-21, 25:7-18.

But the Arabs were not the great multitude of descendants that God promised. And neither are the Jews the great multitude of descendants promised to Abraham. (Jews number less than 25 million today, that's about four-tenths of one percent of the world's population.)

The great multitude that God promised to Abraham will be the redeemed of earth! This number will be in the billions. In other words, the great multitude promised to Abraham are those who would walk with God just as he walked with God. This is why Jesus identified His brothers and sisters as those who do the will of God. (Matthew 12:46-50)

The Apostle Paul tried to convince the Jews that being a descendent of Abraham was beneficial. After all, Israel had been especially favored of God — BUT, he insisted, "A man is not a Jew if he is only one outwardly, nor is circumcision merely outward and physical. No, a man is a Jew if he is one inwardly; and circumcision is circumcision of the heart, by the Spirit, not by the written code...." (Romans 2:28,29)

Back to Jesus' plan for the Hebrews

c. So, about 650 years after the call of Abram, Jesus called a descendent of Abraham to deliver His people from Egypt. This man was Moses. Paul says, "Moses, when he had grown up, refused to be known as the son of Pharaoh's daughter. He chose to be mistreated along with the people of God rather than to enjoy the pleasures of sin for a short time. He regarded disgrace for the sake of Christ as of greater value than the treasures of Egypt, because he was

looking ahead to his reward." (Hebrews 11:24-26)

d. As Israel was about to enter the Promised Land, Moses summoned the Israelites and said, **"The Lord did not set his affection on you and choose you because you were more numerous than other peoples, for you were the fewest of all peoples. But it was because the Lord loved you and kept the oath he swore to your forefathers that he brought you out (of Egypt) with a mighty hand and redeemed you from the land of slavery, from the power of Pharaoh king of Egypt. Know therefore that the Lord your God is God; he is the faithful God, keeping his covenant of love to a thousand generations of those who love him and keep his commands."** (Deuteronomy 7:7-9)

Moses made it quite clear that Israel was not going to receive the land of Canaan from the nations occupying the territory because of their righteousness! **"...No, it is on account of the wickedness of these nations that the Lord is going to drive them out before you. It is not because of your righteousness or your integrity that you are going in to take possession of their land; but on account of the wickedness of these nations, the Lord your God will drive them out before you, to accomplish what he swore to your fathers, to Abraham, Isaac and Jacob... for you are a stiff-necked people."** (Deuteronomy 9:4-6)

When Jesus delivered Israel out of Egypt, He took them to an isolated place to teach them His ways. There were no enemies in the Sinai desert to torment Israel during their early days as a nation for that barren desert could not support life in any form. So, Jesus sent water gushing from a rock and dropped manna from heaven for 40 years. Their clothing did not wear out, neither did their shoes. See Deuteronomy 29:5.

Because Jesus wanted to be close to these people and teach them His ways of truth and righteousness, He commanded Moses, **"...have them make a sanctuary for me, and I will dwell among them. Make this tabernacle and all its furnishings exactly like the pattern I will show you."** (Exodus 25:8,9) Consider the condescension of Jesus. He took this uneducated group of "stiff-necked" slaves and attempted to transform them into a great nation of noble and beautiful examples of His recreative power. There was one condition though. Moses told them, **"If you fully obey the Lord your God and carefully follow all his commands I give you today, the Lord your God will set you high above all the nations on earth.... However, if you do not obey the Lord your God and do not carefully follow all his commands and decrees I am giving you today, all these curses will come upon you and overtake you."** (Deuteronomy 28:1,2,15,16)

Legalism not wanted

Moses did not imply that a "legalistic" relationship with God would bring greatness nor fulfill the purpose of God. Legalism is a term that means legal process. Legal process, by nature is nit-picking and technical. Moses was afraid that Israel would reduce God to a collection of rules, and he wanted Israel to see that their potential to be a great nation could not be fulfilled by merely doing what God said. Oh no. Unless they kept the spirit of God's law in their hearts, they would soon grow weary of obeying God's laws. So Moses said, **"Love the Lord your God and keep his requirements, his decrees, his laws and his commands always."** (Deuteronomy 11:1) **"Love the Lord your God with all your heart and with all your soul and with all your strength. These commandments that I give you today are to be upon your hearts."** (Deuteronomy 6:5,6) **"Because he loved your forefathers and chose their descendants after them, he brought you out of Egypt by his Presence and his great strength.... Acknowledge and take to heart this day that the Lord is God in heaven above and on the earth below. There is no other."** (Deuteronomy 4:37,39) Think about it. If you had been miraculously delivered from slavery and given a wonderful land to inhabit — if you had walked through the Red Sea and eaten manna for 40 years — if you had seen water gush from a rock and seen the powerful manifestations of Jesus at Mt. Sinai — wouldn't you love the Lord your God?

Think it through

Consider for a moment that Jesus, the Creator of heaven and earth, the Holy One of Israel, Jehovah God, The Great I AM, The Almighty, The God of Israel, is also the meek and lowly Jesus of Nazareth. Many Christians are overwhelmed to learn that the one called "Jesus" in the New Testament is the *same* Jesus of the Old Testament! Most Old Testament references about God actually refer to Jesus our Creator instead of the Father! Jesus said to the Jewish scholars, **"...you diligently study the scriptures because you think that by them you possess eternal life. These are the Scriptures that testify about me.... If you believed Moses, you would believe me, for he wrote about me."** (John 5:39,46)

Sanctuary services

The role of Jesus in the plan of salvation is wonderfully explained in the symbols and ceremonies of the Old Testament. Jesus designed that each service teach a special and specific lesson about the process of salvation that would be fulfilled during His first advent as well as His second advent. For this study, we will explore the meaning of three important services:

1. The morning and evening sacrifice
2. The sin offering
3. The Day of Atonement

The morning and evening sacrifice

The morning and evening sacrifices were conducted at sunrise and sunset each day. A flawless year old male lamb was sacrificed on the altar of burnt offering. The priest conducting the service carried some of the lamb's blood into the first room of the sanctuary (the holy place) and sprinkled some of the lamb's blood upon the altar of incense. The service also consisted of burning special incense on coals of the altar.

This sacrifice and its related services became known as the "daily" or "continual" for they took place each morning and evening. The reader must understand what the daily service represents. This involves a short story.

Before sin began, God told Adam (Genesis 2:16) that if he or Eve ate of the tree of the knowledge of good and evil, they were to be executed the moment they ate of the tree. And the only reason they weren't immediately executed is because Jesus stepped between the wrath of God and the guilty pair.

Carefully read the warning that God gave Adam and note the terms of punishment: **"But of the tree of the knowledge of good and evil, thou shalt not eat of it; for in the day that thou eatest thereof thou shalt surely die."** (Genesis 2:17 KJV) Notice again, "for *in the day* that thou eatest thereof thou shalt surely die." A quick comparison of this verse with the Amplified Bible, the New American Standard and the New Revised Standard reveals that an immediate execution of the sentence was to be carried out. The NIV clearly puts the matter in immediate language saying, **"when you eat of it you will surely die."**

Adam and Eve well knew the death penalty for disobedience. They knew about the devil and his intentions to harm them. They also knew they would be safe as long as they obeyed the command of God. They also knew that if they disobeyed, He who had not spared the angels, would not spare them. In short, the tree of knowledge of good and evil represented immediate death to them.

Then one day, Eve saw a beautiful serpent eating the fruit of the forbidden tree. Perhaps one of the greatest inducements to Eve's temptation and fall was the fact that the serpent did not immediately die after eating the fruit. Her amazement with this conflicting evidence was only second to the fact that the serpent could now speak as a result of eating the fruit! Eve was caught by complete surprise on both counts. These two surprises left her speechless and without a rational defense. And in this frame of mind, she entered into a deadly discussion with the serpent.

Eve was no match for the sophistry and cunning of the devil. He had an agenda, she had curiosity. He carefully questioned her knowledge of God's command so that he might entrap her with her own words. It didn't take long. Eve's innocent words to the serpent tell us that she associated the tree with sudden death. She responded to the serpent's inquiry saying, **"...God did say, 'You must not eat fruit from the tree that is in the middle of the garden, and you must not touch it, or you will die.' "** (Genesis 3:3) (Actually, God did not say they could not touch it. He said they could not *eat* of it. The point here is that she associated immediate death even with the touching of the tree.)

Eve cannot deny the evidence

How could Eve argue the surety of God's Word, since the serpent had eaten the fruit and had not immediately died? There he was, smacking his lips and enjoying another piece of fruit. Even more, the serpent now had the power of speech as a result of eating the forbidden fruit! The undeniable evidence before her led Eve to question what God had said. Eve lost faith in God's Word. If we add to her moment of confusion the satanic fantasy of "being like God," we can easily see how temptation overcame her. The devil led Eve to fantasize that she could possess new powers by simply eating the beautiful fruit. He may have used an argument like this, "If this fruit gave me, a mere serpent of the field the power of speech, what would it do for you, Eve?" In this strange and confusing state of mind, Eve took the offered fruit and ate it.

Heaven saw the drama. And, according to God's law, at that very moment, Eve was to be executed. That was the divine decree. But Jesus, Eve's Maker and Friend, stepped between the justifiable wrath of God and guilty Eve. Her execution was stayed—the sentence of death would be imposed, but through other means.

Back on earth, Eve gathered some fruit and ran to Adam. Now Eve became Satan's vehicle of temptation. When Adam saw the fruit, he knew what had happened. As he listened to Eve, he immediately sized up the situation. For the first time in his life, complete sadness filled his soul. He was not under the beguiling influence of a talking snake, yet he faced a great temptation. He knew that separation from Eve was inevitable. He was puzzled by the fact that Eve was not dead, for he well knew the words of His Maker. Adam knew that sudden death had been promised, yet Eve was standing right before him.

He contemplated his wife's predicament for some time and then he made a terrible

decision. He would rather share her fate, whatever it might be, than to live without her. Humanly speaking, we might admire Adam's great love for his wife, except that God asks that we love and obey Him first—even before family. See Matthew 22:37; 10:35-38.

Adam willfully violated the command of God because he wanted to be with Eve more than he wanted to obey God. He saw no solution to her dilemma. He did not trust God to save his wife even though her physical presence before him was proof that God had stayed her execution. So, he took the fruit and in the fullest sense, he bit off more than he and all his descendants would be able to chew. At that very moment, Jesus again stepped between the wrath of God and guilty man. Adam's execution was stayed. Yes, he would also die, but not immediately.

The plan for made for man

God foreknew that Adam and Eve would sin and that's why the plan of salvation was in place before the world was created. Even though they knew better, their sin was not in open defiance of God and this is why their execution was stayed. This is why salvation was offered to man. It is important to note here that the plan of salvation does not lessen the penalty of sin. The penalty still remains and eternal death will be executed at the end of the millennium. It is called the second death. It is also important to notice that the plan of salvation does not alter the consequence of sin—which is called sleep, or the first death. What the plan of salvation offers is pardon from the penalty of sin—not the consequence of sin. Pardon from the penalty of sin is only possible through the mediation of Jesus.

Our need for a mediator

Mediation is the action of "stepping between" God's wrath and man. Ever since that awful day, Jesus has been mediating on behalf of mankind. Paul says, **"For there is one God and one mediator between God and men, the man Christ Jesus."** (1 Timothy 2:5)

See if you can follow this point. Because Adam and Eve came under the condemnation of eternal death, all their offspring are born under the same condemnation. (Children born to slaves are slaves too.) Adam's sin was more serious than Eve's sin for two reasons. First, Adam intentionally chose to disobey. The issues were not misrepresented, nor did he act out of sheer impulse. Secondly, Adam was the trustee of the law. Genesis 2:16 says that God commanded *the man* not to eat of the tree. In other words, Adam is held responsible for sin, for he was put in charge and he willfully disobeyed a direct order from God! Keep in mind that the consequence of sin, whether accidental or willful, is always the same.

Because Adam willfully sinned, his descendants would be sinners. Paul wrote, **"Therefore, just as sin entered the world through one man, and death through sin, and in this way death came to all men, because all sinned."** (Romans 5:12) Because all human beings are under the same curse of sin, all human beings need a mediator if they want to escape the

penalty of sin. For this reason Jesus currently stands between (intercedes) the wrath of God and guilty man. Paul recognized this ministry of Jesus in heaven saying, **"Therefore he is able to save completely those who come to God through him, because he always lives to intercede for them."** (Hebrews 7:25)

The daily

This point is most important: the "daily" (also called the "continual") was designed to teach Israel that it was only through the *daily* intercession of Jesus, the lamb of God, that man could live without being destroyed! See Exodus 29:38-46; 30:7,8. The application of the "daily" provided **corporate** atonement on behalf of the whole nation of Israel and was not directed towards any one individual. See Leviticus 4. Therefore, the daily in ancient Israel symbolizes the daily ministry of Jesus which began the day Adam and Eve sinned and continues to this very day on behalf of the world.

The sin offering

From time to time, offerings were made by leaders or priests for specific sins. This sacrifice was conducted on the altar of burnt offering where the organs were ultimately consumed by the fire of the altar. Here the sinner placed his hands upon the head of his offering and confessed his sin, or if representing his family, the sins of his family. With his own hand, the sinner then took the life of the sacrificial lamb. The priest put some of the blood of the sacrifice on the horns of the altar and then he poured the blood from this offering into a container at the base of the altar. The sinner then carried the offal away from the service and then disposed it.

This sacrifice was designed to teach the Hebrews two things. First, remission for personal sins could only come through shed blood. The death of the lamb pointed forward to the death of Jesus — as a personal sacrifice for those who wanted His salvation. Secondly, God wanted Israel to understand that He had a way of transferring sins away from the sinner. See Leviticus 6:24-30.

The significance of this offering cannot be overstated. This offering brings sin and sinner together and then this offering separates sin from sinner. Jesus wanted each person to understand that each sinner had to confess his sin upon the head of the lamb before the sin could be atoned for. In this setting, Jesus wanted each person to know that his sin could be forgiven.

Now here is a critical point. Neither the daily or the sin offering in ancient Israel had efficacy. *This means that the offerings did not actually bring atonement. Rather, these offerings only demonstrated how atonement would be made.* Paul clearly says, **"...it is impossible for the blood of bulls and goats to take away sins."** (Hebrews 10:4)

Two important contrasts

There are two important differences between the daily sacrifice and the sin offering. First, the daily sacrifice referred to something *that had been done* while the sin offering pointed to something that would be done. In other words, the daily pointed to the fact that Jesus had already stepped between the wrath of God and guilty man. He did this the day Adam and Eve sinned. On the other hand, the sin offering pointed to the fact that Jesus would die "at an appointed time" for the sins of the world. Paul says, **"But when the time had fully come, God sent his Son, born of a woman, born under law...."** (Galatians 4:4)

The second contrast between these two offerings centers on their application. The daily was a corporate offering. It was offered for the camp of Israel as a group while the sin offering was presented by a person or a family. Through these two offerings, the sins of Israel were transferred away from the sinner. Corporately, the sins of Israel were transferred into the sanctuary. Individually, the sins of people were transferred onto the horns of the altar of burnt offering. Then, at the end of the religious year, on the Day of Atonement, the blood which had been deposited on the altars of the sanctuary was removed. Thus, the sanctuary was cleansed of defilement and the record of sin was removed.

The Day of Atonement

The tenth day of the seventh month was a yearly judgment day called the Day of Atonement. The word "atonement" means reconciliation, a bringing together or at-one-ment. This day always fell on the tenth day of the seventh month and it was a special sabbath. No work was done on the Day of Atonement regardless of the day of the week it fell upon. (Leviticus 16:29) All Israel was required to come before God in person on this day to account for their deeds during the past year. Only the high priest officiated in the temple services on the Day of Atonement.

Other priests who normally served in the temple throughout the year could not represent Israel before God on this day. And before the high priest could officiate on this day, he had to go through a qualifying process in the most holy compartment of the sanctuary. *He had to be found worthy of conducting this work before he could officiate on behalf of Israel!* Some discussion on this matter is necessary because the qualification process is intimately connected to an impressive scene in Revelation 4 & 5.

Even though the high priest was chosen by God to serve in His sanctuary, the high priest had to be found acceptable or worthy of service on this annual occasion. The process began on the morning of the Day of Atonement. First, the high priest offered a very expensive sacrifice. He killed a bull and presented the blood before God in the most holy portion of the sanctuary. With trembling and reverence, the high priest entered the second room of the sanctuary to stand in the presence of God. In the brilliance of Shekinah glory, the priest's life and behavior was reviewed and God pronounced approval or rejection on the suitability of the high priest to officiate on behalf of his people. (This preparatory service on the Day of Atonement symbolized a service that would occur in heaven's sanctuary when the judgment of human beings would begin. We shall observe the importance of this preparatory service when we study the seven seals. See Leviticus 16:17 and Hebrews 7:27; 9:7.)

After the high priest was deemed worthy, the service on the Day of Atonement focused on the cleansing of the sanctuary, that is, the restoration of the sanctuary to a sinless condition. All year long, the sins of the people had been transferred to the sanctuary through the blood of the sacrifices and offerings and on this very special day, the sanctuary was restored to its sinless condition by the high priest. This was symbolically done by the high priest when he removed the blood from the horns of both altars. After cleansing the horns of the altars, the high priest then wiped his bloody hands on the head of the scapegoat. Thus the sins of the sanctuary were transferred from the sanctuary to the scapegoat. More will be said about this later.

Notice the relationship?

The daily, the sin offering and the Day of Atonement demonstrate the basic building blocks within the plan of salvation. The daily demonstrates unmerited justification (the gift of God), the sin offering demonstrates sanctification (the response of man) and the Day of Atonement demonstrates the final judgment and disposition of sin (the judgment). These elements will be expanded in our next two studies. For now, we need to look at the sanctuary process to understand the physical process of these things so that we might understand what they represent.

The penalty and the consequence

In the economy of salvation, there is a distinct difference between penalties and consequences. Sin contains both properties. Here are two simple examples: First, if a man rapes a woman and if the rapist is brought to justice, he will receive a penalty for his deed. However, the consequence of his deed will remain with the woman for the rest of her life. In this case, the penalty is upon one person and the consequence is upon another. Secondly, suppose a drunken driver has a wreck. The accident causes the driver to lose his leg. When justice is served, the driver is not only assessed a penalty for driving while intoxicated, he must spend the rest of his life without a leg. In this case, the driver receives both penalty and consequence. The point here is that sin has both a penalty and a consequence. The penalty for sin is eternal death. The consequences of sin can vary from momentary suffering to a life time of remorse.

The sanctuary service addresses both elements of sin. Here's how: After the high priest received the approval of God to serve on behalf of Israel, he went out into the courtyard to select one of two goats as sacrifices for the sins of Israel. One goat was chosen to pay the penalty for sin, the other was left to bear the consequence of sin. The sacrificial goat paid the penalty for sin as a sin offering (Leviticus 16:9) and the other goat received the consequence of sin. This goat, sometimes called the scapegoat, was taken into the wilderness to die after the sins of the sanctuary were placed upon his head. (Leviticus 16:22) This is a major point, for there is an important difference between paying the penalty for sin and reaping the consequences of sin. These two goats symbolize two distinct processes for death. The first goat pointed forward to the death of Jesus. Jesus paid the penalty for the sins of those who receive Him as Savior. The second goat symbolizes the death of Satan. As the father of sin, Satan will not only receive the penalty and consequence for his own sins, but he must suffer the consequences of all the sins committed by the redeemed. These will be added to his account and he will suffer proportionately. God requires complete atonement for sins.

Note: The sanctuary process reveals a valuable lesson. Each wicked person will receive the penalty and reap the consequences for their own sins at the end of the millennium. The penalty will be ultimate death. The consequences will be experienced during the time spent in suffering. (More will be said about this matter in the chapters on the Judgment.) However, the redeemed will escape the penalty of their sins because Jesus, the author of salvation, paid the price. (Goat #1) But, the consequences of their sins will be received by Satan, the author of sin. (Goat #2)

Here's how the atonement service took place: After being found worthy to officiate, the high priest removed the beautiful and lavish garments of his office. In plain white linen, he sacrificed the first goat and then entered the most holy place a second time. The change in clothing symbolizes the work of Jesus on earth for man. To make atonement for man, Jesus laid aside His beautiful clothing in heaven and He came to earth and served before God in the humble garb of man.

When God accepted the atonement presented on behalf of Israel, the high priest then left the most holy place. Next, the high priest washed and removed the accumulated blood on the horns of the altar of incense that stood before the veil in the first compartment (or holy place). Leaving the holy place, the priest then walked out into the courtyard and cleansed the horns on the altar of burnt offering. Then, he proceeded to the remaining goat where he wiped his bloody hands on the head of this animal. This animal was called "Azazel," which is translated as the scapegoat in some versions of the Bible. After wiping his hands on the head of the goat, a very capable man took the second goat miles out into the desert to die. The goat died a slow, agonizing death because the consequences of sin are agonizing to the victims of sin. Ask a woman who has been raped. Ask a child who was sexually molested. Ask a mother whose son was innocently murdered.

Notice the three step process: the penalty for sin was paid by a sacrificial offering, the sanctuary was cleansed of blood and restored to a "sinless" condition, then all record of sin (the blood on the horns) was placed upon the head of the second goat. When the goat was removed from camp, the camp was clean of sin and the high priest joyfully made the announcement.

These services are found in Revelation

The morning and evening sacrifices, the sin offering and the Day of Atonement teach a great deal about the book of Revelation, for Revelation's story centers around heaven's sanctuary! Paul clearly points out that Jesus is directly involved in the heavenly sanctuary services. **"...We do have such a high priest, who sat down at the right hand of the throne of the Majesty in heaven, and who serves in the sanctuary, the true tabernacle set up by the Lord, not by man. ...(for men) serve at a sanctuary that is a copy and shadow of what is in heaven. This is why Moses was warned when he was about to build the tabernacle: 'See to it that you make everything according to the pattern shown you on the mountain.' "** (Hebrews 8:1-5)

In other words, the sanctuary services in the Old Testament are a "shadow" or outline of real events taking place in heaven. The sanctuary services explain the operation or process of saving man. Jesus, the High Priest of the human race, serves in the heavenly sanctuary which God built while the sanctuary built by Moses was only a teaching model based on the true process in heaven. What is Jesus doing up there? How do the services of the Old Testament sanctuary system relate to the end of the world and the great judgment day of the human race?

Here's the heart of the problem. Many Christians miss the entire point of the earthly sanctuary just like as the ancient Jews did. The Jews believed the sacrificial services brought salvation, when in reality, they never made salvation possible! Paul clearly states, **"But those sacrifices are an** annual reminder of sins, because it is impossible for the blood of bulls and goats to take away sins." (Hebrews 10:3,4) God told Isaiah, " 'The multitude of your sacrifices - what are they to me?' says the Lord. 'I have more than enough of burnt offerings, of rams and the fat of fattened animals; I have no pleasure in the blood of bulls and lambs and goats.' " (Isaiah 1:11) The point here is that the sacrificial services were never intended as a means to heaven, rather they only serve as examples of what Jesus is doing for man and why!

A clearer understanding

Carefully consider this point: The sacrifice of animals in the Old Testament was only a "teaching" model. The sacrifice of animals never produced salvation. Rather, God gave the Jews this model so they (and their descendants) might understand the price and process of salvation. The Jews turned the model into a perversion— thinking (like the pagans) that salvation came through religious acts rather than a broken and contrite heart.

When Jesus died on Calvary, the earthly model was finished. Reality had come. Therefore the sacrifices of animals became null and void. The price for sin had been paid, "once for all." But, the *meaning* of the model continues, for the service represented by the Day of Atonement is yet to conclude in heaven.

Think it through

God chose a lamb to symbolize Christ, but the blood of a million lambs cannot

bring salvation. Sanctuary services did not bring salvation to those who observed them, for salvation only comes through faith. (Hebrews 11) Old Testament sanctuary services are still important because they prefigure reality; the shadow helps us understand reality.

Thirty times in Revelation, Jesus is called "The Lamb"; once, Jesus is called a lion. (Revelation 5:5) To those who receive Him, Jesus is a sacrificial lamb. He is gentle and loving. To those who reject Him, Jesus will someday appear as an angry lion, devouring all who have rebelled against Him. (Revelation 19:11-15) As said earlier, the revelation of all that Jesus is—is something the world shall soon see.

Notes

Chapter 7

How the Time of the End is Identified

Those who study prophecy study the deep things of God. The study of prophecy is the pursuit of understanding the purposes and works of God. Unfortunately, most people have a very narrow and limited view of the plan of salvation and this is confirmed when we hear, "Prophecy has little to do with salvation, so why bother with it?" Fact is, prophecy has everything to do with salvation. If the doctrine of salvation reveals the justice and mercy of God, then prophecy reveals the fullness of God's plans to accomplish salvation. Can you imagine a young couple engaged to be married without discussing a date for marriage? Can you image the Church praising God for His great salvation *and* unconcerned about the consummation of salvation? Is it possible for God's people to be anxiously waiting for the Bridegroom *and* indifferent about the timing and events that preface His return?

Nebuchadnezzar's dream

Remember King Nebuchadnezzar's dream? We investigated his vision in Chapter 5. God showed the king the succeeding kingdoms of man outlined in the form of a man made from various metals. A few comments were made in Chapter 5 that are presented here again because they are so sweeping in their meaning:

1. First, the omniscience of God was twice declared to the king. Daniel said, **"...there is a God in heaven who reveals mysteries. He has shown King Nebuchadnezzar what will happen in days to come...."** (Daniel 2:28) And after explaining the vision, Daniel said, **"...The great God has shown the king what will take place in the future. The dream is true and the interpretation is trustworthy."** (Daniel 2:45)

2. By giving this dream to the king, Jesus revealed to the great monarch of Babylon that astrologers, magicians, enchanters and soothsayers are not connected to God, nor do they have the ability to "predict" the future. Their works (back then and today) are simply a collection of clever lies. (Daniel 2:8-11)

3. Daniel revealed the omnipotence of Jesus to the king. Omnipotence means "having all power." Daniel said, **"Praise be to the name of God for ever and ever; wisdom and power are his. He changes times**

and seasons; he sets up kings and deposes them. He gives wisdom to the wise and knowledge to the discerning. He reveals deep and hidden things; he knows what lies in darkness, and light dwells with him." (Daniel 2:20-22) In a later vision Daniel again reminded the king of God's authority: "The decision is announced by messengers, the holy ones declare the verdict, so that the living may know that the Most High is sovereign over the kingdoms of men and gives them to anyone he wishes and sets over them the lowliest of men. ...the Most High is sovereign over the kingdoms of men and gives them to anyone he wishes." (Daniel 4:17,25)

4. The vision and interpretation given to King Nebuchadnezzar contains a broad apocalyptic outline of the future. In other words, the vision lays out a sequence of coming events. As said in Chapter 1, apocalyptic prophecy refers to prophecy that deals with a sequential series of events. Jesus revealed to Nebuchadnezzar that subsequent kingdoms would rise and fall until the time came for the God of Heaven to set up His kingdom on earth.

The kingdoms of man were appropriately represented to King Nebuchadnezzar by the image of a man made of different metals. Babylon was represented by the head of gold and

kingdoms that followed were represented by metals of lesser value.

King Nebuchadnezzar was bluntly told that another kingdom would succeed Babylon. This kingdom was represented by the chest and arms of silver. Afterwards, another kingdom would arise represented by the thighs of brass. The fourth kingdom was represented by the legs of iron. The fifth kingdom was represented by the feet of iron and clay and the sixth kingdom of earth was represented by 10 toes which represents a brief reign of 10 kings (a global confederation) just before Jesus appears. "As the toes were partly iron and partly clay, so this kingdom will be partly strong and partly brittle." (Daniel 2:42)

King Nebuchadnezzar was also told that during the reign of these 10 kings that, "In the time of those kings the God of heaven will set up a kingdom that will never be destroyed, nor will it be left to another people. It will crush all those kingdoms and bring them to an end, but it will itself endure forever." (Daniel 2:44)

So Nebuchadnezzar's dream may be seen as a very broad explanation of the destiny of mankind beginning with his day. Comparing prophecy with history, we discover the following progression of five world empires: Babylon, Medo-Persia, Greece, Rome and the time of many kings. We have yet to see the brief reign of the 10 last kings and the establishment of the kingdom of God. History and prophecy harmoniously combine so that we might understand the plans of God! Even more, a careful study of prophecy allows us to see where we are in the great chain of events.

Daniel has a vision

A few years after the king's vision, Daniel had a vision that covers the same kingdoms and same time periods as the dream of Nebuchadnezzar. In fact, the observant student will soon notice the prophetic process of repetition and enlargement within the books of Daniel and Revelation. The process of repetition and enlargement is indispensable in our search for truth because no one prophecy is complete in itself. In fact, all 18 apocalyptic prophecies in Daniel and Revelation combine to form a harmonious matrix and the operation of this matrix explains two things. First, we can locate the chronology of each prophetic element. Secondly, we can better understand one prophecy by adding those elements from other prophecies that occur at the same time. So, God gave the king a broad picture of future events and then God gave Daniel a view of the same thing with more detail!

Daniel saw a lion, bear, leopard and a terrible beast

Daniel's vision is recorded in Daniel 7. You should study this chapter in your Bible before continuing so that you can appreciate all that Daniel saw. Basically, Daniel's dream contained four strange beasts. They were unusual beasts in that features were added to their bodies to highlight certain characteristics. They were:

1. A lion with eagle wings
2. A bear with three ribs in its mouth
3. A leopard with four wings and four heads
4. A terrible beast with 10 horns

Daniel was told that these four beasts were four great kingdoms that would rise from the earth. (Daniel 7:17) Given the limited number of kingdoms that would rise before the world would come to an end outlined in Daniel 2, we naturally ask if these beasts parallel the kingdoms revealed in Daniel 2. Most Bible historians agree that the four beasts represent the *first four kingdoms* seen by Nebuchadnezzar. As said earlier, the Bible parallels prophetic sequences with other sequences to help us understand the meaning of a prophecy. So, as the lion is king of beasts and gold is king of metals, the kingdom of Babylon was represented to Daniel as a lion. The bear with three ribs in its mouth represents the savage rise of the Medo-Persian empire. The three ribs symbolize the skeletal remains of last three provinces that impeded its rise to power: Egypt, Lydia and Babylon. The leopard, swift and cunning, represents the rise of Grecia. The four heads represent the division of Greece after the death of its first king, Alexander the Great. The terrible beast represents the fourth kingdom that would rule over the world: Rome. The harmony of the chronological sequence and the contents of the visions with historical confirmation places the meaning of these symbols beyond reasonable controversy.

The fourth beast

Even though Daniel observed four beasts in his vision, he was distressed and awed by the fourth beast, for it was very different than the other beasts. This beast specifically persecuted the saints of God. (Daniel 7:21,25) The following is a brief summary of the specifications concerning the fourth beast in Daniel 7 and the little horn that came up later:

1. It starts out as the fourth world empire.
2. It is unusual in strength and furious with enemies.
3. It has teeth of iron.
4. Out of this kingdom 10 horns (or kings) arise.
5. After the 10 kings appear, a little horn arises and, in so doing, uproots three of the original 10 kings.
6. This new horn has all the fierce qualities of its parent, the terrible fourth beast.
7. The little horn power becomes a great horn—much stronger than any of the remaining seven horns.
8. The little horn power blasphemes the God of Heaven.
9. The little horn power wars against the saints for a specified time.
10. The little horn power "thinks" to change times and laws.

11. The little horn power endures until the end of the world.

The fourth beast has been historically recognized as Rome for more than 1,500 years. Rome followed the empire of Grecia. The little horn power (items 5-11 above) has likewise been identified by students of prophecy for more than 700 years as an antichrist power. There is no question concerning the character of the little horn. It is anti-God. The correct identity of this antichrist power is necessary because the time of the end begins when the little horn power is broken. (This point will be demonstrated later.) Also, the reader should know that the little horn power will play a leading role just before Jesus comes.

The little horn power is the great spiritual power that came out of the fourth kingdom, that is, Rome. For more than 700 years students of prophecy have called the little horn power the universal Christian Church or the Roman Catholic Church.

Note: The following is a brief description of what happened in the course of history to the Christian Church as it moved farther and farther away from the truth of God's Word by replacing the teachings of the Bible with man-made traditions or doctrines. The author sincerely believes there are many wonderful and dedicated Christian people within the Roman Catholic Church who love their church and faithfully practice its teachings. Many of its members have not had an opportunity or sufficient reason to consider the Protestant view of the Church's history. Even further, many Catholics have little or no knowledge concerning the origins of its doctrines or teachings. Upon examination, many Catholics are shocked to learn that many Church doctrines have no biblical basis whatsoever.

Process of identification

How did Protestant reformers identify the Catholic Church as being the little horn power? A collection of writings calling for Church reform began to circulate about A.D. 1300. As time passed, the number of people calling for change significantly increased because the abuses of the Church were open and defiant. Those denouncing the teachings or doctrines of the Church became known as "protestors" or "protestants." Their united plea was simple, "Away with the harsh and unjust rule of Roman clerics teaching man-made traditions. Give us the Bible alone as the Word of God. *Sola Scriptura.*" The cries of protestors provoked powerful church officials so that eventually, all protestors were condemned to the dungeon, stake or sword. Persecution, torture, discouragement and death are some of Satan's most persuasive tools.

Some of the better known Protestant reformers involved in the call for reformation were Wycliff, Huss, Jerome, Luther, Calvin, Knox, and Tyndale. As the conflict between Protestants and the Catholic Church grew, educated men throughout Europe began identifying the little horn power in Daniel 7 as the Papacy. Their conclusions were supported by the following:

Rome - fourth beast

The terrible fourth beast in Daniel 7 is historically confirmed and widely recognized as civil Rome, the fourth universal kingdom of the world. Civil Rome became a dominate power around 168 B.C. with the overthrow of Macedonia at the battle of Pydna. The powerful teeth of iron belonging to the terrible beast (remember, the legs of Nebuchadnezzar's image representing this fourth kingdom in Daniel 2 were also made of iron) fittingly described the unusual strength of Rome's military legions since they were first to extensively use iron weapons.

Ten horns overtake Rome

True, Rome was a world empire, but the world is made up of many ethnic groups. By the turn of the fifth century A.D., 10 ethnic nations were warring against the iron-clad authority of Rome. By A.D. 476, civil Rome was overrun and her power broken into pieces. The reformers identified the 10 horns as the tribal nations of the Ostrogoths, Heruli, Franks, Vandals, Lombards, Visigoths, Suevi, Burgundians, Alamanni and the Anglo-Saxons.

Little horn uproots three horns

According to Daniel 7, the little horn power was to become prominent after the appearing of the 10 horns. While it may be said the Christian Church began at the time of Christ, it must be understood that the Church in Rome grew from infancy to great political power over a period of about five centuries. According to Daniel's prophecy, the little horn power would start small, but become stronger than any of the 10 kingdoms represented by the 10 horns! A critical point must be made that *after* the 10 horns are in power, *then* the little horn rises to power, and in so doing, it uproots three of the first 10 horns.

According to the prophecy, the little horn would distinguish itself from the other horn kingdoms by "uprooting" three of the original 10 horns by their roots. History confirms that the Roman Church (the little horn) uprooted three tribal nations known as the Ostrogoths, Vandals, and Heruli. These were utterly destroyed for political reasons that involved a theological dispute on the deity of Christ. This dispute is well known and is called the Arian Controversy. Arius, a theologian from Alexandria, taught that Jesus was not equal to the Father. This, the Roman Church claimed, was blasphemy. And in a struggle for power and dominion, the Roman Church achieved the destruction of those who followed the teachings of Arius. The dominating influence of the Roman Christian Church upon the remaining seven tribal

nations is clearly confirmed through a thousand years of recorded history.

Little horn wages war on saints

According to Daniel, the little horn power would have the same fierce qualities as its parent, the fourth beast. The little horn would become "stouter" than all the other horns. It would have a mouth that spoke against the Most High and it would have eyes like a man. The mouth on the little horn indicates that the Church would make claims that the other horns could not make. The eyes indicate that the Church would "see" things that the other horns did not understand. In short, the little horn would be very intelligent and therefore, more responsible to God for its acts than the other horns.

Back in those days, religion attracted the best minds much like science does today. Whereas scientists are the high priests of our age, clerics commanded that kind of respect in years past. As the Church became politically powerful, she became lord over the nations of Europe. It was the Church that appointed kings and queens. The Church decided political issues. The Church controlled the kings of the world. The Church claimed the right to determine eternal life or death upon her subjects.

The Church was as determined and cruel in conquering her foes as her pagan parent was. To expand her power and influence, popes promised forgiveness of sin — past, present and future along with eternal salvation to anyone willing to fight for the expansion of the Holy Roman Empire. Millions perished in crusades fought in the name of God. Eventually, the Roman Catholic Church conquered Europe, and she ruled with an "iron" fist for almost 13 centuries.

At its high-water mark, the Church exercised a number of spiritual prerogatives that blasphemes God's truth. For example, the Church claimed infallibility for its leader! "We teach and define it to be a dogma divinely revealed that the Roman Pontiff, when he speaks *ex cathedra*, that is, when action in his office as pastor and teacher of all Christians, by his supreme Apostolic authority... he enjoys that infallibility with which the divine Redeemer willed His Church to be endowed in defining doctrine concerning faith and morals; and therefore such definitions of the said Roman Pontiff are irreformable of themselves, and not from the consent of the Church" (Quoted from a booklet titled *The Papacy, Expression of God's Love*, page 29, published by the Knights of Columbus).

Little horn empowered 1,260 years

Daniel predicted the little horn power would persecute the saints of God for a time, times and half a time. This phrase represents three and a half years. A "time" equals one year. "Times" represent two years, and "half a time" represents half a year. We know these terms represent 1,260 days because John uses these time periods interchangeably. Compare Revelation 12:6 and 12:14. Because this time-period occurs during the operation of Jubilee cycles, we must use the day/year principle to determine the length of this time period. (See section in appendix on Secrets of the Jubilee calendar.) Consequently, the 1,260 days of this prophecy represent 1,260 literal years. The point here is that God set a limit; He decreed a length of time that the Papacy could persecute His saints.

The beginning of the 1,260 year period was established by Protestant reformers as taking place in the middle of the sixth century A.D. Specifically, the dates of A.D. 533-538 seemed plausible, for the pope began exercising authority of life and death over the subjects of the fragmented Roman empire at that time. Absolute power as "Corrector of Heretics" was granted to the pope by Emperor Justinian through an imperial decree in A.D. 533. A few years later, the Church moved to solidify her gift. Roman Pontiffs began a reign that would become known as the "Dark Ages."

If A.D. 538 is the correct commencement date of papal authority, and if the day/year principle is applicable, a break or termination in the power of the Papacy should occur 1,260 years later in 1798. A significant number of Protestants reached the conclusion that papal rule should end before the arrival of the 18th century. Writers such as Thomas Parker, 1646; Increase Mather, president of Harvard, 1723; William Burnet, 1724; Richard Clark, 1759, and others anticipated the prophetic collapse of the Roman Church power during the late 18th century!

And sure enough, General Berthier and a French army unwittingly fulfilled the 1,260 year prophecy by capturing the pope and putting him in prison in February, 1798. Thus, the predicted time of little horn rule and persecution was fulfilled.

Little horn "thinks" to change law of God

Daniel predicted the little horn power would "think" to change times and laws. In A.D. 787, at the Second Nicean Council, the second commandment was entirely removed from the Ten Commandments and the tenth commandment was divided into two separate commandments so that 10 would remain. This was done so questions about the use of images or icons in worship would not come up. In addition, the fourth commandment was reduced to just a few words so questions would not be raised about the day of worship. Compare the Ten Commandments (Exodus 20:3-17) with a Catholic Catechism for confirmation on these changes.

Little horn claims to be God on earth

As a capstone for identification, Protestants for more than 400 years have argued that the blasphemous title of the pope, which in Latin is "Vicarious Filii Dei," and means "in place of the Son of God," was a fulfillment of prophecy. In English,

differing forms of this title are used: for example, "Vicar of Jesus Christ" or "Vicar of God." Regardless of the term used, the meaning is still the same, "in place of the Son of God." This title becomes particularly meaningful when the reader understands that popes claim divine authority. In other words, they can decide all matters regarding the work of God on earth, even whether a person is sent to hell or to heaven.

"Anti" Christ

Historically, Protestants found only one organization that met all the specifications of the little horn power of Daniel 7. It was the papacy. (Even though there is debate within Protestantism today as to who the little horn power is, the chronological and historical harmony of Daniel 7 leaves no room for doubt.) The tragic point here is that Satan succeeded. He so corrupted the Christian Church that it became "anti" Christ. How clever of the devil. He corrupted the very institution that Jesus established for the salvation of souls. Some have estimated that the Roman Church sentenced over 50 million people to death during its millennial reign for refusing to receive its doctrines. During those dark years, the devil enjoyed a tormenting rule over earth. And, he even obtained it through the agency that Christ had established. The devil ever works to ruin the plans of God.

The reader should know that Revelation predicts the future appearing of the Antichrist (notice the capital A). This appearing is not the rise and appearing of the Catholic Church. Yes, the Catholics will play a part in final events, but so will the Jews, Protestants, Moslems, and all other religions. The devil himself will appear on earth and claim all power and authority that rightfully belongs to God! This will be the final blasphemy, and the Antichrist to come is none less than the physical appearing of the devil! He will claim to have the power and authority of God and his miracles will deceive hundreds of millions of people.

History repeated

Again, it is said that Satan is the Antichrist. He led the Jews to become anti-christ and he succeeded in causing the Christian Church to do the same in about the same length of time! In both cases, the devil achieved his goals by putting self-centered, ambitious and unprincipled men into leadership. Love of money and power hold far greater reward and satisfaction to the carnal nature than following the teachings of the humble and meek Carpenter from Nazareth.

Jesus starts over a final time

Jesus did not give up His work of saving man because the Jews and the Christian Church became "anti-Christ." Just as He called men and women out of Judaism to begin the Christian Church, He called those who loved and sought truth out of the Christian Church to a new movement. Historically, this movement is called the Protestant Reformation. Thus Jesus passed the privilege of giving the gospel to the Protestants. Admittedly, the Protestant movement of the 19th century started out with great success. But Protestantism has miserably failed. Today, faithful church attendance has reached an all time low in America.

(Note: The term Christian as used in this review of history applies to the Roman Catholic Church which still claims to possess the one and only true Christian faith. Even though Protestants claim to be Christians, there are vast differences between Catholics and Protestants.)

Incredible timing

The timing of prophetic events is incredible. As predicted, the little horn was "wounded" in 1798 when Napoleon captured the pope and placed him in prison. The iron grip of Rome was broken. As a result, the Protestant movement rapidly grew and became a dominant world influence. Truth could now flourish for the Dark Ages were over. The printing press had been invented and Bibles could be printed. The Word of God could be owned and read by ordinary people. No longer was the Bible cloistered away in a monastery or a monk's library. Jesus raised up the Protestant Movement so that men and women could hear greater Bible truth—truths such as salvation by faith, the ministry of Jesus in heaven's temple, the second coming, and the prophetic meaning of 1798! In the simplest of terms, the Roman Catholic Church was brought down so that Bible truth might prosper. Freedom of conscience and worship became basic human rights. No longer would people have to be separated from the knowledge of God by a priest. Everyone could own a Bible and have the liberty to search God's Word for themselves.

The time of the end

The Bible speaks of a specific time period that exists at the end of the world. In general terms, it is called "the Great Day of the Lord," and in most cases, this term refers to a time period when the authority and glory of Almighty God shall be revealed. In the book of Daniel, this time period is called "the appointed time of the end." Notice these texts (emphasis mine):

Daniel 8:17 **As he [Gabriel] came near the place where I was standing, I was terrified and fell prostrate. "Son of man,"** he said to me, *"understand that the vision concerns the time of the end."*

Daniel 8:19 **He said: "I am going to tell you what will happen later** *in the time of wrath,* **because the vision concerns** *the appointed time of the end."*

Daniel 11:35 **Some of the wise will stumble, so that they may be refined, purified and made spotless** *until the time of the end, for it will still come at the appointed time.*

Daniel 11:36 **The king [of the North] will do as he pleases. He will exalt and magnify himself above every god and will say unheard-of things against the God of gods. He will be successful** *until the time of wrath is completed, for what has been determined must take place.*

Daniel 11:40 *At the time of the end the king of the South* **will engage him [the king of the North] in battle, and the king of the North will storm out against him with chariots and cavalry and a great fleet of ships. He will invade many countries and sweep through them like a flood.**

Daniel 12:9 **He replied, "Go your way, Daniel, because the words [of this prophecy] are closed up and** *sealed until the time of the end."*

These six verses clearly say that God has appointed *when* the end shall be. This is good news. God never sleeps even though we may think the hour is late or overdue.

Paul knew about the appointed time of the end and he knew it was involved with the judgment of human beings. He says, "For he [the Father] has set a day when he will judge the world with justice by the man [Jesus] he has appointed. He has given proof of this to all men by raising him from the dead." (Acts 17:31)

Lastly, Jesus clearly confirms the fact that the Father has *pre-set* the time allotted for sin much like a cook sets the time allotted for roasting something in the oven. He said to the apostles shortly before His ascension, **"It is not for you to know the times or dates the**

Father *has set* by his own authority." (Acts 1:7)

Two points must be made from this text since it is widely misunderstood. First, Jesus affirms that the Father has set times and dates by His own authority. Even before sin began, the Father had already decided what the time limits of sin would be. But the next point is more difficult to understand. Jesus told His disciples that it was not for them to know dates and times *that were not relevant* to them. In His statement to the disciples, Jesus did not mean that His disciples in centuries to come could not know the dates and times that were relevant to them; rather, Jesus is revealing an important principle. This principle is that *on or about the time of fulfillment, specific prophecies are understood.*

This is a critical point. The 1,260 and 2,300 year time periods of Daniel 7 and 8 were far from fulfillment when Jesus made this statement to His disciples. *He did not want them to know* that the 1,260 years of Daniel 7 were yet future. He did not want them to know that the 2,300 years of Daniel 8:14 were under way either. Jesus knew that such information would have destroyed the early church before it got started. This principle helps to explain why the book of Daniel was sealed up until the time of the end because time *only becomes important* when the time for prophetic fulfillment arrives.

If we paraphrased the thoughts of Jesus in Acts 1:7, we could say, "My friends, it is not for you to know about specific dates and times the Father has set by His own authority. However, when a specific date or time does arrive, then the Holy Spirit will lead you to understand the timing and what is yet to come." See John 16:13 for support of this conclusion.

1798 marks the beginning of the end

In the prophecy of Daniel 7, an apocalyptic sequence unfolds that reveals when the beginning of the end occurs. Read Daniel 7:1-11 and notice the following progression:

1. Lion
2. Bear
3. Leopard
4. Terrible monster
5. Ten horns - little horn
6. Judgment scene in heaven
7. Beasts destroyed in fire

According to the rules of interpretation presented in Chapter 1 (and confirmed by history), these events occur in their order. According to Daniel 7:20,21 the judgment scene *begins at the end* of the 1,260 years of little horn terror. The proof of this statement is found in two selections of text. First, Daniel says, "**I also wanted to know about the ten horns on its head and about the other horn that came up, before which three of them fell—the horn that looked more imposing than the others and that had eyes and a mouth that spoke boastfully. {21} As I watched, this horn was waging war against the saints and defeating them, {22}** *until the Ancient of Days came* **and pronounced judgment in favor of** the saints of the Most High, and the time came when they possessed the kingdom." (Daniel 7:20-22) When did the Ancient of Days come to the court described in verse 9? Also notice that verse 22 indicates that persecution will resume and last until the *saints possess the kingdom.*

Secondly, Daniel says, "He [the little horn] will speak against the Most High and oppress his saints and try to change the set times and the laws. The saints will be handed over to him for a time, times and half a time. {26} But the court will sit, and his power will be taken away and completely destroyed forever." (Daniel 7:25-26) Here, the saints are handed over to the little horn until the court sits. Again we ask, when did the court sit?

The reader will notice from verses 21 and 22 that the little horn wages war against the saints *until* the Ancient of Days, the Father, came and convened the heavenly court which is described in Daniel 7:9,10. Again, in verse 25, the Bible says the saints will be persecuted for 1,260 years but the court will sit and take away the great authority of the little horn. *The court brings the persecution of the little horn to an end.* The point here is that the court in heaven convenes at the end of the 1,260 years. At this point in time, the Father grants a restraining order against the little horn power and the saints are freed for a season (until the deadly wound is healed). And, we know from Revelation 13, the persecution of the saints will resume when the trumpets begin. This coming

persecution will last until the saints possess the kingdom. (Revelation 13:5-7)

We can't see into heaven

Consider this. When Jesus gave the prophecy to Daniel recorded in Daniel 7, He connected the end of the little horn's power with the Ancient of Days convening the court scene. Knowing that human beings cannot look up into heaven and see events taking place there, Jesus tells us to watch for certain events on earth so we can know the timing of events in heaven. Isn't this neat?

Again, the point is made: The judgment scene in Daniel 7:9,10 began in 1798 — at the end of the 1,260 years. The little horn power was wounded — not because 1,260 years had passed — but because the Ancient of Days pronounced a restraining judgment in favor of the saints. In other words, the Papacy received the deadly wound because the Father ordered it. The 1,260 year time period tells us when to look for the end of papal persecution so that we can know that heaven's court has convened.

Revelation chimes in

If the reader will consider the possibility that the scenes in Daniel 7:9 and Revelation 4 and 5 began in 1798, two things will make a lot of sense. First, just assume that Daniel and John saw the *same* service. John's attention is focused on the book sealed with seven seals and the search for someone worthy to open the book. Daniel is focused on the persecution of the saints and the court scene. Now observe how these two elements are directly connected! Daniel reveals the timing of the court (at the end of 1,260 years). Daniel also tells us that after the court convenes, the books are opened and judgment begins. (But, Daniel doesn't say how long after court convenes that the books are opened.)

On the other hand, John reveals the test of worthiness that our High Priest must pass before He can officiate on behalf of human beings. And, we know from Leviticus 16 that the High Priest had to be found worthy before he could officiate on behalf of Israel on the Day of Atonement. In short, we can therefore say that Jesus was determined worthy to receive the book sealed with seven seals when the court convened in 1798.

There is excellent evidence to demonstrate that the seven seals began opening shortly after 1798. In fact, the third seal opened right on time in 1844, and the fourth seal is about to open. (These matters will be discussed more fully in Chapter 11.)

We're at the end

If we assemble all of the pieces, we can be sure that heaven is in its final phase of the redemption of man. Notice the historical progression:

1. Lion - Babylon - 605 B.C.

2. Bear - Medo/Persia - 538 B.C.

3. Leopard - Grecia - 331 B.C.

4. Monster - Rome - 168 B.C.

5. Ten horns - A.D. 476

6. Little horn - A.D. 538

7. Judgment scene - 1798

We are well into the appointed time of the end. In fact, it is almost over. The service in heaven has been going on for almost 200 years and soon, the final awful moments of the great tribulation will begin. God will use this coming time period to test the faith of every person. Then, those who really trust in God will be revealed.

Summary

For 1,260 years the Christian Church had a wonderful opportunity to accomplish what the Jews failed to do. But alas, the Roman Church became as evil and anti-Christ as their predecessors the Jews. Right on time, the Holy Roman Empire was brought down at the end of 1,260 years in 1798 by a would-be world dictator refusing to believe in God. Even though Napoleon, like King Nebuchadnezzar, didn't know the God of Heaven, history and Waterloo confirm again that there is a God that sets up kings and takes them down. (Daniel 4:17,25)

With the failure of the Roman Church complete, Jesus then raised up the Protestant movement. The Protestants received the opportunity to proclaim the truth of God's Word. This point is most important because somebody on earth has to be able to tell the rest of the world about "the appointed time of the end." And, looking at the degenerate condition of Protestantism today, we may be able to guess why Revelation does not call the saints living at the end of the world "Protestants." Rather, we will see that yet another group of people are to appear. They are called the "remnant" in Revelation.

Chapter 8

The Mystery of Daniel 8

There is another prophecy in Daniel that collaborates the certainty of 1798 and the appointed time of the end. This prophecy identifies 1844 as a very important year. Because these two dates harmonize, we can be certain that we are nearing the end of time that God has allotted for the existence of earth. (Acts 17:26) This prophecy helps to confirm the nearness of Christ's return because it solidly builds upon the events described in Daniel 7. This prophecy is found in Daniel 8.

As said in the introduction to this book, *no one prophecy is complete within itself and this prophecy is no exception.* In fact, this prophecy is best understood after it is put in the context of other prophecies. Therefore, a correct interpretation of this prophecy may not be immediately obvious.

To make this prophecy easier to understand, an interpretation of the prophecy is given first, and then the prophecy is studied in detail. At the end of this chapter, some additional notes are included for those who require more explanation. The reader should ever keep in mind that prophetic pieces are like pieces of a puzzle—that is, each piece has several sides. In other words, the prophecy of

Daniel 8 aligns with other prophecies in Daniel and Revelation to produce a harmonious result. Thus, the prophetic matrix becomes more important as we study because no one prophecy is complete within itself.

The prophecy interpreted

Daniel 8 is a very important story. It serves three purposes. First, it identifies the timing of the judgment of human beings. Secondly, this prophecy contains the first mention of the physical appearing of the devil during earth's last days. The third purpose of this prophecy is most essential. This prophecy (in cooperation with the prophecy in Daniel 9) establishes a solid historical reference that is indispensable for understanding God's long-range timetable. This prophecy clearly reveals that Medo-Persia and Greece would follow Babylon. While this may not appear significant at first, this fact provides a valuable reference point so that we can harmonize the chronology of Daniel's visions with John's visions recorded in Revelation. Of course, all apocalyptic prophecies work in harmony with each other, for God is the Revealer of mysteries. If we properly assemble the data, we not only behold historical progression as fulfillments occur, we can also locate our position and identify those events that are just before us.

Important relationships

The timing of the judgment of the living and the physical appearing of the devil are intimately connected. Here's how: In the days just before the second coming, a series of devastating judgments will fall upon the earth. (See the section on the seven trumpets.) These "acts of God" will completely change life as we now know it. As a result of these coming horrific calamities, the living will have to make some very hard choices. During this time the devil will physically appear. He will deceive millions of willing people. Each person will have to decide whether to obey Jesus and trust in Him for survival, or receive a permit (the mark of the beast) so that one can buy and sell and thus survive.

The appearing of the devil and the judgment of the living are intimately related because the devil's appearing and his subsequent success in gaining control of the world will force everyone to make a decision for or against the commandments of God. The development of this matter will unfold as we progress into Revelation's story. For now, we must investigate the prophecy found in Daniel 8.

The prophecy (Daniel 8:1-12)

Sometime during the third year of Babylon's last king, King Belshazzar, Daniel received this vision. (The reader should read Daniel 8:1-12 before continuing.) A summary of Daniel's vision follows:

1. "I was standing beside the Ulai Canal.... Before me was a ram with two long horns standing beside the canal. One of the horns was longer than the other but grew up later. I watched the ram as he charged toward the West, North and the South. No animal could stand against him.... He did as he pleased and became great." {v1-4}

2. "As I was thinking about this, suddenly a goat with a prominent horn between his eyes came from the west, crossing the whole earth without touching the ground. He came toward the two-horned ram... and charged at him with great rage. I saw him attack the ram furiously... and shatter his two horns. The ram was powerless to stand against him; the goat knocked him to the ground and trampled on him." {v5-7}

3. "The goat became very great, but at the height of his power his large horn was broken off, and in its place four prominent horns grew up toward the four winds of heaven." {v8}

4. "Later, out of one of the four winds another horn arose. It started small, but grew in power to the South and East and toward the Beautiful Land. It grew until it reached the host of the heavens, and it threw some of the starry host down to the earth and trampled on them." {v9-10}

5. **"This horn set itself up to be as great as the Prince of the host; it took away the daily sacrifice from him and the place of his sanctuary was brought low."** {v11}
6. **"Because of rebellion, the saints and the daily sacrifice were given over to it. It prospered in everything it did, and truth was thrown to the ground."** {v12}

The interpretation

The vision only contains three symbols: The ram, the goat, the horn power. Whom do these symbols represent? The ram represents the kingdom of Medo-Persia {v20}. The two horns represent the coregent reign of two kings, the king of the Medes and the king of the Persians. The goat represents the kingdom of Greece {v21}. The great horn represents the first king of Greece when it became a world empire. That king was Alexander the Great. The four horns represent the four generals that eventually took Alexander's place when he died. (Historians widely agree the kings were Cassander, Lysimachus, Ptolemy and Seleucus.) Also see Daniel 11:4. But whom does the horn power represent? In the context of Daniel 8, horns represent *specific men* and this horn power is no exception. The horn power of Daniel 8 represents a great man that will become a king upon earth during the appointed time of the end.

Most commentators on prophecy today conclude that the horn power is Antiochius Epiphanes IV, a Seleucid king that defiled the temple in Jerusalem in 168 B.C. Others teach that the horn power in Daniel 8 is the Papacy which is also represented by the little horn in Daniel 7. Both views have some superficial merit if Daniel 8 is separated from other prophecies that deal with this subject or if most of the specifications of the horn power are ignored. However, both of these views have one thing in common. Their combined effect is that this prophecy has nothing (or very little) to do with the final days of earth's history. How can this be? Twice Gabriel tells Daniel that this vision *concerns* the appointed time of the end. (Daniel 8:17,19)

This author believes that the horn power is *neither* Antiochius IV or the Papacy. The horn power of Daniel 8 is the physical appearing of the devil which is yet to come. The devil will soon appear on the earth in the form of a man—the man of sin predicted by Paul in 2 Thessalonians 2. He will be glorious, brilliant and possess great powers. He will resemble the description of Jesus given in Revelation 1. Without getting too deeply involved at this point, here are a few reasons for this view. (Later, when Revelation 5, 13 and 17 are studied, the reader may better understand this writer's conclusion.)

The horn power specifications examined

As we review the specifications of the horn power, remember that God revealed these matters to Daniel in terms that Daniel was familiar with. This means that God used concepts that

Daniel understood so that Daniel could faithfully record everything he saw. (This point is also true for King Nebuchadnezzar.) Notice the following specifications about the horn power in Daniel 8:9-12:

1. This writer understands, for reasons following, that the horn power appears out of one of the four *winds*. Some interpret the phrase, "out of one of *them*," to mean out of one of the four horns. There is confusion in the agreement of gender with nouns and pronouns in the Hebrew text. However, the point has to be made that this horn power *is not* an extension of the goat, the empire of Grecia. This horn is not an extension of any beast. The horns on the ram and goat belong to specific kingdoms. However, this horn power doesn't belong to any animal. This powerful entity literally appears out of one of the four winds.

2. This horn power starts small but grows toward the South, East and the Beautiful Land (the West). In other words, this horn power comes out of the North. And when this horn power appears, it begins in a small way.

Note: In Daniel's day, geography was reckoned by the Jews differently than we understand it today. For example, Egypt was reckoned as the "South" even though it is southwest from Jerusalem. (Luke 11:31, 1 Kings 10)

Babylon was reckoned as the "North" even though Babylon is geographically northeast. (Jeremiah 4:6, 25:9) Because the Mediterranean Sea formed the western boundary of civilization, the land of Canaan (the Beautiful Land) was considered to be the "West." Today, we call the land of Canaan the Middle East. Isn't it interesting how points of reference change? Directions in the Bible are referenced from Israel's view of the world. There were kingdoms geographically above them: to the North; kingdoms below them: to the south; a great desert to the east and a great sea to the west.

The northern origin of this horn power is important. Why? Because destruction always comes out of the North. This was true for Israel, Egypt and for Babylon! Notice these few texts:

"This is what the Lord says [to Israel]: 'Look, an army is coming from the land of the North; a great nation is being stirred up from the ends of the earth.' " (Jeremiah 6:22)

" 'I will summon all the peoples of the North and my servant Nebuchadnezzar king of Babylon,' declares the Lord, 'and I will bring them against this land and its inhabitants and against all the surrounding nations. I will completely destroy them and make them an object of horror and scorn, and an everlasting ruin.' " (Jeremiah 25:9)

"Egypt is a beautiful heifer, but a gadfly is coming against her from the North." (Jeremiah 46:20)

"Announce and proclaim among the nations, lift up a banner and proclaim

it; keep nothing back, but say, 'Babylon will be captured; Bel will be put to shame, Marduk filled with terror. Her images will be put to shame and her idols filled with terror.' {3} A nation from the North will attack her and lay waste her land. No one will live in it; both men and animals will flee away." (Jeremiah 50:2,3)

The origin of this horn power, coming from the North is not coincidental. This horn power is a king, a stern-faced king that understands intrigue (manipulation) and according to Daniel 8:25; 11:36,44, this particular king of the North will cause enormous destruction.

3. Now we come to a specification that no ordinary man can accomplish. This horn starts small, but it rapidly grows until it reaches the starry host of the heavens and then it throws some of them down and tramples them. This language means that this horn power will grow in recognition among all nations until he is more highly respected than their gods whose dwelling is not on earth. Notice how this works. The pagans knew about and worshiped gods that lived in the heavens. See Daniel 2:11,28. In fact, their idols of wood and stone *were representations* of their gods who were believed to be superior to the gods of their enemies. Notice a few of the texts that explain who the starry hosts are:

"They [Israel] forsook all the commands of the Lord their God and made for themselves two idols cast in the shape of calves, and an Asherah pole. They bowed down to all the starry hosts, and they worshiped Baal." (2 Kings 17:16)

"He [King Manasseh] built altars in the temple of the Lord, of which the Lord had said, 'In Jerusalem I will put my Name.' In both courts of the temple of the Lord, he built altars to all the starry hosts. He sacrificed his own son in the fire, practiced sorcery and divination, and consulted mediums and spiritists. He did much evil in the eyes of the Lord, provoking him to anger." (2 Kings 21:4-6)

"He [King Josiah] did away with the pagan priests appointed by the kings of Judah to burn incense on the high places of the towns of Judah and on those around Jerusalem—those who burned incense to Baal, to the sun and moon, to the constellations and to all the starry hosts." (2 Kings 23:5)

"You alone are the Lord. You made the heavens, even the highest heavens, and all their starry host, the earth and all that is on it, the seas and all that is in them. You give life to everything, and the multitudes of heaven worship you." (Nehemiah 9:6)

"And when you look up to the sky and see the sun, the moon and the stars—all the heavenly array—do not be enticed into bowing down to them and worshiping things the Lord your God has apportioned to all the nations under heaven." (Deuteronomy 4:19)

The scriptural evidence is very clear. The term starry hosts refers to highly exalted deities which the heathen worshiped. The ancients worshiped the starry hosts and gave them names such as Baal, Mercury, Zeus, Hermes, Venus, Ra, Sol and many others. See Acts 14:12.

The meaning of verse 10 is that this horn power grows in recognition until it is respected above all deities worshiped by men. This horn power will prove himself greater than the deities of heaven because he will perform great signs and miracles at will. This is how he tramples upon (shows inferior) the gods of men. See Revelation 13:13,14 and 2 Thessalonians 2:9.

4.   After establishing himself, showing that he is greater than all the gods of men, the devil will set himself in direct opposition to the Prince of the host. Who is the Prince of the host or the army? (2 Chronicles 18:18) In Daniel 8:25, the Prince of the host is called the Prince of princes (or King of kings). In Revelation 17:14 we find a direct confrontation between the armies of the earth led by the devil and Jesus and His army. Could this be the conflict that Daniel saw? If the horn power is the physical appearing of the devil, and if this vision concerns the time of the end, the answer is yes.

Daniel 8:11 says this horn power will take the daily away from the Prince of the host and the place of His sanctuary will be brought low. What does this mean? The reader should remember our study on the ministry of Jesus. The daily is a term that refers to the constant intercession of Jesus on behalf of man. This intercession began the day Adam and Eve sinned and continues to this very day. It was symbolized in the temple services by offerings of atonement morning and evening. This prophecy is not concerned with the end or cessation of temple services on earth. Those things were only symbolic of realities. They did not bring salvation. (Hebrews 8:1-5; 10:1-4) This vision is concerned with the cessation of Christ's intercession, and His work comes to an end in one of four ways:

● When a person dies, his life ends. There is no more intercession, for life is over. (Hebrews 9:27, 2 Corinthians 5:10)

● If a person commits the unpardonable sin, there is no more intercession. (Hebrews 10:26, Matthew 12:32)

● When a nation exhausts the limits of God's patience. (Genesis 15:16; Leviticus 4:13,14; 18:24-28)

● When Jesus terminates His patience with the nations of earth and begins the great tribulation. (Ezekiel 24:14; Revelation 8:2-5, 6:7,8)

How can the horn power of Daniel 8 take away the daily intercession from Jesus who serves in heaven's sanctuary? Answer: By leading the people to forfeit or despise the intercession of Jesus. (2 Thessalonians 2:11,12; Romans 1:18-32; Hebrews 10:29) How can the devil bring down Christ's sanctuary or make His dwelling low? Answer: By leading the people of the world to reject the terms of salvation offered by Jesus during the outpouring of the Holy Spirit. In fact, the devil will fully persecute those who hold to the salvation of Christ. In the place of God's salvation, the devil will offer his deceptive salvation which will be based on cunning lies and supported by clever manipulation. More about this when we study Revelation 13.

5.   Gabriel said, "Because of rebellion, the saints and the daily were given over to it. He prospered in everything he did and truth was thrown down to the ground." What does this mean?

As said before, this vision concerns the appointed time of the end. During the last days of earth, the great tribulation will occur. This time period is a time of rebellion because the law of God will run contrary to the laws of men. Many would rather receive the mark of the beast than obey Jesus. This is the test that is coming upon the whole world. Who will obey God and trust in His promises to provide for them? This point will be clearly demonstrated in Revelation. But for now, just

consider that the second coming of Jesus does not occur until the great rebellion occurs. Paul says, **"Don't let anyone deceive you in any way, for that day will not come until the rebellion occurs and the man of lawlessness is revealed, the man doomed to destruction."** (2 Thessalonians 2:3)

6.   As Gabriel talks to Daniel about the ram, goat and horn power, we run into a puzzling situation. Daniel 8:22-24 requires a little explanation. Gabriel said: **"The four horns that replaced the one that was broken off represent four kingdoms that will emerge from his nation but will not have the same power. {23} In the latter part of their reign, when rebels have become completely wicked, a stern-faced king, a master of intrigue, will arise. {24} He will become very strong, but not by his own power. He will cause astounding devastation and will succeed in whatever he does. He will destroy the mighty men and the holy people."**

Verse 23 says that in the latter part of the reign of the four kings that follow Alexander, this stern-faced king (the devil) will arise. This statement eliminates the possibility that the horn power could be Antiochus IV or the Papacy. Here's how: The four generals (four horns) that gained control over Alexander's empire were long gone before Antiochus IV appeared on the scene in 175 B.C. and the Papacy didn't emerge until A.D. 500.

Some will respond saying, but the four horns are four kingdoms not the four generals who ruled after Alexander. Here is part of the puzzle. If the great horn of the goat was the first king of Grecia, Alexander the Great, who then are the four horns that follow? The generals or their kingdoms? In other words, the context of this vision clearly says that the great horn of the goat is a man (first king) who falls at the height of his power and the beast (goat) to which the horn belongs is the nation of Greece. Therefore, the four horns that follow must also be four men.

But history resolves the problem. When Antiochus IV appeared on the scene, there weren't four kingdoms nor four kings. Seleucus defeated and killed Lysimachus in 281 B.C. and overtook his territory. Thus, Greece was a nation of three provinces (not four) for more than 100 years when Antiochus IV brought destruction to Jerusalem in 168 B.C.

Those who teach that Antiochius IV was the fulfillment of this prophecy misapply verses 22 and 23 and then they diminish all the specifications given in the other verses which the horn power must fulfill. The application of Antiochus IV to this prophecy has no merit if *all* the specifications of this horn power are considered. For example, the horn power takes a stand against the King of kings and the horn power will be destroyed, but not by human power. (Daniel 8:25) Did Antiochius IV fulfill this specification?

No. History says that Antiochius IV died a lonely, frightened and powerless man. (See 1 Maccabees 6, an apocryphal book found in the Douay Version of the Bible.)

The suggestion that the Papacy fulfills this prophecy is somewhat stronger than the arguments used for Antiochus IV. But, the rise and appearing of the Papacy is almost 700 years after the death of the four kings of Greece. The Papacy is not *an extension* of the goat, Greece. Further, the little horn of Daniel 7 is not *one* man as in Daniel 8. but a system of men. The use of horns in Daniel 7 differs from the context of Daniel 8. (Such is not unusual in prophecy. For example, stars in the context of Revelation 12:4 are used much differently than in Revelation 6:13.) But the strongest argument against the Papacy is that the Papacy cannot meet *all* the specifications of this horn power.

A better solution

Gabriel said: {22} **"The four horns that replaced the one that was broken off represent four kingdoms that will emerge from his nation but will not have the same power. {23} In the latter part of their reign, when rebels have become completely wicked, a stern-faced king, a master of intrigue, will arise. {24} He will become very strong, but not by his own power. He will cause astounding devastation and will succeed in whatever he does. He will destroy the mighty men and the holy people."**

There is a rather simple explanation for verses 23 and 24. This explanation is in harmony with all the specifications given in Daniel 8 and 11 about this horn power.

Look at verse 22. It is an explanation of what is going to happen in Greece after the fall of Alexander. And with this verse, the explanation regarding Greece comes to an end.

In verse 23 Gabriel begins to talk about the horn power that would appear in the distant future, the appointed time of the end. {v17,19} Then (loosely paraphrasing verses 23 and 24) Gabriel says, "In the last days, when the last kings on earth shall reign, when people have become completely wicked, a mean and hateful king will arise. He will become very powerful, but his power will not come from within himself. It will come because people willingly give themselves over to him. He will cause unbelievable destruction, and no man can stop him. He will severely persecute the remnant people of God." (Revelation 12:17; 13:5-7, 15)

7. The last specification given by Gabriel is most important. The angel said, **"He will cause deceit to prosper, and he will consider himself superior. When they feel secure, he will destroy many and take his stand against the Prince of princes. Yet he will be destroyed, but not by human power."** (Daniel 8:25) Compare this verse with these two verses: **"The king [of the North] will do**

as he pleases. **He will exalt and magnify himself above every god and will say unheard-of things against the God of gods. He will be successful until the time of wrath is completed, for what has been determined must take place. {45} He will pitch his royal tents between the seas at the beautiful holy mountain. Yet he will come to his end, and no one will help him."** (Daniel 11:36,45)

Three things stand out. First, the horn power in Daniel 8 will be destroyed by Jesus Himself. (Daniel 8:25; 2 Thessalonians 2:8) Secondly, the horn power of Daniel 8 will lead the whole world into a great deception (Daniel 8:25; Revelation 13:14), and lastly, the horn power of Daniel 8 will exalt himself above the different gods that people worship. (Daniel 8:25, 11:36; 2 Thessalonians 2:4)

Intermediate summary

Who is the ram and its two horns? The ram is Medo-Persia and the two horns represent the king of the Medes and the king of the Persians. Who is the goat and its great horn that is broken off when it is at the height of power? The goat is Grecia and the great horn is its first king, Alexander the Great. Who are the four horns that take the place of the great horn? Cassander, Lysimachus, Ptolemy and Seleucus. Who is the horn power that follows? The Bible says:

1. It rises out of one of the four winds (the North).
2. It starts small but rapidly gains respect.
3. It proves that it is greater than the gods of men.
4. It takes a stand against the King of kings.
5. Because of rebellion, it brings an end to salvation and it persecutes the saints.
6. It is a wicked, manipulative king and he destroys everything, including the saints.
7. It exalts himself above all gods. He will come to an end, but not as a result of human power.

Now, place these seven specifications in the appointed time of the end and there is only one conclusion that can satisfy all: The horn power of Daniel 8 symbolizes the physical appearing of the devil in the last days.

What about the 2,300 days?

After beholding the ram, goat and horn power in vision, Daniel heard a conversation. One angel asked the other a five-part question {v13}:

a. How long will it take for the vision to be fulfilled?
b. How will the daily be taken away?
c. How long will the rebellion that causes desolation last?
d. How long will the sanctuary be surrendered?
e. How long will God's people be trampled upon?

An angel called *Palmoni,* answered part of the question. In Hebrew, Palmoni means "holy numberer." This name is especially fitting, for all five questions have numbers for answers! (See marginal reference on Daniel 8:13,14 for Palmoni in older KJV Bibles.)

Daniel heard the answer to the fourth question. He heard the holy numberer say, **"It will take 2,300 evenings and mornings; then the sanctuary will be reconsecrated."** {v14} The reader should keep this length of time in mind, for this prophecy pinpoints the very year when the books in heaven (Daniel 7:10) were opened and when the third seal in Revelation 6 was broken.

Note: In the KJV, Daniel 8:14 interprets the Hebrew term, *ereb boger* as days (plural) even though the term is singular: evening/morning. This is not faulty, for 2,300 *ereb boger* in English has to be plural. However, the Hebrew sense of *ereb boger* is simply a unit of time, "a day." This is proven by the use of the word boger in Judges 19:26 and 2 Samuel 13:4 where boger simply refers to the morning or to the dawn part of the day. The Hebrew word ereb is used in the OT more than 40 times to refer to the evening part of a day. From Genesis 1:5, a day consists of an evening and a morning. That Daniel 8:14 is speaking of 2,300 days is clearly evident given the usage of ereb and boger in many texts.

Conclusion

We come to the end of this chapter deducting several things. We know who the ram, goat and horn power are. But what does the 2,300 days have to do with the vision? In the next chapter, the reader will discover that the 2,300 days is a period of time that separates the ram and goat scenes from the horn power! In other words, the chronology loosely follows this pattern: ram - goat - 2,300 days - horn power. You'll see why in the next chapter.

Additional comments on Daniel 8

Because some insist that Antiochus IV fulfills the prophecy of Daniel 8, a few details about this position are investigated for the sake of discussion. Daniel 8:14 predicts that the temple would be cleansed (KJV) *after* the 2,300 day time-period. However, the text doesn't say which temple would be cleansed. Those holding that Antiochus IV is the horn power of Daniel 8 insist the earthly temple is the object of this prophecy and the 2,300 days are literal and therefore, are not day/years (Jubilee units).

According to 1 Maccabees 1:50-57, Antiochus IV desecrated the temple in Jerusalem on the 15th of Casleu (Jewish month, Kislev; our month, December) in 168 B.C. And 1 Maccabees 4:52-54 says the rebuilt temple was purified and reconsecrated, and the services resumed three years later on December 14, 164 B.C. In 2 Maccabees 10:1-8, it confirms that the temple was cleansed and services resumed at this time. The problem is that the Bible says the sanctuary would

be cleansed *after* 2,300 days expired. If the purification of the rebuilt temple by Judas Maccabee occurred on December 14, 164 B.C., this would have required the commencement of the 2,300 days in 171 B.C. — a full 3.3 years prior to the desecration of the temple by Antiochus. Such a claim for the fulfillment of the 2,300 days is therefore invalid.

Others terminate the 2,300 days with the death of General Nicanor on March 27, 160 B.C. to mark the end of the 2,300 days. But wait, this places the beginning of the 2,300 days in 166 B.C. And nothing of significance begins in 166 B.C. But the question that goes unanswered is why date the 2,300 days from the death of Nicanor? What made his death a prophetic fulfillment? History shows that the hostilities against Israel did not end with his death. For example, King Demetrius was successful in killing Judas Maccabee (1 Maccabees 9:18) about two months *after* Nicanor was killed and the wars against Israel didn't end there. In May, 159 B.C., about one year after the death of Nicanor, "Alcimus ordered the wall of the inner court of the sanctuary to be torn down, thus destroying the work of the prophets." (1 Maccabees 9:54)

In 1 Maccabees 9:64, it reveals that numerous wars continued against Israel for some time after the death of Judas Maccabee. The "threat" (as some put it) against the temple did not disappear with the death of Nicanor. History clearly disputes the claim that "threats" against Jerusalem disappeared when Nicanor died. So how can there be a fulfillment of the prophecy when the time required by the prophecy was not met? Isn't it fair to say that God meant 2,300 days when He revealed the prophecy?

These matters of record are presented to demonstrate that there is no historical substance to the assertions of many that Antiochus Epiphanes IV fulfilled this prophecy. The facts surrounding Antiochus are so distant from the specifications of the prophecy, one wonders why so many defend this conclusion.

The Papacy

Because a number of scholars insist that the horn power of Daniel 8 is the Papacy, a few remarks about this conclusion are included for the reader's consideration.

Protestantism was born within the Roman Catholic Church in much the same way that Christianity came from the cradle of Judaism. If history teaches anything, it is this: Religious organizations, by nature, place loyalty and allegiance above the importance of truth. The reason for this is simple. All religious organizations embrace a collection of teachings which they believe to be God's truth and deviation from that body is considered schismatic and counterproductive.

As Protestantism developed, its followers greatly suffered from the wrath of the Church. Protestants appealed to the Bible alone as the rule of faith. This claim, of course, only

brought more condemnation from Church leaders who were determined to defend ecclesiastical rules and man-made doctrines. When Protestants began to see that the Church was unwilling to change, a number of Protestant expositors came to understand that the little horn of Daniel 7 was the Papacy. They could clearly trace the history and power of the apostate Church back to its Roman origin. Because there is a great deal of similarity between the little horn of Daniel 7 and the horn power of Daniel 8, Protestants just *assumed* that Daniel 8 was a repetition and enlargement of Daniel 7.

In the late 16th century, two Jesuit scholars from Spain, Francisco Ribera and Luis Alcasar, introduced prophetic theories to refute the claims of Protestants that the Papacy was the little horn of Daniel 7 or the horn power of Daniel 8. Their intention was to meet Protestants on their own ground *Sola Scriptura* and refute their charges against the Roman Catholic Church. As a result of their works, two conflicting schools of prophetic thought emerged. Alcasar's primary position was based on the assumption that Revelation's story was descriptive of the victory of early Christians over the Jewish nation and the overthrow of pagan Rome. His conclusion was that Nero was the Antichrist. (Incidently, Alcasar concluded that Antiochus Epiphanes IV fulfilled the prophecies of Daniel 8 & 9.)

Ribera also introduced a prophetic concept that was designed to redirect the accusations of the Protestants that the pope was the Antichrist. Ribera concluded that Antichrist is a single individual who will appear just before the Second Coming of Jesus. He claimed that Antichrist would bitterly persecute the saints, abolish the Christian religion and rebuild the temple in Jerusalem. He would be received by the Jews and pretend to be God and then conquer the world in three and one half years.

These opposing views were put before Protestants to dissuade them from identifying the Papacy as the Antichrist. For about 200 years, Protestants stood firm on the prophetic position: The Roman Catholic Church is the Antichrist of Daniel and Revelation. In the early part of the nineteenth century, Protestantism began to change its mind. A survey of prophetic literature by Protestants since 1826 shows that Protestant expositors began to drift away from their long-standing claim that the Roman Catholic Church was the Antichrist. Today, most Protestant expositors deny that the Roman Catholic Church is prophetically significant. And, without a historical setting or chronological process by which to mark the passage of time, Protestants have arrived at a number of prophetic conclusions that are without any merit. It is ironic that today, most Protestants have adopted a modified version of the Ribera's counter-reformation claim.

Here are five reasons why some Protestants teach that the little horn

of Daniel 7 and the horn power of Daniel 8 is the Papacy:

1. The attitudes and activities of both horns toward God are similar.
2. Both entities are symbolized as horns.
3. The arrogant claims of both horns are blasphemous.
4. Both horns build on deception.
5. The historical conflict between Protestants and Catholics led Protestants to conclude that most everything in the Bible regarding the Antichrist is the Papacy. (The prophetic discovery that the devil himself will appear on earth claiming to be God is a relatively new prophetic concept. For this reason, the term The Antichrist has taken on an even greater meaning.)

Not the same

Here are six reasons (also review the seven specifications in this chapter) why the little horn of Daniel 7 and the horn power of Daniel 8 cannot be the same:

1. The little horn of Daniel 7 comes up out of the fourth beast, Rome. The horn power of Daniel 8 does not derive its strength from any nation. It just appears out of nothing.
2. The little horn of Daniel 7 arises after the 10 horns have become dominate in world history (around A.D. 500). The horn power of Daniel 8 is not an extension of the

goat, Greece. In fact, Daniel 8 only has three symbolic elements within it: a ram, a goat, and the horn power. Twice Gabriel says the vision of Daniel 8 concerns the distant future, the appointed time of the end. We know that the ram and goat occurred between 538 and 168 B.C. This leaves the final symbol to occur at the appointed time of the end.

3. The context of Daniel 7 requires that the little horn is a kingdom that lasts for a time, times and half a time. However, the context of Daniel 8 requires this horn power to be one man, a stern-faced king.

4. Daniel 8 says describes the horn power as taking his stand against the Prince of princes (King of kings). While one could say that all the armies of the world will take their stand against the God of Heaven, the point of Daniel 8 is that this horn power is the *leader* of the conflict against the Prince of princes.

5. The horn power of Daniel 8 is brought to his end by divine power — not by man. This point stands in contrast to the fact that the little horn is quite mortal. It was almost destroyed by Berthier in 1798.

6. Daniel 11:36-45 is a parallel passage that describes the works and activities of this horn power *at the appointed time of the end* which is a time of great wrath (compare Daniel 8:19 and 11:36). We also find a very close harmony of these events explained in 2 Thessalonians 2, Revelation 9 and 13.

The sum total of this matters is not yet complete. There is more about the horn power in Daniel 11 and Revelation 9, 11, 13, and 17. This much is certain. Anyone or any system opposed to the teachings of Jesus as revealed in the Bible is anti-Christ. Antiochus IV was anti-Christ. The Papacy is anti-Christ and so are all of the religious systems of the world. However, the father of this attitude is the soon-to-appear devil, the great Antichrist.

Chapter 9

God's Great Clock Revealed in Daniel 9

The vision is not finished

After Daniel beheld the ram, goat, horn-power and the holy numberer, Gabriel was sent to Daniel with the instruction, "tell this man the meaning of the vision." So, Gabriel flew to Daniel and began talking. (Daniel 8:15) Before explaining the vision to Daniel, Gabriel *twice* emphasizes to Daniel that this vision actually concerns "the appointed time of the end" (verses 17 and 19). This vision took place about 25 centuries ago and the phrase, "the appointed time of the end," means exactly what it says. This phrase indicates that God has appointed a time to end the problem of sin. Have we reached the appointed time of the end? Are we living in the last decade? How can anyone tell? Just as a navigator looks at the stars to know his latitude and longitude, there has to be some type of evidence showing our chronological position if we are to know when the appointed time of the end arrives. Without chronological markers, we are left with nothing to mark our position in the passage of time.

Many people challenge the idea that we are living at the end of the world's history. They ask, "What evidence do you have to show that the end has come?" The world has seen WWI, WWII and dozens of smaller wars since. So, how can we know for sure that we are living at the end of the world? Bible prophecy holds the answer. Jesus has declared the end from the beginning. (Isaiah 45:21) And the Holy Spirit reveals what is going to happen to those who are diligent students of the Scriptures. (John 16:13)

The vision of Daniel 8 serves an important function. The vision reveals two events and connects them with one time-period. The first event is on earth. The second is in heaven. By connecting events in heaven with events on earth, God allows us to know the dates of events in heaven which we can't see with the naked eye! Think about this. Because we can't see what is going on in heaven, we can know what is going on in heaven by understanding prophetic fulfillments on earth. This point will be demonstrated shortly.

The vision of evenings and mornings

The vision in Daniel 8 is called the vision of the evenings and mornings because this is its central point. (Daniel 8:26) For example, a letter of approval is so called because it is a letter of approval. The details concerning the approval are secondary. So it is. The primary purpose of this vision is about 2,300 mornings and evenings.

To appreciate the value of this vision, the reader needs a little background information about Israel at the time of the vision.

By 605 B.C., God had reached His limit with Israel's long history of rebellion. He consequently sent them into Babylonian captivity. Through the prophet Jeremiah, God let Israel know their captivity would last 70 years. **"For twenty-three years... the word of the Lord has come to me and I have spoken to you again and again, but you have not listened.... Therefore the Lord Almighty says this: 'Because you have not listened to my words, I will summon all the peoples of the North and my servant Nebuchadnezzar, king of Babylon... and I will bring them against this land and its inhabitants and against all the surrounding nations.... This whole country will become a desolate wasteland, and these nations will serve the king of Babylon seventy years.' "** (Jeremiah 25:3,8,9,11)

When Daniel saw the Ram and Goat in vision, he already knew that Babylon was going to fall and he also knew that the 70 years of captivity predicted by Jeremiah were about to expire. Later, Daniel wrote, **"...I, Daniel, understood from the Scriptures, according to the word of the LORD given to Jeremiah the prophet, that the desolation of Jerusalem would last**

seventy years. So I turned to the Lord God and pleaded with him in prayer and petition, in fasting, and in sackcloth and ashes." (Daniel 9:2,3)

Daniel was anxious for his people to be set free so they could return to Jerusalem. The hope of returning to the homeland and the destiny of his people burned deeply within his heart for Daniel loved his God, his people and his homeland. Since Gabriel's remarks didn't address the destiny of Israel, Daniel fasted and prayed for more information. Some time later, Gabriel returned for a second visit with Daniel. He brought good news and bad news. This visit is recorded in Daniel 9.

Very broad plan

When Gabriel returned to Daniel, he didn't say very much. But the conversation between them sounds as though their discussion picked up where it last ended. Daniel says, **"While I was still in prayer, Gabriel, the man I had seen in the earlier vision, came to me in swift flight about the time of the evening sacrifice."** (Daniel 9:21)

Remember, in the earlier vision, Gabriel explained to Daniel that the ram with two horns represented the kings of Media and Persia. Since the time of that vision, Daniel had heard reports about their successful conquests. He also knew within his heart that they would eventually overthrow Babylon. So, Daniel was not surprised when time came for fulfillment. (See the story of Belshazzer in Daniel 5.) When Gabriel returned to Daniel the second time,

Babylon had fallen. Daniel had witnessed the fulfillment. Daniel now began to put some perspective on the plans of God because he knew that other kingdoms must rise and fall too. These things had been clearly laid out in his vision of the ram and goat (Daniel 8), the vision of the four beasts (Daniel 7) and King Nebuchadnezzar's vision of the image (Daniel 2).

Now the old prophet realized that God's timetable was much more encompassing than just 70 years of captivity in Babylon. So, by the time Gabriel returned for the second visit, Daniel was beginning to wonder about the larger view of God's purpose for Israel. (It is hard for humans to grasp the scope of God's plans! We think small because we are small. For us life is short, and so are most of our plans.)

So, Gabriel explained to Daniel that God's purpose for Israel was much greater than just setting Israel free to return to Jerusalem. *God wanted Israel to accomplish something for Him.* However, before we can examine what God wanted of Israel, we need to demonstrate a harmony that exists between history and the fulfillment of prophecy.

Historical harmony

It is widely accepted that Babylon fell to the Medes and Persians in the autumn of 538 B.C. Although the Medes and Persians conquered Babylon, they were no better at remaining in power. In time, they too fell. About two centuries after their rise

to power, Alexander the Great finally defeated the Persians at the decisive battle of Arbela. Historians generally agree that Alexander established Greece as a world empire by 331 B.C. The fall of Babylon, the rise and fall of Medo-Persia and the rise and fall of Grecia are very important points in this study because history not only confirms the three kingdom sequence, the names of the rising kingdoms are also confirmed by history.

Daniel was shown that the goat (Greece) would become very great, but at the height of its power the large horn would be broken off and in its place four prominent horns would grow up. History confirms that at the zenith of world power, Greece's first king, Alexander the Great, died an untimely death at age 32. Daniel was also shown that Alexander's kingdom would not be given to his heirs (Daniel 11:4) and history confirms that it was not. About 25 years after Alexander's death, his empire was divided among his four leading generals: Cassander, Lysimachus, Seleucius and Ptolemy. The point here is that history confirms the sequence and chronology of the vision. This is important because we see a pattern emerging. An apocalyptic prophecy always has a beginning and an ending point in time, and the events between the beginning point and the ending point always follow chronologically! This consistent rule can be observed throughout the 18 prophecies of Daniel and Revelation.

The second visit - good news, bad news

When the angel Gabriel appeared before Daniel at the second visit (Daniel 9), he said, **"I have now come to give you insight and under- standing.... Therefore, consider the message and understand the vision [of the evenings and mornings you saw earlier]."** (Daniel 9:22-23)

Two items must be mentioned. First, Daniel's primary concern at the time of Gabriel's second visit was the restoration of Israel. Daniel knew that the 70 years of Babylonian captivity were just about over and he privately longed to see an immediate fulfillment of the prophecy. (Daniel 9:19) Daniel wanted to go home. Daniel wondered how the vision of the evenings and mornings related to the restoration of Israel, so he consequently sought the Lord for greater understanding with fasting and prayer. When Gabriel showed up, the angel immediately began talking about Israel, the restoration of Jerusalem and the temple because this was the burden on Daniel's heart.

Secondly, it is important to know that Jeremiah's prophecy about the Babylonian captivity was fulfilled the year of Gabriel's second visit. Right on time, Cyrus, King of Persia, released Israel from the 70 years of captivity. The decree is recorded in Ezra. **"In the first year of Cyrus king of Persia, in order to fulfill the word of the Lord spoken by Jeremiah, the Lord moved the heart of Cyrus king of Persia to make a proclamation...[freeing Israel]."** See Ezra 1:1-11.

The future of Israel

As the second visit began, Gabriel said, **"As soon as you began to pray, an answer [to your petition about your people Israel] was given, which I have come to tell you, for you are highly esteemed. Therefore, consider the message and understand the (first segment of the) vision."** (Daniel 9:23) Then, the angel outlined six major points concerning the future of Israel (Daniel 9:24-27):

1. Seventy "sevens" are granted to your people to:
   a. pay the penalty for their wicked deeds as a nation
   b. put an end to national apostasy
   c. bring in everlasting righteous- ness
   d. seal up the vision and proph- ecy
   e. anoint the Most Holy
2. From the issuing of the decree to restore and rebuild Jerusalem until the Anointed One appears would be 69 "sevens".
3. In the middle of the 70th week, the Anointed One would be cut off from His people. He would also confirm the covenant with His own blood and He would put an end to sacrifices and offerings.
4. Jerusalem and its sanctuary would be destroyed after they are rebuilt.
5. Wars and desolations would continue until the end of Jerusalem.
6. The one who causes desolations upon the earth will continue until the very end of time.

Note: The Hebrew word in Daniel 9:24 translated "weeks" (KJV) and "sevens" (NIV) is "shabua." Shabua means a week or a seven. There are 17 instances where this word is used in the Old Testament and all of them refer to a literal week or seven days. Daniel 10:2,3 and Daniel 9:24 use the *same* word: shabua. This little point will become important in our study because the Jubilee calendar is necessary for calculations that follow.

Comments

Gabriel informed Daniel that the Anointed One (the Messiah) would appear 69 weeks after a decree was given to restore and rebuild Jerusalem. This indicated to Daniel that yes, Jerusalem would be restored and that the Holy One of Israel would now come "at a specific moment in time."

The Jews well knew that the Anointed One (Messiah) would come through Israel, for Isaiah had prophesied: **"...The virgin will be with child and will give birth to a son, and will call him Immanuel. ...in the future he will honor Galilee of the Gentiles... The people walking in darkness have seen a great light; on those living in the land of the shadow of death a light has dawned. ...And he will be called Wonderful Counselor, Mighty God, Everlasting Father, Prince of Peace."** (Isaiah 7:14, 9:1,2,6)

Daniel was both disappointed and thrilled with the information given him. Daniel was thrilled to learn that Messiah, the promised King of Israel would come at an appointed time. Daniel also recognized that Messiah's appearing was still several centuries away. But the news that crushed Daniel was the fact that someday, Jerusalem and the temple would be fully destroyed *again*. (See item 4 above.) Daniel wondered, would God entirely forget His people?

An appointment with Messiah

Gabriel told Daniel that from the decree to restore and rebuild Jerusalem until Messiah the Prince appears would be 69 weeks (literally 69 sevens). What does this mean? The Jews reckoned time in two ways. First, there was literal time. A week was seven evening and mornings. Secondly, they also reckoned time in Jubilee units. For example, a Jubilee week is seven years in length; a year for each day of the week. This system of time was given to Israel at the time of the Exodus and is explained in Leviticus 25 and 26. So, under this system, 69 weeks represents 483 years (69 x 7 = 483).

The Jubilee rule

Although not stated in the Bible, there is a consistent process for prophetic dating. (See Appendix A for a larger discussion on Jubilee cycles.) It appears to this author that God established the Jubilee calendar for three reasons: First, it was a recurring cycle of time that renewed His affection for Israel through events that transpired every 50th year.

Secondly, Jubilee cycles kept all other timing cycles together in a synchronous form. Lastly, God implemented Jubilee cycles so that He could provide the mathematics and events necessary for prophetic calculations over long periods of time without requiring a lot of dates and events outside the Bible.

It appears to this writer that there is a consistent use of the day/year principle in prophecy. It works as follows: *If a time period falls within the operation of the Jubilee calendar and that time period occurs in one of the 18 apocalyptic prophecies of Daniel and Revelation, then the time period requires the use of the day/year principle.*

This simple principle explains why some time periods are day/year and others are not. For example, this writer believes the Jubilee calendar expires in 1994. This means that the 3.5 years of Daniel 7:25 are to be interpreted as 1,260 literal years while the 1,000 years of Revelation 20 are to be interpreted as 1,000 literal years.

Jubilee weeks

As said before, God associates events in heaven with events on earth so that we might understand the timing of things in heaven. According to the prophecy, Jesus was going to leave heaven and come to earth as a baby. Gabriel told Daniel to start counting down the 69 weeks when the decree to restore and rebuild Jerusalem was given.

Did God mean 69 literal weeks or 69 Jubilee weeks? Answer: History proves that God meant Jubilee weeks. Notice how the story unfolds.

Which decree?

To be sure, four decrees were granted to the Jews for restoration to their homeland! The first was given in 536 B.C. by Cyrus (Ezra 1). The second was given in 519 B.C. by Darius (Ezra 6). The third and fourth decrees were given by Artaxerxes in 457 and 444 B.C. (Ezra 7 and Nehemiah 2). But which of these decrees did God intend that the Jews should count from?

It is this writer's opinion that God intentionally kept this question shrouded in a mystery just as He has intentionally kept the date of Christ's second advent a mystery. The knowledge of timing—of both advents—belongs to those who are studying, watching and praying. And, as in the days of Christ's first advent, the negligent will be caught by surprise at the second coming—even though they may be highly respected religious officials.

God did not reveal *which* decree that would start the prophecy. The question of which decree kept the Jews watching and wondering. For example, 69 weeks after 536 B.C. is 53 B.C. (a little early); 69 weeks after the second decree in 519 B.C. is 36 B.C. (still too early). And 69 weeks after 457 B.C. is A.D. 27 (right on time as will be seen shortly). **Note:** The 444 B.C. decree is not historically plausible because A.D. 40 is too late for the historical appearing of Messiah.

The Jews well knew Daniel's prophecy. And, prophetic interest must have been piqued as 53 B.C. drew near. But, Messiah didn't appear. Then, 36 B.C. must have raised prophetic interest too. But, again, there was no Messiah. So, it is understandable that when A.D. 27 arrived, prophetic interest was greater than before. Notice that Luke carefully documents the beginning year of Christ's ministry by telling who is ruling: **"In the fifteenth year of the reign of Tiberius Caesar — when Pontius Pilate was governor of Judea, Herod tetrarch of Galilee, his brother Philip tetrarch of Iturea and Traconitis, and Lysanias tetrarch of Abilene.... The people were waiting expectantly and were all wondering in their hearts if John might possibly be the Christ."** (Luke 3:1,15) In this very year, Jesus was baptized, being 30 years of age. Jesus was anointed by the Holy Spirit and the Father commended Jesus for His faithfulness to the plan of salvation. (Luke 3:21-23)

The wise men

Here is an interesting matter. Each time the story is told of the birth of Jesus, the wise men are mentioned. Many people don't know that the wise men were students of prophecy. They came from the East (area around Babylon) where they had found and studied Daniel's writings. By understanding that a priest in Israel had to be 30 years of age before beginning his ministry, they had calculated an approximate time when the 483 years should end and then they

subtracted 30 years from their conclusion to determine the year of Jesus' birth.

When we consider that their round-trip journey to see Baby Jesus could have taken up to two years, we detect the intensity of their desire to see the Messiah. Wise men do not go to such extremes on a whim. Like the prophets Simeon and Anna, they, too, longed to *personally* behold the Savior of the world. Their presence at the birth of Jesus is another confirmation that the decree of Artaxerxes in 457 B.C. is the correct decree for starting the count down. The presence of the wise men in Jerusalem at time of Jesus' birth is a strong statement, for there is no other prophecy in the Bible pinpointing the time of Messiah's appearing other than Daniel 9.

What is so ironic is that these "Gentiles" were watching and waiting for the sign of Messiah while the Jewish leaders were in total ignorance. Perhaps some of the Jewish elders had experienced false Messianic excitement before. Why should they be excited now? What does this say about trusting religious leaders?

A special year

There is one more point about the 457 B.C. date of the decree to restore and rebuild Jerusalem. Although we can't discuss it in detail here, the decree of Artaxerxes in 457 B.C. is the only decree that occurs in a Jubilee year. The intersection of Artaxerxes' decree with a Jubilee year is not coincidental. Seventy weeks equal 490 years (70 x 7

= 490). Seventy weeks also equal 10 Jubilee cycles (49 x 10 = 490). The importance of Messiah dying in the middle of the 70th week confirms something larger than the 70 week prophecy. Later we will see that the Jubilee year is both symbolic of God's restoration and redemption and symbolic of God's retaliation upon His enemies.

Three keys explain the 2,300 evenings and mornings

We now return to Gabriel's second visit. Gabriel told Daniel that the 70 weeks were *decreed* upon Israel. The Hebrew word translated "decreed" comes from the Hebrew word *chathak* and it means to cut off, as from a larger item. For example, if you granted your son one hour to play outdoors, you may require that he first take out the trash. In this illustration, the time required to take out the trash is part of his one hour — thus, the trash gets removed quickly. So, Gabriel informed Daniel that 70 weeks had been cut off of something. What was it? Answer: The longer prophecy containing 2,300 evenings and mornings which Daniel had previously seen. This small detail solves a big problem, for in his first visit, Gabriel did not reveal *when* the 2,300 evenings and mornings began. Now that we know that the 70 weeks are cut off of some time-frame, we can assume (for the moment) two things. First, the 70 weeks are cut off from the 2,300 evenings and mornings. And secondly, both prophecies share the same beginning point

The keys explained

Here are six reasons why this author believes the 70 weeks are a subset of the longer 2,300 evenings and mornings vision. Even more, they begin at the same point in time.

1.   Daniel 8:13 asks five questions. Each of the five questions is answered with a number of days. The fourth question about the length of time the sanctuary will be surrendered is answered with a specific length of time, namely, 2,300 evenings and mornings. (Daniel 8:14) Nothing is said about the commencement or conclusion of this time period. It is just identified. However, we can be sure that the 2,300 evenings and mornings have something to do with the context of the vision. That is, this time period has something to do with the historical setting of the ram and the goat, and it has something to do with the appearing of the horn power at an appointed time.

2.   Daniel does not mention a sanctuary in the vision of Daniel 8. So, what does the five-part question in verse 13 have to do with the symbols of this vision? Answer: The 2,300 days separate the ram and goat from the appearing of the horn power. Because apocalyptic prophecies are not complete within themselves, apocalyptic prophecies are dependent upon each other to complete the picture. The point here is that the five-part question

in Daniel 8:13 reveals five "numerical" issues that involve timing. And the remaining four questions are answered with numbers by Palmoni in Daniel 12.

3. The time period of 2,300 evenings and mornings refers to a span of 2,300 years. Here's how: Ever since creation, a day is made up of an evening and a morning. (Genesis 1) So, the holy numberer is talking about 2,300 days, and evenings and mornings are translated as days in the King James Version. Under the operation of the Jubilee calendar, a day equals a year. In fact, our discussion about 70 weeks clearly reveals that God is reckoning time in Jubilee units. So, if the 70 weeks are day/years, the 2,300 days must be 2,300 years. But when do they begin?

4. The absence of a clearly stated starting point for the 2,300 days has caused considerable discussion. A number of scholars have *suspected* that the 70 weeks and the 2,300 days begin at the same time; however, there is a way to conclusively demonstrate this point. There is evidence that the 70 weeks are cut off from the 2,300 days, but are they cut off at the beginning of the 2,300 days? In other words, do both time periods share the same starting point? The answer is yes. Even though the subject of the seven

seals has not been presented thus far, they provide the confirming key. Here's how: The judgment scene in Daniel 7:9 began in 1798, at the end of the 1,260 years. If we calculate the date for the cleansing of the sanctuary as 1844 (2,300 years after 457 B.C.), there is complete harmony from the sum of the prophetic parts. In 1798 Jesus began opening the seven seals and the third seal, containing the judgment hour message, was opened in 1844. Notice how the elements come together. The 70 weeks began in 457 B.C. (Daniel 9) and Jesus personally confirmed this date by appearing and dying on time. The judgment scene in Daniel 7 began in 1798 because we find the little horn power is broken right on time. If the reader will consider the idea that Jesus began opening the seals in 1798, the timing of the third seal will easily fit into 1844 because the third seal is a *heavenly* sanctuary message! The harmony of these points demonstrates that the only place for the 2,300 years to start is with the decree that starts the 70 weeks. In this case, three separate prophecies link together to confirm the operations within each other!

5. What is the surrender of the sanctuary? What is the cleansing (KJV) or reconsecration (NIV) of the sanctuary? What does the response by Palmoni in Daniel 8:14 mean? "**...It will take 2,300 evenings and mornings; then the sanctuary**

will be reconsecrated." (Daniel 8:14) What sanctuary is Palmoni talking about—the sanctuary in Jerusalem that was lying in ruins or the sanctuary in heaven where Jesus serves? (Hebrews 8:1-5) Answer: Palmoni is talking about the sanctuary in heaven for it is the true sanctuary at the time of the fulfillment of this vision. In short, Palmoni is saying that 2,300 years after the decree to restore and rebuild Jerusalem, then heaven's sanctuary will begin to be restored. The restoration of heaven's sanctuary is the removal of sin from heaven's sanctuary. This occurs as Jesus decides the case of each person. For example, the sins of each person are either placed upon the sinner's head or Jesus places them upon the scapegoat, the devil. The point is that they are no longer remain in the books of heaven. This is the cleansing, the judgment scene that Daniel saw in heaven. (Daniel 7:10)

6. We know that the 70 weeks began with the decree of Artaxerxes in 457 B.C. We also know that the 70 weeks were cut off from a longer time frame. We will shortly demonstrate that Jesus fulfilled the 70 week prophecy by dying in the middle of the 70th week. The point here is that His death confirms the decree given in 457 B.C., which is also connected to the timing of His ministry as our High Priest in heaven's sanctuary. If the 2,300 year prophecy began when the 70 weeks prophecy began, then 1798 and 1844 fully synchronize. This point will be seen in its beauty in the study on the seven seals.

Summary

At this point, we need to bring all the details together so we can clearly see where we are headed. Study the chart below and then identify the following relationships:

1. The death of Jesus confirms the decree of Artaxerxes in 457 B.C.

The relationship between the 70 Weeks, 2,300 day/years and the 1,260 day/years of the little horn power dominion.

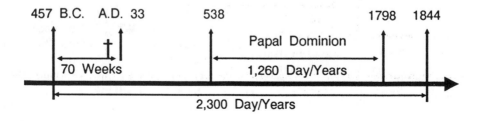

2. When 2,300 years are added to 457 B.C., the result is 1844.
3. The intimate relationship between events terminating on earth in 1798 and the judgment scene taking place in 1844 is shown below.
4. Daniel 8 contributes to the historical matrix by giving additional information about the Medo-Persian and Grecian empires. This prophecy also introduces the appearing of a great king at the "appointed time of the end" which is not shown on this diagram.

The point here is that the 2,300 days of Daniel 8 and the 70 weeks of Daniel 9 are established chronologically by the earthly ministry of Jesus. There are three keys that make these conclusions possible:

KEY I - A day for a year

The Bible consistently follows this rule: All 18 *apocalyptic time periods* occurring during the operation of the Jubilee calendar are to be interpreted in day/year units. After the Jubilee calendar expires, all apocalyptic time periods are to be interpreted in literal units of time. (See Appendix A.)

If we apply this rule, we find consistent harmony between history and prophecy. For example, most historians now calculate the fifteenth year of Tiberius Caesar as A.D. 27, which is exactly 483 years from the decree in 457 B.C. by Artaxerxes. Should this surprise us? Jesus, who set the time of His appearing and had the information delivered to Daniel, appeared when He said He would. Right on time.

KEY II - Jesus dies on time

Gabriel said that in the middle of the 70th "seven" the Anointed One would be cut off (literally cut down), that He

The Harmony Between Daniel 2, 7, 8 and 9

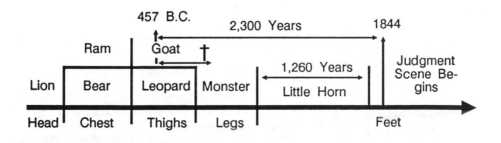

would also confirm the covenant with many and He would put an end to sacrifices and offerings.

Since a "seven" represents seven years, the 70th week of this prophecy is seven years long. The 70th week began with A.D. 27 and reaches to A.D. 33 because a week is measured from Sunday to Saturday *inclusively*. The middle day of every week is Wednesday. Consequently, Jesus died in the spring of A.D. 30 which is the Wednesday year or middle of the 70th week. Here's how:

1. Sunday year   = A.D. 27
2. Monday year   = A.D. 28
3. Tuesday year = A.D. 29
4. **Wednesday year = A.D. 30**
5. Thursday year = A.D. 31
6. Friday year   = A.D. 32
7. Sabbatical year = A.D. 33

Several points support A.D. 30:

1. The decree to restore and rebuild Jerusalem was given in the Spring of 457 B.C. (Ezra 8) The 70th week began in the Spring of A.D. 27. Jesus was crucified in the Spring, at Passover, which was always celebrated in the Spring. (John 19:14)

2. It appears that Passover, the 15th day of the first month, fell on Saturday in that year. (John 19:31)

3. Gabriel indicated that Messiah was to be "cut off" (literally

translated: cut down or cut off). Was He cut down by His own people? Stephen, the first Christian martyr knew that his people had killed the Messiah. He cried out to the Sanhedrin regarding the crucifixion of Jesus, **"...you have betrayed and murdered him!"** (Acts 7:52)

4. Did Messiah put an end to sacrifices and offerings? Paul says, **"God ...canceled the written code, with its regulations, that was against us and that stood opposed to us; he took it away, nailing it to the cross."** (Colossians 2:13,14)

5. Did Jesus confirm the covenant? Jesus said, **"This is my blood of the covenant, which is poured out for many for the forgiveness of sins."** (Matthew 26:28) Paul wrote, **"...This salvation, which was first announced by the Lord, was confirmed to us by those who heard him."** (Hebrews 2:3)

History agrees

According to the prophecy, Jesus died *exactly on time*. The year was A.D. 30. At the very moment the High Priest was about to slay the Passover lamb in Jerusalem's temple, Jesus, hanging from the cross—the Passover Lamb of God, died for the sins of the whole world.

An angel immediately flew to the temple and tore the heavy temple veil from top to bottom that separated the Holy place from the Most Holy place. This act signified the end of the sacrificial system. Jesus had confirmed the covenant of salvation with His own blood. The religious services which had been required of Israel were now fulfilled. Their primary meaning was fully explained. The penalty for sin which they had pointed to was now paid in full. And the shadow of the earthly temple disappeared in the glory of Christ's resurrection. The ceremonies that pointed to Calvary were left behind at the cross.

Note: When the temple veil was torn open, the great multitude that had gathered in the courtyard of the temple for the Passover service stood in awe at the scene. For the first time ever, ordinary people peered into the Most Holy room of the temple and the sole property of the room was darkness. The ark of the covenant which had been hidden by Jeremiah at the time of the Babylonian captivity had not been found and, in fact, remains hidden to this very day! How symbolic. Darkness not only filled the inner place of Israel's religious shrine, darkness filled the hearts of the worshipers, too.

Conclusion

It is necessary to sum up a few things from this chapter to see how all the prophetic pieces interlock:

1. There was a great deal of expectation in Israel in A.D. 27, the fifteenth year of Tiberius Caesar. Many Jews *anticipated* the appearing of Messiah because they understood the timing of Messiah's appearance as predicted by Daniel. See Luke 3:15. Even the Samaritans knew that Messiah was coming. The woman at the well said: **"...I know that Messiah (called Christ) is coming... when he comes, he will explain everything to us."** (John 4:25) Mathematically, A.D. 27 is the 483rd year from the decree given by Artaxerxes in 457 B.C. In addition, most scholars today generally agree that Jesus would have been 30 years of age in A.D. 27 because Herod, the king who tried to kill Him, died in 4 B.C.

2. Jesus was baptized and anointed by His Father in A.D. 27, being about 30 years of age. It was customary for a man to be 30 years old before he could serve Israel as a priest. See Numbers 4:3.

3. "Elijah," as promised in Malachi 4:5, preceded the baptism of Jesus in A.D. 27. John the Baptist came in the spirit and power of Elijah to prepare the "way of the Lord." See Matthew 11:14.

4. Jesus, who gave this vision to Daniel 550 years before He was born, understood the timing and fulfillment of the prophecy, for He said at the beginning of His ministry on earth, **"The time has come...."** (Mark 1:15) Again, Jesus speaking after His baptism in Nazareth said, **"The Spirit of the Lord is on me... to proclaim the**

year of the Lord's favor." (Luke 4:18,19)

5. Christ died precisely on time. Jesus, The Passover Lamb of God, died on the *very day* the ceremonial service had pointed forward to for centuries. The Passover Lamb was slain in the Spring of the year, on the 14th day of the first month. Jesus died in the Spring of the year, at the time of Passover. The Spring of A.D. 30 is the middle year of the 70th week of seven years.

The fullness of time

Paul succinctly sums up Daniel's prophecy by saying, **"But when the time had fully come, God sent his Son...."** (Galatians 4:4) Can any question remain that God's timing is less than perfect?

So, we have applied two valuable keys — both centered on Jesus. First, we see the operation of Jubilee cycles. Under this system a day equals a year. This discovery allows us to accurately calculate the timing of the birth, ministry and death of Jesus. The second key is historical evidence. Jesus appeared right on time and this not only demonstrates the synchronism of the Jubilee calendar and the day/year principle, it also confirms our understanding of the prophecies. These two keys tell us we are on the right track. In the next chapter we'll examine the third and most profound key!

Chapter 10

The Failure of Israel

Even though the prophecies of Daniel 8 and 9 span several centuries and predict several events, their primary purpose is to provide a means for identifying *when* the appointed time of the end arrives. Daniel 8 establishes a historical footing in the days of the Medo-Persian empire. Artaxerxes was a Persian king and his decree took place in 457 B.C. God, in His foreknowledge of coming events, chose this decree as an earthly marker for the Hebrews to begin their count down to the appearing of Messiah. In addition, God chose this decree as a beginning point to date the cleansing of heaven's sanctuary. The most impressive point about both prophetic dates is that they center on the date of Christ's ministry. Therefore, we may safely establish the chronology of Christ's ministry in the judgment scene of Daniel 7.

Thus far, we have established three important dates. These are the decree of Artaxerxes in 457 B.C., the baptism of Messiah in A.D. 27 and the death of Jesus in A.D. 30. The ministry and death of Jesus not only confirms the accuracy of 457 B.C., but it also confirms the synchronism of the Jubilee calendar. Therefore, we know the location of the days within the week of years. Jesus died in the Wednesday year, the middle of the week. By knowing the synchronism of the weekly cycles within the Jubilee calendar, we can accurately locate other important events. More will be said about this later.

Back to Daniel

When Gabriel told Daniel that 70 "sevens" were *cut off* for Israel, he spoke of God's timing mechanism of Jubilee cycles. The reader should observe that 490 literal years are exactly 10 Jubilees (49 x 10). The appearing of Messiah, exactly 483 years (69 "sevens") after the decree of Artaxerxes, to be baptized of John in A.D. 27 confirms the accuracy of this conclusion.

The second key to understanding Daniel 9 is that Christ's death in A.D. 30 confirms the accuracy of 457 B.C. Jesus died precisely on time in the middle of the 70th week to confirm God's covenant with man: The plan of salvation.

There are some very strange views about the 70th week. For example, some teach that the 70th week contains a historical time period of 3.5 years, a gap of many centuries, and then a final 3.5 years. If this is true, the *middle* of the 70th week cannot be determined! For example, we can only compute the middle of the 70th week because we know the beginning and ending dates. The middle year between A.D. 27 and 33 is A.D. 30. If the 70th week is not seven consecutive years, mathematically speaking, the middle of the 70th week cannot be calculated.

Other people teach that there is a long gap of about 2,000 years between the 69th week and the 70th week. These disconnect the 70th week from the previous 69 weeks and move the 70th week down to the end of time for one basic purpose. They believe that the 70th week applies to the Jews living at the end of time. This is why the restoration of Israel as a state in 1948 stands so prominently in their eschatology. But, if the 70th week is disconnected from the previous 69 weeks, how can one be sure that the 68th week is consecutive with the 69th week, and so forth? Weekly cycles, whether in literal time or Jubilee time, follow in order. They cannot be disconnected for each other. If the 70th week is disconnected from the 69 weeks, then, what is the prophetic purpose of the decree to restore and rebuild Jerusalem and the following 69 weeks?

If the 70th week is disconnected from the 69 weeks, the timely value of the 69 weeks, the baptism and death of Jesus are completely eliminated. In addition, the date of the decree to restore and rebuild Jerusalem in 457 B.C. cannot be confirmed and ultimately, we are left without a historical marker to know when the 2,300 year prophecy begins. And, the

ministry of Jesus in heaven—the cleansing of the heavenly sanctuary—is just as important as His ministry on earth!

The 70 weeks of 490 years stand together as one unit of consecutive time. The Bible does not support the idea that the 70th week is disconnected from the 69th week in any text. Ten Jubilee cycles or 70 "sevens" of 490 literal years were allotted to the Jewish nation to accomplish certain things and Jesus Himself confirmed the beginning of the 70th week of seven years in A.D. 27. He again confirmed the middle of the week by dying three and a half years later in A.D. 30.

Now, the third and last key that unlocks this portion of Daniel's prophecy relates to the end of the 70th week—A.D. 33. This date is extremely important for God's election of the Jewish nation ended in this year.

KEY III - The destiny of the Jews

Let's review Gabriel's comments to Daniel concerning the Jews:

Seventy "sevens" (or weeks) are granted to your people to:

a. pay the penalty for their wicked deeds as a nation
b. put an end to national apostasy
c. bring in everlasting righteousness
d. seal up the vision and prophecy
e. anoint the Most Holy

The very first thing Gabriel said is that 70 "sevens" are granted to "your people," Daniel. The importance of this time period and the people to whom it applies must not be overlooked. Look at the five specifications. The first two elements relate to Jewish behavior within the specified time-period and the last three elements refer to promised glory if the Jews would cooperate with God.

The Jews knew they were special to God. They knew that they, through Abraham, had been elected as trustees of God's covenant. They knew that Messiah would come through their bloodline. But they forgot that God's covenant with them as a people was conditional. More about this in a moment.

Gabriel's words to Daniel address the covenant relationship that had existed between Jesus and the Jews for almost 800 years. If Israel would turn away from their idolatry and rebellion, they could still fulfill God's purpose, for God had promised to rescue a remnant of them from Babylon. (Jeremiah 27:22) God wanted Israel to know that their rescue from Babylon did not lessen their covenant responsibilities, nor did it mean that all was well between them. Gabriel's message addresses God's concerns for Israel. He clearly said that Israel would have the opportunity to anoint the Most Holy One of Israel and to bring in everlasting righteousness during the probationary period of 490 years.

If the Jews had cooperated with the Lord, the history of the world would have been far different than we now know it. If the Jews had fulfilled their calling, they could have "sealed up the vision and prophecy" so that the destruction described in this prophecy would not have to take place. If – if – if...

The covenant(s)

The prophecy of Daniel 9 is complex. It will only fit together properly when a number of other things (outside the prophecy) are correctly understood. So, a word about God's covenant with man is necessary.

We often hear about the old and new covenants, and much of what we hear is not biblical. Even though it is not possible to explore the depths of the covenant at this time, two items must be correctly understood about the covenants if we are going to understand the prophecy of Daniel 9.

First, the basic element of the covenant between God and man is this: "If you will be my people, I will be your God." This thought and these words are found many times throughout the Scriptures. The contents of the everlasting covenant are comprehensive and have always existed, for God's covenant is unchanging and everlasting! Man's knowledge of the contents of the covenant has developed through the centuries because God has revealed more about the covenant as circumstances warranted.

The essential elements of the everlasting covenant were first revealed to Adam and Eve after they sinned. The covenant was repeated and enlarged at the time of the flood and then, it was repeated and enlarged with Noah. It was further renewed and enlarged with Abraham, Moses, etc. The point is that God's everlasting covenant is *everlasting*. It has always existed and will always exist. As time passes, God expands man's understanding of His covenant concept so that man can understand His Maker more completely, and even more, understand the properties of salvation. Knowledge is cumulative. This means that human beings can learn from earlier generations if they are willing. God's covenant is both universal and everlasting. This means that it applies to everyone everywhere, and that it has never changed. This is a profound point that must be examined carefully.

The plan of salvation has never changed. Men and women, boys and girls of all ages have *always* been saved by faith and the same is true today. (Hebrews 3:7-19;11:1-40, Ephesians 2:8,9)

The second point that must be understood about God's covenant is that God, at the time of Abraham, chose the descendants of Abraham to be trustees of the covenant. They were to carry the good news of the everlasting covenant to the ends of the world. They were chosen because God loved Abraham. God knew that many people working together could accomplish more than a few people working separately. So, He chose the family of Abraham because Abraham was His friend. God wanted a nation of "Abraham-like people." But the

Pharisees didn't understand. They said to Jesus, " 'Abraham is our father,' they answered. 'If you were Abraham's children,' said Jesus, 'then you would do the things Abraham did.' " (John 8:39)

Understand that Israel's election as the trustees of the covenant was conditional. See Deuteronomy 7-9. And Moses warned Israel on a number of occasions that if they were unfaithful to their calling, God would reject them. See Deuteronomy 28.

Understand how the covenant works:

God's covenant is immutable or irrevocable. On the other hand, the election of Israel as trustees was revocable because they had to meet certain terms in order to be trustees of the gospel. (The same is true of trusts today. Trustees must comply with certain terms in order to remain trustees of a trust.)

God's covenant contains a condition. It says: *If* you will be my people, THEN, I will be your God. In other words, no one is forced to accept the covenant. It is each person's choice. It is the responsibility of the trustees of the covenant to see that everyone properly understands the everlasting covenant so that all may decide for or against the covenant.

Israel not only violated God's covenant, they did not live up to the terms of being trustees of the covenant. So, God sent them into Babylonian captivity. (2 Chronicles 36:16) From their captivity,

God revealed that He would give them one more chance to fulfill His purpose for them. This last chance was for a limited time. It would last 490 years.

The newer covenant

The everlasting covenant was renewed and enlarged when Jesus was upon earth. This expansion does not do away with any of the previous elements of the covenant. Jesus said, **"Do not think that I have come to abolish the Law or the Prophets (the Scriptures); I have not come to abolish them but to fulfill them. I tell you the truth, until heaven and earth disappear, not the smallest letter, not the least stroke of a pen, will by any means disappear from the Law (the Scriptures) until everything is accomplished."** (Matthew 5:17,18)

New truths were revealed from the covenant by Jesus. And, after He ascended to heaven, even more truth was revealed to His disciples. One of the most exciting truths that has been revealed is the ministry of Jesus in heaven as man's High Priest. This will be carefully examined in our next study.

Very important distinction

A very important distinction has to be made between the covenant and the rules of trusteeship. God's everlasting covenant with man is unilateral. This means it is His covenant, and the terms are created by Him. Man is in no position to negotiate an agreement with God. Not once in all the Bible is God's everlasting covenant called "our" covenant. God always refers to it as "My" covenant. See Genesis 17 for ownership of the covenant. The basic element of God's covenant to man is extremely simple: If you will be my people, I will be your God.

The rules of trusteeship are vastly different, distinct and separate from the terms of the covenant. Most people mix these things together and then get very confused with the whole subject. So, the following example may be helpful: A wealthy couple learned they were going to have a child. So, they set up a trust for the child before it was born. When the child was 10 years of age, both parents were killed in a plane crash. Since the child was a minor, he could not take possession of his inheritance. Therefore, according to the terms of the trust, the court appointed a trustee for the child until the child should reach maturity.

Here's the point. The rules binding upon the trustee are separate and distinct from the trust held for the child. The trust dictates that several things are to be done for the child and the trustee is responsible for seeing that they are done. So it is. When God gave circumcision to Abraham, circumcision was not the everlasting covenant. Circumcision is not part of the everlasting covenant for the covenant says, "If you will be my people, I will be your God." However, Abraham was willing to be a trustee of the gospel and God mandated to Abraham and his descendants that circumcision was a *token or sign* of this responsibility. Later, through Moses, God required His trustees to do other things. He required a sanctuary system of ceremonial services so that in ages to come, people could investigate and understand the properties of His salvation. But, like the Jews, many Christians today still misunderstand the purpose of the ceremonial system. It never was part of the everlasting covenant. The ceremonial system was part of *their* responsibilities as trustees of His covenant. God wanted to teach Israel and later, the world about the plan of salvation.

Because Israel continuously violated the covenant of God for centuries, His patience finally ran out. God used sword, famine, plague and wild beasts upon Israel to redeem them, but to no avail. Finally, God granted them 10 Jubilees of time, 490 years to "straighten up." But, in the end, Israel lost their right to be trustees of the covenant. This is why circumcision came to mean nothing. See Romans 2:28,29.

When Jesus died on Calvary, the ceremonial services that pointed forward to the confirmation of the salvation were fulfilled. This is why they were nailed to the cross. See Colossians 2:14,15; Galatians 4:9,10. And because Israel failed to fulfill their responsibility as trustees, God's election of literal Israel ended.

But the everlasting covenant remains unchanged. In fact, it was renewed and enlarged again through the apostle Paul for the sake of all who would believe in His name. Jesus revealed to

Paul that He was our High Priest. And as our mediator in the heavenly sanctuary, He was the mediator of a better, more complete covenant. Complete in the sense that humans beings now understood more about the love of God. Complete in the sense that God would now reckon anyone a descendant of Abraham if they were willing to live by faith in Jesus. (Galatians 3:29)

Back to Daniel again

Because God knows the future, Daniel's prophecy predicts the outcome of the 490 years of probationary time. God, having all foreknowledge, knew that Israel would not measure up. But keep in mind that God does not deal with us on the basis of His foreknowledge; rather, He deals with us considering our time and place. Because He is love, He does not use His foreknowledge to manipulate us to His advantage or our disadvantage.

Because Jesus knew Israel would forfeit their probationary time of 490 years, He decreed that Jerusalem would again be destroyed and wars and desolations would continue to the destruction of Jerusalem (A.D. 70.) Even more, the "evil one" who causes wars and desolations would be free to continue his work until the very end of time.

During the 70 "sevens," Israel was to atone for their wicked ways as a nation by turning to the Lord in repentance. Repentance means the forsaking of sin! During their probationary time of 490 years (457 B.C. to A.D. 33), the Jewish nation was to "bring in everlasting righteousness" by measuring up to the high calling as trustees of the gospel set forth by Jesus. The Jews were to fully develop the loving characteristics of their Messiah so that when He appeared, they could recognize Him by His character!

70 "sevens" - a measure of forgiveness

The Jewish people clearly knew the 70 "sevens" were probationary. They knew national apostasy brought on the Babylonian captivity. See Daniel 9:1-20. They knew that they had been given a final opportunity. In fact, Jesus used the 70 "sevens" mentioned in Daniel 9 as an expression of forbearance when Peter asked, **"...Lord, how many times shall I forgive my brother when he sins against me? Up to seven times? Jesus answered, I tell you, not seven times, but seventy times seven."** (Matthew 18:21,22) Peter caught the meaning. He was to forgive his brother just as God had forgiven Israel (70 x 7).

The last year of the 70th "seven" occurred in A.D. 33. This year is important for it marked the last year of Jewish probation. Here the clock of mercy stopped. Frankly, Jewish interest in doing God's will expired long before A.D. 33. Jesus knew this. He therefore pronounced divine sentence upon 1400 years of Jewish history when He proclaimed, **"Your house is left to you desolate."** (Matthew 23:38) The Jews were no longer trustees of the covenant and

recorded history won't let anyone deny that the Jews rejected the Messiah. (John 1:11)

Like Sodom and Gomorrah, Jericho and the wicked nations of Canaan, Israel passed the point of divine forbearance. They had been forgiven "seventy times seven." Yet, the Jewish nation like the heathen nations before them, came to the end of divine mercy and Jesus dealt with them accordingly. Jesus had clearly warned Israel of His actions on the heathen and made it clear He would do the same to them saying, **"...so I punished (the land of Canaan) for its sin and the land vomited out its inhabitants.... And if you defile the land, it will vomit you out as it vomited out the nations that were before you."** (Leviticus 18:25,28)

Israel abandoned

A series of events transpired the following year showing that Jesus terminated His covenant with the nation of Israel. Before looking at them, review Israel's relation to Jesus:

● The Jews rejected Jesus as the Messiah, the Savior of the world. They could not see beyond the shadows of ceremonies and services. For purposes of salvation, they preferred the blood of animals to faith in the blood of Messiah. What makes this so sad is that the sacrifices of animals never once provided atonement for sin. Paul said, **"...it is impossible for the blood** of bulls and goats to take away sins." (Hebrews 10:4)

● The Jews failed to bring in national repentance; thus their corporate rebellion led them to crucify Jesus and persecute those who represented His work on earth. Their religious pride blinded them in their transgressions. Jesus said to the Pharisees, **"You belong to your father, the devil, and you want to carry out your father's desire. He was a murderer from the beginning, not holding to the truth, for there is no truth in him. When he lies, he speaks his native language, for he is a liar and the father of lies."** (John 8:44)

● Jesus, before his death knew the Jews would reject the covenant, saying, **"If they do not listen to Moses and the Prophets, they will not be convinced even if someone rises from the dead."** (Luke 16:31)

The straw that breaks the camel's back

Perhaps, the most significant historical event recorded in the Bible during the last year of probationary time was the stoning of the Christian deacon, Stephen. The Sanhedrin (the Jewish supreme court) sentenced Stephen to death for preaching that "Jesus has risen from the dead." The killing of Stephen initiated a calculated and open persecution of all Christians by the Jews. (See Acts 7)

Jesus chooses others to carry His gospel

What did Jesus do from heaven in A.D. 34 to demonstrate the termination of the trusteeship of the Jews?

1. Jesus gave Peter a vision about unclean animals. While in vision, Peter thought the command to "kill and eat" the unclean animals had dietary implications. Peter said, **"I have never eaten anything impure or unclean."** (Acts 10:14) But a voice from heaven said, **"...do not call anything impure that God has made clean."** (Acts 10:15) Three times this happened. Peter wondered about the vision. What did it mean? While thinking about the meaning, the Holy Spirit said, **"...Simon, three men are looking for you. So get up and go downstairs. Do not hesitate to go with them, for I have sent them."** (Acts 10:19,20)

The apostle Peter was invited to the home of a Roman centurion, Cornelius. Cornelius was a Gentile and as such, was regarded as "unclean" by the Jews. But Cornelius wanted to hear the gospel. He was a God-fearing man.

Peter was very perplexed about going into the home of a Gentile (which was unlawful for a Jew to enter), but the Holy Spirit had said, "Go!" Upon arriving at the home of Cornelius, Peter said, **"...you are well aware that it is against our law for a Jew to associate with a Gentile or visit him. But God has shown me that I should not call** any man impure or unclean. So when I was sent for, I came without raising any objection. May I ask why you sent for me?" (Acts 10:28,29) Peter now understood the meaning of the vision. A great change was taking place. He dimly began to see that the commission of representing God on earth belonged to the Christians — instead of the Jews. (Compare Acts 10, Matthew 28, and Acts 15.)

2.   Perhaps the strongest response of Jesus to Israel's final rejection was to take one of Israel's brightest and best and "make" a Christian out of him. The conversion of Saul to the apostle Paul, and his life of dedication and service is a story only excelled in the Bible by the life of Jesus. Saul, the Jewish persecutor, became Paul, the persecuted Christian, an apostle sent specifically to the Gentiles. Jesus told Ananias concerning Saul, "...This man is my chosen instrument to carry my name before the Gentiles and their kings and before the people of Israel. I will show him how much he must suffer for my name." (Acts 9:15,16)

Knowing that Israel had failed as trustees of His covenant, Jesus raised up a new group of trustees — people called "Christians." Jesus set out to accomplish through the Christian Church what the Jews had failed to do. He gave the Christians a renewed and expanded covenant, a bold faith, an understanding of His character and most of all, a theology based on His life, death, resurrection and priestly ministry. And as early Christians went, Paul became a brilliant and energetic champion of the cross.

Will the Jews change?

Many people today believe that the Jews are still God's chosen people. This is not true. Their probation ended in A.D. 33 without accomplishment. They were rejected by God as trustees of His covenant. Paul understood this very well. He told the Romans, **"A man is not a Jew if he is only one outwardly, nor is circumcision merely outward and physical. No, a man is a Jew if he is one inwardly; and circumcision is circumcision of the heart, by the Spirit, not by the written code. Such a man's praise is not from men, but from God."** (Romans 2:28,29) Paul told the Galatians, **"There is neither Jew nor Greek, slave nor free, male nor female, for you are all one in Christ Jesus. If you belong to Christ, then you are Abraham's seed, and heirs according to the promise."** (Galatians 3:28,29)

Jesus, speaking as Lord, clearly transferred the trusteeship of the gospel to His disciples saying, **"But you will receive power when the Holy Spirit comes on you; and you will be my witnesses in Jerusalem, and in all Judea and Samaria, and to the ends of the earth. Therefore go and make disciples of all nations, baptizing them in the**

name of the Father and of the Son and of the Holy Spirit, and teaching them to obey everything I have commanded you. And surely I am with you always, to the very end of the age." (Acts 1:8, Matthew 28:19,20)

Lastly, Paul knew that Israel, as a nation, had been cut off from the covenant of God. He sincerely hoped that some of its people would repent and find God's favor again. He said, **"And if they do not persist in unbelief, they will be grafted in, for God is able to graft them in again."** (Romans 11:23)

It is this writer's opinion that God has a very important reason for allowing the rise of the state of Israel in these last days. Jesus wants the world to fully behold the character and nature of a religious people who refuse to accept Him as their Savior. By observing their attitudes and conduct toward their neighbors, one can easily see what happens when trustees of His covenant fail to live up to the terms set forth.

Three keys confirm historical footing

Now we have three keys. The three keys now work together to unlock the longest time prophecy in the Bible. Note that the decree of Artaxerxes in 457 B.C. fully meshes with the dates of three events. First, Jesus began His ministry 69 weeks after the decree (A.D. 27). Secondly, Jesus died in the middle of the 70th week (A.D. 30). Lastly, Israel lost their position as trustees of the Gospel at the end of the 70 "sevens" (A.D. 33). The

promised destruction of the city and the temple also mentioned in the prophecy (Daniel 9:26) occurred in A.D. 70. Rome completely destroyed Jerusalem in that siege. What a sad ending to such a glorious beginning.

The appointed time of the end

As you can now see, the visions of Daniel 8 and 9 are comprehensive. The Bible is a storehouse of treasures and those who study prophecy study the deep things of God. Now that the accuracy of 457 B.C. has been *nailed* down, we can be certain of the origin and purpose of the 2,300 days. They end in 1844.

What is the cleansing of the sanctuary?

3.   If we proceed 2,300 years from a confirmed 457 B.C. we arrive at 1844.

2300

- 457

1843

From mathematics alone, we note the date would be 1843. This is because math uses a number scale that includes a zero. Notice the following scale:

-2 -1 0 1 2

You will notice that two years (or two spaces) exist between -1 and 1, for this scale moves from -1 to

0 to 1. When the dating of time relative to Christ's birth was put together, the 0 year was left out. It is not possible to say 0 B.C. or A.D. 0. So, any periods of time that span B.C. to A.D. must have an additional year added to be mathematically correct. So 1843 +1 equals 1844.

4. What does the Bible mean when it says that the sanctuary will be reconsecrated or cleansed after 2,300 evenings and mornings?
The sanctuary to which this part of the vision relates is in heaven, where Jesus serves as our High Priest. Paul said, **"...we do have such a high priest, who sat down at the right hand of the throne of the Majesty in heaven, and who serves in the sanctuary, the true tabernacle set up by the Lord, not by man."** (Hebrews 8:1,2) Remember, this vision focuses on the "appointed time of the end" and the time frame connects to the judgment scenes found in Daniel 7:9,10. As we learn more from this prophecy, we'll discover that the most important things concerning the destiny of the human race take place in the heavenly sanctuary and not on earth.

Even though the temple of the Jews was restored by the decree of Artaxerxes, it was destroyed again in A.D. 70 by the Romans because the privilege of being God's chosen nation

was forfeited by the Jews at end of the 70th week. Ironically, the rebuilt temple of the Jews was just that — not a house of prayer for all people. It doesn't matter if the Jewish temple will be rebuilt again. The Jews are no longer the chosen servants of God. So, the vision of the 2,300 days is connected to the services of Jesus, the High Priest of the human race, serving in the only temple that matters: the heavenly sanctuary in heaven.

The sanctuary restored

The Christian faith is built upon the achievement of Jesus. He came to earth, was tempted beyond anything humans will ever face, yet He lived a sinless life and willingly died at the hands of His own people to pay the penalty of sin. He returned to heaven and at the right time, He sat down at the right hand of the Father to intercede through the merits of His blood for the human race. Christ's work in heaven from His ascension to 1844 may be thought of as that of a priest in the earthly sanctuary.

Since the Old Testament sanctuary built in the wilderness was a representation of the one in heaven, services back there represented or "shadowed" processes of services actually taking place in heaven! Paul clearly understood this point. Talking about the role of priests, he says, **"They serve at a sanctuary that is copy and shadow of what is in heaven. This is why Moses was warned when he was about to build the tabernacle: 'See to it that you make everything according** to the pattern shown you on the mountain.' " (Hebrews 8:5)

Since the Jews failed to measure up to the probationary time period of the 70 "sevens," the *intended* purpose of the rebuilt temple and restored services was never fulfilled. Consequently, Jesus said, "Your temple is left desolate." Here is a profound point: What Jesus intended to do in the earthly temple has to be done in the heavenly one!

In a later chapter we will learn that Jesus was coronated as High Priest in heaven in 1798 and when 1844 arrived, He began a very special work at that time. It is His coronation and work as our High Priest that reconsecrates or restores the sanctuary process! This is not to say that Jesus wasn't busy with heavenly business from His ascension in A.D. 30 to 1844. No! Jesus was very intimately involved with the trustees of the gospel, the Christian Church. Jesus also showed Daniel that certain events would develop during the "times of the Gentiles." Some of these prophetic matters are very fascinating and will be looked at in our next chapter.

The point is made that Jesus clearly placed a long span of time between Daniel's day and the "appointed time of the end." We know that the appointed time of the end began in 1798, and 1844 collaborates to clearly prove we are living in the final phase of Christ's ministry in heaven. The longest time prophecy in the Bible has been fulfilled—all 2,300 years to be exact. Since Jesus personally confirmed the accuracy of the 70 weeks prophecy

(beginning in 457 B.C.) with His baptism and death, 1844 is just as certain too, for both time periods began at the *same* time. We shall soon see that 1844 figures prominently in Revelation's story.

Summary

Daniel 7, 8 and 9 are inseparably linked together to show us when the "appointed time of the end" arrives chronologically. The accuracy of 1798 and 1844 is as certain. The former date is historically confirmed by the works of man. The latter date is confirmed by works of Jesus. Can there be any doubt? The resulting harmony between the 1,260 years, the 70 "sevens" and the 2,300 years is both scriptural and historical.

Isn't it interesting that what the Jews forfeited, the Christians inherited? In the next chapter, we will look into prophetic events that took place after 1844. We will also see that history repeats itself!

Chapter 11

The Day of Judgment
Part I

Thus far we've studied the prophetic mechanism that reaches to 1844 chronologically. Why is 1844 so important? What docs the Bible mean when it says, "then shall the sanctuary be restored?" The answer to this question is not complicated when the underlying issues involved are properly understood.

Even though the prophetic importance of 1844 is not appreciated by many people at this time, this will change when God breaks His silence with the affairs of man! Interest in this subject will rise from obscurity to intense interest overnight because the seven seals of Revelation are directly related to this time-period! As we will see, God has ordained that the living shall know that "the appointed time for the end" of the world has come! For the sake of review, notice that the longest time prophecy in the Bible is built solidly upon four historical moments confirmed in scripture:

1.   The decree to restore and rebuild Jerusalem occurred in the Jubilee year of 457 B.C. (Ezra 7)

2.   At the beginning of the 70th week (483 years after the decree to rebuild) Jesus was baptized and anointed by the Holy Spirit in A.D. 27. (Luke 3)

3.   Jesus, the Passover Lamb, was crucified in the middle of the week, A.D. 30, at the time of the annual Passover feast. (John 19)

4.   Probationary time for the Jews as a nation ended in A.D. 33 when the privilege of representing God was transferred to the Christians. (Acts 7-10)

So, according to Daniel 8:14, the cleansing of the heavenly sanctuary began 2,300 years after the decree to restore and rebuild Jerusalem. The restoration of the heavenly sanctuary is very similar to the ancient Day of Atonement service conducted in the wilderness sanctuary. What does this mean to us right now?

Another look at Daniel 7

We need to study Daniel 7 more thoroughly because we're looking for information on the importance of 1844. How can we know for sure that 1798 marks the beginning of the "appointed time of the end?"

Daniel's four beasts, discussed in Chapter 7, parallel the same kingdoms that Nebuchadnezzar saw. These were Babylon, Medo-Persia, Greece and Rome. Even though history removes any doubt about the identity and chronological progression of these kingdoms, Daniel 7 reveals more than the rise and fall of kingdoms. It reveals an important sequence:

1. Lion

2. Bear

3. Leopard

4. Monster beast

5. Ten horns

6. Little horn

7. Judgment scene

8. Beasts burned by fire

Two verses in Daniel 7 connect the beginning of the judgment scene with the ending of the little horn. Notice: **"As I watched, this horn was waging war against the saints and defeating them, {22} until the Ancient of Days came and pronounced judgment in favor of the saints of the Most High, and the time came when they possessed the kingdom."** (Daniel 7:21-22)

Notice in the previous text that the little horn wages war against the saints *until* the Ancient of Days *came* and pronounced judgment in favor of the saints. Now, we know that the little horn's time period of persecution ended after 1,260 years, in 1798. The point here is that the Ancient of Days *came* to the scene described in Daniel

7 and He pronounced judgment (a "temporary restraining order") against the little horn at that time — and persecution ended. The 1,260 years connects to the judgment against the little horn, thus 1798 marks the date of the "temporary restraining order." It is called a "temporary restraining order" because persecution by the little horn will resume at the very end of time. In Revelation 13:3 the wound inflicted upon the little horn will be healed, and in verse 7, war commences again upon the saints. The point here is that Daniel 7:21,22, in a veiled way, alludes to this resumption of persecution by saying, **"and the time came when they possessed the kingdom."** The saints don't possess the kingdom until Jesus comes. So yes, persecution ended in 1798 by divine decree from heaven and yes, persecution will rise again and end again by the appearing of Jesus Himself.

The judgment scene

The Bible offers enough information to connect 1798 with the judgment scene of Daniel 7. But what does this have to do with 1844 and the cleansing of the sanctuary?

Daniel 7 contains an important key that unlocks the significance of 1844. Notice what Daniel says, **"As I looked, thrones were set in place, and the Ancient of Days took his seat. His clothing was as white as snow; the hair of his head was white like wool. His throne was flaming with fire, and its wheels were all ablaze. A river of fire was flowing, coming out from before him.**

Thousands upon thousands attended him; ten thousand times ten thousand stood before him. The court was seated, and the books were opened." (Daniel 7:9,10)

What did Daniel see taking place in heaven? What is the meaning of this courtroom scene? Daniel saw the judgment of mankind! Reread the verses above and reflect on the following points for a moment:

1. Thrones (plural) were put in place or arranged. Heaven was made ready for a great event.
2. The Ancient of Days, the Father, presides. His appearance is greater than the brightness of the sun. His throne (compared to the other thrones) is so bright that it appears to be on fire. The glowing angels that encircle Him appear to Daniel as wheels of fire.
3. This is no ordinary convention in heaven. Billions of angels throughout the universe have been summoned to this special occasion.
4. The Father takes His seat. The court was seated. And the books of record were opened.

But the scene doesn't end with these verses. There's more. Daniel says, "In my vision at night I looked, and there before me was one like a son of man, coming with the clouds of heaven. He approached the Ancient of Days and was led into his presence. He was given authority, glory and sovereign power; all peoples, nations and men of every language worshiped

him. His dominion is an everlasting dominion that will not pass away, and his kingdom is one that will never be destroyed." (Daniel 7:13,14) These two verses reveal a marvelous mystery that shall be studied shortly.

5. In this vast assembly of angels, Daniel sees a being that looked very different than the heavenly host. This being looked like a "son of man." Consider the significance of this. Billions of angels are gathered in this courtroom and center stage stands a being that looks like one of the human race! This "son of man" can only be Jesus.
6. Jesus is taken before the Ancient of Days by a retinue of holy angels.
7. As Daniel watches, Jesus receives authority, glory and sovereign power.
8. Daniel concludes the vision saying that Jesus is ultimately worshiped by everyone in heaven and on earth and His kingdom will never pass away or be destroyed. (Contrast this with the four beasts that rise and fall.)

Daniel sees the judgment of human beings

What did Daniel see? In a sentence, Daniel was permitted to see the services that mark the beginning of the judgment day of the human race! The Bible speaks in many places about the judgment day as being in the future. Notice these few texts:

1. "For God will bring every deed into judgment, including every hidden thing, whether it is good or evil." (Ecclesiastes 12:14)

2. "For he (the Father) has set a day when he will judge the world with justice by the man he has appointed...." (Acts 17:31)

3. "For we must all appear before the judgment seat of Christ, that each one may receive what is due him...." (2 Corinthians 5:10)

4. Peter understood that the day of judgment would be future: "...The Lord knows how to rescue godly men from trials and to hold the unrighteous for the day of judgment...." (2 Peter 2:9)

5. Paul anticipated the judgment day saying, "This will take place on the day when God will judge men's secrets through Jesus Christ...." (Romans 2:16)

6. Jesus told the Pharisees that the great judgment day was in the future saying, "The men of Nineveh will stand up at the judgment with this generation and condemn it; for they repented at the preaching of Jonah, and now one greater than Jonah is here. The Queen of the South will rise at the judgment with this generation and condemn it; for she came from the ends of the earth to listen to Solomon's wisdom, and now one greater than Solomon is here." (Matthew 12:41,42)

7. Jesus told the Jews that He would someday judge them saying, "...the Father judges no one, but has entrusted all judgment to the Son, that all may honor the Son just as they honor the Father...." (John 5:22,23)

That a judgment day is prophesied in the Bible is beyond dispute. But the big question is, "When does it occur?" When does Jesus actually determine the eternal destiny of each person?

The Day of Atonement

Part of the answer to the question is found in the sanctuary service of the Old Testament! Remember, Israel faced a judgment day count-down each year. According to the Mishna, a collection of Jewish writings, the judgment of Israel began on the first day of the seventh month with the Feast of Trumpets. The judgment ended on the 10th day with the Day of Atonement. Today, the 10th day of the seventh religious month is called "Yom Kippur" which literally means, "day of judgment."

If you review the chapter on the Ministry of Jesus, you will find an explanation of the Day of Atonement and what it meant to the Jews. In short, the Feast of Trumpets began on the first day of the seventh month with trumpets sounding to warn Israel that probation or mercy was closing. Each person was to search his heart and make all wrongs right before the 10th day. All sins had to be transferred from the individual to the sanctuary *before* the 10th day. Failure to have sins transferred to the sanctuary meant the sinner must bear the penalty for his own sins.

The Jews understood the Day of Atonement to be the end of the yearly judgment process. By the evening of the ninth day, all sins had to be confessed and transferred into the sanctuary via the shed blood of an animal so that all sins for that year could be disposed of. On the morning of the 10th day, the sanctuary was cleansed of all accumulated sins by the high priest. Thus, the Day of Atonement was the most significant day in Jewish ceremonies. Jesus told Moses, "...**on the tenth day of the seventh month you must deny yourselves and not do any work; whether native-born or an alien living among you, because on this day atonement will be made for you, to cleanse you. Then, before the Lord, you will be clean from all your sins. It is a sabbath of rest, and you must deny yourselves; it is a lasting ordinance.**" (Leviticus 16:29-31)

Back to Daniel 7

Daniel obviously saw a courtroom setting with the Ancient of Days presiding. Daniel saw the books of record opened. The record books contain every motive, deed and thought of all that have ever lived. Each person that lived on earth will be examined and a determination for eternal life or eternal death will be made. All heaven attends this solemn meeting. Daniel mentions that ten thousand times ten thousand angels are present. Every angel anxiously watches as Jesus reviews each record and arrives at a decision that will last for eternity! It is an awesome occasion.

Note: Many people are surprised to discover in John 5:22 that Jesus is the One who makes the eternal decision upon each person. The Father has granted both the position of *advocate and judge* to Jesus. This is only fair, for Jesus has walked where we walk, He has suffered more than we suffer and He was tempted more than we are tempted. (Hebrews 4:15) The beauty of this point might be understood by comparing our judicial system with heaven's judicial system. In our judicial system, we are judged by our peers. In other words, a person is judged by a jury of people having the same background as the accused. In a similar way, the people of earth are judged in heaven by one like us, a "son of man"! Daniel saw Jesus approach the Father and receive authority and sovereign power for this express purpose. Sovereign power means unlimited power.

When does the court convene?

How do 1798 and 1844 collaborate? Answer: The judgment scene of Daniel

7:9,10 began in 1798. From Revelation we will learn that Jesus was found worthy to receive the book sealed with seven seals in 1798. Jesus immediately began opening the seals. (These matters will be covered in the chapter on the seven seals.) The point here is that Jesus opened the third seal in 1844 — which marks the beginning of the judgment of man.

A short explanation is given here that might be helpful. When Jesus began His earthly ministry, one of the first things He did was to cleanse the earthly temple. See John 2. After cleansing the temple, the Pharisees taunted Him asking how He could reconstruct the temple in three days since it had taken 46 years to build. (John 2:20) Here is a parallel. Just as it took 46 years to build the temple that Jesus cleansed on earth, it took 46 years (1798-1844) to set the stage on earth so that people might understand that Jesus was beginning His high priestly ministry in heaven! The first two seals of Revelation 6 have to do with setting earth's stage so that people might understand the event occurring during the third seal. More will be said about this in our study on the seven seals.

Putting the pieces together

If we combine information from Daniel 7, information from Daniel 8 and 9, information on the Day of Atonement and the texts on the day of judgment we discover four wonderful points:

1. The judgment of human beings takes place in heaven after four world empires have risen and fallen and after the little horn power has waged war on the saints for 1,260 years.
2. Jesus is the Judge. He is granted authority, glory and sovereign power to conduct this process.
3. The restoration or cleansing of the heavenly sanctuary began at the end of the 2,300 years in 1844. The courtroom scene can be nothing less than the judgment of human beings. It is the final event in the heavenly sanctuary. The service began in 1798 and the opening of the books in 1844 indicates that the time to review the records of each person has come!
4. The Old Testament Day of Atonement provides valuable information that helps us understand what the cleansing of the "true" sanctuary in heaven means.

Repetition and enlargement

Understand that Daniel 7, like Daniel 2, is a broad sweeping prophecy. All details regarding the little horn power are not included in Daniel 7. There are other things to learn that specifically relate to our day. As mentioned before, the Bible uses the process of repetition and enlargement to unfold the prophecies. Daniel 7 enlarges the details of Daniel 2. Likewise, Daniel 8 expands some of the details of Daniel 7, and we will see that the entire book of Revelation enlarges upon Daniel 8-12!

The process of the judgment examined

What happens in the judgment process? How are we judged? Solomon, the wise man, wrote, "...**here is the conclusion of the matter: Fear God and keep his commandments, for this is the whole duty of man. For God will bring every deed into judgment, including every hidden thing, whether it is good or evil.**" (Ecclesiastes 12:13,14)

In 1844, Jesus began cleansing the sanctuary in heaven. What defiled the heavenly sanctuary so that it needed cleansing? The recorded sins of people on earth. Remember how the sins of Israel were *recorded* on the horns of the altars each day so that it had to be cleansed each year on the Day of Atonement? So the sins of each person are accurately and fully recorded in heaven's sanctuary. Those who live up to all the knowledge they have are given the righteousness of Christ. This is the mystery of God! This is how the plan of salvation can save the most vile offender! In 1844, Jesus began going through the books of record. This process is conducted before the host of angels so that nothing is hidden. Jesus thoroughly investigates all aspects of each person's life that lived upon earth. Quite likely, He began with the first to die — Abel.

As Jesus proceeds through the books of record, He makes an irrevocable decision about each person regarding eternal life or death. Those in the books of record who rejected the promptings of the Holy Spirit and refused to receive salvation will be lost.

They stand condemned as "uncovered" sinners before the Father. They refused to live by faith and they refused to heed the promptings of the Holy Spirit. Understand that Jesus intimately investigates every aspect of a person's life to insure that a fair decision is made. Jesus considers what each person knew, what each person had opportunity to know, what each person did with what he knew or believed. He also considers where each person came from, their time and place, how each person treated others and many, many other factors. This is a solemn scene of eternal importance. Millions of reverent angels are in attendance.

Because books of record are used in heaven's court scene, we can conclude that the judgment began with the dead. This process has been going on in heaven for almost 150 years. Soon, the judgment of the living will begin! The work in heaven will turn from the books of records to the lives of the living! Books of record will not be necessary for the living—for they face a test. It will be pass or fail and each person will determine his own fate.

A new problem arises

If the judgment of the dead, that is, the process of determining the eternal destiny of the dead began in 1844, how can dead people be living in heaven or hell prior to 1844?

Many people believe that the sentence of eternal life or of eternally burning in hell is executed at death. Naturally, such a thinking requires that eternal judgment be made at the time of death. Is this what the Bible teaches about the judgment of mankind? No. The Bible clearly says that God has appointed a certain time to judge the world. Even more, no one could be judged until Jesus had first lived as a human being and been tempted in all points as we have been. (Acts 17:31) Further, when Jesus returns at the second coming, He brings His reward with Him indicating that the judgment process is completed! **"Behold I am coming soon! My reward is with me, and I will give to everyone according to what he has done."** (Revelation 22:12)

Does God burn people for eternity?

Through the centuries, Satan has tormented millions of people with the concept that when a person dies, he goes straight to heaven or hell. Many Christians accept this idea today and aren't particularly bothered by it. After all, no one has seen a large pit of fire where loved ones are burning and writhing in pain.

Only in the past century has this doctrine lost most of its terror. In Protestantism today, almost everyone goes to heaven. When was the last time you heard a funeral sermon sending someone to hell?

The doctrine of an eternally burning hell has a terrible history. This teaching was used by the Roman Church to control the masses. The people who lived during the Dark Ages didn't have Bibles, so they lived in constant fear and had many superstitions about God. (For example, a sneeze was believed to be a demon attempting to snatch away one's breath. Thus the quick response "Bless you" was offered since last rites were necessary for salvation.) The superstitious fears of the people were preyed upon by Roman clerics as a way of raising money. Families could both buy deceased loved ones out of the torment of purgatory and purchase eternal life for themselves, regardless of any behavior. The wealthier the family, the higher the price, of course. (In fact, the construction of St. Peter's Basilica was financed entirely from the sale of indulgences in the 15th and 16th centuries. Total sales reportedly reached an equivalent of $48 million in those days. Indulgences were popular because they were "legal documents" from the pope granting eternal life without first going to purgatory.)

Protestants in general still hold to the teaching of the immortality of the soul. There are several problems with the idea that one goes to heaven or hell at death. These are:

1. The Bible does not say that burning forever in hell fire is the penalty for sin. On the contrary, the Bible says that, **"...the wages of sin is death."** (Romans 6:23)

2. If burning in hell forever is the penalty for sin, then Jesus could not have possibly paid the penalty for sin by dying on Calvary for He

was resurrected the third day. Conversely, one could argue, "Jesus didn't remain dead for eternity either." This is true. But the wages of sin is death and once the second death is experienced, the penalty is paid. Jesus was resurrected to life forever because He was sinless.

3. Going to heaven or hell at the time of death presupposes an immediate judgment decision upon that individual. From Daniel 7 and 8 we learned that the judgment did not begin until 1844. Decisions for eternal life or death were not made before that time!

4. If people go to heaven or hell immediately at death, then what is the purpose of the resurrection? Notice that the wicked and the righteous are both resurrected. Paul said, **"And I have the same hope in God as these men, that there will be a resurrection of both the righteous and the wicked."** (Acts 24:15) Some suggest the purpose of the resurrection is to come back and get the earthly body. According to Paul, we won't be able to use the earthly body which is perishable! **"I declare to you, brothers, that flesh and blood cannot inherit the kingdom of God, nor does the perishable inherit the imperishable... the dead will be raised imperishable,** **and we will be changed. For the perishable must clothe itself with the imperishable, and the mortal with immortality."** (1 Corinthians 15:50, 52, 53)

5. Jesus clearly predicts two resurrections, **"...for a time is coming when all who are in their graves will hear his voice and come out - those who have done good will rise to live, and those who have done evil will rise to be condemned."** (John 5:28,29) If people are already burning in hell, why would they be resurrected too? Wouldn't that be a case of being condemned before proven innocent?

6. John saw the redeemed awake from death at the second coming. He says, **"...they came to life and reigned with Christ a thousand years."** (Revelation 20:4)

Death is like sleep

Fifty-three times in the New Testament, death is called sleep. Sleep is simply a condition of unconsciousness. Solomon says, **"For the living know that they will die, but the dead know nothing; they have no further reward, and even the memory of them is forgotten. Their love, their hate and their jealousy have long since vanished; never again will they have a part in anything that happens under the sun."** (Ecclesiastes 9:5,6)

King David knew the saints weren't in heaven praising God. He wrote, **"No one remembers you when he is dead. Who praises you from the grave?"** (Psalms 6:5) **"It is not the dead who praise the Lord, those who go down to silence."** (Psalms 115:17) Jesus said to His disciples concerning Lazarus, **" '...our friend Lazarus has fallen asleep; but I am going there to wake him up. His disciples replied 'Lord, if he sleeps, he will get better.' Jesus had been speaking of his death, but his disciples thought he meant natural sleep. So then he told them plainly, 'Lazarus is dead.' "** (John 11:11-14)

When Jesus resurrected Lazarus from death, Lazarus gave no report of stoking fires in hell or dancing in heaven. No! He'd been sleeping and thus unconscious of anything going on!

In our next lesson, we'll look at the story of the rich man and Lazarus. Does it prove people are burning in hell?

Summary

We have chronologically located the Day of Judgment described by Daniel. The service began in 1798 and the judgment of the dead began in 1844. The courtroom is in heaven. It is the heavenly Day of Atonement to which the wilderness Day of Atonement pointed forward. Since that time, Jesus, the Judge of Mankind, has been involved with determining the eternal destiny of each person as the books of record are reviewed. The books clearly reveal the choices that each person made. The record books contain what the person knew at the time, what they did and why! Everything is exposed in the judgment process.

At the second coming, those who have been granted eternal life will rise in the first resurrection. Later, those who have done evil will rise to meet their Maker and receive their due reward at the end of the millennium. We shall continue our investigation of these things in the next lesson.

Chapter 12

The Day of Judgment Part II

Is there life in death?

From Daniel, we learned that the judgment of the human race began in 1844. The great courtroom scene began with the Ancient of Days taking His seat in 1798. Then after some business was finished, the books of records were opened in 1844 and a review of each person who had died commenced.

The importance of these dates will develop even further as we continue our study in Revelation. However, the fundamental issue of what happens to a person when he dies must be addressed because death, judgment and reward are all connected. The truth on this subject is very important, for it is directly connected to the climactic story of Revelation!

A number of the Eastern Mystic religions believe in the transmigration of the soul. This concept teaches that the soul was once a lower form of life before entering the human being, and at death, life moves on to a higher or lower form depending on how one lived in this life. Many Christians have a theology that parallels this concept. The basic difference between Christians and those believing in the transmigration of the soul is that Christians believe life *begins* with conception in the womb. On the other hand, many Christians and Eastern Mystic religions believe the soul is immortal and thus not subject to death. Both ideas are plainly contrary to the Scriptures. The soul can die! God says, **"...the soul who sins is the one who will die."** (Ezekiel 18:4) If the soul is immortal, when is immortality bestowed upon it?

When does life begin?

The Bible tells us, **"And the Lord God formed man from the dust of the ground and breathed into his nostrils the breath of life, and man became a living being."** (Genesis 2:7)

A living being is a combination of two elements: the body and the breath (power) of life. Separate these two elements, and you don't have a living being! Life may be thought of as light. Connect a light bulb with electricity and there is light. Separate the electricity from the bulb and there is no light.

Some people believe that when a person dies, the spirit (the soul) returns to God. Solomon said, **"Remember him (our Creator) - before the silver cord is severed, or the golden bowl is broken; before the pitcher is shattered at the** spring, or the wheel broken at the well, and the dust returns to the ground it came from, and the spirit returns to God who gave it." (Ecclesiastes 12:6,7) From this scripture, it is clear that the spirit returns to God who gave it. This is true of *both* the righteous and the wicked! The word translated spirit in Ecclesiastes 12:6,7 is the identical word used for breath in Job 27:3. Notice what Job said, "...as long as I have life within me, the breath of God in my nostrils, my lips will not speak wickedness...." In other words, what returns to God is the power to live.

God grants breath to all that live. This is true of animals and man. Of Noah's flood it is said, "Every living thing that moved on the earth perished - birds, livestock, wild animals, all the creatures that swarm over the earth, and all mankind. Everything on dry land that had the breath of life in its nostrils died." (Genesis 7:21,22)

The Greek and Hebrew words for spirit mean wind or breath. The Hebrew word, "ruach" and the Greek word, "pneuma" do not refer to some intelligent entity free of the body. Rather, these words simply apply to the breath of life. The word for breath is often translated spirit and vice versa. The point is that a soul does not exist when the spirit or breath is separated from the body! When breath and a body are brought together, the result is a soul. Our example of the light bulb demonstrated this. When power is applied to the bulb we have light. When power is disconnected, there is no light.

In the same way, when the breath of life is connected to a body, we have an intelligent soul — whether animal or man. When the breath of life is taken from the body, there is no soul.

The Hebrew word for soul is "nephesh" and the Greek word is "psuche." Both of these words mean or imply that a living being is a soul! Solomon wrote, "Man's fate is like that of the animals; the same fate awaits them both: As one dies, so dies the other. All have the same breath (spirit), man has no advantage over the animal...." (Ecclesiastes 3:19)

Other Bible writers agree

Adam and Eve were expressly driven from their Eden home so that they could not eat from the tree of life and live forever! After Adam and Eve sinned, Jesus said, "...the man has now become like one of us, knowing good and evil. He must not be allowed to reach out his hand and take also from the tree of life and eat, and live forever." (Genesis 3:22) The point here is that Adam and Eve were removed from the Garden of Eden for the express purpose of death. As long as they could eat of the tree of life, they would live. So they had to be removed from the garden.

The Bible says that the ability to exist forever comes only through Jesus. John says, "He who has the Son has life; he who does not have the Son of God does not have life." (1 John 5:12)

In Paul's day, many of the early Christians sorrowed thinking there was no resurrection—no life hereafter. To set the matter straight, Paul said, **"According to the Lord's own word, we tell you that we who are still alive, who are left till the coming of the Lord, will certainly not precede those who have fallen asleep. For the Lord himself will come down from heaven, with a loud command, with the voice of the archangel and with the trumpet call of God, and the dead in Christ will rise first. After that, we who are still alive and are left will be caught up with them in the clouds to meet the Lord in the air.... Therefore encourage each other with these words."** (1 Thessalonians 4:15-18) Paul did not comfort those grieving for their deceased friends with the notion their friends were in heaven. No. He pointed them forward to the resurrection.

The devil started it

The one who brought confusion to this point in the very beginning was the devil. Satan told Eve she wouldn't die if she disobeyed God. Today, Satan has twisted the meaning of death 180 degrees so that many people believe that death means life! King David knew the dead weren't in heaven praising the Lord for he said, **"It is not the dead who praise the Lord, those who go down to silence; it is we who extol the Lord...."** (Psalm 115:17)

The apostle Peter also knew the dead weren't in heaven praising the Lord. In his famous sermon on the Day of Pentecost he quoted a number of references from the Old Testament where King David had prophesied about the coming Messiah. Then Peter concluded by saying that David was not in heaven. He said, **"Brothers, I can tell you confidently that the patriarch David died and was buried, and his tomb is here to this day.... For David did not ascend to heaven, and yet he said, 'The Lord said to my Lord: Sit at my right hand until I make your enemies a footstool for your feet.' "** (Acts 2:29,34)

King David knew the dead were not in heaven playing a harp and singing praises to God. He wrote, **"No one remembers you (God) when he is dead. Who praises you from the grave?"** (Psalm 6:5) Solomon understood death just like his father, David. He wrote, **"Whatever your hand finds to do, do it with all your might, for in the grave, where you are going, there is neither working nor planning nor knowledge nor wisdom."** (Ecclesiastes 9:10)

Daniel saw the great resurrection at the end of time. He clearly states that some of the dead will awake to everlasting life and others will awake to shame and everlasting contempt. **"Multitudes who sleep in the dust of the earth will awake: some to everlasting life, others to shame and everlasting contempt."** (Daniel 12:2)

There is consistent harmony throughout the Bible on the nature of death. Man is mortal and death is like sleep. Man, when dead, is unconscious of anything that goes on. The dead are dead! The dead simply remain in a state of unconsciousness. They rest from their labors until the resurrection morning.

(The author once visited with a man that claimed to have died on the operating table for five minutes. He reported that he had an out-of-body experience in bright lights. Does a hallucinogenic experience validate or invalidate the Scriptures?)

What about mediums?

Jesus clearly told the Jews to have nothing to do with mediums or spiritists. These are people who practice and promote communication with the dead. Jesus said, **"Do not turn to mediums or seek out spiritists, for you will be defiled by them.... A man or woman who is a medium or spiritist among you must be put to death. You are to stone them; their blood will be on their own heads."** (Leviticus 19:31; 20:27)

King Saul finds an unhappy medium

A special story is preserved in the Bible to demonstrate three important things. It's conclusion is found in 1 Samuel 28. In brief, King Saul, the first king of Israel, had repeatedly failed to obey the Lord. He was disobedient and rebellious. One day Samuel was sent to Saul telling him the kingdom would be taken from him and given to another. That promised "other" was a young shepherd boy named David. Saul remembered these words from time to time. Time passed, and Samuel died.

One day the Philistines assembled at Shunem to fight the Israelites. When Saul saw the size of their army, he became afraid and terror filled his heart. The Bible tells the rest of the story, **"He inquired of the Lord, but the Lord did not answer him by dreams or Urim or prophets. Saul then said to his attendants, 'Find me a woman who is a medium, so I may go and inquire of her.' 'There is one in Endor,' they said. So Saul disguised himself, putting on other clothes, and at night he and two men went to the woman.**

'Consult a spirit for me,' he said, 'and bring up for me the one I name.' But the woman said to him, 'Surely you know what Saul has done. He has cut off the mediums and spiritists from the land. Why have you set a trap for my life to bring about my death?'

Saul swore to her by the Lord, 'As surely as the Lord lives, you will not be punished for this.' Then the woman asked, 'Whom shall I bring up for you?' 'Bring up Samuel,' he said. When the woman saw Samuel, she cried out of the top of her voice to Saul and said, 'Why have you deceived me? You are Saul!'

The king said to her, 'Don't be afraid. What do you see?' The woman said, 'I see a spirit coming up out of the ground.' 'What does he look like?' he asked. 'An old man wearing a robe is coming up,' she said. Then Saul knew it was Samuel, and he bowed down and prostrated himself with his face to the ground.

Samuel said to Saul, 'Why have you disturbed me by bringing me up?' 'I am in great distress,' Saul said. 'The Philistines are fighting against me and God has turned away from me. He no longer answers me, either by prophets or by dreams. So I have called on you to tell me what to do.'

Samuel said, 'Why do you consult me, now that the Lord has turned away from you and become your enemy? The Lord has done what he predicted through me. The Lord has torn the kingdom out of your hands and given it to one of your neighbors - to David. Because you did not obey the Lord or carry out his fierce wrath against the Amalekites, the Lord has done this to you today. The Lord will hand over both Israel and you to the Philistines, and tomorrow you and your sons will be with me. The Lord will also hand over the army of Israel to the Philistines.'

Immediately, Saul fell full length on the ground, filled with fear because of Samuel's words...." (1 Samuel 28:6-20)

Three important points are made:

1. The Lord had turned His back on Saul and refused to answer him by prophets or dreams. Neither did the Lord answer Saul through the medium of Endor. In his desperation, Saul sought out the devil. What he saw and heard was a demon in the form of Samuel, the deceased prophet.

2. Notice that Satan's remarks were quite accurate about Saul's condition. Even though Satan doesn't precisely know the future (he is not omniscient), he is very smart. He had carefully studied Saul and in the medium's house he succeeded in destroying whatever courage the abandoned king may have had.

3. Satan clearly gave Saul the idea that Samuel was in the grave (not in heaven or in hell) and that he would soon join Samuel in death.

The doctrine that deceased people are in heaven or hell opens the door to communication with spirits. The Bible is absolutely clear that such communication is not with angelic beings but with demons.

Jesus - now alive forever and ever

In Revelation, Jesus told John, **"...do not be afraid. I am the First and the Last. I am the Living One; I was dead, and behold I am alive for ever and ever! And I hold the keys of death and Hades (the grave)."** (Revelation 1:17,18) Jesus clearly holds the keys to death and the grave. He has the power of life within Himself! Jesus will use the key of life and open the graves of all the righteous at the resurrection during the second coming. Paul said, **"For the Lord Himself will come down from heaven, with a loud command, with the voice of the archangel and with the trumpet call of God, and the dead in Christ** will rise first. After that, we who are still alive and are left will be caught up with them in the clouds to meet the Lord in the air. And so we will be with the Lord forever." (1 Thessalonians 4:16,17)

Problem texts

There are two texts in the Bible that can be particularly confusing on the matter of death. We'll look at these briefly:

"For Christ died for sins once for all, the righteous for the unrighteous, to bring you to God. He was put to death in the body but made alive by the Spirit through whom also he went and preached to the spirits in prison who disobeyed long ago when God waited patiently in the days of Noah while the ark was being built...." (1 Peter 3:18-20)

Some people interpret this text to mean that Jesus, during the time He was dead, went to a prison where evil people had been held since the flood and there preached forgiveness to them.

Such a view opens up insurmountable questions. For example, after a person is once consigned to hell, can he be set free? The Roman Church taught for centuries that freedom from hell was possible for a contribution to the Church. But look at the flip side of the coin. Suppose you were in heaven and for a fee, you could be sent to hell by someone who didn't like you. As you quickly see, the actions of other

people cannot determine nor control your eternal destiny whether in heaven or hell.

Consider this too. What would be the point of Jesus preaching forgiveness to people who had been burning in hell for 2,000 years? Can they now repent and go to heaven? Jesus preaching repentance to someone burning in hell for 2,000 years is anticlimactic isn't it? How persuasive would Jesus (or anyone for that matter) have to be to persuade those burning in hell for 2,000 years that they need to repent? The whole idea is absurd. The Bible teaches that we have only one chance for salvation. It is during this life. (Hebrews 4:7)

Peter, in our problem text, is making the point that Jesus was put to death in the body and made alive by the Spirit of God. By this *same Spirit,* Jesus patiently waited for 120 years in the days of Noah to save ány and all who would get on board. (See Genesis 6:1-8) Then Peter says, **"For this is the reason the gospel was preached even to those who are now dead, so that they might be judged according to men in regard to the body, but live according to God in regard to the spirit."** (1 Peter 4:6) In other words, Peter says the gospel is preached to those who are now dead to spiritual things (the Jews) so they might see their need to live in harmony with the spirit and receive life and the approval of God! The true meaning of 1 Peter 3 does not conflict with other scriptures on death when rightly understood. There is harmony in the sum of the parts!

The rich man and Lazarus

No parable has caused more discussion than this one. Luke records the story, "There was a rich man who was dressed in purple and fine linen and lived in luxury every day. At his gate was laid a beggar named Lazarus, covered with sores and longing to eat what fell from the rich man's table. Even the dogs came and licked his sores. The time came when the beggar died and the angels carried him to Abraham's side. The rich man also died and was buried.

In hell, where he was in torment, he looked up and saw Abraham far away, with Lazarus by his side. So he called to him, 'Father Abraham, have pity on me and send Lazarus to dip the tip of his finger in water and cool my tongue, because I am in agony in this fire.' But Abraham replied, 'Son, remember that in your lifetime you received your good things, while Lazarus received bad things, but now he is comforted here and you are in agony. And besides all this, between us and you a great chasm has been fixed, so that those who want to go from here to you cannot, nor can anyone cross over from there to us.'

He answered, 'Then I beg you, father, send Lazarus to my father's house, for I have five brothers. Let him warn them, so that they will not also come to this place of torment.' Abraham replied, 'They have Moses and the Prophets; let them listen to them.' 'No, father Abraham,' he said, 'but if someone from the dead goes to them, they will repent.' He said to him, 'If they do not listen to Moses and the Prophets, they will not be convinced even if someone rises from the dead.' " (Luke 16:19-31)

A casual look at the story raises several questions:

1. Assuming there are people in heaven and hell, can they actually carry on a conversation?
2. Can people in heaven carry water to those in hell?
3. Do the rich go to hell and the poor go to heaven?

Josephus, a Jewish historian who lived shortly after Christ, tells us this story was in vogue at the time of Christ. It's a tale of theological contrasts within Judaism. For example, the Sadducees rejected the idea of a resurrection believing that one went straight to their eternal reward at death while the Pharisees believed in the resurrection. See Acts 23:6-9. The Pharisees believed a wealthy person was blessed of God for his righteousness while a poor person was rewarded for some evil, either hidden or hereditary. See John 9.

Jesus took this well-known tale of many opposites and tied it together with some very important points—none of which has to do with burning in hell or dancing in heaven. Notice:

1. The Jews were wealthy. They had been given God's richest blessings. They had been enlightened with

truth. They had been chosen as a special people.

2. The poor Gentiles did not have the opportunities of the Jews. But circumstances do change! The Jews would become destitute and the Gentiles would become enlightened! (Remember the end of the 490 years, A.D. 33?)

3. With roles and opportunities exchanged, the converted Jew in torment cries out to the Gentile in heaven, " 'I have five brothers. Go warn them of things to come.' Abraham replied, 'They have Moses and the Prophets; let them listen to them.' 'No, father Abraham,' he said, 'but if someone from the dead goes to them, they will repent.' He said to him, 'If they do not listen to Moses and the Prophets, they will not be convinced even if someone rises from the dead.' " (Luke 16:19-31)

Jesus concludes the tale by placing Himself in the heart of the story saying, "even if someone rises from the dead, they will not be convinced — they are that hard-hearted."

Like Peter's vision of the unclean animals, the story of the rich man and Lazarus is designed to teach an important lesson. It is not designed to confirm a theological point. As we have seen in this series of studies, the Bible offers a consistent message. It's inspiration comes from One that changes not.

The destiny of the wicked

Since the Bible says burning in hell forever is not the penalty of sin, what is the penalty of sin? The Bible says, "...the wages of sin is death." The Bible clearly says there will be a hell fire! "...But fire came down from heaven and devoured them. And the devil, who deceived them, was thrown into the lake of burning sulfur...." (Revelation 20:9,10)

Malachi, the Old Testament prophet, saw the total destruction of the wicked. He writes, " 'Surely the day is coming; it will burn like a furnace. All the arrogant and every evildoer will be stubble, and that day that is coming will set them on fire,' says the Lord Almighty. 'Not a root or a branch will be left to them. But for you who revere my name, the sun of righteousness will rise with healing in its wings. And you will go out and leap like calves released from the stall. Then you will trample down the wicked; they will be ashes under the soles of your feet on the day when I do these things,' says the Lord Almighty." (Malachi 4:1-3)

Two more difficult texts

Revelation 20:10 says, "...they will be tormented day and night for ever and ever," and Revelation 14:11 says, "...and the smoke of their torment rises for ever and ever...."

Do these texts imply an eternally burning hell? At first glance they seem to! Will Jesus burn and scorch people for ever and ever? Is this the unquenchable wrath of God?

First, we have determined that the wages of sin is death. Death, by definition of many Bible writers, means sleep or a state of unconsciousness. The destruction of the wicked cannot last eternally because in this scenario, they would never die, thus the penalty of sin would never be paid.

The second text (Revelation 14:11) literally indicates that the smoke from the destruction of the wicked rises for ever and ever. If the complete destruction of the wicked means an end to sin and sinners, the scriptures then indicate that the smoke of their torment can not be put out. The lake of fire will consume sin and sinners until nothing remains.

Revelation 20:10 seems to say on the surface that the wicked are tormented day and night eternally. Actually though, John was expressing two important ideas. First, sinners burn differing lengths of time and secondly, while they burn, they feel the torment of their suffering.

From Malachi 4 we know the wicked will be eventually reduced to ashes. From John, we know the wicked will be burned up and that there will be a new heaven and a new earth for the first earth is passed away! (See Revelation 21:1.) From 2 Peter 3 we know the earth and everything in it will melt and be laid bare with great heat. From the weight of all Bible evidence, John's comments in Revelation 20:10 indicating the wicked

are tormented day and night forever can be interpreted to mean "as long as they exist." Like marriage (forgive the comparison), it lasts forever for as long as both shall live.

Hell fire is not the greatest punishment

In a later lesson, we will study the sequence of events that take place before the final destruction. We will look further into the resurrections and the final death.

But the greatest punishment that Jesus gives to His created beings at the very end is not hell fire. Rather, the greatest punishment placed upon the wicked at the end of the millennium is a revelation of God's tender love for each person. Here's the story:

1. At the second coming, the saints are taken to heaven and the wicked remaining upon the earth are slain by the brightness of Jesus' glory. The earth is desolated by the splendor of righteousness!

2. The saints (the resurrected and the living) are caught up with Jesus in the air and they return to heaven for 1,000 years. The purpose of this 1,000 years is very simple: Jesus wants each redeemed person to clearly see that His decision on those not in heaven was fair. In other words, the saints now get to review the books of record. They learn, first hand, why a loved one or friend was not granted eternal

life. Every mystery will be laid open. After reviewing each case to their satisfaction, all the saints are convinced that Jesus was loving, just and merciful in His judgment on each person. Even more, the saints will determine the amount of suffering that each wicked person is to receive! God requires that full atonement for sins be made. This is why vengeance is His to repay.

3. At the end of the 1,000 years, the saints return to earth with Jesus. Jesus resurrects the wicked. They come forth to gaze upon the New Jerusalem and the saints within the city. Satan, who was bound to the desolate earth, now stirs the wicked to attack the New Jerusalem and rob the redeemed of their home. As the mob rushes toward the city, Jesus stops the vast throng just as He commanded the storm on Galilee to be still.

4. Then every eye is drawn to the sky where a great panorama of salvation's story is played. Each person (saints and sinners) watches the drama, for the most incredible event to ever happen is now to take place. The giant screen-play in the heaven not only tells the big story of God's love, it replays each person's life before its owner. Both saint and sinner stand in awe. Now they see as never before the extended mercy of salvation—the mystery of God.

Now they comprehend what they dimly understood before. Now the saints see the humility of Jesus and sinners see Paradise lost. The wicked behold the One who loved them beyond understanding, the One who died that they might have the opportunity of salvation!

5. Every knee bows before Jesus, the Father and the Holy Spirit. They are righteous. They are fair. They are love! The wicked bow before their justice. The saints bow before their mercy. Now, at this grand moment, before all human beings that ever lived, the seventh and final seal is broken on the book of life. The book is opened. Now the multitude beyond number understand a new dimension about God. He foreknew all this. His written record, sealed before the world was created, is *exactly* the same as the story contained in the books of record and reviewed in the sky!

6. Now God is exonerated before His creatures. God has been proven as a God of love. He freely granted His creatures the power of choice. Now, Satan stands before the vast multitude as a despicable liar. The evidence clearly shows that God does not use His foreknowledge to manipulate or control the outcome of any event. His creatures truly have the greatest power outside of divinity: the power of choice.

The saints rejoice with unbounding joy at the choices they made: the choice to live by faith, the choice to follow Jesus, the choice to struggle against sin, the choice to be what Jesus wanted them to be, the choice to do what He wanted, and the choice to go wherever He directed!

On the other hand, the sinners are crushed. In despair beyond words they see the tragic result of their choices. They look upon the Holy City, Jesus and the saints and a grief beyond comprehension overtakes them. They have no anger against the Godhead. They are love and the wicked stand before God with regret beyond understanding. Their regret is not based on heart-felt repentance; rather, it is based on the consequence of seeing what they have lost. The seeds of rebellion are so deep that repentance is impossible. In agony beyond description they turn upon each other to vent their anguish. In mercy, Jesus sends fire down from heaven and ends the nightmare. Sin and sinners will be gone.

And now we behold something of the justice of God. Would He require someone to burn for 10 billion years (and this is just the beginning of eternity) for a life of sin lasting only 70 years? No. In God's system of justice, the penalty is *always* commensurate with the crime. Fairness requires no more and no less.

Notes

Notes

Chapter 13

Introduction to Revelation

Comments

The book of Revelation may be likened to the fuse box in your house. As all wires meet and end in the fuse box, so all books of the Bible meet and end in Revelation. For this reason, a number of references have been used in this book. Revelation can only be understood with the help of other scriptures. It cannot stand alone. For example, one authority states that Revelation makes more than 450 allusions to phrases or ideas from the Old Testament!

Revelation's story is intimately connected to all the books in the Bible. For this reason, four essential doctrines have been covered thus far because a proper understanding of these four doctrines is necessary to understand Revelation's story. These doctrines are:

1. The second coming of Jesus
2. Salvation and sanctification by faith
3. The work of Jesus in the heavenly sanctuary
4. The pre-advent judgment and the state of the dead

One more essential doctrine remains to be studied: the truth about worship. Revelation predicts that all the world will worship the great antichrist system that shall soon appear on the earth, "except those whose names are written in the book of life!" Why most of the world will obey this system will be explored later.

Revelation's story begins with a reward to all that study the book: **"Blessed is the one who reads the words of this prophecy, and blessed are those who hear it and take to heart what is written in it, because the time is near."** (Revelation 1:3) When prophecy reaches the moment of fulfillment, its language becomes potent with meaning. A special blessing *now* belongs to those who study Revelation because the final days just before Christ's return have come!

Don't overlook the details

To the untrained eye, Revelation is a confusion of symbols and beasts. However, Revelation follows a very careful progression in its story. To appreciate the order, the student must consider two important elements. First, there are 12 apocalyptic prophecies in Revelation. Each prophecy has a beginning point and an ending point in time. Secondly, each prophecy is cross-linked with other prophecies so that if some element within the prophecy is obscure, another prophecy will help explain the meaning.

One of the most common faults found among students of prophecy is that they often fail to satisfy *all* of the specifications that go with a particular element. For example, in Revelation 13, John saw a composite beast rise from the sea. The beast had seven heads and 10 horns. In the first few verses, John explains that the seven heads have blasphemous names. He also says that one of the heads had been wounded, but the deadly wound had been healed when this beast rises from the sea! But wait, there's more! In Revelation 17, an angel tells John that the seven heads are seven hills. They are also seven kings. John is also told that five have fallen, one is, and one is yet to come. In addition to these specifications, John is told that the beast from the Abyss is an eighth king, but he belongs to the seven heads. My point here is that *all* specifications about the heads have to be satisfied before a correct interpretation can be made.

Language types

As you already know, the gospel of salvation is not hard to understand. It can be summed up in a coined word: GOBEDO. In other words, if you are willing to GO where God directs; BE all that God requires; DO all that He commands, you are living by faith! (More than five billion people will hear

the gospel and understand it in a very short time, so it can't be that hard to understand!)

However, the story within Revelation is more difficult to comprehend since the events predicted within the book have not yet happened. But once the judgments of God begin to fall, the story of Revelation will be quite easy to explain. So, for now, the hardest part of understanding Revelation is getting a handle on the cryptic language. Revelation is written with three types of language. These are:

1. Symbolic or spiritual language
2. Analogue or analogous language
3. Literal language and terms

These three language types are mixed throughout the book of Revelation and discerning whether language is literal, symbolic or analogous can be difficult and confusing. So, here are some samples of each language type for you to observe:

1. Symbolic language

"...There I saw a woman sitting on a scarlet beast that was covered with blasphemous names and had seven heads and ten horns.... This title was written on her forehead: Mystery, Babylon the Great, The Mother of Prostitutes and of the Abominations of the Earth." (Revelation 17:3,5)

Who is this woman wearing the title Babylon? The Bible says, **"The woman** you saw is the great city that rules over the kings of the earth." (Revelation 17:18)

Very important rule: If the student suspects language to be symbolic, a relevant text must clearly define the symbol. The key word here is *relevant.* A symbol can have different meanings at different times! (Compare Revelation 12:9 with Numbers 21:9 & John 3:14)

Notice this example of symbolic language: **"Their bodies (the Two Witnesses) will lie in the street of the great city, which is figuratively called Sodom and Egypt, where also their Lord was crucified."** (Revelation 11:8)

It is a historical fact that Jesus was not crucified in Sodom or in Egypt. He was crucified just outside the gates of Jerusalem. Revelation predicts the Two Witnesses will lie in the street of "the great city." From Revelation 17:18, we know who the great city is. It is the harlot, Babylon.

This verse says that Babylon will be like Sodom and Egypt. Sodom was noted for unrestrained evil and Egypt was known for hardness of heart (as manifested by Pharaoh). Both the people of Sodom and the ruler of Egypt passed the point of no return—they committed the unpardonable sin. Babylon will do the same. Babylon's leaders and followers will war against the saints.

The point here is Revelation uses symbolic language to say things that are very potent in just a few words.

Revelation is a very small book (only 17 pages in my Bible), but it says volumes about the end of the world! In a later chapter, we will examine these verses in detail.

2. Analogous language

"The locusts looked like horses prepared for battle. On their heads they wore something like crowns of gold, and their faces resembled human faces." (Revelation 9:7)

The language of this text is a comparison or analogy. The locusts *looked like horses,* but they aren't horses! They don't symbolize horses either, for if they did, the scripture would clearly define the meaning of the horses with relevant scripture. John describes this scene using the analogy of a swarm of locusts. Later, we will discover that John actually saw a swarm of evil angels coming out of the Abyss much like a swarm of locusts arriving to destroy vulnerable crops. John says these evil angels are prepared for battle much like war horses were in his day, and they were led by the commanding angel of the Abyss. John says that whether it is Greek or Hebrew, the name of the commanding angel means destruction. This text has many of the same analogous attributes described in Joel 2. Read all of Joel 2 and notice the parallel in the use of language. Joel 2 talks about the second coming of Jesus with all His holy angels.

3. Literal language

"And I saw a beast coming out of the sea. He had ten horns and seven heads... and on each head a blasphemous name." (Revelation 13:1)

The numbers 10 and seven are literal. John literally saw 10 horns and seven heads. The horns and heads are symbolic for they are discussed and explained in Revelation 17. But numbers in Bible prophecy are always literal and real. What they refer to may be symbolic. Remember rule 3? In this case the heads and horns are symbolic because the meaning of the symbols is given later.

Numbers cannot be symbolic for two reasons. First, a number always specifies a certain quantity. For example, there are seven seals in Revelation. That seven is literal is confirmed by counting. Secondly, what would be the value in using one number to represent another. For example, would it make sense if the 1,000 years of Revelation 20 was symbolically represented as 37 years?

In a secondary sense, numbers can indicate something beyond their literal meaning. For example, the number seven is often used to demonstrate the fullness of something. There are seven days in a week, seven colors in the rainbow, seven notes to the musical scale, seven trumpets in Revelation, seven sayings of Jesus on the cross, etc. Again, the point is emphasized that the number seven is literal in each case,

but we can also see that seven implies fullness or a state of completion.

Sometimes mixed up

One thing that makes interpretation difficult is that language types are sometimes mixed in the same sentence! Notice this one:

"The great city split into three parts, and the cities of the nations collapsed...." (Revelation 16:19) Remember the verse used earlier? **"The woman you saw is the great city that rules over the kings of the earth."** (Revelation 17:18) The harlot of Revelation 17 is the great prostitute that rules over the nations. In Revelation 16:19, we learn that the great city that rules over the world (symbolically Babylon) will be split into three parts at the second coming of Jesus while the (literal) cities of the nations collapsed.

How can we tell which type of language is being used? How can we know if a term is literal, symbolic or analogous? Since mixing language can result in bizarre interpretations, we must be very careful. We need a set of rules to govern our methods of interpretation.

Rules of interpretation

The rules we use for interpretation of Revelation naturally affect our conclusions. Anytime we change the rules, we change the conclusions. Discerning the rules of interpretation is not easy. The only way to discover them is to first read and study extensively, and then look for recurring patterns. If a pattern constantly appears, it may be a rule of interpretation. Since the Bible does not specifically state the rules of interpretation, we are still left with the element of faith for no one can prove something that hasn't happened! At best, we can hold to that which has been demonstrated to be trustworthy.

Distinctive treatment necessary

As explained in Chapter 2, each of the five prophecy types deserve distinctive treatment. Mixing the prophecies or merging their respective rules of interpretation renders interpretation impossible. Since we are studying apocalyptic prophecy, we need to discuss the rules that apply to this type of prophecy.

1. Apocalyptic prophecy always has a beginning point and ending point in time. Because apocalyptic prophecies have a beginning and ending point in time, they cannot have multiple fulfillments. An apocalyptic sequence can only occur once. Apocalyptic prophecy often contains events within the beginning and ending points whereby progression towards consummation can be determined. Intermediate events within the prophecy must happen in the order in which they are presented.
2. All other prophecies of the Bible are subordinate to the chronological structure of apocalyptic

prophecy. This means that apocalyptic prophecy holds greater weight in terms of chronology than non-apocalyptic prophecies. No one prophet has been shown *everything* that God intends to bring about. (1 Corinthians 13:9) Each time God speaks to a prophet about the end of time, more detail is provided. Those living the last days can therefore organize the visions of the prophets and fit the pieces together much better than they could. Today's generation can look backwards for almost 6,000 years and see much more detail about God's dealing with man than prophets of old could. Because of this, we can organize the fulfillments of apocalyptic prophecy much more clearly. Keep in mind, an apocalyptic prophecy is not fulfilled until all the specifications and the chronology of the prophecy are both met.

3. When a prophecy becomes applicable, the language of the prophecy becomes potent. For example, John begins Revelation by saying, **"The Revelation of Jesus Christ, which God gave him to show his servants what must soon take place...."** (Revelation 1:1) The words "must soon take place" cannot mean 2,000 years. Reason requires that words mean what they say. The point is that when a prophecy becomes present truth, the language of the prophecy becomes potent with meaning. If the language is symbolic, the meaning of the symbol must be

explained by relevant scripture. Students cannot makeup their own interpretations of symbols. The Bible must interpret itself.

The first rule above warrants some discussion. As stated before, apocalyptic prophecy is prophecy that lays out a sequence of events. According to rule 1, there are only a 18 apocalyptic prophecies in the Bible.

It is very important to understand the primacy of apocalyptic structure. For example, the trumpets of Revelation are numbered and follow in consecutive order. If a student demonstrates an interpretation for trumpet five, that interpretation must recognize the chronological timing of trumpet four because trumpet four must occur before trumpet five does!

If we apply rule 2 to the interpretation of trumpet five, all specifications regarding trumpets one through four must be met too since all aspects of the trumpet prophecy have to be met in order to have a true fulfillment. Since there is only one second coming of Jesus, prophecies having chronological sequences that lead up to that event can only have one fulfillment. Said another way, if trumpets one through five occur, trumpet three can't happen again because trumpet six is next sequentially.

Historical applications

Through the centuries, a number of so-called "fulfillments" have been claimed. The problem with these claims is that they cannot satisfy rule 2 which calls for fulfillment of all the details relevant to the prophecy! Since God gives the details to the prophets, a fulfillment can only occur when all the specifications are met. Read Revelation 9:13-21 in your Bible and then follow this interesting story:

In the 19th century, Dr. Josiah Litch, a Methodist minister, concluded that trumpets five and six (Revelation 9) concerned Mohammedanism. He was convinced that the sixth trumpet predicted the fall of the Ottoman Turkish empire. Dr. Litch wrote a book in 1838 titled, *The Probability of the Second Coming of Christ About A.D. 1843,* and in it he wrote, "But the duration of their dominion (the Moslems) over the Greek empire... (is) 541 years and 15 days.... If the time for commencing the periods was at the time of the first onset of the Ottomans upon the Greeks, July 27, 1299, then the whole period will end in August, 1840." (p. 134) As August, 1840, drew near, Litch calculated the actual date to be August 11.

Casual students of world history are aware of the powerful Ottoman Turkish empire. For several centuries, these fierce Moslems were undisputed rulers of the Middle East. But, the kingdoms of man come and go. Ottoman glory faded due to a number of humiliating wars. In 1774, Turkey signed a treaty with Russia allowing Russia the right of approval in certain Turkish internal affairs. In 1833, Turkey signed another treaty with Russia which made the ruler of Turkey subject to the Russian tsar. In exchange, Turkey was given protection from an old enemy, Egypt. But in 1839, Egypt seized the Turkish navy as well as a great deal of land. Turkey quickly appealed for help. Four nations (England, Russia, Austria and Prussia) came to the rescue and forced a treaty between Turkey and Egypt, and it was signed in London in July, 1840. The treaty required Egypt to release the Turkish navy, reduce the size of its army, withdraw from Syria and resume paying tribute to Turkey.

On August 11, 1840, the treaty was presented to Mehemet Ali, the pasha of Egypt. The point made by some historians is that Egypt's acceptance of the treaty left Turkey without sovereignty. Thus, the Ottoman Turkish empire fell. But does this fulfill the specifications of the prophecy of the sixth trumpet? The fact that something of political importance happened on an anticipated day in August, 1840, sent shivers among some prophetic students of that time. They were fully convinced that the sixth trumpet had been fulfilled! But was it? Were all details of the prophecy met? A number of matters prevent this conclusion from being regarded as a fulfillment. Four distinct problems stand out:

1. There is no question that the sixth trumpet is a great war. But this trumpet does not identify which political power rises or falls as a result of the war. Litch thought the feud between Egypt and Turkey qualified, but the Ottoman Empire did not fall or collapse in August of 1840. Most historians agree that the Ottoman empire fell at the end of World War I. But, this isn't the end of Turkey; in fact, Turkey is a sovereign nation today.

2. In October of 1582, under Pope Gregory's approval, 10 days were eliminated from the calendar to correct cumulative error caused by the absence of a leap year of 366 days in the Julian calendar. Dr. Litch did not adjust the timing of his conclusions to compensate for this loss of 10 days, thus the August 11 date is invalid even if we follow his rules or concepts of interpretation.

3. Dr. Litch assumed that the phrase, "an hour, a day, a month and a year" in Revelation 9:15, represented a quantity of 391 years, 15 days. He arrived at this conclusion by assuming the phrase was cumulative and then he applied the day/year principle. Today, we know that the phrase is translated incorrectly in the KJV. The phrase actually represents a specific moment in time rather than a sum of years. Most translations of the Bible this century support this corrected understanding. The phrase is punctiliar. It says that the angels who were kept ready *for this hour, day, month and year* were released.

4. The final and greatest obstacle to Dr. Litch's claim is that fulfillment

of the first five trumpets cannot be demonstrated from history. If we follow the sequence of the seven trumpets, trumpet six can only occur after the first five trumpets have been fulfilled!

To his credit, Dr. Litch withdrew his announcement that the sixth trumpet had been fulfilled in August, 1840. He became convinced that what had appeared to be a fulfillment, was not a fulfillment. By 1873, Dr. Litch published a book titled, *A Complete Harmony of Daniel and the Apocalypse,* in which he wrote, "the trumpets are yet future and will occur shortly before the second coming of Christ."

This short story is told to point out a very important issue. Throughout the centuries, many people have attempted to explain Revelation's story and show that some piece or part has been fulfilled. But time has proven them to be wrong. However, this does not lessen the value or the meaning of Revelation, for God has had a lesser and a greater purpose for this book. First, the book was not sealed like the book of Daniel until the time of the end, so that people down through the centuries could do what Dr. Litch did. In other words, God has wisely kept interest in Revelation and the second advent alive by allowing people to reach conclusions or applications of Revelation that seem to apply in their day. The second and greater purpose for the book of Revelation is to reveal God's actions at the end of the world. Revelation has *one correct* message and

this message will only be understood in its totality by the final generation that live during the events predicted within it. This is why we, the final generation, must maintain fidelity to rules of interpretation that are now revealed. Unless the rules are satisfied, we don't have fulfillment!

Revelation's timing

In order to appreciate and understand Revelation's story, the student has to determine a place in time where the story begins. Expositors from the Historical School of thought assume the story began with the ascension of Christ (A.D. 30). After all, there are no specific dates mentioned in Revelation. On the other hand, Futurists assume that most of Revelation begins with the rapture! So, where does it start?

Remember, there is a demonstrated prophetic mechanism: Prophetic things are understood on or about the time of fulfillment. We will see in the next chapter that Revelation's story has two parts. The first part applies to the seven churches and the second part begins with 1798. If you aren't clear on the importance of 1798 and 1844, you should review the chapters on the Judgment Day.

New light in 1844

The year 1844 did not come and go unnoticed upon earth. As the year 1840 approached, a significant number of people in Europe and America came to understand the importance of the

2,300 days of Daniel 8:14. In America they were generally called Millerites or followers of William Miller. Miller, a licensed Baptist minister, set northeastern America astir with his prophetic message that Jesus was returning to earth "on or about 1843." Miller understood the *cleansing* of the sanctuary to be the cleansing of earth from sin—thus, he concluded, the second coming must occur at the end of the 2,300 days of Daniel 8:14 which would be sometime during 1843. Later the date was revised to 1844. At the height of his popularity about 100,000 people of various denominations subscribed to his prophetic conclusion that Jesus was about to return!

Miller was not a single voice preaching on the imminent return of Jesus even though his prophetic views largely dissipated after 1844. The 19th century is a high water mark for spiritual interest in America. Great preachers of the era include Charles G. Finney, Dwight L. Moody and Billy Sunday. These and many others contributed to the spiritual revival of America and Europe at that time. Thousands in the eastern part of America "got religion" and dedicated their lives to the Lord. Camp meetings began in Kentucky and thousands attended. A large number of Americans were "spiritually revived."

When Jesus didn't come as anticipated in 1844, the Millerite revival essentially died. Protestant churches in general became disillusioned with prophetic study and skepticism about prophecy would characterize Protestantism for a

century. Then, in the early 1970's, prophetic interest began to come alive. Suddenly, Hal Lindsey's book, *The Late Great Planet Earth* became a best seller. But prophecy is only interesting if there is imminent fulfillment. For this reason, prophetic study seems to polarize people. It is either a topic of considerable interest, or it is a waste of time.

So when does Revelation's story begin?

There are two answers to this question. Notice what John is told, **"Write, therefore, what you have seen, what is now and what will take place later."** (Revelation 1:19)

Just like Daniel's visions (Daniel 8-12), John's vision had information for "his day" and information for "our day." Because some of the information given to the seven churches related to immediate problems within the churches, John was clearly told to, **"...write on a scroll what you see and send it to the seven churches: to Ephesus, Smyrna, Pergamum, Thyatira, Sardis, Philadelphia and Laodicea."** (Revelation 1:11)

The messages to the seven churches initially belonged to the churches *at the time they were sent to them.* But, in a larger sense, the messages to the seven churches are timeless and universal because the seven churches still exist—not in the same place, nor with the same people. People come and go. Times change, but the seven churches remain. The point is that the seven churches represent the body of believers in Christ! The problems with sin haven't changed and the promises and threatenings Jesus gave each church still stand. In fact, Jesus concludes his message to each church saying, **"He who has an ear, let him hear what the Spirit says to the churches."**

The seven churches are not numbered one through seven. They are not sequential or chronological in order. They are not apocalyptic. They do not represent seven time periods since the ascension of Jesus. They simultaneously existed in John's day and they simultaneously exist now.

Something old, something new.

We need to notice three things in the messages to the seven churches and see if they apply to us. We need to comprehend the description of Jesus as He is represented to each church; we need to understand the things said to each church and we need to notice the promise given to each church. Notice:

Descriptions of Jesus

What does each description of Jesus reveal? How does each description relate to the problems faced by each church?

1. **Ephesus:** Jesus holds the seven stars in his right hand and walks among the seven lampstands. {1:20-2:1}

2. **Smyrna:** Jesus is the First and Last, who died and came to life again. {2:8}
3. **Pergamum:** Jesus has the sharp, double-edged sword. {2:12}
4. **Thyatira:** Jesus is the Son of God, whose eyes are like blazing fire and whose feet are like burnished bronze. {2:18}
5. **Sardis:** Jesus holds the seven spirits of God and the seven stars. {3:1}
6. **Philadelphia:** Jesus has the key of David. What He shuts—no one can open. What He opens—no one can shut. He sets before us an open door that no one can shut. {3:7,8}
7. **Laodicea:** Jesus is the faithful and true witness, the ruler of God's creation. {3:14}

Timeless words

Notice what Jesus says to each church:

1. **Ephesus:** You have forsaken your first love. {2:4}
2. **Smyrna:** You are afflicted and poor—yet you are rich. Be faithful unto death. {2:9,10}
3. **Pergamum:** You sin by gluttony and sexual immorality Balaam style. ("Balaam style" refers to immoral sins committed with heathen who don't know any better. See Numbers 22-24.) {2:14}
4. **Thyatira:** You sin by gluttony and sexual immorality Jezebel style. (This refers to sins committed within the church by those knowing better. Compare with 1 Kings 21 and 2 Kings 9.) {2:20}
5. **Sardis:** You are dead. Wake up! {3:1,2}

6. **Philadelphia:** You are weak but you are faithful. Hang on. {3:8,10,11}
7. **Laodicea:** You are neither hot nor cold. Repent! {3:15,19}

A promise is a promise

Notice what the overcomers receive:

1. **Ephesus:** Those overcoming will have the right to eat of the tree of life, which is in the paradise of God. {2:7}
2. **Smyrna:** Those overcoming will not be hurt by the second death. {2:11}
3. **Pergamum:** Those overcoming will receive some of the hidden manna and a white stone with a new name on it. {2:17}
4. **Thyatira:** Those overcoming will have authority over the nations. {2:26}
5. **Sardis:** Those overcoming will be dressed in white and their names will never be erased from the book of life. {3:5}
6. **Philadelphia:** Those overcoming will become a pillar in the temple of God. {3:12}
7. **Laodicea:** Those overcoming will have the right to sit with Jesus on His throne. {3:21}

To the sincere in all churches

Here's an important question. When will the promise to each church be realized? Answer: When Jesus comes. This little point will be important in a future lesson. So, just remember the seven promises will be fulfilled when Jesus comes.

Jesus says, **"He who has an ear, let him hear what the Spirit says to the churches."** The messages to the seven churches are timeless. As the number seven denotes fullness or wholeness, the seven churches represent all children of God—scattered over the face of the earth. Which church describes your experience in the Lord? The glory of Jesus is not dimmed by time. Even though He clearly sees the frailty and weakness of His people, He blends encouragement with divine warning. His promised rewards far surpass any price we have to pay. To God be the glory!

Summary

Revelation follows a very careful outline. The story within Revelation was designed to do two things: First, an understanding of the story will change your life. God wants His people prepared for the things He is about to do. Secondly, Revelation will provide credibility to the message that God's people will give just before the second coming because people everywhere are going to see that Bible prophecy can be trusted when rightly understood!

The story, the language and the meaning of Revelation combine in an integral way to reveal who Jesus really is and to reveal *all* that Jesus is! Hence the last book in the Bible is called, "The Revelation of Jesus."

Rules of interpretation are vitally important. Rules are directly connected to conclusions, and rules are no respecter of bias, scholarship or denomination.

Revelation had information for the seven churches that existed in John's day, and Revelation contains information for the final and last generation upon earth. The core message to each of the seven churches is still applicable today. Which church do you belong to? Will you be found among the overcomers when Jesus returns?

Notes

Chapter 14

The Seven Seals

Introduction

There are hundreds of interpretations about the meaning of the seven seals in Revelation. However, when the story of the seals is set into the prophetic matrix (see Appendix), the timing and the meaning of the seals becomes quite easy to understand. This writer believes that a correct understanding of the seals can only be found by correlating the operation of the seals with other prophecies, especially the timing of the seals. For this reason, the rules of interpretation will be very important in this study.

Conclusion

To help the reader see where this study is going, the meaning of the first three seals is given here. Then, as this chapter unfolds, the reader can see how these conclusions were reached.

The seven seals of Revelation are similar to graduation diplomas. When a child completes the eighth grade, he receives a diploma. Then, upon graduating from high school, he receives another. When he graduates from college, he receives another diploma. If he goes on to graduate

school and graduates, he receives another. Thus, diplomas represent specific accomplishments by the graduate. With each diploma, the skills of the graduate becomes more valuable and demand for his accomplishments grow (meaning, his annual income usually increases).

Before angels or human beings were created, the Father wrote a book revealing everything that would happen in the universe. He perfectly sealed up the book with seven seals so that no one could see what was in the book. The Father designed that when the time was right, this book would be opened and the contents revealed. His purpose for the book is that He wants everyone to see that He knew about Lucifer's evil actions, Adam and Eve's fall into sin, and even the details of our lives before we came to be. More importantly, He wants everyone to see that even though He knew that sin was going to happen, He never once prevented any angel or person from exercising their right to make choices. (More about this shortly.)

The Father also designed that when the time came to open the book, there would be a careful process connected to exposing the contents. This process is the full disclosure of all that Jesus is; namely, that Jesus is just as much God as is the Father. Jesus possesses every power that the Father has. However,

Jesus has always kept His glory and authority veiled from angels as well as men. But, the plan of salvation requires the full disclosure of Jesus. So, the opening of each seal is connected to a brighter and clearer revelation of all that Jesus is. As each seal opens, more about Jesus is seen, both in heaven and on earth. (This is why the last book of the Bible is called the *Revelation of Jesus*.)

This is why the parallel. The seven seals are similar to seven diplomas. As each diploma reveals more about the accomplishments and worthiness of the graduate, so each broken seal reveals more about Jesus.

The seals reveal Jesus

The opening of the seals is directly connected to events transpiring on earth. Notice how this works: The first seal represents the salvation of Jesus. This seal was opened shortly after 1798. The setting was this: For 1,260 years, the Roman Catholic Church had claimed to hold the keys of life and death. The Church taught that salvation was only possible through her application of sacraments. Shortly after the Church fell in 1798, Jesus opened the first seal and sent a revival message throughout the world that salvation was only available through Him—not any Church. Historically, we find the effect of the first seal on earth called the "great awakening" which took place in Europe and America during the first half of the 19th century.

The second seal represents the translation, printing and distribution of the Bible throughout the world. This seal complements the work begun under the first seal, for people upon hearing about the salvation of Jesus, wanted Bibles so that they could study into Christ's full salvation for themselves. And, the formation of Missionary and Bible Societies rapidly grew—both in Europe and America. Thus, this seal reveals the supremacy of the teachings of Jesus over the vain teachings of men.

The third seal represents the proclamation of the judgment-hour message that began in 1844. This seal fully exposes the ministry of Jesus in heaven's sanctuary. It reveals that He has been found worthy to conduct the judgment of human beings. And, a body of people were raised up to proclaim this truth to the world.

Looking at the first three seals, we find a beautiful process. The first seal represents the salvation of Jesus contrasted against salvation controlled by the Church. The second seal represents the supremacy of the Word of Jesus contrasted against the foolish teachings of men. And, the third seal reveals the ministry of Jesus in heaven which began in 1844. Thus, the opening of the seals reveal the accomplishments and worthiness of Jesus. In fact, when the next seal (the fourth) is opened, the authority of Jesus will be suddenly and shockingly revealed to the whole world. This point will be explored in a moment. For now, we need to investigate how these things come together.

The rules of interpretation

The previous chapter discussed three rules of interpretation for apocalyptic prophecies. These will be come very valuable as we apply them in this chapter. In shortened form they are:

1. Apocalyptic prophecies have beginning and ending points in time. Events within the prophecy must occur in the order in which they are presented.
2. Apocalyptic prophecy is not fulfilled until all the specifications and the chronology of the prophecy are both met.
3. Those elements believed to be symbolic must be interpreted by applicable scripture for the Bible must interpret itself.

When does Revelation's story begin?

In order to understand any of Revelation's prophecies, we must have a beginning point in time. Because apocalyptic prophecy deals with a predicted sequence of events, a chronological beginning date is extremely important. We saw this point confirmed in our study on Daniel 8 and 9. The decree to restore and rebuild Jerusalem in 457 B.C. marked the beginning of the 490 years as well as the 2,300 year prophecy!

We know that Revelation (like Daniel) contains some information for John's day *and* information on things that will occur in the future. For example, the seven churches existed in John's day. And we know something about their problems and the warnings from Jesus.

(Revelation 1:11,19; 2:1-3:22) And, we also know that Revelation deals with events that will happen in the future. But, where do these events begin?

Revelation 4 starts an important prophecy. This prophecy tells of a great convocation in heaven where Jesus is found worthy to take a book sealed with seven seals. Upon receiving the book, Jesus begins to open the book by breaking one seal open at a time. What is this book? What is inside it? Why is it sealed up? When does this scene take place?

The all important ceremony

Stop! You need to read all of Revelation 4 and 5 in your Bible before proceeding. This is necessary so that you are acquainted with the details of the story.

The elders?

Who are the 24 elders sitting on thrones around the throne? The Bible doesn't explain who they are in direct terms. They are mentioned 12 times in Revelation. However, there are some very strong clues that reveal their identity. First, the term elder means *one who has gone before,* or someone of greater experience. Revelation 5:9 indicates that the elders have been redeemed by the blood of Jesus. Paul tells us that Jesus took some resurrected people to heaven with Him at the time of His ascension. (Matthew 27:51,52; Ephesians 4:7,8) But perhaps the greatest evidence supporting the idea that these are people who once lived on earth is the location of their thrones. Understand that billions of angels are in this assembly. The judgment of human beings is about to begin. The year is 1798 and who should be given a front row seat to observe the fairness and mercy of Jesus as He judges the human race? Those who have been redeemed — peers of those who shall be saved and condemned.

The Lamb's book

John clearly saw the Lamb deemed worthy to take this all important book from the right hand of the Father. (Revelation 5:7) Even though John does not call the book sealed with seven seals the "book of life" in Chapter 5, he clearly refers to this book as the "Lamb's book of life" in other places in Revelation. John calls it the "Lamb's book of life" because it is the only book the Lamb receives in Revelation's story! Notice:

"All inhabitants of the earth will worship the beast - all whose names have not been written in the book of life belonging to the Lamb...." (Revelation 13:8)

"...The inhabitants of the earth whose names have not been written in the book of life from the creation of the world will be astonished when they see the beast...." (Revelation 17:8) (Note when the book of life was written.)

"Nothing impure will ever enter it (New Jerusalem), nor will anyone who does what is shameful or deceitful, but only those whose names are written **in the Lamb's book of life."** (Revelation 21:27)

Daniel knew of this special book even though he does not call it by name! Speaking about the close of probation, Daniel says, **"At that time Michael, the great prince who protects your people, will arise. There will be a time of distress such as has not happened from the beginning of nations until then. But at that time your people - everyone whose name is found written in the book - will be delivered."** (Daniel 12:1)

King David knew of this book. **"Your eyes saw my unformed body. All the days ordained for me were written in your book before one of them came to be."** (Psalm 139:16) Moses knew of this book. (Exodus 32:32) And Jesus spoke to His disciples of this book. (Luke 10:20)

There is only one place in the Bible that tells us when this book is opened: at the end of the 1,000 years. This is when the seventh seal is broken. John says, **"And I saw the dead, great and small, standing before the throne, and books were opened. Another book was opened, which is the book of life...."** (Revelation 20:12)

The book of life was written by the Father and perfectly sealed up before the creation of anything, including the angels. It contains the story of Lucifer and his rebellion, the fall of Adam and Eve, and the implementation of the plan of salvation. This book contains a record of everything and everyone before anything came to be. And when the great day of final reckoning comes at the end of the thousand years, the hosts of earth and heaven will be brought together to stand before God. At this one and only time in earth's existence, all members of the human race will be alive! It's a grand and terrible moment. See Revelation 20.

When the wicked of earth are resurrected, Satan immediately stirs the vast multitude with rebellion. He convinces the numberless crowd that God intends to do them harm. He incites an angry rebellion to destroy the New Jerusalem and the saints within. As the wicked rush upon the city, Jesus speaks. The multitude is stopped in their tracks. Silence overtakes the breathless mob for about half an hour. (Revelation 8:1) Jesus, as King of Kings and Lord of Lords, speaks. The anger and rebellion of the numberless mob is suspended. As lightning pierces darkness, the wicked realize they stand before their Maker. He is not a tyrant. He is not angry. He speaks in a voice that is gentle but firm.

Then, Jesus unfolds the plan of salvation before the multitude. The wicked behold the extended love of God. Each person understands the economy of salvation. Each person's life is presented from the books of heaven's record. The wicked behold their deeds just as God saw their deeds. Each person sees the spiritual influences of good and evil upon their life. They see the choices they made. He who sees the hearts and reads the motives reveals their sinful lives to them with unvarnished clarity. The wicked know why they are condemned.

All justification for sin is expelled in the light of God's records. With every motive fully exposed, sin is seen as nothing more than love for self. The wicked now know what the love of Jesus is, why He died on Calvary and most of all, they know why they cannot be saved. At the end of this revelation, every knee bows before Jesus with deepest emotion. The wicked admit Jesus is fair and just in His eternal decision.

While the wicked see their lives pass before their eyes, the righteous see the same from their position in the Holy City. They too behold the story of salvation. They too see their own sinful lives pass before them. And at the end, they too kneel before Jesus. But instead of confessing the fairness and justice of God, the saints confess that Jesus is unbelievably merciful. Think of it. One group kneels before His justice, the other before His mercy! But, every knee bows.

Jesus predicted long ago, **"...before me every knee will bow; by me every tongue will swear. They will say of me, 'In the Lord alone are righteousness and strength.' All who have raged against him will come to him and be put to shame. But in the Lord all the descendants of Israel will be found righteous and will exult."** (Isaiah 45:23-25) Even though the wicked admit the justice and love of God, they cannot change their evil course, for outside of God's power there is no power to overcome sin! Such is the heinous nature and cancer of sin.

John says, "Then another book was opened which is the book of life." At last, the breaking of the seventh seal allows the mysterious book of life to be opened. Heaven's most intriguing book has been sealed for thousands of years and it contains not only the history of everything, it contains the names of those who shall live forever (angels included). This is why the book is called the book of life. Sinners and victors stand around the throne with deepest interest.

What a moment! What a day! A hush falls upon the audience as they see that the books of record, those books recorded by unerring angels, are identical to the book of life! In other words, God precisely wrote down everything that would happen before it came to be and the books of record confirm that God knew in advance what choices His creatures would make!

If the number of the redeemed of all ages is 14,567,259,123,382, then that's the exact number of names remaining in the book of life! The names of the wicked were blotted out when the book was written. Both the wicked and the righteous look into the book with amazement. The wicked have no argument with the salvation of the saints, for the mercy and justice of Jesus has been revealed to them. And the righteous stand in awe that Jesus knew them by name before the world existed!

Book of life is evidence

The opening of this book proves two very important things. First, it unquestionably proves the omniscience of God. He knows everything about everything. The contents of the book, written before anything was made, clearly describes what has taken place in heaven and upon earth. Each angel and member of the human family beholds the story written in the book of life, and knows the story is accurate, for he sees himself as a character in the story. The book of life is identical to the book of records with one exception. The names of the wicked are blotted out of the book of life.

Secondly, the book of life unquestionably proves that God granted the power of choice to each person. Each angel and member of the human family will see from the books of record that his eternal reward was his own choice. Those inside the New Jerusalem know they are only there because they chose Jesus as their Savior. Those outside the city know they are there because they chose to reject the promptings of the Holy Spirit. The net effect is this: Even though God knows everything about everything, He does not manipulate His subjects on the basis of foreknowledge. The power of choice was freely bestowed upon all His children and the opening of this book fully confirms it! In other words, God knew what was going to happen, God knew the price sin would extract, and yet, He went forward with the creation of angels and human beings giving them the power of choice.

The book will be studied for eternity. The contents of this book will be compared with the Bible and the books of record throughout the ages, for the redeemed will never cease to marvel at the love and works of God.

One last and very important point. The greatest punishment God gives an angel or a human being is the "reality of forfeiture." When the wicked behold with their own eyes what they *chose* to forfeit, words will not be able to describe their anguish. The wicked, in deepest grief, will turn and vent their remorse upon each other. (Zechariah 14:12,13) They will begin to attack one another and to finish the carnage, Jesus sends fire from heaven and burns them up. Sin and sinners are no more. The universe is free at last! Free of sin.

Back to the book with seven seals

So, when does Jesus take the book sealed with seven seals in Revelation 5:7? There are three choices for the answer to this question.

    a. Shortly after His ascension
    b. 1798
    c. Sometime in the future

The Bible answers the question! In fact, Daniel provides the key. Notice Daniel's vision recorded in Daniel 7:

"As I looked, thrones were set in place, and the Ancient of Days took His seat. His clothing was as white as snow; the hair of His head was white like wool. His throne was flaming with fire, and its wheels were all ablaze. A river of fire was flowing, coming out from before Him. Thousands upon thousands attended him; ten thousand times ten thousand stood before Him. The court was seated, and the books were opened.... And there before me was one like a son of man, coming with the clouds of heaven. He approached the Ancient of Days and was led into His presence. He was given authority, glory and sovereign power; all peoples, nations and men of every language worshiped him. His dominion is an everlasting dominion that will not pass away, and His kingdom is one that will never be destroyed." (Daniel 7:9-14)

Here, the Ancient of Days takes His seat and the court scene in heaven begins. When did this happen? Answer: In 1798, at the end of the little horn power's reign. Notice: **"As I watched, this horn was waging war against the saints and defeating them, until the Ancient of Days came and pronounced judgment in favor of the saints of the Most High, and the time came when they possessed the kingdom."** (Daniel 7:21-22) We know from Daniel 7:25 that the little horn power would persecute the saints for 1,260 years. We know that Napoleon inflicted a deadly wound upon the Papacy in February, 1798, when he captured the pope and put him in prison.

Because we can't see what is going on in heaven, God has connected events on earth with events in heaven. Bible prophecy is our connection between the two. Thus, the court scene in heaven begins when the time allotted to the little horn power expires — namely, 1798.

Consider the parallels

Several important parallels exist between Daniel 7 and Revelation 4 and 5. The most important parallel in these two scenes is that Jesus is especially honored. According to Daniel, Jesus receives authority, glory and sovereign power *when the court scene commences* in 1798. According to John, Jesus is given the seven attributes of God—wealth, wisdom, glory, honor, power, praise and authority—when He is found worthy to receive the book of life. (Revelation 5:12) The point is that according to Daniel, Jesus receives sovereign power in 1798 and according to John, Jesus receives all the attributes of God when He is found worthy to receive the book sealed with seven seals. Are these two events related? Do they occur in the same service? Yes.

Daniel and John favorably compare:

Daniel 7:9 and Revelation 4:2,4

- I looked, thrones were set in place.

- Before me was a throne with 24 thrones surrounding it occupied by 24 elders.

Daniel 7:9 and Revelation 4:3,4

- The Ancient of Days took His seat. His clothing was as white as snow, the hair of His head was white like wool.

- The One who sat there had the appearance of a jasper and (the brilliance of a ruby). The elders were dressed in white.

Daniel 7:9,10 and Revelation 4:5

- His throne was flaming with fire and its wheels were all ablaze. And the books were opened.

- From the throne came flashes of lightning, rumblings and peals of thunder. Before the throne seven lamps were blazing.

Daniel 7:13 and Revelation 5:7

- I saw one like "a son of man." He approached the Ancient of Days.

- The Lamb approached the Father sitting on the throne and took the scroll from His right hand.

Daniel 7:14 and Revelation 5:9,12

- He was given authority, glory and sovereign power.

- The Elders sing of Jesus, "You are worthy to take the scroll and open its seals." Billions of angels sing, "Worthy is the Lamb, who was slain, to receive power and wealth and wisdom and strength and honor and glory and praise!"

The parallel between the scenes is close. Daniel and John saw the same heavenly courtroom scene. Daniel saw a human being, "a son of man," approach the Father sitting on His throne, and John saw "a Lamb looking as though it had been slain" come before the Father as He sat upon His throne. Daniel saw thrones put in place and the court convene with billions of angels in attendance. He saw the Father take His seat, and eventually, the books of records were opened in 1844. (This is when the cleansing of heaven's sanctuary begins.) Daniel saw Jesus approach the Father and receive sovereign power and glory.

John also saw a great convocation in the throne room of the universe and specifically mentions seeing 24 thrones around the Father's throne. Billions of angels were in attendance. Heaven's most important book was in the right hand of the Father. A search through the universe was conducted for someone worthy to receive this most important book—for some heavenly process cannot continue until *this book* is received. John wept because he knew that no one could receive eternal life until someone was found worthy to receive the book of life and exonerate the Father. After an intensive investigation throughout the universe, Jesus was *judged* worthy to receive the book. The elders along with billions of angels sang enthusiastically as power, wealth, honor and praise were conferred upon Jesus.

Jesus received book of life in 1798

After comparing the two visions, there is no question that Daniel and John saw *special recognition given to Jesus when He received power, wealth, strength, wisdom and praise from the Father.* From Daniel we learn that Jesus is promoted at the time heaven's court convenes in 1798. From John we learn that Jesus is promoted at the time He receives the book sealed with seven seals. The honor conferred upon Jesus in these scenes confirms that John and Daniel saw the same scene. Thus, the book of life was given to Jesus shortly after 1798.

Two other matters confirm 1798 as the correct date. First, on the Old Testament Day of Atonement, the high priest had to be found worthy to officiate on behalf of Israel before he could conduct the service. (See the chapter on the Ministry of Jesus.) If we understand that the courtroom scene described by Daniel and John symbolizes the concluding services in the heavenly sanctuary, it is appropriate that Jesus must first be found worthy to conduct the judgment of human beings which is related to this occasion.

The last point confirming 1798 as the date when Jesus received the book sealed with seven seals comes from the internal harmony of Revelation's story. Since the story has not been studied yet, this point is not helpful at the moment. However, as we study Revelation, the harmony of the sum of the parts will continue to confirm the importance and significance of 1798. As we look into the various sequences that involve chronology and timing, the significance of this point will be easily realized.

What are the seven seals?

According to Webster, a seal is a device that secures an object. In this case, the seven seals perfectly secures the contents of the book of life. This means no one can get into the book and change its contents. What was written down in the book cannot be altered. In fact, the contents of the book of life are not described in Revelation's story. The contents are not revealed until every person who ever lived stands before Jesus! John saw *when* the book was opened (Revelation 20:12), but he did not see *what* was in the book.

The opening of the seals implies two things. First, as each seal opens, the contents of the book are nearer to exposure. The seals are numbered consecutively, thus when the fourth seal is opened, the events that occur under this seal confirm where in the sequence we are. When the sixth seal is opened, the second coming of Jesus occurs—but keep in mind, the book still has one more seal to be opened. The book is not opened at the second coming because everyone involved is not alive at that time.

Secondly, and more importantly, the opening of the seals only have meaning when we understand their relationship to the book that is sealed up. *What point is made unsealing the book of seven seals if the exposure of the contents of the book is not the object of the sequence?* The seals progress in a definite sequence towards the climactic moment when the book of life is opened. The progression of the seals is viewed from heaven by billions of attending angels (remember, they haven't seen inside the book) and on earth by people studying Revelation's story! These things may not be easy to understand at first, but those who study will understand. Daniel was told, **"None of the wicked will understand, but those who are wise will understand."** (Daniel 12:10)

A brief outline of the seven seals:

1. Rider on white horse—set out on conquest.
2. Rider on red horse—carries sword throughout earth.
3. Rider on black horse—tells of judgment.
4. Rider on pale horse—brings devastation.
5. Martyrs for truth's sake.
6. The Lamb's second coming.
7. Silence for about a half hour.

Jesus received the book of life in 1798 and began opening the seals at that time. We will see that the first three seals were opened during a short period of time and that these seals prepare the world for the events described in the next three seals!

Before we examine the seals, we must understand an important point that is often overlooked. John is in vision and he has been taken to the heavenly throne room to view things that occur at the appointed time of the end. In other words, John was zoomed forward in time to behold events that occur at the end of the world. Remember John was told,

"Write the things you have seen, what is now and what will take place later." Revelation 4:1-6:17 begins an apocalyptic sequence that begins with 1798 and ends with the second coming.

The four horses

The four horses of the first four seals are not unique in Revelation, for Zechariah saw four horses having the same colors! Zechariah was told the four horses represent the four spirits of heaven that stand in the presence of the Lord of the whole world. (Zechariah 6:5) These spirits go throughout the earth at God's command to accomplish His will. (Zechariah 1:10,11) Zechariah saw the black horse go north, the white horse go west, the pale or dappled horse go south and the red horse, by inference, go east. (Zechariah 6:6) These four horses go throughout the whole world. These four horses symbolize the work of the four living creatures that stand in the presence of God. These four living creatures are seraphim or "senior angels" having great responsibilities. See Revelation 4:8. The four living creatures are a special order of beings, created by God for service throughout His universe. These angels insure that

God's desires are carried out. (For more study on the seraphim and their responsibilities see Ezekiel 1 & 10.)

The seals begin

Each horse represents the works or actions of the four living creatures as they are commissioned by Jesus. As Jesus opens each seal, He initiates a process from heaven which each living creature carries out. All of these processes lead to the consummation of the plan of salvation. Very important point: The effect and influence of the seals is cumulative. This means that the conquering begun in seal one is concluded in seal six. The process begun during seal two reaches its climax during seal five, and the proclamation during seal three prepares some 144,000 special people for the events that transpire during seal four.

In other words, a seal doesn't begin and end so that the next seal can begin and end. Rather, the first three seals begin certain processes which remain in motion until their counterpart concludes their work. It was for this very reason that Jesus was given sovereign power! He starts three processes upon earth that He personally manages. Even more,

Relationships Between First Six Seals

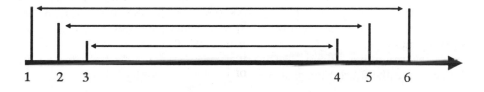

He must direct the processes so that the gospel accomplishes its intended task. Matters as serious as salvation don't happen in random order. Paul says of Jesus, **"For by him all things were created: things in heaven and on earth, visible and invisible, whether thrones or powers or rulers or authorities; all things were created by him and for him. He is before all things, and in him all things hold together."** (Colossians 1:16-17)

Just as the rider of each horse controls the action of the horse, Jesus sends the four living creatures to earth with special assignments. As each "senior angel" prepares to do his work, John is invited to observe. Each invites John saying, "Come."

First seal

"I watched as the Lamb opened the first of the seven seals. Then I heard one of the four living creatures say in a voice like thunder, 'Come!' I looked, and there before me was a white horse! Its rider held a bow, and he was given a crown, and he rode out as a conqueror bent on conquest." (Revelation 6:1,2)

The first horse goes out of the heavenly sanctuary to conquer something on earth. Nothing is conquered in the first seal. No one event on earth marks the opening of this seal. Rather, this seal marks the beginning conquest of Jesus. In 1798, Jesus was given all authority to conclude the sin problem by bringing the plan of salvation to its climax. Time had come to put the everlasting gospel in final form, for soon, it must go to every person on earth.

Because 1798 was almost 200 years ago, the reader needs to understand certain contrasts. At that time, the Church of Rome claimed to be the representative of God on earth. The Church claimed to hold the keys of salvation. The Church controlled its members either through excommunication (and the forfeiture of salvation) or through political adversity. God decreed the limits of the little horn power to be 1,260 years. When the little horn power was brought down, a vacuum for truth and salvation existed. Into this vacuum, Jesus sent a great revival or spiritual awakening. This phenomenon is historically verifiable both in America and Europe.

Remember, the processes set in motion by the seals are additive in nature. Thus, the great revival in America and Europe in the early 19th century prepared the way for the next seal, and the first two seals prepared the way for the understanding of the third seal which would occur in 1844.

The work that began under the first seal though sets the stage for the final presentation of the gospel. The entire world must hear the true gospel and the gospel is a revelation of Jesus. John saw the consummating victory of the gospel. He says, **"And I saw what looked like a sea of glass mixed with fire and, standing beside the sea, those who had been victorious over the beast and his image and over the number of his name...."** (Revelation 15:2)

Second seal

"When the Lamb opened the second seal, I heard the second living creature say, 'Come!' Then another horse came out, a fiery red one. Its rider was given power to take peace from the earth and to make men slay each other. To him was given a large sword." (Revelation 6:3,4)

The second horse goes out of the heavenly sanctuary with a large sword. This sword eventually causes men to slay each other. A number of Bible students are reluctant to identify this event as having a heavenly origin, but John's vantage point is clearly in heaven. But, the heavenly origin is not a problem. Jesus told his disciples, "Do not suppose that I have come to bring peace to the earth. I did not come to bring peace, but a sword." (Matthew 10:34) The sword of Jesus is the Word of Truth. Hebrews 4:12 says, "The word of God is living and active. Sharper than any double-edged sword...." Paul said, "Take the helmet of salvation and the sword of the Spirit, which is the word of God." (Ephesians 6:17) In Revelation 2:12, John describes Jesus to the church in Pergamum as, "Him who has the sharp, double-edged sword." Jesus said to this church, "Repent therefore! Otherwise, I will soon come to you and will fight against them with the sword of my mouth." (Revelation 2:16)

We will later study the war and bloodshed that occurs all over the earth as a result of the Word of God. The coming war will be a contest between truth and falsehood. This seal culminates in the fifth seal, a time when people will kill one another over God's truth! Here is a subtle but very important point. Notice that the text describing the second seal does not have to mean that the slaying occurs *at the time* the second seal is opened. (Neither is the conquering described in the first seal accomplished during the time of the first seal.) Rather, the consequence of the second seal is seen *when peace is taken from the earth and men slay each other* on account of the sword!

What is the sword? Allowing the Bible to interpret itself, we must conclude from the texts above that the sword represents the "Word of God."

Can we look back to the time period following 1798 and find anything that historically marks the opening of this seal? Yes! The formation of Bible societies that began during the early 19th century by Protestants fulfills the meaning of this seal! The gospel commission belonged to Protestants after 1798. The translation and distribution of the Bible into every nation on earth has grown immensely since 1800. In those days a large number of Protestant churches in Europe and North America formed Bible and Missionary Societies to carry the gospel to all the world! By the time we reach the end of the 19th century, we reach a high-water mark for the establishment and activity of mission service by Protestant denominations. People gave liberally to the printing and distribution of the Bible. In fact, no book on earth has ever been translated and distributed to the extent the Bible has. No other book on earth has overcome the popularity of the Bible and the Bible will be the book upon which the coming great controversy will be focused!

Third seal

"When the Lamb opened the third seal, I heard the third living creature say, 'Come!' I looked, and there before me was a black horse! Its rider was holding a pair of scales in his hand. Then I heard what sounded like a voice among the four living creatures, saying, 'A quart of wheat for a day's wages, and three quarts of barley for a day's wages, and do not damage the oil and the wine!' " (Revelation 6:5,6)

The third horse leaves the heavenly sanctuary with a pair of scales and a message. The scales imply judgment. Indeed, we know from Daniel that the books of record were opened at the end of the 2,300 years in 1844 and that Jesus began an investigation of the records of those who have died. The work of the third living creature is to see that people on earth become aware of what Jesus is doing in the heavenly sanctuary. During the past 148 years, the understanding and awareness of the investigative judgment has mightily grown around the world. Even though general knowledge of the ongoing judgment process is not yet widespread among the ever increasing population of the earth, several million people already know about it! Those who understand this truth will soon be in a position to explain the even more

important judgment process that is coming: the judgment of the living!

A promise of wages accompanies this seal. A full day's wages are promised to those who will help spread this special message. Just as Solomon paid the builders of his temple in wheat, barley, oil and wine (2 Chronicles 2:10,15), the teachers of heaven's temple will be fully paid by Jesus Himself. Even though many years have passed since the judgment hour message first began, and thousands of those who have labored to carry the judgment hour message are now dead, they will receive their full reward! God is fair!

First three seals set global stage

These three seals have been opened. There is historical evidence to support this claim. As each seal opened, there was a progressive revelation of Jesus in heaven and on earth. Who Jesus is, what He is and how He intends to conclude the gospel commission becomes clearer to the watching angels and to a growing number of people on earth. Truth is ever progressive and the seals demonstrate just that. The first two seals were opened shortly after 1798. In 1844, the third seal was opened. By 1874, the judgment hour message was organized well enough to be proclaimed in foreign lands! And for almost 200 years, the activities described in these three seals have influenced the earth, in effect, setting the stage for what is about to happen!!!

Fourth seal

"When the Lamb opened the fourth seal, I heard the voice of the fourth living creature say, 'Come!' I looked, and there before me was a pale horse! Its rider was named Death, and Hades was following close behind him. They were given power over a fourth of the earth to kill by sword, famine and plague, and by the wild beasts of the earth." (Revelation 6:7,8)

The opening of the fourth seal brings global devastation. See Chapter 2. This living creature is the angel of death. Perhaps this is the same angel that flew over Egypt and killed the firstborn children and animals of the Egyptians. (Exodus 12-13) Perhaps he is also the same angel that killed 185,000 of Sennacherib's army. (2 Kings 19) Regardless of his identity, his influence upon the earth is unmistakable.

Jesus sends this senior angel to earth with four terrible judgments to arrest the attention of the world. These judgments are identified as: sword, famine, plague and wild beasts. Twenty-five percent of the earth will perish in these judgments! For a clearer understand about these four dreadful judgments, you must read Ezekiel 14:12-23.

The fourth seal is the next one to open. This is self-evident. From the perspective of chronological timing alone, the devastating results of this seal have not been observed upon earth since the seals began opening. We will also see that the events during this seal are a great catalyst marking the beginning of the judgment of the living! The death and destruction attending the fourth seal is fully explained in Revelation's story on the seven trumpets and seven last plagues. These will be studied in considerable detail in future lessons.

One last point. The first four seals are actions carried out by senior angels (the four living creatures). The fifth seal is carried out by the followers of Jesus on earth, and the sixth seal is carried out by Jesus Himself!

Fifth seal

"When he opened the fifth seal, I saw under the altar the souls of those who had been slain because of the word of God and the testimony they had maintained. They called out in a loud voice, 'How long, Sovereign Lord, holy and true, until you judge the inhabitants of the earth and avenge our blood?' Then each of them was given a white robe, and they were told to wait a little longer, until the number of their fellow servants and brothers who were to be killed as they had been was completed." (Revelation 6:9-11)

The opening of the fifth seal ushers in a period of martyrdom. Why would Jesus allow martyrdom to come upon His people? There are two reasons. First, persecution separates pretense from substance. When the price for being a Christian is great, who will be willing to bear the cross and follow the teachings of Jesus? Answer: Only the pure in heart that love God's truth.

In America, the cost of being a Christian has been for the most part, easy. We have religious liberty. We can worship without intimidation or fear. We have freedom of speech. We can teach and believe whatever we want. We are truly blessed! But this blessing has brought a curse. We have become lazy, weak and in many instances, corrupt. Christianity today is comprised of many fair-weather Christians filled with external piety. Protestant America has become degenerate and looks more like a hospital for sin-sick people than an army of soldiers prepared for the final conflict with Satan!

The second reason the fifth seal brings martyrdom is that when the fifth seal is opened, Satan is personally upon earth claiming to be God. Those following Jesus will recognize the devil for what he is and will do everything possible to tell the world of his supreme deceptions. Think of it! With much of the world receiving the devil as God, those who fearlessly identify the imposter as the devil will not be looked upon favorably! How would you feel if someone called your God "the devil?" If ever there was an unholy war, this will be it. Those killing the followers of Jesus will actually be told by the evil imposter that they are doing God a service!

Sixth seal

"I watched as he opened the sixth seal. There was a great earthquake. The sun turned black like sackcloth made of goat hair, the whole moon turned blood red, and the stars in the sky fell to earth, as late figs drop from a fig tree when shaken by a strong wind. The sky receded like a scroll, rolling up, and every mountain and island was removed from its place. Then the kings of the earth, the princes, the generals, the rich, the mighty, and every slave and every free man hid in caves and among the rocks of the mountains. They called to the mountains and the rocks, 'Fall on us and hide us from the face of him who sits on the throne and from the wrath of the Lamb! For the great day of their wrath has come, and who can stand?' " (Revelation 6:12-17)

The opening of the sixth seal brings Jesus to the rescue of His people. The opening of the sixth seal is the second coming. John describes King Jesus as riding on the white horse, having the title, "King of Kings and Lord of Lords" upon His sash. (Revelation 19:11-16)

Just as the work of the first seal began on a white horse in 1798, so the work of the sixth seal is concluded on a white horse. Jesus set out to conquer in 1798 and at the second coming, He conquers! John says, "I saw heaven standing open and there before me was a white horse, whose rider is called Faithful and True. With justice he judges and makes war.... Out of his mouth comes a sharp sword with which to strike down the nations. He will rule them with an iron scepter....' " (Revelation 19:11,15)

Seventh seal

"When he opened the seventh seal, there was silence in heaven for about half an hour." (Revelation 8:1)

The opening of the seventh seal occurs at the end of the 1,000 years and the story within the book of life—now unsealed—is fully exposed. The importance of this seal will be seen again in later lessons.

Summary

The first three seals prepare the world stage for the development of the next three seals. The relationships within the seals become quite evident if the student will compare each seal with its corresponding partner. For example, the work begun under the first seal is fulfilled under the sixth seal. The work begun under the second seal is fulfilled with the fifth seal. And, the message begun under the third seal culminates with the opening of the fourth seal. The breaking open of each seal reveals a new dimension about Jesus! For example:

Seal 1: The salvation of Jesus
Seal 2: The supremacy of His Word, the Bible
Seal 3: The ministry of Jesus in heaven as Judge
Seal 4: The authority of Jesus over earth
Seal 5: The faith of Jesus in His people
Seal 6: The sovereignty of Jesus as King of Kings
Seal 7: The deity of Jesus exposed

The first seal reveals the salvation of Jesus (in contrast to the controlled salvation offered by the Church), the second seal reveals the supremacy of the Word of Jesus (not the supremacy of man's word about Jesus), the third seal reveals the ministry of Jesus in heaven's sanctuary, the fourth seal reveals the authority of Jesus over the world, the fifth seal reveals the faith of Jesus in His followers, and the sixth seal reveals the sovereignty of Jesus as King of Kings. The seventh seal reveals that the name of Jesus is above every name. (But, Jesus returns His sovereignty and His kingdom to the Father after the revelation of the seventh seal! See 1 Corinthians 15:24-28.)

For now, we need to remember that the opening of each seal moves us chronologically towards the second coming and the great day of reckoning for all human beings at the end of the 1,000 years. Consider this point: Billions of people will sleep on through the second coming because the wicked are not resurrected until the 1,000 years are ended. They will be resurrected to behold the opening of the seventh seal. What a day that will be for them.

In the next lesson, we will study the consequences of the seals in more detail. You will see how the opening of the fourth seal marks the beginning of the judgment of the living!

Notes

Chapter 15

The Seven Trumpets Part I

Review

Our previous chapter focused on the seven scals. Because the seals are chronological in nature, it is critically important that we establish when the seals begin to be opened if we are to identify their relationship to time. In our last lesson, we saw how Daniel and Revelation harmoniously combine and bring us to the conclusion that 1798 is the year that Jesus received the book sealed with seven seals. The harmony of the sum of prophetic parts brings encouragement and enlightenment to students of prophecy! Even more, we shall again see that Revelation's sequences internally harmonize with 1798 and 1844.

The issue of the worthiness of Jesus as our High Priest also brings us to 1798. Remember, in the Old Testament, the high priest had to be found worthy and his sacrifice accepted *before* he could officiate on behalf of Israel! (Leviticus 16)

The previous lesson also stated that two seals were opened within a short time period following 1798 and the third seal opened in 1844. As every drama requires a stage, the first three seals set earth's stage for the next three seals. In addition, there is historical evidence confirming the operations conducted under the first three seals. The cumulative influence of the first three seals has been steadily growing around the world. We will discover in this lesson just how well the senior angels of the first three seals have done their work!

The fourth seal

Carefully review the fourth seal: **"When the Lamb opened the fourth seal, I heard the voice of the fourth living creature say, 'Come!' I looked, and there before me was a pale horse! Its rider was named Death, and Hades was following close behind him. They were given power over a fourth of the earth to kill by sword, famine and plague, and by the wild beasts of the earth."** (Revelation 6:7,8)

The strongest internal evidence that the fourth seal is the next one to be opened is that the devastation described in this seal has not yet occurred *at any time in earth's history*. The fourth seal indicates that 25% of the earth will be destroyed by these four dreadful judgments of God. Why will Jesus open the fourth seal and send these four terrible judgments throughout the earth?

An angry God?

There is much confusion about the character of God in the world today. By misrepresenting the character of God, the devil has lead many people to either hate or ignore God. Even worse, the devil has lead most of the Protestant world to regard Jesus much like a heavenly Santa Claus. By over-emphasizing the great compassion and mercy of Jesus, and diminishing the legitimacy of God's Ten Commandments, many are ignorant of the teachings of Jesus that require obedience. As the bumper sticker says, "Jesus is either Lord over all or He's not Lord at all!"

Think about your own character for a moment. Have you ever had someone misrepresent you before people who didn't know you? Even worse, has someone spread lies about you among those who knew you? How hard is it to overcome slanderous falsehoods?

The Bible declares that God is love. Divine love is the balance between justice and mercy. Jesus is all-merciful, and yet, He requires obedience and justice. He wants people to live as He lives. The prophet Micah wrote, **"He has showed you, O man, what is good. And what does the Lord require of you? To act justly and to love mercy and to walk humbly with your God."** (Micah 6:8)

The Bible tells us that Jesus is very capable of anger, and in times past, His wrath has broken out upon individuals, cities, nations and even the world! Review these four stories in your Bible that demonstrate the wrath of Jesus:

1. Individuals: Korah, Dathan and Abiram (Numbers 16)
2. Cities: Sodom and Gomorrah (Genesis 19)
3. Nations: The Philistines (Joshua 5:13-6:27)
4. Earth: The Flood (Genesis 6,7)

Each of these stories bring out a very important truth. Jesus rises up in anger and wrath when His mercy and patience no longer have a redeeming effect.

The truth hurts

Satan is delighted when people believe that salvation comes by assumption. Many popular preachers and evangelists preach "Christ without the cross" and consequently become popular. They excite multitudes with stories of powerful miracles. They proclaim ecstatic messages about the power of Jesus and talk extensively about healing from sickness or blessings that eliminate poverty. But few preachers clearly define sin and even fewer say that we can and must obtain victory over it. People don't like to have their sins pointed out! Think about it. If Jesus were alive upon the earth today, His teachings would meet with the same rejection as when He walked upon the earth. When it comes to sin, the truth hurts today just like it hurt when He walked upon the earth.

The problem is that we human beings have a hard time seeing our own faults.

Even worse, many of us don't want to know our faults! Without a clear definition of sin we can't appreciate or understand the malignancy of sin. By watering down the high standard of righteousness, Satan has led this nation (and all the others) into greater sin. Consequently, problems without solutions escalate.

We cannot appreciate the salvation of Jesus without an understanding of the offensiveness and power of sin. Until we comprehend something of the magnitude of sin, we cannot appreciate the meaning of "being saved." Until we admit our helplessness to overcome sin, we cannot appreciate the transforming power of Jesus nor can we realize our desperate need for His great love. Satan has cleverly worked through the large religious systems of the world to disguise sin. In general, people don't understand what sin is, nor do they know how to obtain victory over it! But the everlasting gospel has the answer! This is another reason why the gospel must go to the world. It must expose the religious systems of the world for what they are!

The devil has encompassed the seven great religious systems in the world so that they serve his purposes. In very general terms, the premise of each system is:

1. **Atheism:** This system teaches there is no God. Man is the supreme being.

2. **Heathenism:** This system is ignorant of the living God and creates its own god(s) as needed.
3. **Eastern Mysticism:** This system teaches that man is immortal and can become God.
4. **Judaism:** This system teaches that man is saved by obedience or compliance with the laws of God.
5. **Islam:** This system teaches that man is saved through obedience and compliance with the teachings of Mohammed.
6. **Catholicism:** This system teaches that man is saved through obedience and compliance with the teachings of the Church.
7. **Protestantism:** For the most part, this system teaches that man is saved by believing that he is saved.

As you look at these seven systems, you'll notice they neatly fit into one of three categories:

1. There is no salvation, for there is no God.
2. Man saves himself through obedience.
3. Man is saved by assuming he is saved.

The world's seven religious systems are built on false assumptions. (This is not saying that God does not have sincere people within each system. Those living up to all they know to be right are claimed by God as His children.) But falsehoods, once assumed or accepted, lead people away from God's truth and ultimately, people do terrible things in the name of God. Jesus warned His disciples, "**They will put you out of the synagogue; in fact, a time is coming when anyone who kills you will think he is offering a service to God. They will do such things because they have not known the Father or me.**" (John 16:2,3)

Back to the fourth seal

Jesus has prepared a final test for the world to find out who loves Him *and* His truth. The test has been carefully prepared to test our love for principles of righteousness. It will not be enough to be sincere and dedicated when the test is applied. Hitler was sincere and dedicated to his terrible ideas and the world suffered at his hands. Sincerity is not the most important element in life. The most important point is TRUTH. Who loves and seeks for more of God's Truth? Who lives up to all the truth he knows? Who loves the truth of God so much that he would be willing to suffer or die for its sake?

John saw the saints struggling to defend truth at the end of the world. He says, "**Then the dragon was enraged at the woman and went off to make war against the rest of her offspring - those who obey God's commandments and hold to the testimony of Jesus.**" (Revelation 12:17) As he watched the war, John saw the suffering and martyrdom of the saints that occurs during the fifth seal, for John was told, "**This calls for patient endurance on the part of the saints who obey God's commandments and remain faithful to Jesus.**" (Revelation 14:12)

In 1844, Jesus began judging the dead from the books of record. But how does Jesus judge the living? Their lives are still being lived out. They continue to make choices. Because the world is so diverse with languages, cultures and religious beliefs, God has designed the judgment of the living in such a way that the living will choose their own eternal destiny. As each person makes his decision about the gospel, Jesus eternally seals them in it! Here's a brief scenario:

Jesus sends His four dreadful judgments to awaken and arouse the earth to the sinfulness of its course. These four judgments (also described in Ezekiel 14) arrest the indifference of the people of earth to the gospel so they can hear the final gospel call. These four judgments are so extensive that every mind on earth is forced to consider them. While people are considering the meaning of the judgments, they will be open to hear the everlasting gospel which contains an explanation of these judgments. As the people of earth contemplate the full gospel, they are invited to do something that most have never done—yield their lives to the truth contained in the Word of God, the Bible. The gospel clearly calls for obedience to the King of Kings. This is how the Bible becomes the center of a great controversy. This is why John contrasts the saints with the followers of the devil, he says, "**...[the saints] obey God's commandments and remain faithful to Jesus.**" (Revelation 14:12) Satan, on the other hand, sees to it that circumstances will be so difficult that no one will be able to obey God's commandments unless they are willing to live by faith! The saints won't be able to buy or sell! Much more will be said about this in future chapters. The point is that salvation has always come by faith and during the great tribulation, the saints will have the faith to obey God rather than men! (Acts 4:19)

Trust and obey

James clearly saw the true relationship between obedience and faith. He says, **"You see that a person is justified by what he does and not by faith alone. ...I will show you my faith by what I do."** (James 2:24,18)

So what moves God to send judgments upon peoples and nations? Notice what Jesus said to Isaiah, **"See, the Lord is going to lay waste the earth and devastate it; he will ruin its face and scatter its inhabitants.... The earth will be completely laid waste and totally plundered. The Lord has spoken this word. The earth dries up and withers, and the world languishes and withers, the exalted of the earth languish. The earth is defiled by its people; they have disobeyed the laws, violated the statutes and broken the everlasting covenant. Therefore a curse consumes the earth; its people must bear their guilt. Therefore earth's inhabitants are burned up, and very few are left."** (Isaiah 24:1-6)

Isaiah was well aware of the hardness of people's hearts. He said, **"...When your judgments come upon the earth, the people of the world learn righteousness. Though grace is shown to the wicked, they do not learn righteousness; even in a land of uprightness they go on doing evil and regard not the majesty of the Lord."** (Isaiah 26:9,10)

Jesus loves mercy and He loves justice

Jesus holds each person accountable for his deeds. When people get away with murder, lying, stealing and cheating, evil rapidly grows. The land becomes defiled. Sin is like nuclear fission—once started, it can't be stopped. The runaway result is that sin spreads until almost every person is controlled or contaminated with it. When people, cities, nations or even the world reaches a point where love has no redeeming effect, Jesus sets His mercy aside and steps in with redeeming judgments. These judgments are sent to arouse people with the sinfulness of their course!

Ezekiel 14:12-27 gives a very clear explanation of the four judgments used in the fourth seal. **"The word of the Lord came to me: 'Son of man, if a country sins against me by being unfaithful and I stretch out my hand against it to cut off its food supply and send famine upon it and kill its men and their animals, even if these three men - Noah, Daniel and Job were in it, they could save only themselves by their righteousness, declares the Sovereign Lord.**

Or if I send wild beasts through that country and they leave it childless and it becomes desolate so that no one can pass through it because of the beasts.... Or if I bring a sword against that country and say, 'Let the sword pass throughout the land'.... Or if I send a plague into that land and pour out my wrath upon it through bloodshed, killing its men and their animals....

How much worse will it be when I send against Jerusalem my four dreadful judgments - sword and famine and wild beasts and plague; to kill its men and their animals. Yet there will be some survivors - sons and daughters who will be brought out of it. They will come to you, and when you see their conduct and their actions, you will be consoled regarding the disaster I have brought upon Jerusalem - every disaster I have brought upon it... for you will know that I have done nothing in it without cause." (Ezekiel 14:12-23)

Notice the prophecy of Hosea: "The days of punishment are coming, the days of reckoning are at hand... because your sins are so many and your hostility so great, the prophet is considered a fool, the inspired man a maniac." (Hosea 9:7)

Through Moses, God warned the Israelites, "If you obey the Lord your God and keep his commands and decrees that are written... the Lord thy God shall bless you in the land you are entering to possess. But if your heart turns away, and you are not obedient, and if you are drawn away to bow down to other gods and worship them... you will certainly be destroyed...." (Deuteronomy 30:10-18)

New Testament warnings

If you think that the above warnings only apply to Old Testament days, consider the following warnings from the New Testament:

Peter said, "For if God did not spare angels when they sinned, but sent them to hell, (the Greek word translated hell is "tartarosas" - the Greek equivalent to the bottomless pit), putting them into gloomy dungeons to be held for judgment; if he did not spare the ancient world when he brought the flood on its ungodly people, but protected Noah, a preacher of righteousness, and seven others; if he condemned the cities of Sodom and Gomorrah by burning them to ashes, and made them an example of *what is going to happen* to the ungodly... the Lord knows how to rescue godly men... and to hold the unrighteous for the day of judgment." (2 Peter 2:4-9)

Revelation says, "...Come out of her (Babylon), my people, so that you will not share in her sins, so that you will not receive any of her plagues; for her sins are piled up to heaven, and God has remembered her crimes.... Therefore in one day her plagues will overtake her: death, mourning and famine. She will be consumed by fire, for mighty is the Lord God who judges her." (Revelation 18:4,5,8)

John says, "I saw in heaven another great and marvelous sign: seven angels

with the seven last plagues - last, because with them God's wrath is completed." (Revelation 15:1)

From the above examples, it is evident that God has sent and will send judgments upon the world either in an effort to save or to punish. We need to notice two specific points.

First: In the case of corporate judgments (judgments upon groups of people) mentioned above, God extended mercy to those who would turn from wrong. In Noah's day, the ark was open to whomsoever would get on board. In Sodom and Gomorrah, God couldn't even find 10 righteous people, but did save Lot and some of his family. In Jericho, the harlot Rahab and hcr family were saved. In Nineveh, the entire city was saved through repentance!

While cities, nations and earth itself may fill up their cups of iniquity, God seeks to save those who love Him and spares them from His judgments. In 2 Peter 3:9, it says that, **"(Jesus) is patient with you, not wanting anyone to perish, but everyone to come to repentance!"** This is divine mercy.

Secondly: God sends judgments upon people when their wicked acts take them *beyond* redeeming love. It is important to understand that there is a point of NO return where divine mercy is no longer available. It can be called the point of no return, the unpardonable sin or the close of probation (mercy). A person, city, nation and even earth itself can commit

the unpardonable sin! When this point is reached, destruction follows.

Consider this interesting verse from Revelation 16:5,6: **"Then I heard the angel in charge of the waters say: 'You are just in these judgments, you who are and who were, the Holy One, because you have so judged; for they have shed the blood of your saints and prophets, and you have given them blood to drink as they deserve.' "**

The context of this verse is found during the seven last plagues which are yet future. In this text, an angel has just poured out the third of the seven *last* plagues upon earth. More will be said about these horrible plagues later; but for now, it is important to notice that the angels, impartial observers of human conduct, declare God to be true and righteous for having punished humans in this manner! "This is divine justice," the angel proclaims. We ask, "How can this be?" The balance between divine mercy and divine justice is divine love.

This is a hard thing to understand at times. How can God be all merciful, all forgiving, and yet be able to execute punishment?

Review the reasons for judgments

Judgments are not pleasurable acts to God. The Bible calls them, "His strange work." See Isaiah 28:21. Why then does He send them? *God sends punishments upon people or nations for at least two reasons:*

First: He tries to bring evil-doers to repentance through warnings. But if the warnings go unheeded, He sends destruction to sober evil-doers. If they defiantly refuse to turn from their evil, a point is finally reached where mercy is no longer meaningful. In fact, extended mercy only allows evil, violence and suffering to needlessly continue.

Some argue that the God of the Old Testament is not the same God described in the New Testament. This is not true! Jesus is always the same, yesterday, today and tomorrow. (See Malachi 3:6 and Hebrews 1:10-12.) He is long-suffering, yet, as in the eviction of Satan and his angels from heaven (Ezekiel 28:14-17, Revelation 12:7,9), Jesus has clearly demonstrated that even in heaven there is a point where mercy becomes meaningless and justice must prevail.

As said earlier, Satan would have us misunderstand God's love. He would have us picture God as either a vengeful tyrant that zaps those who disagree with Him or a God that does not concern Himself with our sins. Either concept is wrong. The first concept is the foundation of the doctrine of an eternally burning hell. The second concept is the basis for amoral and decadent behavior. Those who understand that they will meet their Maker and have to give account for their deeds are careful with their actions! Jesus warned, "Do not be afraid of those who kill the body but cannot kill the soul. Rather, be afraid of the One who can destroy both soul and body in hell." (Matthew 10:28)

Secondly: God sends judgments upon earth to get man's attention. People forget God. They forget He owns the universe. We can forget that God means exactly what He says. Satan leads the world to distort or magnify God's patience incorrectly. His long-suffering is taken for granted and sinners become bold in their acts of sin (Ecclesiastes 8:11 and Zephaniah 1:12). We may forget or even deny that judgments and justice eventually come, but the Bible record is not obscure on this matter. The fate of Sodom and Gomorrah, Jericho, and the people who lived before the Flood prove that God rises up when violence and sin reaches an intolerable level.

The great tribulation begins with opening of fourth seal.

The final test of mankind involves a time of great tribulation. Jesus spoke to His disciples about the magnitude of these judgments at the end of the world. He said, "For there shall be great tribulation such as was not since the beginning of the world to this time, no, nor ever shall be." (Matthew 24:21) The time of trouble grows with intensity too. When the seven last plagues occur, it is tribulation beyond our comprehension. Daniel says, "...There will be a time of distress such as has not happened from the beginning of nations until then." (Daniel 12:1) Revelation clearly predicts and describes the coming events that comprise the great tribulation. We are not left to guess what the trouble is or why it comes. As you can now understand, global trouble begins when Jesus opens the fourth seal and sends the fourth living creature to earth with His four judgments: sword, famine, plague and wild beasts.

Earthquake marks the opening of the fourth seal

Revelation does not leave us in darkness wondering how the judgments of the great tribulation occur! The fourth seal will begin when the censer in Revelation 8:2-5 is thrown down. Then, the seven first plagues (the trumpets) will take place. The seven first plagues are followed by seven last plagues so there are 14 in all. Each plague has a special purpose and meaning.

A time of wrath

Before we examine the contents of the seven trumpets, we need to understand that the short time period between the fourth seal and the sixth seal is appropriately called, "a time of wrath." Remember Gabriel's visit with Daniel? Review what Gabriel said, **"...I am going to tell you what will happen later in the time of wrath, because the vision concerns the appointed time of the end."** (Daniel 8:19) On a later visit with Daniel, Gabriel told Daniel that Satan would appear in person upon earth! He said, **"The king (Satan) will do as he pleases. He will exalt and magnify himself above every god and will say unheard-of things against the God of gods. He will be successful until the time of wrath is completed, for what has been determined must take place."** (Daniel 11:36)

The time of wrath is mentioned twice in Daniel's vision and John saw it too! Compare Daniel's verses above with Revelation 15:1 in which John says, **"I saw in heaven another great and marvelous sign: seven angels with the seven last plagues - last, because with them God's wrath is completed."** In other words, God's wrath is completed or finished during the seven last plagues!

Two Phases of God's Coming Wrath

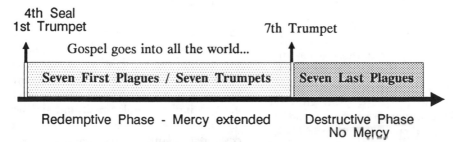

4th Seal
1st Trumpet   7th Trumpet

Gospel goes into all the world...

Seven First Plagues / Seven Trumpets   Seven Last Plagues

Redemptive Phase - Mercy extended   Destructive Phase
                                          No Mercy

Study the chart on the previous page and notice that the trumpets mark a time period of redemptive judgments because mercy is mixed with them. This underscores the purpose of the trumpets to awaken and arouse people to the sinfulness of their course, and to prepare them for the close of mercy.

Back to the Day of Atonement

The time period of the seven trumpets marks the judgment of the living. We have studied the importance of the Day of Atonement in the wilderness. The Day of Atonement was the most important day in the Jewish year for the 10th day of the seventh month marked the close of Israel's judgment for that year.

To warn the Jews of this final and most important day of the year, the Feast of Trumpets began nine days earlier—on the first day of the seventh month. (Leviticus 23:24) Each day, according to Jewish records, trumpets sounded throughout the camp announcing the closing of mercy. On the 10th day, the actual Day of Atonement, the trumpet sounded throughout the land (Leviticus 25:9) to signify that probation had ended.

The close of judgment was not a surprise in the wilderness and neither will it be a surprise to those living upon earth. In fact, Jesus is desirous that the close of probation come upon earth with ample warning so that all necessary preparations can be made by any desiring eternal life!

A clarion call

The Bible uses the trumpet as a symbol of warning or announcement. Notice the following references:

"Blow the trumpet in Zion; sound the alarm on my holy hill. Let all who live in the land tremble, for the day of the Lord is coming. It is close at hand." (Joel 2:1)

"I appointed watchmen over you and said 'Listen to the sound of the trumpet!'... I am bringing disaster on this people, the fruit of their schemes, because they have not listened to my words and have rejected my law." (Jeremiah 6:17,19)

"...If anyone hears the trumpet but does not take warning and the sword comes and takes his life, his blood will be on his own head." (Ezekiel 33:4)

When Jesus returns, He will use the trumpet to announce His appearing! **"...For the trumpet will sound, the dead will be raised imperishable, and we will all be changed."** (1 Corinthians 15:52)

Since ancient times, the trumpet has not only been an instrument of music, it has been a means of communication. For example, generals in battle directed their armies with trumpets. The trumpet was ideal because its penetrating sound could rise above the din of war or pierce the dark of night. Night watchmen were required to sound the trumpet if the enemy approached. Specific tunes were used to indicate assignment and signals. The apostle Paul says: **"...If the trumpet does not sound a clear call, who will** get ready for battle?" (1 Corinthians 14:8).

So it will be. The sounding of the seven trumpets will be a clarion call. The seven trumpets of Revelation are symbols of warning or announcement. Their purpose is to awaken the world with the fact that Jesus is about to appear. Their message is, "Get ready! Get ready! Get ready!" Since the trumpet is the loudest of all musical instruments and the number seven is usually considered to be a full or comprehensive number, these trumpets have global application. After all, God wants to awaken and arouse all people of earth that Jesus is coming back to earth to gather up those whose names are written in the book of life!

What occurs as each trumpet sounds?

Notice the events that will occur as each of the seven trumpets sound:

1. John saw a meteoric shower of burning hail mixed with blood, probably of men and beasts. A third of the earth, trees, and all the green grass was burned up. (Revelation 8:7)
2. John saw a rock as big as a mountain strike the sea. A third of the sea turns to blood, a third of the sea creatures die, and a third of the ships are destroyed. (Revelation 8:8,9)
3. A flaming star impacts a continent. A third of the rivers and the springs of waters turn

bitter, and many people die from the waters. The name of this plague is "Wormwood" or bitterness. (Revelation 8:10,11)
4. John saw one third of the sun, moon and stars struck, and they turn dark. A third of the day will be without light as well as a third of the night. (Revelation 8:12)
5. The angel king of the bottomless pit is let out. He brings a terrible affliction for five months upon those who are rebelling against God. The torment is so bad that **"men will seek death, but will not find it; they will long to die, but death will elude them."** (Revelation 9:1-12)
6. Satan conducts a great war to conquer the world. Four angels hold back the war until the very hour, day, month and year arrive. A third of those who fight in the war will die. The number of troops will be myriads (200,000,000 NIV). (Revelation 9:13-19)
7. Jesus concludes His special work in the heavenly sanctuary. There is an earthquake, lightning, rumblings, peals of thunder, and a great hailstorm. (Revelation 11:15-19)

The fourth seal opens and the first trumpet sounds

Jesus opens the fourth seal and initiates the great tribulation upon the world by sounding the first trumpet. These seven warning plagues fall in response to our unrestrained evil and hardness of heart. " Why has the Lord decreed such a

great disaster against us? What wrong
have we done? What sin have we
committed against the Lord our
God?... '(Your) houses are full of
deceit; (you) have become rich and
powerful and have grown fat and sleek.
(Your) evil deeds have no limit.' "
(Jeremiah 16:10; 5:27,28)

Thus, the opening of the fourth seal
will attract the attention of everyone
on earth that God's wrath has broken
out upon earth. These trumpet plagues
are not man-made; rather, these will
be rightly called, "Acts of God" and
will be correctly recognized as such.
As in the days of Pharaoh, God says
the world will know, "I am the Lord
that do these things." (Exodus 7:5)

Summary

From the Bible we have seen that Jesus
has sent judgments upon the world in
times past. Judgments from heaven
come with warning. Jesus uses
judgments to awaken and arouse
people with the sinfulness of their
course. His judgments can be
redemptive or punitive. They can be
a means of salvation or a means of
destruction.

The opening of the fourth seal marks
the beginning of the tribulation that is
coming upon the earth. At the close
of mercy, an even greater tribulation
comes upon the earth in the form of
seven last plagues! (Daniel 12:1)

Our next chapter will closely investigate
each of the seven trumpets. Their
effects will be worldwide. The

awakening will be unlike anything ever
seen on earth. The people of earth are
about to be suddenly awakened to hear
a very sobering message! The reader
should also realize that the devil is
preparing to use these events to his
advantage. It's going to be a most
interesting time.

Notes

Chapter 16

The Seven Trumpets Part II

Review

The previous chapter surveyed the great tribulation that marks the end of the world. Daniel 8 and 11 refer to this time-period as "a time of wrath." We will understand the importance of this term more fully in this lesson.

In effect, the trumpets are designed to arrest the attention of the world so that everyone can hear the gospel. What is called "gospel" today is only a portion of the full gospel! Jesus says when everyone has heard the gospel of the kingdom, "then the end will come." (Matthew 24:14) The full gospel story hasn't been told yet because the everlasting gospel contains certain elements that accompany the revelation of Jesus! The full gospel contains an explanation of the trumpets, the seals, the seven last plagues and the four beasts of Revelation. Because truth is constantly unfolding, the gospel continues to develop in size and value even though the principles of the gospel remain unchanged. Salvation has always and shall always come by faith in God. Love to God and fellowman is the foundation of the gospel and the transformation of every

life under the influence of the Holy Spirit is proof that God can restore His image in fallen man.

John clearly saw that the remnant would have to give the gospel *again* to the world! (Revelation 10:8-11.) The reason the gospel must go again throughout the world is that in its final form, the gospel contains a special message that is not applicable at any other time in earth's history. This timely message not only explains the purpose of the trumpets, it contains a call to worship the living God. The call to worship God consists of a very important test that affects the whole world! The final gospel will separate those who really love God from those who hate the light of truth. Those who are now living up to all the light they have will rejoice and move forward with the greater light of the full gospel that is soon to light up every corner of the world!

Seven trumpets begin

Carefully read the following verses from Revelation:

"And I saw the seven angels who stand before God, and to them were given seven trumpets. Another angel, who had a golden censer, came and stood at the altar. He was given much incense to offer, with the prayers of all the saints,

on the golden altar before the throne. The smoke of the incense, together with the prayers of the saints, went up before God from the angel's hand. Then the angel took the censer, filled it with fire from the altar, and hurled it on the earth; and there came peals of thunder, rumblings, flashes of lightning and an earthquake. Then the seven angels who had the seven trumpets prepared to sound them." (Revelation 8:2-6)

A number of important things stand out in these verses. We will study two of them. First, observe the chronological sequence. Notice that the seven angels who serve God are given seven trumpets (compare with Revelation 1:20); THEN the angel at the golden altar (of incense) hurls down a censer; THEN there is thunder, rumblings, lightning and an earthquake on earth; and THEN the seven angels prepare to sound their trumpets.

Secondly, notice that the angel at the altar places much incense on the altar BEFORE the trumpets sound.

What do these things mean?

As pointed out in the previous chapter, the fourth seal and the trumpets commence together. The primary purpose of the fourth seal is to reveal the authority of Jesus. The revelation of His authority exposes our accountability to His authority. The primary purpose of the seven trumpets is to awaken and arouse the world so people will listen to the everlasting gospel. Every religious system and

church has its own authority and center for doctrine. For this reason, Baptists don't listen to Methodists, and Jehovah Witnesses don't pay any attention to Mormons. But Jesus is about to overrule all religious processes. The throwing down of the censer and the commotion that follows on earth simultaneously marks the beginning of the trumpet sequence and the end of an atonement process in heaven. This will quickly get people's attention and who will have a full explanation of these things? One group of people: the 144,000. More will be said about them in the next chapter.

There is an important subject that needs to be explained. When the censer of Revelation 8:2-5 is thrown down, this act symbolizes the end of God's patience with the nations (not the people) of the world.

In ancient times, God's patience with the existence of sin was expressed through the "daily or continual" offering. Each morning and evening, a sacrifice was offered on the altar of burnt offering. This sacrifice was offered on behalf of the *nation* of Israel and not for any particular individual. In other words, this sacrifice was a corporate sacrifice. (See Numbers 15:22-31 and Leviticus 4 for a clear distinction between corporate and individual sacrifices.)

In Israel's day, the morning and evening sacrifices provided corporate atonement on a continual or daily basis. This atonement was necessary so that Israel could dwell in God's consuming presence. God requires full atonement for every sin! Without atonement morning and evening, the nation of Israel could not exist! From heaven, Jesus has been interceding on behalf of the world. A guilty world has been sheltered from the righteous justice of Almighty God through the daily or continual merits of Jesus' intercession. Just before the seven trumpets begin, the censer in heaven is thrown down indicating the sudden end of corporate intercession. A sinful and defiled world will suddenly and unexpectedly reap the deserving wrath of God. As in the days of Noah, earth in a corporate sense, will reach a point of no return. When that point is fully reached, the fourth seal is opened, and the earthquake follows. Then, the trumpets commence, and the great tribulation begins.

The first four trumpets are warning judgments sent to the world saying, "Get ready, get ready. Prepare to meet your Maker." The last three trumpets are curses that God sends upon specific people. The one point to keep in mind is that during the trumpets, God's hand is stretched out to save those who want to be saved.

Much incense

The angel at heaven's altar was given much incense to put on the altar before the seven trumpets sound. The fragrance of the incense along with the prayers of the saints goes up before God. What does this symbolize? In the wilderness sanctuary, a special incense was offered before the Lord each morning and evening as the daily sacrifice was being applied. (Exodus 30:7,8,37) On the Day of Atonement, the high priest carried a censer full of burning coals with two handfuls of this incense into the Most Holy Place. Jesus said, **"He (the high priest) is to put the incense on the fire before the Lord, and the smoke of the incense will conceal the atonement cover above the Testimony (the mercy seat on top of the ark), so that he will not die."** (Leviticus 16:13) That which separated the high priest from the consuming glory of God was only a thin veil of smoke!

From Revelation 8:5 we conclude that the censer is thrown down because its usefulness is finished. The daily atonement conducted with this censer is ended. Now, extra incense is added to the fire on the altar to sustain the atonement period a little longer than usual. This is necessary for the judgment

The 1,260 Day Ministry of the 144,000

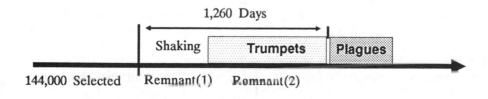

of the living is about to take place. The prayers of the saints come up before the Lord with the fragrance of the incense because the saints are knowledgeable, ready and prepared for the hour of trial that is about to occur. In other words, there will be a body of people on earth anticipating the trumpets before they take place. They know that time for the judgment day of God has come. And, appropriately, the first people to be judged during the trumpets will be those who have had an opportunity to know and prepare for these things! (1 Peter 4:17)

This point brings up the issue of the 144,000 which will be studied later. For now, study the diagram on the previous page and see how the 144,000 and their support group (hereafter called *remnant(1)*) are prepared to go throughout the world during the time period of the seven trumpets to gather in the remaining children of God (hereafter called *remnant(2)*) which are in Babylon.

The first three trumpets

"The first angel sounded his trumpet, and there came hail and fire mixed with blood, and it was hurled down upon the earth. A third of the earth was burned up, a third of the trees were burned up, and all the green grass was burned up. The second angel sounded his trumpet, and something like a huge mountain, all ablaze, was thrown into the sea. A third of the sea turned into blood, a third of the living creatures in the sea died, and a third of the ships were destroyed. The third angel sounded his trumpet, and a great star, blazing like a torch, fell from the sky on a third of the rivers and on the springs of water. The name of the star is Wormwood. A third of the waters turned bitter, and many people died from the waters that had become bitter." (Revelation 8:7-11)

The first three trumpets are caused by meteors and asteroids. God is going to shake the heavens! It is quite possible for these events to commence during the latter part of 1994. The threatening presence of meteors and asteroids has been known for many years. Millions of chunks of cosmic debris travel through space. In fact, the rings about the planet Saturn are rings of asteroids. An asteroid is a piece of cosmic debris that can range in size from a golf ball to several miles in diameter.

At the annual meeting of the American Geophysical Union in December, 1989, Dr. Clark Chapman of the Planetary Science Institute in Tucson, Arizona, and Dr. David Morrison, chief of the space science division at NASA's Ames Research Center in Mountain View, California, shocked their audience of 4,000 scientists by suggesting that, "the risk of death from a wandering asteroid from outer space is somewhat greater than the risk of an individual American dying in an airplane crash." Their calculations are based on the fact that more than 100 major meteors have recently impacted the surface of the moon. In March of 1989, a half-mile wide asteroid came within 500,000 miles of earth. If it had hit the earth, astronomers said, "it would have crashed with enough violence to destroy a good-sized country."

John's description of the first trumpet is a hail-storm, not of ice, but of fire! This fire burns up a third of the land and trees and all the green grass. Because the next two trumpets are caused by large meteors, this author believes the first trumpet is caused by a large amount of cosmic debris such as baseball-size meteors which enter our atmosphere and impact the earth thus causing a large number of fires all around the world. Men will be powerless to stop the fires because there are so many and they are so scattered. The death and destruction described in this trumpet cannot be stopped.

When the second angel sounds his trumpet, John saw a large meteor, perhaps a mile or two in diameter, hit the sea. The effect is immediate. The resulting tidal wave destroys a third of the ships on the ocean — not to mention seaports! The intense heat of the meteor vaporizes the oxygen in the water and destroys a third of the marine life in the area. Perhaps the "blood" John saw is the red tide or red algae that thrives in deoxygenated water.

When the third angel sounds his trumpet, a large meteor hits a continent or land mass. Perhaps an instantaneous series of groundwaves and earthquakes follow to redistribute tectonic forces beneath the surface of the earth. The "shaking" of the ground, the movement of hugh tectonic plates collapses

thousands of water wells that provide cities with drinking water. What drinking water is available would likely be contaminated by sewage, refuse and toxic waste that has been buried in the ground. Many people will die from drinking the water.

Note that each of the first three trumpets affects 1/3 of whatever they fall upon. If we add together the 1/3 of each trumpet, this could mean that 3/3 or all of the earth will be affected by these trumpets. This would be consistent with the idea that all the world must be awakened to hear the gospel message. We don't know just how earth was represented to John in this vision. Maybe 1/3 of the area he was viewing was affected or perhaps, 1/3 of the total earth will be affected. Either way, the result of the first three trumpets is awful.

The student may be somewhat skeptical of the first three trumpets occurring as a result of meteorites. Such skepticism is respected. For further study on this subject, the reader should obtain a copy of the June, 1989 issue of *National Geographic Magazine*. In this edition, *National Geographic* features an article on the subject of "Extinctions." The hypothesis of this article is that mass extinctions occurred in the distant past due to large meteors impacting the earth. (The face of the moon clearly reveals a history of many large meteoric impacts.) During the past 13 years, scientists have become quite confident that large meteors have impacted the earth in the past and they speculate that dinosaurs became extinct because of them. What is so ironic is that while scientists are studying the past, the Bible predicts mass extinctions in the **future** in this very same fashion!

Rick Gore, the author of the *National Geographic* article wrote, "Most scientists now concur that at least one great extraterrestrial object struck the planet around the time the dinosaurs died out.... The idea that large objects could strike our planet and cause mass extinctions was considered radical until just a decade ago. Then a team of researchers at the University of California found high levels of iridium—a metal rare on earth but common in meteorites—in a thin layer of clay laid down about the time dinosaurs became extinct. Their conclusion—that an asteroid hit earth 66 million years ago, wreaking environmental havoc—shocked the scientific world. Further analysis of the iridium layer has supported the impact, although scientists are widely divided over its effects." Ibid., page 665, 666.

There is no question that very large meteors have impacted this planet in the past. A number of craters clearly indicate such impacts. (The largest in North America is in Manson, Iowa. It's about 18 miles wide.) What is so interesting about the scientific pursuit of this idea is that scientists have created computer models of what could happen if a large meteor hit the sea or hit the land. See if you notice any parallels from *National Geographic* and John's description in Revelation: "A huge plume would push the atmosphere aside.... Winds of hundreds of kilometers an hour would sweep the planet for hours, drying trees like a giant hair dryer. Two-thousand degree rock vapor would spread rapidly. It would condense to white hot grains that could have started additional fires.... Volcanoes erupt, tsunamis crash into the continents. The sky grows dark for months, perhaps years... (water sources) become anoxic or toxic... creatures die." Ibid., page 673.

The fourth trumpet

"The fourth angel sounded his trumpet, and a third of the sun was struck, a third of the moon, and a third of the stars, so that a third of them turned dark. A third of the day was without light, and also a third of the night." (Revelation 8:12)

This trumpet obviously marks a phenomenal event in the heavens. Just how this is done, John doesn't say. Following the scenario in *National Geographic* the darkening of the sun, moon and stars could come as a result of the previous three trumpets. Even more likely would be a chain of enormous volcano eruptions in response to the shift in tectonic plates caused by the third trumpet. With the sun darkened, vegetation would become stunted. Food crops which were destroyed as a result of the fires in the first trumpet, could not recover. The prospects of life on earth after the first four trumpets will be questionable. And this is God's primary purpose. He wants to see who will trust in Him even though the heavens fall!

As the people of earth witness these terribly awesome things, they will be desperate about survival. In their suffering, they will seek the meaning of these events. Clearly, these calamities are "acts of God." Regardless of race, creed, color or religious belief, each person will be alarmed and interested. As people begin to hear about the first four trumpets of Revelation, the truthfulness and meaning of Revelation's story will quickly blossom. Thus, God will reach the minds of people in every nation, kindred, tongue and people. Now people will listen to a prophetic explanation of what these events are all about. In short, millions of people all over the world will be anxious to hear the everlasting gospel!

Now, three curses

As if the asteroids weren't bad enough, the next three trumpets are even more painful. John says, **"As I watched, I heard an eagle that was flying in midair call out in a loud voice: 'Woe! Woe! Woe to the inhabitants of the earth, because of the trumpet blasts about to be sounded by the other three angels!' "** (Revelation 8:13) This eagle is the fourth living creature that John saw earlier. (Revelation 4:7) The message from this living creature says that the next three trumpets are curses or woes. That is, they directly fall upon certain people and not the physical elements of earth.

Take a close look at the fifth trumpet

The first woe is the fifth trumpet. This trumpet marks the physical appearance of Satan who will claim to be God. He is the "angel king" of the Abyss. Notice John's description:

"The fifth angel sounded his trumpet, and I saw a star that had fallen from the sky to the earth. The star was given the key to the shaft of the Abyss. When he opened the Abyss, smoke rose from it like the smoke from a gigantic furnace. The sun and sky were darkened by the smoke from the Abyss. And out of the smoke locusts came down upon the earth and were given power like that of scorpions of the earth. They were told not to harm the grass of the earth or any plant or tree, but only those people who did not have the seal of God on their foreheads. They were not given power to kill them, but only to torture them for five months. And the agony they suffered was like that of the sting of a scorpion when it strikes a man. During those days men will seek death, but will not find it; they will long to die, but death will elude them. The locusts looked like horses prepared for battle. On their heads they wore something like crowns of gold, and their faces resembled human faces. Their hair was like women's hair, and their teeth were like lions' teeth. They had breastplates like breastplates of iron, and the sound of their wings was like the thundering of many horses and chariots rushing into battle. They had tails and stings like scorpions, and in their tails they had power to torment people for five months. They had as

king over them the angel of the Abyss, whose name in Hebrew is Abaddon, and in Greek, Apollyon. The first woe is past; two other woes are yet to come." (Revelation 9:1-12)

The language of this trumpet is generally analogous. John best describes the things he saw with analogies of his own or with analogies used by Old Testament writers. Actually, the meaning of this trumpet is better understood when it is compared to Joel 2, for Joel saw a very similar scene. The difference between Joel and John is that John saw the coming of Satan (the angel king from the Abyss) while Joel saw the coming of the Lord! Notice Joel's remarks:

"Blow the trumpet in Zion; sound the alarm on my holy hill. Let all who live in the land tremble, for the day of the LORD is coming. It is close at hand— a day of darkness and gloom, a day of clouds and blackness. Like dawn spreading across the mountains a large and mighty army comes, such as never was of old nor ever will be in ages to come. Before them fire devours, behind them a flame blazes. Before them the land is like the garden of Eden, behind them, a desert waste— nothing escapes them. They have the appearance of horses; they gallop along like cavalry. With a noise like that of chariots they leap over the mountaintops, like a crackling fire consuming stubble, like a mighty army drawn up for battle. At the sight of them, nations are in anguish; every face turns pale. They charge like

warriors; they scale walls like soldiers. They all march in line, not swerving from their course. They do not jostle each other; each marches straight ahead. They plunge through defenses without breaking ranks. They rush upon the city; they run along the wall. They climb into the houses; like thieves they enter through the windows. Before them the earth shakes, the sky trembles, the sun and moon are darkened, and the stars no longer shine. The LORD thunders at the head of his army; his forces are beyond number, and mighty are those who obey his command. The day of the LORD is great; it is dreadful. Who can endure it?" (Joel 2:1-11)

Compare their views

- Joel saw a great army of locusts that looked like horses. John saw the same.

- Joel saw the sun and moon darkened. John saw the same.

- Joel marveled at the power of the army. John marveled at the same.

- Joel saw the Lord at the head of His army. John saw the angel king of the Abyss at the head of his army.

Two important connecting points are presented regarding the appearing of Satan:

1. Satan is let out of the Abyss (spirit world) in Revelation 9 and is returned to the Abyss in Revelation 20. "And I saw an angel coming

down out of heaven, having the key to the Abyss and holding in his hand a great chain. He seized the dragon, that ancient serpent, who is the devil, or Satan, and bound him for a thousand years. *He threw him into the Abyss and locked and sealed it over him...."* (Revelation 20:1-3)

2. From the fifth trumpet we learn that Satan is allowed to come up out of the Abyss and physically appear upon earth during the fifth trumpet. What will he do after he appears? **"They were told not to harm the grass of the earth or any plant or tree, but only those people who did not have the seal of God on their foreheads. They were not given power to kill them, but only to torture them for five months...."** (Revelation 9:4,5) It is interesting to note from these verses that Satan and his angels cannot harm the physical things of earth that have been already hurt during the first trumpet.

Why do Satan and his angels torment the wicked and not the saints? To make the world violently angry with the Two Witnesses and their followers!

Two Witnesses have great power

We will study the Two Witnesses in our next chapter. For now, we need only to understand that they are God's representatives upon earth during the trumpets. They have great powers and the earth is afraid of them! Notice what John says about them, **"If anyone tries to harm them, fire comes from their mouths and devours their enemies. This is how anyone who wants to harm them must die. These men have power to shut up the sky so that it will not rain during the time they are prophesying; and they have power to turn the waters into blood and to strike the earth with every kind of plague as often as they want."** (Revelation 11:5,6)

So, Satan, after appearing upon earth torments the wicked beyond what the Two Witnesses have already done and the devil lays the blame upon God's representatives. Thus, the world becomes even more *enraged* with the Two Witnesses and their followers and ultimately concludes that they must be destroyed.

Who is the angel king, the beast from the Abyss?

Only once in Revelation's story does an "angel king" come out of the Abyss. Twice in Revelation, a "beast" ascends out of the Abyss. Since Revelation 12:9 clearly tells us that the dragon-like beast is a fallen angel called Satan, we can safely say the "angel king" that ascends from the Abyss in Revelation 9 is the devil. After all, the devil is a fallen star. When we compare Joel's account of the second coming with the appearing of the angel king from the Abyss, we can be safe in concluding that Satan is the angel king.

What does the beast from the Abyss do? Notice the following verses: **"Now** when they (the Two Witnesses) have finished their testimony, *the beast that comes up from the Abyss* will attack them, and overpower and kill them." (Revelation 11:7)

"The beast which you saw... will come up out of the Abyss and go to his destruction. The inhabitants of the earth whose names have not been written in the book of life from the creation of the world will be astonished when they see the beast...." (Revelation 17:8)

When Satan appears on earth claiming to be God, the world will be astonished. He will almost deceive the entire world with his miracles and great supernatural powers. Satan will eventually "kill" the effectiveness of God's representatives by appearing to be so powerful and so much greater than those representing God's cause. Each person will have to make a very hard decision: follow the teachings of the Jesus and receive the wrath of Satan or obey the commands of Satan (claiming to be God) and receive the wrath of God.

Revelation 17:8 clearly says that those whose names *are not* written in the book of life will be astonished at the appearing of Satan. But the saints will be expecting him. After all, the fifth trumpet clearly explains when he appears. We'll study Satan's appearing and work more closely in a later lesson. For now, consider that he physically appears during the fifth trumpet.

A close look at the sixth trumpet

The second woe is a great war. John says, "The sixth angel sounded his trumpet, and I heard a voice coming from the horns of the golden altar that is before God. It said to the sixth angel who had the trumpet, 'Release the four angels who are bound at the great river Euphrates.' And the four angels who had been kept ready for this very hour and day and month and year were released to kill a third of mankind. The number of the mounted troops was two hundred million. I heard their number. The horses and riders I saw in my vision looked like this: Their breastplates were fiery red, dark blue, and yellow as sulfur. The heads of the horses resembled the heads of lions, and out of their mouths came fire, smoke and sulfur. A third of mankind was killed by the three plagues of fire, smoke and sulfur that came out of their mouths. The power of the horses was in their mouths and in their tails; for their tails were like snakes, having heads with which they inflict injury. The rest of mankind that were not killed by these plagues still did not repent of the work of their hands; they did not stop worshiping demons, and idols of gold, silver, bronze, stone and wood—idols that cannot see or hear or walk. Nor did they repent of their murders, their magic arts, their sexual immorality or their thefts. The second woe has passed; the third woe is coming soon." (Revelation 9:13-21, 11:14)

This trumpet describes a great war into which Satan leads his deceived followers. Satan sets out to establish a one-world government and he succeeds for a short time. Satan will overcome all political opposition and crush those who obey the commandments of God. He, Satan, claiming to be God, will ultimately sit on a throne as King over the kings of earth, and Lord of lords over the religious systems of earth. He will rule the world through deception and force. Daniel saw the conclusion of this great war in his vision (Daniel 11:21-45). The outcome is that Satan temporarily wins. The war under the sixth trumpet, like all wars, forces everyone to take sides. At the close of the sixth trumpet, the whole world will stand in two camps: those obeying Satan, and those obeying Jesus!

A look at the final trumpet

Now comes the close of salvation. Everyone has made his decision. John says, **"The seventh angel sounded his trumpet, and there were loud voices in heaven, which said: 'The kingdom of the world has become the kingdom of our Lord and of his Christ, and he will reign for ever and ever.' And the twenty-four elders, who were seated on their thrones before God, fell on their faces and worshiped God, saying: 'We give thanks to you, Lord God Almighty, the One who is and who was, because you have taken your great power and have begun to reign. The nations were angry; and your wrath has come. The time has come for judging the dead, and for rewarding your servants the prophets and your saints and those who reverence your name, both small and great— and for**

destroying those who destroy the earth.' Then God's temple in heaven was opened, and within his temple was seen the ark of his covenant. And there came flashes of lightning, rumblings, peals of thunder, an earthquake and a great hailstorm." (Revelation 11:15-19)

This trumpet announces the close of salvation. God's mercy has been extended as long as possible. Every person has made his decision for or against the gospel. Those who side with Satan will receive the mark of Satan—a mark necessary to conduct business, a physical permit to buy and sell! Those who side with the gospel appear frail, weak and helpless against the devil and his forces. The saints can't buy or sell. All forms of life-support are cut off. Satan will see that every means of earthly survival is removed from them. In fact, during the sixth plague (that is, the 13th event of all 14 plagues) the devil will lead the world in a united effort to exterminate the saints with a universal death decree.

But don't think the story of persecution is one sided. It is a terrible thing to fall into the hands of the living God. Jesus will deal with the devil and his followers. He will break apart the consolidated powers of Satan by sending seven last plagues upon them. Whereas the first two woes were single events, the last woe contains the seven last plagues. The awful and terrible plagues containing the full fury of God's wrath will fall upon all who receive the number or the name of the devil.

Trumpets parallel seven last plagues

There are some obvious comparisons between the trumpets and the plagues. Notice:

Seven trumpets

1. Hail, fire, and blood upon 1/3 of earth
2. One third of the sea turns to blood
3. One third of the drinking water becomes bitter
4. Sun, moon and stars affected (1/3 of heaven struck)
5. Satan appears bringing affliction on the wicked
6. Great War — millions killed
7. Hailstorm, earthquake

Seven last plagues

1. Terrible sores upon all rebelling against God
2. Sea turns to blood — everything in it dies
3. Drinking water and rivers turn to blood
4. Sun scorches people with intense heat
5. Great affliction on the government of Antichrist
6. Final war upon saints — Armageddon
7. Great hailstorm, earthquake and final destruction of earth

The parallel is important in this respect. The trumpets (seven first plagues) are samples of what the seven last plagues will be. The essential difference between these two groups of plagues is God's mercy. During the trumpets, there is mercy because a person can turn from their rebellion against God and be saved. During the seven last plagues, there is no mercy. The wrath of God will fall full force upon the wicked.

Those that keep the commandments of God and remain faithful (faithful means faith-full) to Jesus during the great tribulation will live by this precious promise: **"He who dwells in the shelter of the Most High will rest in the shadow of the Almighty. I will say of the Lord, 'He is my refuge and my fortress, my God, in whom I trust.' Surely he will save you from the fowler's snare and from the deadly pestilence. He will cover you with his feathers, and under his wings you will find refuge; his faithfulness will be your shield and rampart. You will not fear the terror of night, nor the arrow that flies by day, nor the pestilence that stalks in the darkness, nor the plague that destroys at midday. A thousand may fall at your side, ten thousand at your right hand, but it will not come near you. You will only observe with your eyes and see the punishment of the wicked. If you make the Most High your dwelling— even the LORD, who is my refuge— then no harm will befall you, no disaster will come near your tent."** (Psalm 91:1-10)

Summary

The seven trumpets will suddenly and unexpectedly come upon most of the people living upon earth. The meteoric impacts will arrest the world's attention so that all may hear the everlasting gospel. Outside the context of such dramatic events, the gospel has little momentum among earth's 5.4 billion people. So, the primary purpose of the trumpets is the revelation of true salvation. Revelation's story will come into sharp focus when the trumpets begin because people all over the world will seriously investigate the things taking place right before their eyes! Thus, the full gospel will go the ends of the earth in a very short time period.

One final point, the trumpets are "samples" of the wrath of God. The seven trumpets are followed by seven last plagues that are much more destructive. The severity of the trumpets will cause every human being to carefully consider the warning message contained in the everlasting gospel. This warning will be studied later.

Notes

Notes

Chapter 17

The 144,000 and Two Witnesses

The purpose of the trumpets has been examined. Jesus will awaken and arouse all the world with spectacular events from the heavens to draw attention to the gospel story so that it can go to every nation, kindred and tongue in a short period of time. Notice the words of Jesus, **"And this gospel of the kingdom will be preached in the whole world as a testimony to all nations, and then the end will come."** (Matthew 24:14)

The phrase "as a testimony to all nations" in the NIV is translated "for a witness unto all nations" in the KJV. The point is that the gospel is a witness or a testimony that either saves or condemns! Think about this. The preaching of the gospel offers salvation to those who receive it and condemns those who reject it. Jesus told Nicodemus, **"Whoever believes in him (the Son) is not condemned, but whoever does not believe stands condemned already because he has not believed in the name of God's one and only Son. This is the verdict: Light has come into the world, but men loved darkness instead of light because their deeds were evil."** (John 3:18,19)

The gospel of Jesus is polemical. The word polemical means "opposite" or "poles apart." Jesus said, **"Do not suppose that I have come to bring peace to the earth. I did not come to bring peace, but a sword."** (Matthew 10:34) The power and clarity of the gospel during the time period of the trumpets will be greater than anything the world has ever witnessed. John says the entire world will be enlightened with the full gospel message. This message exposes the false or fallen teachings of Babylon. John saw a messenger from heaven bearing a powerful message. He says, **"After this I saw another angel coming down from heaven. He had great authority, and the earth was illuminated by his splendor. With a mighty voice he shouted: Fallen! Fallen is Babylon the Great!..."** (Revelation 18:1,2)

A trumpet in one ear, the gospel in the other

Who is worthy to give the full gospel message during the trumpets? This is a very important question. The answer, like most answers from Revelation, requires some background information. Revelation identifies a very special group of people who will present the plan of salvation to every nation, kindred, tongue and people during earth's final hours.

Wonderment about the 144,000 has occurred ever since John wrote about them. Who are the 144,000? What do they do? Why are they so special in Revelation's story? Some denominations believe the 144,000 are the only ones saved at the second coming. Others believe the 144,000 are converted Jews that proclaim the gospel to all the world during the tribulation before Jesus comes. Some people believe the number 144,000 is symbolic and therefore, not a literal count or number of people but actually a number that represents the people that will be redeemed.

The Bible answers all these questions after some careful investigation. From Revelation we learn seven important points concerning the 144,000. They are:

Point 1

The 144,000 are selected and sealed *prior* to the sounding of the seven trumpets and the opening of the fourth seal. **"After this I saw four angels standing at the four corners of the earth, holding back the four winds of the earth to prevent any wind from blowing on the land or on the sea or on any tree. Then I saw another angel coming up from the east, having the seal of the living God. He called out in a loud voice to the four angels who had been given power to harm the land and the sea: 'Do not harm the land or the sea or the trees until we put a seal on the foreheads of the servants of our God.' Then I heard the number**

of those who were sealed: 144,000 from all the tribes of Israel." (Revelation 7:1-4) The four winds that are held back until the 144,000 are ready are the four terrible judgments contained in the fourth seal; sword, famine, plague and wild beasts. In other words, Jesus delays the opening of the fourth seal until the development and selection of the 144,000 is completed. Then the angels having the seven trumpets begin their work. Notice that the first four angels of the seven trumpets harm the physical elements of earth. Specifically, the first two angels have the power to harm the land, trees and sea! (Revelation 8:7,8)

Point 2

The 144,000 come from each of the 12 tribes of Israel. Are these literal tribes in Israel today? No. We have already concluded that literal Israel failed at the end of the 490 year probationary period and the gospel was given to the Christians. The Jews are not going to receive the gospel commission during a future period of seven years, for the 70th week of Daniel 9 occurred between A.D. 27 and A.D. 33. Even more, the gospel commission was taken from the Christian faith and passed on to the Protestants in 1798. We also know that a true remnant of Israel remains, that is, true Israel belongs to Christ. Paul wrote, **"If you belong to Christ, then you are Abraham's seed, and heirs according to the promise."** (Galatians 3:29) This is why Paul says, **"For there is no difference between Jew and Gentile—the same Lord is Lord of all and richly blesses all who call on him."**

(Romans 10:12) And lastly, **"There is neither Jew nor Greek, slave nor free, male nor female, for you are all one in Christ Jesus."** (Galatians 3:28)

The origin and identity of the 144,000 have caused much discussion through the years. Some religious groups are certain the 144,000 come from their denomination since they claim to possess all of God's "truth." A compelling point might be reached on the identity of the 144,000 by drawing a comparison from the book of Numbers. When Israel was about to cross over into the Promised Land, a census was taken of men 20 years and older and the tribes totaled approximately 603,000 men. (See Numbers 2.) Israel failed to enter the Promised Land at that time due to the failure of the spies to give an encouraging report, so 38 years later, when Israel prepared to enter the Promised Land, a census was taken again. This time the number of men 20 years and older came to approximately 624,000. The second census included the Levites who were not counted in the earlier census. (See Numbers 26.)

In Revelation's story, a definite parallel exists. Before the people of God enter the heavenly Promised Land, God assures the saints that 12,000 from each tribe will be selected as firstfruits or choice specimens! This means that each of the 12 groups of people will have 12,000 glorious representatives!

The beauty of this process is that when the Israel of God is redeemed at the second coming, it will be a numberless multitude! (Revelation 7:9) The number of people that make up spiritual Israel will be like the sands of the sea. But the people who gather the great multitude together during the time-period of the trumpets will be the 144,000.

Who constitutes the true Israel that shall be saved? The Apostle Paul says, **"A man is a Jew if he is one inwardly.... For it is not those who hear the law who are righteous in God's sight, but it is those who obey the law who will be declared righteous."** (Romans 2:29,13) Paul's identity of who God's "chosen people" are clearly harmonizes with John's remarks on the identity of the saints. He says, **"...they have the testimony of Jesus and obey the commandments of God,"** and **"...the saints remain faithful to Jesus."** (Revelation 12:17; 14:12)

The word "Jew" is normally interpreted today as meaning a race or nation of people. The actual origin and meaning of the word refers to "those chosen or selected." James, the author of the New Testament book bearing his name, understood the literal meaning of "those chosen or selected." His book is expressly addressed to early Christians suffering from persecution by saying, **"...to the twelve tribes scattered among the nations...."** (James 1:1) James was not referring to the Jewish race, but to those early Christians who had fled because of persecution. The concept of being chosen is clearly seen in Peter's epistle too. He says, **"To God's elect, strangers in the world, scattered throughout... who have been chosen**

according to the foreknowledge of God the Father...." (1 Peter 1:1,2)

Note: Following the ascension of Jesus, the Jews and Romans severely persecuted the followers of Christ. (Historians believe eight of the 12 apostles were either crucified or beaten to death.) After Jerusalem was destroyed in A.D. 70, persecution of the Christians continued three more centuries, for the Romans intensely hated the Christians because they preached a divisive doctrine. They refused to worship the Emperor. As a result of persecution, Christians were scattered all over the world. When James and Peter penned their epistles, they clearly addressed them to their brothers who were suffering persecution.

Point 3

What is the "Christian" significance of the 12 tribes? As each of Jacob's 12 sons were different and unique, each of the 12 tribes represents a unique character and experience in knowing, loving and serving God. See Genesis 49. Jesus has apparently created 12 varieties of people and He appreciates the unique make-up of each type person. It is reasonable to say that upon receiving Jesus as our personal Savior, we are joined to one of the 12 tribes of Israel by our personality type and experience in the Lord.

Point 4

John describes the characters of the 144,000, **"These are those who did not defile themselves with women, for they kept themselves pure. They follow the Lamb wherever he goes. They were purchased from among men and offered as firstfruits to God and to the Lamb. No lie was found in their mouths; they are blameless."** (Revelation 14:4,5)

Comments on purity

What a statement! **"They kept themselves pure.... No lie was found in their mouths; they are blameless."** In the past, some popular TV evangelists have caused some embarrassment among Christians due to impropriety with women. Men claiming to be "servants of God" have been caught in slavery to Satan. Perhaps the greatest sin in these cases is that these men did not come forward to confess their sins until "caught." One wonders how sincere a confession can be after being "caught in the act." Even further, God rightfully expects those "talking the talk should be walking the walk." John says of the 144,000, **"they are not defiled with women."** This doesn't mean they are unmarried for the marriage relationship is holy, ordained by God. This statement indicates that these people are morally pure — fully committed to Jesus. The pure in heart shall represent God! See Nehemiah 13:26,27.

One thing is certain about these 144,000 servants of God, they are blameless before God. Even the Old Testament prophet Zephaniah says of the remnant,

"The remnant of Israel shall not do iniquity, nor speak lies; neither shall a deceitful tongue be found in their mouth...." (Zephaniah 3:13)

According to John, the Father's name is written in their foreheads. (Revelation 14:1) The Father's stamp of approval was represented to John as the Father's name on their forehead. The Father places this stamp on them because He approves what is going on inside the forehead! According to the Apostle Paul, those filled with the Holy Spirit possess the mind of Christ. (1 Corin- thians 2:16)

The phrase "blameless before God" means that these men and women walk humbly in uprightness before God just like Noah, Abraham and others. They speak truth, live truth and as a result of living by faith, they fully reflect the loving character of Jesus. They are sinners who have overcome besetting sins. The key to their being selected as one of the 144,000 is their perseverance for "overcoming." Review the promises Jesus made to each of the seven churches in Revelation 2 and 3. Jesus said to the church in Laodicea, "To him who overcomes, I will give the right to sit with me on my throne, just as I overcame and sat down with my Father on his throne." (Revelation 3:21)

John also says these are "offered as first fruits to God and to the Lamb." What does this mean? First fruits is a term describing a special offering presented to the Lord at various feasts. This was particularly true at the final feast of the religious year, the Feast of Tabernacles. This feast was a feast of thanksgiving to God for the crops had been harvested and the choice or best fruits were offered to the Lord at this time. The best or "first fruits" became the property of the high priest after they had been presented at the sacred service. The term "first fruits" does not refer to fruit presented first. Rather, it refers to the best or "choice" fruits of the harvest. We use similar words today. For example, the wife of our president is called the "First Lady." This doesn't mean she is chronologically the first lady in America; rather, she is the most exalted lady in our land!

The sanctuary sequence on earth follows the pattern of the heavenly sequence. So, after the seven trumpets and the close of mercy, just before the second coming, Jesus will receive the first fruits of the harvest. He will receive the 144,000 as "firstfruits" or choice fruits of earth's harvest and they will become the special property of Jesus, our High Priest. This elite group will form a special entourage accompanying Jesus throughout the eternal universe! John says, "They follow the Lamb wherever He goes." (Revelation 14:4) Think of the privilege that belongs to this group of people—being a personal attendant to Jesus!

The Holy City, New Jerusalem, has 12 gates and 12 foundations. Each gate bears the name of a tribe and each foundation, the name of an apostle. (Revelation 21:12,14) Apparently the saints will enter the Holy City through the gate corresponding to their tribe or experience in the Lord! A group of

12,000 elite servants of God from each tribe leads the way through each gate! Everyone will belong to a tribe! Everyone will have a family. Think about the generosity of God. There will be an elite group from each character-type of the human family. Even more, God finds perfection in differing character types!

Point 5

The 144,000 sing a new song in heaven which no one else can learn. What does this mean? Upon leaving Egypt, Israel faced an excruciating moment on the shore of the Red Sea. Said in today's vernacular, "Israel was between the devil and the deep blue sea" as Pharaoh's army rushed to recapture the fugitives. On one side Israel faced impassable mountains, on the other side open desert, before them was the Red Sea and behind them was Pharaoh's advancing calvary of 600 chariots. What a predicament! What a moment of extremity!

The anguish of the moment was so great that the Hebrews cried out in terror for deliverance! The Lord looked upon His children and delivered them! God parted the waters of the Red Sea and the children of Israel walked through on dry ground. When Pharaoh's army pursued the Israelites, God relaxed the parted waters and swallowed Pharaoh's best soldiers, thus terminating Israel's worry with Egypt. **"Then Moses and the Israelites sang this song to the Lord: 'I will sing to the Lord, for he is highly exalted. The horse and its rider he has hurled into the sea. The Lord is my strength and my song; he has become my salvation.... Pharaoh's chariots and his army he has hurled into the sea. The best of Pharaoh's officers are drowned in the Red Sea. The deep waters have covered them; they sank to the depths like a stone.' "** Exodus 15:1-5. This song of deliverance relates to a specific experience. Only those who went through this experience can spontaneously sing the words!

The 144,000 servants of God live through the most extreme circumstances of earth. Because they are special servants of God, the wrath of Satan is especially fierce against them. John saw them as more than conquerors—they are victorious over Satan even though a number of them will die. They sing a new song that no one else can sing. No one else can sing their song for no one else has ever had their experience. No one else can join in, for no one else can sing the words!

Point 6

What do the 144,000 accomplish that is so great? They proclaim the gospel to every nation, kindred, tongue and people during the seven trumpets. Because they walk with God as Enoch did, these people reach a level of spiritual maturity above all other people. These understand better than any others the sufferings and works of Christ. The highest honor God can bestow upon a Christian is to allow the Christian to enter into Christ's suffering. (2 Corinthians 6:3-10, Mark 10:38,39)

What does spiritual maturity involve? The 144,000 know what it means to live by faith as Jesus lived by faith. These people know what complete and full submission to the will of God means. These would rather die than willfully commit a sin. These carry the responsibility of the gospel during the judgment hour to a reeling world — a mission which many people can't understand. These people are serious students of God's Word. These are recipients of the latter rain or outpouring of the Holy Spirit. These are both a demonstration and proclamation of the character of Jesus. These are the choice fruits of heaven's harvest. These might be thought of as 144,000 clones of the Apostle Paul!

When does this maturity occur? Before the first trumpet takes place. **"Do not harm the land or the sea or the trees until we put a seal on the foreheads of the servants of our God."** (Revelation 7:3) Since these people are yet to appear, and it is obvious the first trumpet has not sounded, it is self evident that the sealing of the 144,000 is taking place right now! Jesus says, **"My eyes will be on the faithful in the land, that they may dwell with me; he whose walk is blameless will minister to me."** (Psalm 101:6)

One last comment on the identity of the 144,000. In Revelation 12, the story of the true church (represented by a woman) and a terrible dragon is told. The woman wears a crown of 12 stars on her head. From the Greek, we learn that these stars are set in a *stephanos* or crown of victory. Stars symbolize messengers or angels and by applying the words of Daniel 12:3 to Revelation's symbolism we find a very beautiful fit. **"Those who are wise (or teachers) will shine like the brightness of the heavens, and those who lead many to righteousness like the stars for ever and ever."** In other words, the crown of victory is set with 12 stars that represent the glorious triumph of the 12 tribes. The 144,000 are "stars" in every sense of the word!

Point 7

Is 144,000 a literal number? If the number is symbolic and does not represent a literal number of people, then the scripture must tell us the meaning of the symbol according to the rules of interpretation. Since no such description exists for any number in Revelation, we can feel free to regard the number as literal.

Numbers cannot be symbolic. For example, in Revelation 17, John saw a beast having seven heads and 10 horns. The heads and horns are symbolic — not the numbers! The number 144,000 is a literal number. The term "servants of God" suggests that these people will powerfully lead the proclamation of the everlasting gospel. In fact, in Revelation 10:7 the servants are called prophets! So, the work of the 144,000 will be to first gather *remnant(1)* and then when the trumpets begin to sound, the will march into Babylon to gather *remnant(2)*.

Two Witnesses control the 144,000

This brings us to the heart of Revelation's story: The Two Witnesses. Who are they? How do they relate to the 144,000?

Notice all of the following specifications from Revelation 11 about the Two Witnesses:

1. The Two Witnesses prophesy for 1,260 days in sackcloth. {v3}
2. These are the two olive trees and two lampstands that stand before the Lord. {v4}
3. Anyone that tries to harm them must die by fire. {v5}
4. These men have power to shut up the sky and prevent rain (during the 1,260 days) and they have power to turn water to blood and strike the earth with any plague as often as they want. {v6}
5. After 1,260 days are ended, the beast that comes up from the Abyss will attack them and kill them. {v7}
6. Their bodies lie in the street of a city called Sodom and Egypt, where Jesus was crucified. {v8}
7. The earth will rejoice that the Two Witnesses are dead. {v10}
8. After three and a half days they live again. {v11}
9. They go up to heaven in a cloud. {v12}

Revelation 11 is a chapter describing the two instruments God uses in the conclusion of the plan of salvation. These two powerful instruments used together might be compared to a cutting torch. When oxygen and acetylene are mixed together, a hotter and more penetrating flame is obtained than when using either gas alone. In these last days, God is going to use the Two Witnesses to cut through the barriers of sin. The Two Witnesses are brought into prominent focus in the final days of earth because sin has almost destroyed the sensibilities of people. The distress caused by the trumpets is carefully designed to give opportunity and credibility to the Two Witnesses. They will offer salvation to all who want to be saved!

The term "witness" is very important—understanding that the Two Witnesses accomplish their work during the time-period of the trumpets. Since the gospel will go to every person during this time, the gospel becomes a witness for or against every person! This is a crucial point. The gospel either offers salvation or brings condemnation! There is no middle ground at the time of the revelation of the gospel. The point here is that in days ahead, as in ancient Israel, no one could be sentenced to death on the testimony of one witness. God told Moses, **"One witness is not enough to convict a man accused of any crime or offense he may have committed. A matter must be established by the testimony of two or three witnesses."** (Deuteronomy 19:15) So, God will send two witnesses to each person so that no one may miss salvation. If a person chooses to reject salvation, then both witnesses will testify against him and he will be condemned.

The Two Witnesses are:

1. The Bible (the two lampstands)
2. The Holy Spirit (the two olive trees producing the oil)

The Bible appeals to the intellect and the Holy Spirit appeals to the heart. It is through these cooperative agencies or "witnesses" that God works for the salvation of man. **"...I will put my laws in their minds and write them on their hearts...."** (Hebrews 8:10) This verse clearly shows a relationship between the intellect and the affections.

In Zechariah 4, we learn that God's work on earth will be completed through the power of the Holy Spirit. **"...'Not by might nor by power, but by my Spirit,' saith the Lord Almighty."** (Zechariah 4:6)

Consider the vision of Zechariah: **"He asked me, 'What do you see?' I answered, 'I see a solid gold lampstand with a bowl at the top and seven lights on it, with seven channels to the lights. Also there are two olive trees by it, one on the right of the bowl and the other on its left.' I asked the angel who talked with me, 'What are these, my lord?' He answered, 'Do you not know what these are?' 'No, my lord,' I replied."** (Zechariah 4:2-5)

Notice the indirect answer to Zechariah: **"So he said to me, 'This is the word of the Lord to Zerubbabel: Not by might nor by power, but by my Spirit,' says the Lord Almighty."** (Zechariah 4:6) But, Zechariah's curiosity wasn't satisfied. **"Then I asked the angel, 'What are these two olive trees on the right and the left of the lampstand?' Again I asked him, 'What are these two olive branches beside the two gold pipes that pour out golden oil?' He replied, 'Do you not know what these are?' 'No, my lord,' I said. So he said, 'These are the two who are anointed (chosen) to serve the Lord of all the earth.' "** (Zechariah 4:11-14)

Synthesizing

Zechariah saw one lampstand with seven lights and two olive trees with golden pipes connected between the trees and the lights. He was told these two symbols serve the Lord of all the earth. Now, Zechariah knew the following: Clear olive oil was daily used for the seven lamps in the temple and priests put the oil in them every morning and evening. But the specifications of Revelation 11 are slightly different. John saw:

1. Two olive trees
2. Two lampstands
3. [They stand or serve] before the Lord of the earth.

Important differences

In the wilderness sanctuary, there was one lampstand with seven lights on it in the tabernacle. One lampstand represents one agency from which the light of God's truth shines — and the light is complete (seven lights). The lampstand in the ancient tabernacle represented the "anointed" agency of God of spreading His truth: His *chosen people*. They were the means by which

His Word was to be carried to the Gentiles. (Isaiah 42:6)

In Zechariah's day, there was still one lampstand with seven lights on it. But Zechariah saw something different about the lampstand as it *stood before the throne of God in heaven*. Instead of priests putting the oil into the lamps, God had two olive trees automatically filling the lamps with oil. In other words, God kept the lamps burning by having living trees fill the lampstand.

God wanted Zechariah to understand that the living trees, producing ever-flowing oil, represented the work of the Holy Spirit. This is how God kept truth alive — not by man's power. This is why Zechariah was told, "Not by might (human means) but by My Spirit (God's means)," that God's truth would be kept shining throughout the earth. Those two trees producing oil represent the work of the Holy Spirit throughout the earth. There were two trees because there are two works of the Holy Spirit: the early rain and latter rain.

Seven hundred years later, John saw seven distinct lampstands before God instead of one lampstand. This reflects an important transition: God had abandoned Israel as His chosen agency and had turned to His seven churches. Again, seven is a perfect number. And to assist each church in its special work, God appointed an attending angel to help keep its lamp brightly burning. (Revelation 1:20)

When John enters into the experience of the 144,000, in Revelation 10 (John eats the book that is given to him) there is another important transition. Instead of seven lampstands, there are only *two* lampstands standing before the Lord, but the two olive trees remain unchanged.

What does this transition mean?

With the selection of the 144,000, God abandons the agency of the seven churches and turns to the agency of last resort: the agency of His Word. Carefully consider this. The remnant will be identified by their allegiance to God's Word, not by membership in some church organization. (The value of a tree is known by its fruit not by its name.) The two lampstands represent the final agency of God that lights up the whole world with His truth. This agency is the Bible. Observe the connection. The 144,000 will present the final prophetic message that comes from the open book taken from the hand of Jesus. (Revelation 10:8-11) John ate the book which is the prophetic messages coming from Daniel (the Old Testament) and Revelation (the New Testament). The eating of the book means that John "digests" the message contained in the book. Thus, the two lampstands represent the Old and New Testaments — from which comes the final message of mercy, the everlasting gospel.

Therefore...

Witness 1 is two Lampstands = OT/NT = Bible = Word of God = Agency 1.

Witness 2 is two olive trees = Early/Latter Rain = Ministry of Holy Spirit = Agency 2.

These two witnesses are God's anointed means for presenting His truth in coming days. **"And I will give power to my two witnesses, and they will prophesy for 1,260 days, clothed in sackcloth (distressing circumstances). These are the two olive trees and the two lampstands that stand before the Lord of the earth."** (Revelation 11:3,4) Understand that God's Word and the Holy Spirit serve the Lord as the final agencies of salvation. For 1,260 literal days the Bible and Holy Spirit will mightily work under most distressing circumstances. They will suffer great rejection, but they will gather the elect of God from all corners of the earth.

"If anyone tries to harm them, fire comes from their mouths and devours their enemies. This is how anyone who wants to harm them must die." (Revelation 11:5) The Two Witnesses testify of present truth. In coming days, their message to the world will be a life and death matter. Some who first reject the Bible, may later accept the conviction of the Holy Spirit and be saved. Some who reject the impress of the Holy Spirit at first, may later see the truth in God's Word and be saved. Two points must be made here:

1. No one will be sentenced to eternal death by rejecting one witness. It takes the rejection of both. (Jesus saves anyone willing to listen.) (Deuteronomy 19:15)

2. "Fire came out of the mouths of the Two Witnesses...." This may be a figure of speech having to do with final reward much like the sword that comes out of Jesus' mouth at the second coming. Revelation 19:15 says, **"Out of his (Jesus') mouth comes a sharp sword with which to strike down the nations. 'He will rule them with an iron scepter.' He treads the winepress of the fury of the wrath of God Almighty."**

"These (144,000 men and women, young and old — Joel 2:28) have power to shut up the sky so that it will not rain during the time they are prophesying; and they have power to turn the waters into blood and to strike the earth with every kind of plague as often as they want." (Revelation 11:6) Supernatural powers will be given to the 144,000 so that their message will have credibility. No rain for 1,260 days? Notice this text: James 5:17 says, **"Elijah was a man just like us. He prayed earnestly that it would not rain, and it did not rain on the land for three and a half years."**

The 144,000 will have powers like Moses before Pharaoh: "They can strike the earth with every kind of plagues as often as they want." These manifestations will be going on at a time when the earth is greatly suffering from the devastation of the trumpets. By the time of the fifth trumpet (the appearing of the devil), you can see why the world will put their hopes in the lies of the devil. Satan will claim that the suffering of the wicked is directly due to the satanic powers of the 144,000. Thus, the anger of the wicked will be directed at God's people.

Killed by beast from abyss

"Now when they (the Bible and Holy Spirit) have finished (fully completed giving) their testimony, the beast that comes up from the Abyss will attack them, and overpower and kill them." (Revelation 11:7) Two points must be made: First, how can the Bible and Holy Spirit be killed? Consider what they do. What is the unpardonable sin? Isn't it rejecting the influence of the Holy Spirit so that His influence is not felt in your life? What follows after rejection of the Holy Spirit? Open rebellion against the Word and authority of God. What sin cannot be forgiven? (Matthew 12:31)

At the close of mercy, everyone will have either received or rejected the saving message of the Two Witnesses. Thus, their work will be fully and completely accomplished and their saving influence will come to an end. As far as the salvation of mankind goes, the work of the Two Witnesses will be finished. Their influence will be made of no-effect by the physical appearing of the devil, the beast that ascends from the abyss.

Secondly, the beast from the abyss kills them. Who is the beast from the abyss? The physical appearing of the devil.

In the book of Revelation, there are four beasts: a lamb and a lamb-like; a dragon and a dragon-like. These will be investigated in a later chapter, but for now, just consider the possibility that when the devil physically appears upon the earth, he will lead the world to reject God's Two Witnesses: Bible truth and Holy Spirit conviction, through his deceitful miracles.

Review

Let's review the order of events so this makes sense:

1. The 144,000 are chosen and empowered.
2. They prophesy 1,260 days under difficult circumstances but fully accomplish their work. Revelation indicates that some of the 144,000 will die just as John the Baptist died after completing his task. And many of the saints will die, too. (Fifth seal martyrdom)
3. The beast from the abyss (the devil himself) will kill the influence of the Bible and Holy Spirit by deceiving many and forcing the rest of mankind (sixth trumpet war) to obey him. Those who will not live by faith will have to receive his mark for survival.

The great city

"Their bodies will lie (for some months) in the street of the great city, which is

figuratively called Sodom and Egypt, where also their Lord was crucified." (Revelation 11:8) Notice these figurative terms: bodies; great city; Sodom; Egypt. The first term we need to understand is "the great city." What is the great city?

"The woman you saw is the great city that rules over the kings of the earth." (Revelation 17:18) We know the following about the woman of Revelation 17. She is a whore. She rides upon the dragonlike beast having seven heads. She holds her cup of iniquity in her hand and it is full. She is drunk with the blood of the saints. Without covering the details right now, the whore represents the global union of church and state that will occur during the sixth trumpet. At the time of the seventh trumpet, the close of salvation, the people of earth will be like those in the days of Sodom — having hearts full of unrestrained evil, and as in the days of Egypt — they will have hardness of heart. In other words, the world will have committed the unpardonable sin and the people of earth will then either be citizens of Babylon the Great or New Jerusalem.

Their work done, the outpouring of the latter rain finished, the 144,000 run as Elijah did from Jezebel after Mt. Carmel. They head to the forests and mountains for safety. The wicked, abandoned by God to the devil, cheer, "Good riddance!" No more conscience. No more calls to obey the Bible or the God of Heaven.

Seven last plagues begin

A few terrible months pass. The wrath of God is poured out in the first four plagues. **"For three and a half days men from every people, tribe, language and nation will gaze on their bodies and refuse them burial."** (Revelation 11:9) How can the Two Witnesses have bodies? Simple. Those who accept the truth of God will press together and form small companies or bodies in various places.

After the fifth plague is poured out upon the throne of the devil, a universal death decree will be agreed upon by the entire world. The date of the universal execution of God's people will be agreed upon. The day of agreement will be three and a half days before the appointed time for their execution. (Example: Suppose the U.N. passed a decree on Wednesday at noon and the effective date of the decree was Saturday night at midnight.)

When the agreement is made, God's people, as far as the wicked are concerned, are dead. The slaying of God's people is the final solution to stopping the plagues the devil claims. Evil angels will direct angry mobs to the remote locations of God's people. For the saints, there is no escape. Even though the saints haven't been killed yet, the wicked know where they are. This is why the text says the people of God aren't buried, for they aren't dead yet.

"The inhabitants of the earth will gloat over them and will celebrate by sending each other gifts, because these two prophets had tormented those who live

on the earth." (Revelation 11:10) A great party will be given by the devil after the universal agreement is reached. Meanwhile, the saints will have to patiently wait for the deliverance of the Lord. Man's extremity is God's opportunity.

"But after the three and a half days a breath of life from God entered them, and they stood on their feet, and terror struck those who saw them." (Revelation 11:11) When the universal death decree is to be enacted (1,290 days after the censer of Revelation 8:2-5 is thrown down, Daniel 12:11), the tide of evil suddenly turns. Jesus speaks (thunders) from heaven and He announces the deliverance of His people. As His words roll through the earth, His people hear their Master speak and the inexpressible joy of deliverance breaks onto their faces. The hostages of the wicked are set free. The saints, who were moments before powerless to stop the angry rush of the wicked, now behold a miraculous delivery from the death decree. Jesus bids His people to watch with their own eyes the destruction of the wicked. Psalms 91:7 says, **"A thousand may fall at your side, ten thousand at your right hand, but it will not come near you."**

God remembers Babylon

As Jesus begins to take Babylon apart—piece by piece—the saints stand in awe. **"Then they (the 144,000) heard a loud voice from heaven saying to them, 'Come up here.' And they went

up to heaven in a cloud, while their enemies looked on."** (Revelation 11:12)

There is a special resurrection of all the martyrs who died during the fifth seal. Jesus invites His martyrs to behold His appearing. They died for Him, He lives for them! Imagine the terror of the wicked murderers beholding their victims coming forth from graves. The resurrected people will be clothed with immortality and great power! Then, the 144,000, those people who fearlessly bore the testimony of Jesus to the world, are taken to heaven *before* the gathering up of the rest of the dead. These are special trophies that belong to Jesus and they will attend Him when He appears a few days later. Remember, the 144,000 are firstfruits.

"At that very hour there was a severe earthquake and a tenth of the city collapsed. Seven thousand people were killed in the earthquake, and the survivors were terrified and gave glory to the God of heaven." (Revelation 11:13) Babylon's great power will come from 10 kings of the world. (The world will be divided in 10 parts during the sixth trumpet war.) On the 1,290th day, the strongest sector of Babylon falls first; thus, one tenth of Babylon, the great city, collapses. A great earthquake destroys 7,000 wicked people. These may be the staff of Babylon, Satan's evil administration. God's people who are in that geographic area are terrified, but none are hurt. In fact, they rejoice to see a deadly blow sent to Babylon. The fall of Babylon takes about 45 days (elapsed time between the 1290 and the 1335, Daniel 12:12), enough time for

Satan's followers to feel the dread of personally meeting the Lamb of God on His throne.

The once powerful enemies of God now become powerless. They cannot proceed with their evil plot of the universal death decree. They realize they are doomed by a power greater than their leader, Lucifer. Then, the seventh plague is executed. The rich, the powerful, the great men of earth cower before the appearance of the Father and the Lamb. (Sixth seal) They cry out, **"Fall on us and hide us from them... for the great day of their wrath has come."** (Revelation 6:17) There is a most important point here. Sooner or later, every person will have to behold the face of Jesus for himself.

Some of the 144,000 will die?

The Bible suggests that some of the 144,000 will die during the great tribulation. Here's the evidence: Revelation 7:3 says, **"Do not harm the land or the sea or the trees until we put a seal on the foreheads of the servants of our God."** Notice that the 144,000 are called *servants*.

Revelation 10:7 says, **"But in the days when the seventh angel is about to sound his trumpet, the mystery of God will be accomplished, just as he announced to his servants the prophets."** Notice that in this text, the servants are identified as *prophets*.

Revelation 10:11 says, **"Then I (John, in the experience of the 144,000) was told, 'You must prophesy again about many peoples, nations, languages and kings.' "** Notice in this text, that those who proclaim the message contained in the open book are to *prophesy* again. Prophets prophesy, don't they?

Revelation 11:18 says, **"The nations were angry; and your wrath has come. The time has come for judging the dead, and for rewarding your servants the prophets and your saints and those who reverence your name, both small and great — and for destroying those who destroy the earth."** Notice in this verse, concerning the seventh trumpet, that the servants of God are again identified as prophets. Notice also that the prophets are a distinct group from the saints in this verse.

But Revelation 16:5-7 says, **"Then I heard the angel in charge of the waters say: 'You are just in these judgments, you who are and who were, the Holy One, because you have so judged; for they have shed the blood of your saints and prophets, and you have given them blood to drink as they deserve.' And I heard the altar respond: 'Yes, Lord God Almighty, true and just are your judgments.' "** In these verses, the third plague falls on those who shed the blood of saints during the fifth seal *and* who also shed the blood of prophets. This time, the distinction between saints and prophets is very clear!

Add to the above this text. Revelation 18:24 says, **"In her (the whore) was found the blood of prophets and of the saints, and of all who have been killed on the earth."** Again, the distinction is made between prophets and saints in this verse. The point is that prophets have died all down through the ages for their testimony. Even the greatest prophet of all, John the Baptist was beheaded. Why should the 144,000 be given an exemption from martyrdom? Why should they escape the fate of many they lead to Christ?

Summary

The 144,000 and the Two Witnesses are God's final means of gathering His sheep. Think about the combination brought to this time: a fine group of people from all parts of the world, educated in the knowledge of the Scriptures, especially the prophecies of Daniel and Revelation, and empowered by the Holy Spirit. Put this combination in the setting of world-wide havoc caused by the trumpets and some amazing things are bound to happen!

Notes

Chapter 18

The Four Beasts of Revelation Part I

It takes a minimum of two

It is interesting to know that in Old Testament times, a person accused of murder could not be put to death on the testimony of one witness. Notice the importance and responsibility of being a witness: **"On the testimony of two or three witnesses a man shall be put to death, but no one shall be put to death on the testimony of only one witness. The hands of the witnesses must be the first in putting him to death, and then the hands of all the people...."** (Deuteronomy 17:6,7)

During the time-period of the trumpets, the gospel goes as a "testimony" to every nation and person. Jesus said, **"And this gospel of the kingdom will be preached in the whole world as a testimony to all nations, and then the end will come."** (Matthew 24:14) Who gives this life or death testimony? God's Two Witnesses—the Bible and the Holy Spirit! It is vital to know that in Revelation's story, no one will be condemned for rejecting the testimony of one witness. There will be two witnesses appealing for salvation. One appeals to the mind, the other to the heart.

The unpardonable sin

According to the Bible, there are two types of sin! The first type is accidental or sin that occurs without willful intention. Hitting your finger with a hammer and saying a bad word could be described as an accidental sin. Sometimes we say things that are untrue (or not altogether true) without intending to do so. John was aware of both types of sin when he wrote, **"If anyone sees his brother commit a sin that does not lead to death, he should pray and God will give him life. I refer to those whose sin does not lead to death. There is a sin that leads to death. I am not saying that he should pray about that. All wrongdoing is sin, and there is sin that does not lead to death."** (1 John 5:16,17)

The second type of sin is deadly and comes from persistent wrong-doing! Paul wrote, **"If we deliberately keep on sinning after we have received the knowledge of the truth, no sacrifice for sins is left, but only a fearful expectation of judgment and of raging fire that will consume the enemies of God."** (Hebrews 10:26,27)

Jesus told the Pharisees, **"And so I tell you, every sin and blasphemy will be forgiven men, but the blasphemy against the Spirit will not be forgiven. Anyone who speaks a word against the Son of Man will be forgiven, but anyone who speaks against the Holy Spirit will not be forgiven, either in this age or in the age to come."** (Matthew 12:31,32)

An unpardonable sin is committed when a person persistently refuses to yield to the prompting of the Holy Spirit. According to Webster, the word blasphemy means, "taking the prerogatives of God." The work of the Holy Spirit is to lead us into *all* truth, but if we refuse to be led into *all* truth, we reject the work and ministry of the Holy Spirit. Israel persistently refused to follow the leading of the Holy Spirit and their hearts and minds became hard as stone. God promised Ezekiel that He would forgive the sins of Israel if they would cooperate. He said, **"I will give them an undivided heart and put a new spirit in them; I will remove from them their heart of stone and give them a heart of flesh."** (Ezekiel 11:19) Israel's heart of stone led them to kill Jesus and then justify their deed! And, Revelation says the condition of the world will be like Sodom and Egypt in the days of the Two Witnesses. Sodom signifies unrestrained evil and Egypt signifies hardness of heart. These terms from Revelation indicate that much of the world will commit the unpardonable sin! Much of the world will reject the testimony of the Two Witnesses. Those who receive them will receive the gospel and be saved. Those

who reject the testimony of the Two Witnesses will have to receive the mark of the beast. It will be that simple.

Satan's plans revealed

Thus far in our study, we have investigated the activities of Jesus in heaven. We have learned about the book with seven seals and the seven trumpets. As we begin our investigation of Revelation 12, John changes the focus of the story to tell us about the response of the devil to the seven trumpets. God wants His people to be aware of this wicked foe for we need to know about his actions and his plans for the last days!

The rules again

Revelation tells of four beasts. All four beasts play a very important role in the final days of earth and a correct identification of the four beasts is not only required, it is mandatory. If they are not properly identified, our prophetic conclusions will be faulty and who wants to head into the great tribulation with a faulty road map? If we hold to faulty conclusions, we will not be able to satisfy the specifications attributed to each beast. And speaking of specifications, the reader must understand that *all* specifications regarding the beasts are of equal importance. In fact, God so designed the story of Revelation that there is only one correct solution for the identity of each beast. This point will be made toward the end of this chapter. Before we begin this investigation, review the rules of interpretation that shall be used:

1. An apocalyptic prophecy is identified by the presence of a beginning and an ending point in time and the events in the prophecy must occur in the order in which they are given.
2. A fulfillment only occurs when all the specifications of the prophecy are met, including chronological order.
3. If a prophetic element is declared symbolic, the meaning of the symbol must be revealed with applicable scripture.

Four beasts

The following beasts are mentioned in Revelation:

1. Lamb — 31 times

2. Lamblike — 15 times*

3. Dragon — 12 times

4. Dragonlike — 21 times*

*count varies slightly depending on interpretation

We will begin our investigation of the beasts with the first beast: the Lamb. Please notice these four texts:

Revelation 5:6 "Then I saw a Lamb, looking as if it had been slain, standing in the center of the throne, encircled by the four living creatures and the elders. He had seven horns and seven eyes, which are the seven spirits of God sent out into all the earth."

Revelation 5:12 "In a loud voice they sang: 'Worthy is the Lamb, who was slain, to receive power and wealth and wisdom and strength and honor and glory and praise!' "

Revelation 6:16 "They called to the mountains and the rocks, 'Fall on us and hide us from the face of him who sits on the throne and from the wrath of the Lamb!' "

Revelation 14:1 "Then I looked, and there before me was the Lamb, standing on Mount Zion, and with him 144,000 who had his name and his Father's name written on their foreheads."

The obvious representation of this beast is Jesus. Why do you think Jesus is symbolized as a lamb in Revelation? Notice these six specifications that identify the Lamb (many more could be given):

1. Lamb was slain
2. Lamb has seven horns
3. Lamb has seven eyes
4. Lamb is found worthy to receive seven-fold gift: power, wealth, wisdom, strength, honor, glory and praise
5. Lamb is angry at second coming (compare with Revelation 19:15)
6. Lamb is seen with the 144,000 wearing His name and His Father's name

Jesus is represented as a lamb in Revelation's story for at least two reasons. First, Jesus was the Lamb of God, the sacrifice of God for the sins of man. (John 1:29) Secondly, God always puts simple matters first. Look at the book of Daniel. Wouldn't you agree that the simplest prophecy in the book is the first one (Daniel 2)? So, the interpretation of the first beast in Revelation is easy to grasp.

The book of Revelation centers on the revealing of Jesus — this is why it is called, "The Revelation of Jesus." Jesus is going to be fully exposed so that all may see who He really is. Not even the angels of heaven have seen all that Jesus really is, for they have not seen Him reigning over the universe as King of Kings and Lord of Lords — yet. The plan of salvation not only has to do with the redemption of man, but on a cosmic scale, a universal scale, the plan has to do with the full disclosure of Jesus. He really is God! He has the same powers and authority as the Father, but He was willing to lay everything aside and become a man, to be beaten and crucified by men, so that man might have eternal life. And, in order to do this, Jesus laid aside His divine authority. He became a servant of the plan of salvation like a son is subject to his father. But, the revelation of all that Jesus really is has already begun. The Father stepped aside when the court scene began in Daniel 7:9,10 so that Jesus might take center stage and be fully revealed before the hosts of the universe as ALMIGHTY GOD.

One more point must be made. In the book of Revelation, Jesus is called the "Lion of the tribe of Judah." (Revelation 5:5:) How can Jesus be symbolized as both beasts: a lion and a lamb? Aren't these opposites? When Jesus comes in all His glory, He will appear with the strength and ferocity of a lion to those who oppose His truth. (Hosea 5:14, Revelation 19:15) On the other hand, those who stand firm for His truth will rejoice to see the Lamb that took away their sins and paid the price for their salvation.

A beast is not necessarily a nation

Some people assert that a beast in Bible prophecy is *always* a nation. This rule of interpretation, they argue, is clearly revealed in Daniel 7 where four beasts represent four world empires and in Daniel 8 where two beasts represent two world empires. Agreed, beasts represent world empires in Daniel 7 and 8, but this does not mean they *always* represent world empires in the rest of the Bible. In the symbolism of Revelation, the Lamb cannot represent a nation for Jesus is represented as *a Lamb that was slain* and is found worthy to receive the book sealed with seven seals. How could a nation have been slain? How could a nation have been in heaven and received the book sealed with seven seals? Jesus is not a nation nor does Revelation's use of a beast imply that Jesus is one. (Most people agree that a lamb is a beast just like a lion, leopard or bear.) Therefore, the claim that beasts are *always* nations cannot be a rule of interpretation, for the rule cannot be applied *always*. A rule is something that is *always* true.

This point is also confirmed in Revelation 12:9. In this text we learn that the great red dragon (certainly a horrible beast) is *Satan the angel* that was cast down from heaven. If you will review rule 3 above, you will notice that when elements are symbolic in nature, the Bible reveals the meaning of the symbol. Can there be any doubt that Jesus is the Lamb? Is there any doubt that the great red dragon of Chapter 12 is the devil himself? If the great red dragon represents pagan or papal Rome as some suggest, we have a real problem, for Revelation 12:4 says the great red dragon's tail swept a third of the stars out of the sky and flung them to the ground. How did pagan or papal Rome do that?

Another point should be raised about pseudo rules of interpretation. Some people say that a horn in Bible prophecy *always* represents a kingdom or a nation. This is verified, they say, in Daniel 7:24. The 10 horns are usually identified as 10 tribal nations that finally overran Rome by A.D. 476. However, the Bible says the 10 horns are 10 kings. Well, it is true that in order to be a king, one must have subjects, and subjects constitute a nation. So, in a round-about way, it's not hard to see why people associate horns with nations. However, there is a gottcha: Who is the large horn between the eyes of the goat in Daniel 8:8? According to Daniel 8:21, that horn is the *first* king — not the first kingdom of Greece nor the succeeding kings of Greece. In the context of Daniel 8, a horn consistently represents a single person. In fact, the four horns that replaced the first horn refer to four persons! (This matter is very important because the horn power that appears out of the four winds (Daniel 8:9) is one person and not a chain of persons. More will be said about this in the next chapter.)

Horns in Daniel 7 and 8

Now, contrast the use of a horn in Daniel 8 with the little horn of Daniel 7. In Daniel 7, the little horn power does not represent one person, but rather the office of "king." We know this to be true for the little horn power operates for a period of 1,260 years — certainly longer than one life-time.

My point about these things is that the student must respect the context of each prophecy and attempt to understand how the elements are used. The uses of elements change. Therefore, there are no rules about prophetic elements — the context of the prophecy has to be our guide. This point will be confirmed later when we discuss the meaning and use of stars.

So, in Daniel 7, the 10 horns are 10 kings, and the little horn is also a king. But the little horn continues for 1,260 years, so it must represent the office of a king and not one man. However, in Daniel 8, the notable horn is one person that dies and the four horns that take his place are four persons. The context of the prophecy makes the difference on how the elements are to be interpreted. Context has to be our guide. With these things said, we will now begin our investigation of a prophecy that begins in Revelation 12:1 and reaches to Revelation 14:5.

A glorious woman

Revelation 12:1,2 "A great and wondrous sign appeared in heaven: a woman clothed with the sun, with the moon under her feet and a crown of twelve stars on her head. {2} She was pregnant and cried out in pain as she was about to give birth."

We naturally ask, "What does this text mean?" Notice these six points:

1. Woman?
2. Sun?
3. Moon?
4. Crown?
5. Pregnant?
6. When does this scene occur?

In these first two verses, God highlights six great themes which are often overlooked or reduced in meaning:

Point 1

Woman = a bride; God's people

Obviously, this prophecy is symbolic. Who is the woman? What does she represent? According to Daniel 9, the Messiah was to appear 483 years (69 Jubilee weeks) after the decree of Artaxerxes to rebuild the temple and the city of Jerusalem. When Jesus gave this prophecy to Daniel, He hoped for a great wedding and reception. The bride, Israel, and the bridegroom, Messiah, were to be married.

John the Baptist knew he was sent to announce the wedding! John said to his disciples: **"You yourselves can testify that I said, 'I am not the Christ but am sent ahead of him.' The bride belongs to the bridegroom. The friend who attends the bridegroom waits and listens for him, and is full of joy when he hears the bridegroom's voice. That joy is mine, and it is now complete."** (John 3:28-29)

But the wedding of Messiah and Israel didn't happen because Israel turned her affection to other gods. Despite God's great love and mercy for Israel, she continued in her rebellion. Does the following sound like a broken heart? **"Go and proclaim in the hearing of Jerusalem: 'I remember the devotion of your youth, how as a bride you loved me and followed me through the desert, through a land not sown. ...(Does) a bride (forget) her wedding ornaments? Yet my people have forgotten me, days without number."** (Jeremiah 2:2-3,32)

God's original plan (Plan A) failed. But, there is Plan B. **"Let us rejoice and be glad and give him glory! For the wedding of the Lamb has come, and his bride (the woman) has made herself ready."** (Revelation 19:7) The Messiah is going to get married anyway. The wedding of the Lamb is still on. But this time, the bride will be those from every nation, kindred, tongue and people who want to be married to the Lord. Here's the offer: **"He came to that which was his own, but his own did not receive him. Yet to all who received him, to those who believed in his name, he gave the right to become children of God — children born not of natural descent, nor of human decision or a husband's will, but born of God."** (John 1:11-13)

The point is that the wedding is still to come. The bride of Jesus will be made up of those who love Jesus so much that they completely yield their lives to Him.

Applying these verses to Revelation 12, we conclude that the bride represents God's people. Now, here is a gottcha: Does the bride represent literal Israel at the time of Christ's birth or does the woman represent spiritual Israel? Your answer is important for it sets the stage for the whole of Chapter 12. Are we dealing with spiritual concepts that are larger than life, or are we dealing with representations of real things that can be historically identified? Again, we must let the context be our guide.

Point 2

The woman was clothed with the (brightness of the) sun: Her garment represents the righteousness of Jesus.

Notice this text: **"Fine linen, bright and clean, was given her (the bride) to wear." (Fine linen stands for the righteous acts of the saints.)"** (Revelation 19:8) At first glance, the reader might interpret this text to mean that the righteous acts of saints is clothing enough. But, before getting too far into wearing your own righteousness, consider these texts: God told Moses, **"Make linen undergarments as a covering for the body, reaching from the waist to the thigh. Aaron and his sons must wear them whenever they enter the Tent of Meeting or approach the altar to minister in the Holy Place, so that they will not incur guilt and die...."** (Exodus 28:42,43)

God required special underwear for the priests who served in the sanctuary, and God requires special "inner-wear" for those going to His wedding banquet. **"But when the king came in to see the guests, he noticed a man there who was not wearing wedding clothes. 'Friend,' he asked, 'how did you get in here without wedding clothes?' The man was speechless. Then the king told the attendants, 'Tie him hand and foot, and throw him outside, into the darkness, where there will be weeping and gnashing of teeth.' "** (Matthew 22:11-13)

The meaning, then, is that the bride of Jesus wears fine linen, bright as the sun. This represents the righteousness of Jesus which is made manifest by those who receive it by righteous deeds.

The people of Jesus will rejoice singing: **"I delight greatly in the Lord; my soul rejoices in my God. For he has clothed me with garments of salvation and arrayed me in a robe of righteousness, as a bridegroom adorns his head like a priest, and as a bride adorns herself with her jewels."** (Isaiah 61:10)

The bride of Jesus (the saints) will wear a garment of light even brighter than Adam and Eve — as bright as the sun. The adornment of God is complete, beautiful and more glorious than pen can tell.

Point 3

The woman stands on the moon. The moon represents God's promise or covenant of marriage.

Psalms 89:34,37 says, **"I will not violate my covenant or alter what my lips have uttered. ...it will be established forever like the moon, the faithful witness in the sky."**

God's covenant is the basis of marriage between the lamb and the woman. Can two be married without a mutual covenant of fidelity? No. Understand how the marriage covenant works: God says, "IF you will be my people, I will be your God, AND there will be marriage." (Hebrews 8:10) Jesus told His disciples, **"In my Father's house are many rooms; if it were not so, I would have told you. I am going there to prepare a place for you. And if I go and prepare a place for you, I will come back and take you to be with me that you also may be where I am."** (John 14:2-3)

Many people are confused about God's *everlasting* covenants with mankind. One man recently told me that God's covenant with Israel was irrevocable because God's promises are irrevocable. While it is true that God's promises are irrevocable, some promises require a relationship with man. These *always* contain qualifying conditions. For example, the everlasting covenant, "If you will be my people, I will be your God" begins with *If*. I do not find that God's covenant with Abraham or Moses or Israel was unconditional. See

Deuteronomy 28 and Leviticus 18 and 26. Rather, I consistently find them conditional — a point confirmed by Paul. (Romans 2 & 11; Galatians 3 & 4; Hebrews 10 & 11)

When the marriage of the Lamb and the woman occurs, the everlasting covenant changes! The "IF" part of the covenant will be eliminated for it will be unconditional. **"He who overcomes will inherit all this, and I will be his God and he will be my son."** (Revelation 21:7) No more if's, and's or but's. No conditional element will remain in the covenant. The bride will forever be sealed in holy matrimony to the Bridegroom for eternity. Hallelujah!

Here is an interesting point. The woman wears a garment as bright as the sun, and she stands on the moon. Given the physics of the sun and moon, the following seems reasonable: The people of Jesus, wearing His gift of righteousness, stand by faith on His covenant of promised marriage. As the moon has no light of itself, the covenant of marriage has no meaning by itself. However, when the gift of Christ's righteousness is properly understood, this light brings the glorious opportunity of entering the marriage covenant with Jesus into clear focus. Again I say, Hallelujah! What have we done that Jesus should want to enter into a covenant to spend eternity with us? What unbelievable honor!

Point 4

Crown = Victory / 12 stars = 144,000

The woman wears a *stephanos* crown. In the Greek language this is a crown of victory. This crown stands in contrast to the Greek *diadema* which is a crown of authority. The bride wears a crown of victory because she represents those down through the ages who have overcome the devil and his schemes. Remember the seven promises given to the seven churches? "To him that overcomes, I will...." Remember the conditional nature of the covenant: "If you will be my people..."? The point here is that God's people can overcome anything through the power of Jesus.

Notice John's admiration for the victory of the bride: **"And I saw what looked like a sea of glass mixed with fire and, standing beside the sea, those who had been victorious over the beast and his image and over the number of his name. They held harps given them by God and sang the song of Moses the servant of God and the song of the Lamb: 'Great and marvelous are your deeds, Lord God Almighty. Just and true are your ways, King of the ages.' "** (Revelation 15:2-3)

So the bride is entitled to wear the crown of victory because she is not only victorious through the ages, she is victorious over the dragon, his image and his number.

But, what do the 12 stars represent? Before we answer this question, remember the discussion earlier about context guiding us? Please look up these two groups of texts about stars:

1. Revelation 1:20; 12:4; 14:6-12 and Daniel 12:3
2. Revelation 6:13; 8:12

Here we find prophetic elements meaning one thing in one group of texts, and then meaning something else in another. If you *did* look up the texts, you will notice that no consistent statement can be made about stars in prophecy. Sometimes, stars represent messengers or angels doing the work of God and sometimes, stars represent meteors that fall out of the sky. But, the context in each case explains the use of stars so that we can make sense out of it.

For example, who are the angels of the seven churches in Revelation 1:20? Answer: *Heavenly* messengers of God assigned to each church. Who do the three angels in Revelation 14:6-12 represent? Answer: *Earthly* messengers of God carrying the final offer of mercy to a dying world. Notice how Daniel's testimony collaborates with this last thought: **"Those who are wise (margin: teachers) will shine like the brightness of the heavens, and those who lead many to righteousness, like the stars for ever and ever."** (Daniel 12:3)

The 144,000 will not be movie stars, rock stars, or political stars. They will be "gospel stars" among the jewels of God on the day that He makes up His crown. Fascinating point: Using figurative speech, if the woman represents the people of Christ, and the head of the body is Jesus, it seems fitting (pun intended) that surrounding the Head are the 144,000 who were victorious just as

He was victorious. These are forever His closest friends. Isn't it beautiful that the relationship between the bride and Jesus is compared to the closest of human relationships: marriage?

Point 5

The woman is pregnant and in pain.

The burning hope of God's faith-full people has ever been the appearing of Jesus, either in His first advent as a baby or in the second as King of Kings. The pregnant condition of the woman suggests a particular time for this scene in Revelation. Ever heard the expression, "Pregnant with expect-ation?" Notice what Luke says of the fifteenth year of Tiberius Caesar (A.D. 27), **"The people were waiting expectantly and were all wondering in their hearts if John might possibly be the Christ."** (Luke 3:15) Paul, speaking about the timely appearing of Jesus, said, **"But when the time had fully come, God sent his Son, born of a woman...."** (Galatians 4:4) And, Jesus knew that His ministry was on time. He said at the synagogue in Nazareth, **"The Spirit of the Lord is on me, because he has anointed me to preach good news to the poor. He has sent me to proclaim freedom for the prisoners and recovery of sight for the blind, to release the oppressed, to proclaim the year of the Lord's favor."** (Luke 4:18,19)

So, the pregnancy of the woman gives a clue regarding the timing of this vision. Because each apocalyptic prophecy has a beginning and ending point in time, we have to start this prophecy and its sequence at some point in time. In a moment, we will find that Chapter 12 begins with the birth and ministry of Jesus.

Point 6

When does this scene occur?

A few words about rules of interpretation are important because we are about to apply all three in the next few verses. The reader needs to understand that rules of interpretation are not man-made. Rather, it is only our privilege to observe the operation of laws or rules. For example, Sir Isaac Newton did not invent the law of gravity. God did. But Sir Isaac did observe the consistent behavior of gravity and he eventually worked out a formula stating the operation of gravity. Incidently, we refer to the *law* of gravity because it is uniformly consistent wherever you go on earth. A physical law is *always true.*

In the same sense, man can not make up laws or rules for prophetic interpretation. We may only state what the rules are by conducting a careful and prayerful investigation. God carefully designed the scenes in the prophecies, He orchestrated their order, He knew in advance what He wanted them to mean, and He withheld general understanding of the principles by which the prophecies operate until the last generation should arrive. How else would the last generation know they are the final one?

It is obvious from both Daniel and John that neither man understood the meaning of what he saw. Therefore, as writers of things revealed, they could not even venture a personal comment on the meaning of their visions. This point is interesting because their ignorance about their visions preserves the purity of the visions. In other words, they could not interject their own thoughts and thus frustrate the operation of the prophetic process. The result is that now, the precision of the prophecies and their internal linkage is unfolding and the relationship between all 18 apocalyptic prophecies is no less marvelous and no less certain than the behavior of electrons and atoms.

These points have been made because we must now apply the three rules. First, this particular prophecy (Chapter 12:1-14:5) has a beginning point in time and an ending point in time and each element within the story occurs in order. This doesn't mean that every word in every verse or even every verse is in chronological order. It means that the events described in the verses are in chronological order. On a few occasions, both Daniel and John temporarily interrupt the flow of their story to add a few details so that the reader might more clearly understand what they are saying. This does not frustrate the obvious order of the story nor does it cancel the first rule of interpretation. After all, isn't understanding the purpose of this investigation?

According to rule 2, a fulfillment is only possible when all specifications of the prophecy are met. In other words, we have to satisfy *all specifications* in the equation before we can reach a conclusion. Be careful here. Many students attempt to solve one prophecy and ignore the impact their conclusions have on the other 17 prophecies. So, we not only have to satisfy the texts or symbols at hand, we also have to satisfy existing relationships with the other 17 prophecies before we can be relatively certain of our conclusions. Because all 18 prophecies are interlocked, one has to satisfy the whole equation before he can be sure that he has solved the mystery of a specific prophecy. In other words, one has to mentally surround all 18 prophecies before he can be sure that he has the details of any one prophecy correctly interpreted.

Lastly, if something is thought to be symbolic, we have to use *applicable* scripture to explain the meaning of the symbol. THEN, we put all things together and see what the story says.

More specifications about timing of this vision

{3} "Then another sign appeared in heaven: an enormous red dragon with seven heads and ten horns and seven crowns on his heads. {4} His tail swept a third of the stars out of the sky and flung them to the earth. The dragon stood in front of the woman who was about to give birth, so that he might devour her child the moment it was born."

The first four verses of Revelation 12 introduce the story and the main characters of this prophecy. John sets up the story so that we might identify the players and behold their interactions. Please notice the following:

1. John saw another scene in heaven. (Remember, he first saw the woman standing on the moon.)
2. John saw an enormous red dragon having seven heads and 10 horns, and there are seven diadems on the seven heads.
3. John notes that the dragon's tale (O.K., tail) was responsible for the fall of one third of the stars, so that they were flung to earth.
4. John saw the dragon stand before woman to devour the child the moment it was born.

Explanation

The woman and the dragon were seen in the sky and not on earth. This nuance heightens the drama that is about to unfold on earth. The purpose of this perspective is cosmic. This means that the story is much larger than events taking place on earth. This is a story between Jesus and Satan. In fact, if the reader is going to fully appreciate this story, he must first understand that when this story begins, Christ and Satan are foes already. In fact, they had been foes for several millenniums before we even reach the time of the birth of Jesus on earth.

Notice John's description of the dragon: enormous red dragon having seven heads and 10 horns and seven diadems on the heads. Who is the dragon? Who are the stars that were flung to the earth? Who is John describing? Is this pagan Rome and its legions? Is it papal Rome and her priests? Is this a world empire? No. No. No. This dragon is not a nation — either in a primary or secondary sense. This story is not about some nation. Following rule 3, the Bible plainly says who the dragon is. **"The great dragon was hurled down — that ancient serpent called the devil, or Satan, who leads the whole world astray. He was hurled to the earth, and his angels with him."** (Revelation 12:9)

Once the identity of the dragon is correctly made, the Bible makes enormous sense just as it reads. Notice that the following verse reveals what will occur just after the second coming of Jesus: **"He seized the dragon, that ancient serpent, who is the devil, or Satan, and bound him for a thousand years."** (Revelation 20:2) Again, the question is asked, "Who is the dragon that is bound for a thousand years? Is it a nation or world empire?" No. It is simply the devil himself. The enormous red dragon, having seven heads and 10 horns is the devil. Period.

One more time. Notice this verse: **"Then the dragon was enraged at the woman and went off to make war against the rest of her offspring — those who obey God's commandments and hold to the testimony of Jesus."** (Revelation 12:17) This verse clearly reveals that the final warfare against the saints will be led by and controlled by the devil himself

— not by any one nation. Any dilution of the correct meaning of the dragon makes the story of Revelation illogical and confusing. For example, some scholars claim that the dragon in Chapter 12 represents pagan or papal Rome. How such a conclusion can be defended from Revelation is beyond rules of interpretation.

Crowns

A comment must be made about the crowns belonging to the dragon in this prophecy. In Chapter 12, there are seven diadems on seven heads. In Chapter 13, there are 10 diadems on 10 horns. What does this mean? We know that diadems are crowns of authority. This is in contrast to the stephanos, the crown of victory that the woman wears. Here's the operation: In the days of Christ, the devil's authority against the "woman" was exercised through false religion. Notice:

Jesus was condemned by the Jews. Andrew was crucified in Achaia on a cross in the form of an X. Bartholomew was crucified in Armenia. James, the son of Zebedee, was beheaded. James, the son of Alphaeus, was beaten to death. Peter was crucified upside down. Philip, Thaddeus and Thomas were martyrs for their faith. Paul was beheaded for his faith. And millions of saints were murdered during the 1,260 years of persecution by the little horn.

These all died for challenging false religion. In other words, the persecuting authority came from the religious sector. (In a later study, the seven heads will be shown to be seven false religious systems and the 10 horns are 10 kings who conspire with religious leaders to do the work of the devil.) In the coming days before us, after the devastation of the first four trumpets, Satan's authority against the "woman" will come through civil authority, that is, by penalty of civil law. Eventually, a majority in each of the 200+ countries of the world will vote in favor of laws concerning the exercise of religion. State troopers, sheriffs, police and military personnel will have to enforce the laws. This is why the diadems are transferred from the heads in Chapter 12 (religious authorities) to the horns in Chapter 13 (civil authorities). The direction of persecution changes.

John says that a third of the stars were flung to the earth by the tail of the dragon. This refers to the expulsion of the devil and his angel followers before the creation of the world. This happened before the creation of earth, more than 4,000 years before the birth of Jesus. Knowing this helps us to realize that first, the devil has been holding a grudge against Jesus for a long time. Secondly, consider the size of the devil's army. If Daniel saw billions of angels attending the court room scene in Daniel 7:9,10, and this is after the expulsion of the devil, how many angels does Satan have?

The dragon stood before the woman to devour her child as soon as it was born. John saw the devil attempt to kill Jesus. We know that he moved upon the evil heart of Herod to carry out a wicked plan as soon as Herod learned of the birth of Jesus. The point must be made that Herod's attempt to destroy Jesus was not an edict of the Roman empire. Herod acted on his own, using the authority of his office. But, this hideous act was not a deliberate or calculated act of pagan Rome. I emphasize this point because some people don't understand that this prophecy is about the actions of the devil. They try to apply this prophecy to some phase of pagan or papal Rome.

{5} **"She gave birth to a son, a male child, who will rule all nations with an iron scepter. And her child was snatched up to God and to his throne."**

Jesus was born of a virgin. This woman is a virgin. She is the bride-to-be of Jesus. In Matthew 25, the kingdom of heaven (the people of God) is likened unto 10 virgins. However, her offspring, the male child, is no ordinary child. The prophecy specifies that He will rule all nations with an iron scepter. This means that the rulership of the male child cannot be broken, for one does not break an iron rod. Read this text and see if you can identify the male child: **"Out of his mouth comes a sharp sword with which to strike down the nations. 'He will rule them with an iron scepter.' He treads the winepress of the fury of the wrath of God Almighty."** (Revelation 19:15) There is only one person who can meet these specifications: Jesus. And, Jesus *was* a male child, circumcised the eighth day. (Luke 2:21)

The Bible says that the male child was snatched up to God and His throne. Again, the Bible says, **"The point of what we are saying is this: We do have such a high priest, who sat down at the right hand of the throne of the Majesty in heaven."** (Hebrews 8:1) Who else can fulfill the specification but Jesus?

{12:6} **"The woman fled into the desert to a place prepared for her by God, where she might be taken care of for 1,260 days."**

John says that after the devil failed to kill baby Jesus, the devil then moved to destroy the woman. She ran to the desolate places of earth for 1,260 days. (In this instance, a day equals one year because the Jubilee calendar is operational during this time period.)

Stage set

So, we have a short chronological story. The first six verses of Revelation 12 set an impressive stage for the next 29 verses that follow. Before moving on, we must conduct a brief review of symbols and interpretations:

1. Woman = bride = saints
2. Sun = garment of righteousness
3. Moon = marriage covenant
4. Crown = victory / 12 stars = the elite of the 12 tribes
5. Timing = first advent of Jesus
6. Dragon = the devil himself
7. Dragon attempts to kill the male child
8. Jesus snatched up to God's throne
9. Dragon chases woman 1,260 years

Before John continues with the flow of the story, he includes one more detail that is important to the chronology of this story. It's a detail that most people don't understand. So, John backs up a little bit, so that we can see how this event fits into the larger event. Keep in mind, this interruption does not frustrate the obvious flow of the prophecy.

{7} "And there was war in heaven. Michael and his angels fought against the dragon, and the dragon and his angels fought back. {8} But he was not strong enough, and they lost their place in heaven. {9} The great dragon was hurled down—that ancient serpent called the devil, or Satan, who leads the whole world astray. He was hurled to the earth, and his angels with him."

When did this war happen? Answer: Resurrection Sunday. Here's the evidence right from the Bible:

{12:13} "When the dragon saw that he had been hurled to the earth, he pursued the woman who had given birth to the male child." Think about this: When the dragon saw that he had been hurled to the earth — he chases the woman *who had already given birth* to Jesus. Read the text a few times and notice what it really says. We know that Jesus was born in 4 B.C., so this text speaks of the devil being cast out of heaven after 4 B.C.! Contrary to what a lot of people think, John is not talking about the first expulsion of the devil from heaven. This is something else. The Bible is written very clearly. When the devil saw that he had been

hurled to the earth, he chased the woman who had already given birth to Jesus. Notice the order of events:

The next verse says: **{14} "The woman was given the two wings of a great eagle, so that she might fly to the place prepared for her in the desert, where she would be taken care of for a time, times and half a time, out of the serpent's reach."** We know from Daniel 7 that the woman's period of suffering began in A.D. 538. So, when we put verses 13 and 14 together, we find the order of events. When the dragon saw that he was cast out of heaven (Y), he chased the woman (Z) who had already given birth to Jesus (X).

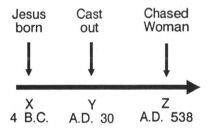

John narrows this matter even further. When the dragon was cast out of heaven, John heard a voice saying, **{10} "Then I heard a loud voice in heaven say: 'Now have come the salvation and the power and the kingdom of our God, and the authority of his Christ. For the accuser of our brothers, who accuses them before our God day and night, has been hurled down.' "** Notice that the dragon is called the accuser of "our brothers." Did you know that angels regard us as brothers? "At this I fell at his feet to worship him. But he said to me, 'Do not do it! I am a fellow servant with you and with your brothers who hold to the testimony of Jesus....' " (Revelation 19:10)

Here's a problem

Some people claim that verses 7-9 refer to the expulsion of the devil from heaven before the world was created. If this is true, how could angels call the devil "the accuser of our brothers" before the world was created? There were no human beings for the devil to accuse when Lucifer was first cast out of heaven! Look again at the text: {10} "Then I heard a loud voice in heaven say: 'Now have come the salvation and the power and the kingdom of our God, and the authority of his Christ. For the accuser of our brothers, who accuses them before our God day and night, has been hurled down.' "

When was salvation actually paid for? Answer: the day Christ died. Notice the words of Jesus: " 'Now my heart is troubled, and what shall I say? 'Father, save me from this hour'? No, it was for this very reason I came to this hour. Father, glorify your name!' Then a voice came from heaven, 'I have glorified it, and will glorify it again.' The crowd that was there and heard it said it had thundered; others said an angel had spoken to him. Jesus said, 'This voice was for your benefit, not mine. *Now* is the time for judgment on this world; *now the prince of this world will be driven out.'"* (John 12:27-31)

Until Calvary, the devil and his angels could enter heaven (not the Holy City) and argue against the salvation of sinners. See Job 1.

The devil and his angels taunted the holy name of God because He offered sinful humans another chance for salvation and did not offer defiant angels "a plan of salvation." So, the devil and his angels were bitter and they determined to destroy the very ones that Jesus loves most: His bride to be. (For a study on the expulsion of Lucifer and his angels, see *Day Star,* Volume 2, Number 6, page 16.)

On resurrection Sunday, Jesus hastily left the tomb and returned to heaven to forever throw the devil and his angels out of heaven. Their argument against man's salvation was ended, for the price of salvation had been paid in full. (This is why Jesus told Mary, "Don't slow Me down, I've got to go to My Father and your Father." See John 20:17) Jesus raced to heaven, and upon the approval of His sacrifice, He received a "permanent restraining order" from the Father. Then the devil and his angels were permanently thrown out of heaven at speeds exceeding 186,000 miles per second, the speed of light. See Luke 10:18. After the devil's speedy exit, John heard someone say these words: {10} "Then I heard a loud voice in heaven say: 'Now have come the salvation and the power and the kingdom of our God, and the authority of his Christ. For the accuser of our brothers, who accuses them before our

God day and night, has been hurled down. They (our accused brothers) overcame him by the blood of the Lamb and by the word of their testimony; they did not love their lives so much as to shrink from death. Therefore rejoice, you (angels in the) heavens and you who dwell in them! But woe to the earth and the sea, because the devil has gone down to you! He is filled with fury, because he knows that his time is short (limited).' "

Now observe the progression

{13} "When the dragon saw that he had been hurled to the earth, he pursued the woman who had given birth to the male child. {14} The woman was given the two wings of a great eagle, so that she might fly to the place prepared for her in the desert, where she would be taken care of for a time, times and half a time, out of the serpent's reach." Point: When the devil realized that he had no more access to heaven, he set out with great anger to destroy the bride. But, the woman survives in the desert for 1,260 years....

THEN...

{15} "Then from his mouth the serpent spewed water like a river, to overtake the woman and sweep her away with the torrent."

The final days of the 1,260 years were marked by bloody warfare upon the woman. As Protestantism grew in popularity, so did persecution. This spewing of water out of the dragon's mouth to overtake the woman refers to sweeping the woman away with the torrents of war and bloodshed. Notice the origin of the language: "if the Lord had not been on our side when men attacked us, when their anger flared against us, they would have swallowed us alive; the flood would have engulfed us, the torrent would have swept over us." (Psalms 124:2-4)

{16} "But the earth helped the woman by opening its mouth and swallowing the river that the dragon had spewed out of his mouth."

As Protestantism grew into a sizeable force, and the 1,260 years were ending, God opened up a new piece of real estate to help the woman. There is no coincidence between 1776 and 1798. The Declaration of Independence in 1776, and the fall of the Papacy in 1798 are integral to God's plan, and He plainly reveals this in prophecy. Today, that part of earth which helped the woman is called the United States of America. Back then, in 1776, it was called the New World. God had a specific purpose for the U.S.A., and indeed, it has uniquely helped the woman. No other nation in the history of mankind has done more for the cause of Christ than the United States. And it deeply saddens me today, that the U.S.A. has lost her former glory because she, like Israel of old, has forgotten her God.

THEN....

When the devil saw that the earth helped the woman, {17} "Then the dragon was enraged at the woman and went off to make war against the rest of her offspring—those who obey God's commandments and hold to the testimony of Jesus."

Three things must be said now. First, the dragon is preparing for war upon the remnant. This coming war obviously occurs after 1776 and it is described in Revelation 13. Secondly, this verse is not the end of the prophecy. In fact, the prophecy is just getting started. Did you know that John did not assign chapter and verse designations to Revelation? So, don't assume that Chapter 13 starts another prophecy, for it doesn't. The story continues uninterrupted!

In just 17 verses, John carries us from the birth of Christ to the time of the remnant! So, stay tuned. Our next study will investigate what happens to the remnant.

And lastly, remember, the story in Chapter 12 is cosmic; that is, it deals with larger issues than what you see before you. For example, note the scorecard of God:

1. God granted the Jews 30 Jubilees of time: they failed.
2. God granted the Christians 36 Jubilees of time: they failed.
3. God granted the Protestants 4 Jubilees of time: they failed.
4. God will grant His Two Witnesses 1,260 literal days, and they will fully accomplish their task.

In closing, consider the scorecard:

Michael versus Lucifer

1. The devil challenged Michael in heaven before the world was created. Lucifer lost.
2. The devil led the world into violent wickedness. Jesus destroyed the world with a flood.
3. The devil tried to kill baby Jesus. The devil lost.
4. The devil tried to keep his place in heaven after Calvary. The devil lost.
5. The devil chased the woman into the wilderness for 1,260 years. The devil lost.
6. The devil tried to destroy the rise of Protestantism through bloodshed and war. The devil lost.
7. The devil is preparing for war on the remnant. Millions of saints will die, but the devil will lose the war. (More about this in the next chapter.)

Is there any doubt as to why the devil is angry with the woman? Just consider that you and I are the objects over which the war between Christ and Satan will be fought. In our next study, we find that John clearly describes the war: "He was given power to make war against the saints and to conquer them. And he was given authority over every tribe, people, language and nation." (Revelation 13:7) Get ready. This verse includes you.

Chapter 19

The Four Beasts of Revelation Part II

A coming time of wrath

Before discussing the last two beasts, we need to review two texts from Daniel 8 to appreciate the term, "the appointed time of the end." Gabriel said something very important about the appointed time of the end to Daniel, "Son of man... understand that the vision concerns the time of the end.... I am going to tell you what will happen later in the *time of wrath,* because the vision concerns the appointed time of the end." (Daniel 8:17,19)

Gabriel clearly indicates there is a period or time of wrath associated with the appointed time of the end. Later in the vision, Gabriel again mentions the time of wrath. Talking about the king of the North, Gabriel said, **"The king will do as he pleases. He will exalt and magnify himself above every god and will say unheard-of things against the God of gods. He will be successful until the *time of wrath* is completed, for what has been determined must take place."** (Daniel 11:36)

Notice that the king of the North is successful until the time of wrath is completed! The king of the North will be studied later. For now, just understand that this king is incredibly successful until the time of wrath is finished.

Notice what John says about the wrath of Jesus at the second coming, **"Then the kings of the earth, the princes, the generals, the rich, the mighty, and every slave and every free man hid in caves and among the rocks of the mountains. They called to the mountains and the rocks 'Fall on us and hide us from the face of him who sits on the throne and from the wrath of the Lamb! For the great day of their wrath has come, and who can stand?' "** (Revelation 6:15-17)

Important questions

When does the time of wrath occur? What is the purpose of the time of wrath? What causes all the anger?

The time of God's wrath begins when the censer is thrown down. This event *in heaven* is marked by a global earthquake *on earth.* (Revelation 8:2-5) The censer is thrown down in heaven because God's forbearance with evil on earth, in a corporate sense, has reached its limit. Just as Moses angrily threw down the two tablets of stone containing the Ten Commandments when he came down the mountain and saw the wickedness of Israel (Exodus 32), so the angel before the altar of incense throws down the censer indicating the time for the wrath of God has come! The throwing down of the censer marks the opening of the fourth seal. The four winds (sword, famine, plague and wild beasts) are held back until the 144,000 are selected, and then they are loosed. The seven trumpets serve to awaken the people of the world that Jesus is concluding His ministry in the heavenly sanctuary. See chart on next page.

The *first* seven plagues (or trumpets) are redemptive and are therefore mixed with mercy. On the other hand, the seven *last* plagues occur after the trumpets sound and all who received the mark of the beast will receive God's wrath full strength! Notice the warning, **"...If any one worships the beast and his image and receives his mark on the forehead or on the hand, he, too, will drink of the wine of God's fury, which has been poured full strength into the cup of his wrath...."** (Revelation 14:9,10) This text indicates that at a point yet future, God's fury will be poured *full strength* into the cup of His wrath which those who received

the mark of the beast will have to drink.

During the trumpets, God's fury is not poured full strength upon the human race because the seven *first* plagues are designed to awaken, arouse and rescue as many people as possible. However, when everyone has made his decision for or against the gospel, probation then closes. Everyone on earth will have heard the everlasting gospel and made a decision. At that point, those in opposition to God's authority will have rejected the clearest revelation of His will through His Two Witnesses: the Bible and the Holy Spirit. At that time, God can do no more to save people.

Then, the seven last plagues follow. These terrible judgments sum up God's terrible wrath. John says, **"I saw in heaven another great and marvelous sign: seven angels with the seven last plagues - last, because with them God's wrath is completed."** (Revelation 15:1)

The wrath of God is reasonable

Revelation is clear that God's wrath is poured out, full strength, upon those

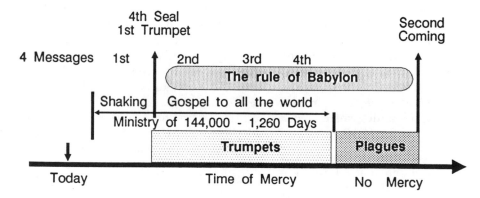

receiving the mark of the beast. Many today deny that God has wrath. Even more, these refuse to believe that He will pour it out upon human beings. Be not deceived. God is going to do exactly what He says. So, why will He pour out the seven last plagues upon those having the mark of the beast?

1.   These have not only rejected His sovereignty and His extended mercy, they have chosen to disobey His direct commands.
2.   All who reject the gospel will knowingly join with the devil in persecuting God's people. There will be no middle ground.

The wicked will become enraged by the demands of the gospel and many saints will die for their faith. This martyrdom is marked in Revelation by the opening of the fifth seal. **"Then I heard a voice from heaven say, 'Write: Blessed are the dead who die in the Lord** *from now on.'* **'Yes,' says the Spirit, 'they will rest from their labor, for their deeds will follow them.' "** (Revelation 14:13)

But the suffering of God's people does not go unobserved for Jesus is a God of justice. He observes each crime against His children and He will see that justice is served at the right time. God has all the time in the world to see that justice is carried out.

When the seven last plagues are poured out on the enemies of God, *they* will suffer in the extreme. Then, the justice of Jesus will be demonstrated. And as

terrible as these last seven plagues are, John heard the angel with the third plague saying, **"...You are just in these judgments... for they have shed the blood of your saints and prophets...."** (Revelation 16:5,6)

Our world has reached the same depth of iniquity as ancient Jerusalem. We only lack a global catalyst to start a chain of horrific events. We will see people betray one another. We will see people killing one another. Right before us is a time of great wrath. We will behold a world of unrepentant and rebellious people! Suffering and bloodshed will be much, much worse than during the French Revolution!

But observe the perplexity of the situation: Those following Satan will receive the wrath of God, while those following Jesus will receive the wrath of the devil. No one can escape the time of wrath. Jesus, knowing what the power of the gospel would eventually do to earth, said, **"Do not suppose that I have come to bring peace to the earth. I did not come to bring peace, but a sword. For I have come to turn a man against his father, a daughter against her mother, a daughter-in-law against her mother-in-law, a man's enemies will be the members of his own household. Anyone who loves his father or mother more than me is not worthy of me; anyone who loves his son or daughter more than me is not worthy of me; and anyone who does not take his cross and follow me is not worthy of me. Whoever finds his life will lose it, and whoever loses his life for my sake will find it."** (Matthew 10:34-39)

Surprise turns to rapid reaction

To more clearly understand why there will be a time of wrath, even a global war against the saints, you must consider the horrific effects of the trumpets.

When the wrath of Jesus breaks out, the entire world will be destabilized. Economic, governmental, social and religious processes all over the world will change overnight! Contingency laws will be made effective in just a few hours for a "state of emergency" will be declared in all quarters of our globe. In just a few days, the people of earth will recognize the judgments to be "acts of God." In desperation, people in every land will inquire, "What does God want?" Priest, rabbi, imam, pastor, guru, bishop, witch-doctor and anyone else claiming to be a spiritual leader will all say the same thing! The clergy of every religious body will say, "God is angry because He is offended with our evil ways."

There is something about an emergency that unites the interests and hopes of people. The first four trumpets create a global emergency. In response, people will seek a common solution, for these judgments are not an issue of people against people, but rather, God against people! Religious and political leaders of earth will quickly respond to seek a common means of appeasing God, for all the world will be hurting! This global union to appease God is called "Babylon" in Revelation. It is a confederation of religious and political powers. On the surface, the ecumenical harmony between all the entities of Babylon will appear to be reasonable. After all, everyone wants the judgments of God to stop immediately!

But, how is God to be appeased? The answer from every quadrant will be "Repent and obey the will of God." But the question rises again, "Obey what?" The Moslems obey the Koran. The Catholics obey the pope. The Jews obey the Torah. The Buddhists obey the teachings of Buddha. Protestants claim to obey the Bible—but what does the Bible actually say? This question will be discussed in more detail in a later study, but for now, understand that this question will become, not only the most important question in the whole world, but the most anxious question ever asked by human beings.

Peace and safety?

Remember the words of Paul? **"Now, brothers, about times and dates we do not need to write to you, for you know very well that the day of the Lord will come like a thief in the night. While people are saying, 'Peace and safety,' destruction will come on them suddenly, as labor pains on a pregnant woman, and they will not escape."** (1 Thessalonians 5:1-3)

Two points need to be made. First, the sudden destruction described in this text comes as a *surprise* to the world. It says that when the world is focused on its need for global peace and safety — sudden destruction will come from God. Ironic, isn't it? Is there any subject of greater importance than peace right now? Changes all over the world are occurring much faster than ever anticipated and the need for peace becomes more acute every day. Even though these rapid movements hold the world's attention and interest, most people do not understand that God foretold our need for peace and safety! Even more, Revelation clearly tells how the sudden destruction will occur! Like a sudden explosion, the trumpets will shatter the hopes and goals of people all over the world in one afternoon.

Secondly, when the sealing of the 144,000 is completed, the four angels holding back the four winds will let go and the seven trumpets will begin. By looking at any newspaper you can see we stand at the door of an irreversible countdown of events, for "peace and safety" is being prominently discussed by the leaders of our world.

The establishment of world order

We have already seen that Revelation 12 brings us chronologically to the time of the end. In verse 17, Satan prepares to make war on the last of God's people. The devil is enraged for he knows his time is short. If you will read Revelation 13:1-10 in your Bible before continuing with this chapter, the following comments will be easier to follow.

Revelation 13:1-10 describes the meteoric rise of a world power. This world power does not yet exist even though all the elements are now present. As a result of the devastation of the trumpets, this world power will rise and take control of earth. As we will see, Revelation identifies this future organization as Babylon even though the actual name it will take still remains to be seen. But one thing is certain, this coming organization will war upon the people of God for 42 months.

John says, **"And the dragon stood on the shore of the sea. And I saw a beast coming out of the sea. He had ten horns and seven heads, with ten crowns on his horns, and on each head a blasphemous name."** (Revelation 13:1)

Note: Some translations say, **"And I (John) stood on the shore of the sea."** The translation problem stems from the use of a Greek pronoun. The pronoun can be translated as "it" or "I." The context seems to better support the idea that John was standing on the shore and he saw the beast rise out of the sea.

The dragonlike beast

What does John see? Carefully read over each of the following points and remember that we are following a chronological sequence:

1. John sees a beast having seven heads and 10 horns rise out of the sea. On each head is a blasphemous name. {v1}
2. This beast not only resembles the dragon of Revelation 12, this beast resembles a leopard, has feet like a bear and a mouth like a lion. {v2}

3. The dragon (from Chapter 12) gave the beast his power, throne and great authority. {v2}
4. One of the seven heads seemed to have had a fatal wound but the fatal wound had been healed when it rises. {v3}
5. The whole world was astonished and followed the beast. {v3}
6. Men worshiped (obeyed) the dragon because he had given authority to the beast and asked, "Who is like the beast? Who can make war against him?" {v4}
7. The beast was given a mouth to utter proud words and blasphemies and to exercise his authority for 42 months. {v5}
8. The beast was given a mouth to diminish God's authority. {v6}
9. The beast was given power to make war on the saints and to conquer them. He was given authority over every tribe, people, language and nation. {v7}
10. All inhabitants of the earth will worship the beast—except those whose names are in the book of life. {v8}
11. He who has an ear, let him hear. {v9}
12. Those going into captivity will go into captivity and those to be martyred will be martyred. The saints are to remain firm, patient and faithful. {v10}

Summarizing

The story which began in Chapter 12 is continued without interruption in Chapter 13. When John wrote

Revelation, he did not divide the story into chapters and verses. That was done later by translators. *The events in Chapter 13 follow Chapter 12 in chronological order.* The war against the remnant that Satan prepares for in 12:17 is described in 13:7. Five major points can be summarized from Chapter 13:

Point 1

In Chapter 13, we move from the dragon beast to the *dragonlike* beast. The dragonlike beast is so called because he not only maintains the *form* of the dragon (seven heads and 10 horns), his *power* comes from the dragon! Think of this beast as a hand puppet. The dragon (the devil) is the hand inside the dragonlike beast.

In this chapter we will behold the purpose and function of the seven heads and 10 horns. In other words, after this beast rises, we will see why there are seven heads and 10 horns. The dragonlike beast is not the dragon; rather, the dragon takes on *earthly* characteristics when it rises from the sea. This beast, then, is more than the dragon in Chapter 12. This beast is made up of earthly kingdoms represented by a lion, a bear and a leopard. These beasts are found in Daniel 7 and here we find a final union of remnant nations, multitudes and languages.

Note: The lion, bear, leopard and terrible beast were allowed to live on after they lost dominion. (Daniel 7:12) This is why: The dragonlike beast is a composite of the remnant of all peoples, nations and languages of the world. It will quickly rise to power in response to the destruction caused by the trumpets. This organization will be global because Satan's warfare against the saints will be global. Revelation clearly predicts that all inhabitants of earth will worship the beast except the remnant. {v7,8}

Point 2

The seven heads and 10 horns represent a confederation or alliance of global powers. As will be seen shortly, the seven heads represent seven false religious systems and the 10 horns represent 10 political rulers that shall appear. The identity of the horns and heads will be studied shortly.

Point 3

Contrary to its powerful claims, Babylon will not last forever! It will be empowered for a maximum time-period of 42 months. The saints will have to stand courageously against this mighty foe. The saints will have to be patient and completely trust in Jesus at this time for they will suffer greatly. {v5,10} This coming time-period of persecution is representative of the 1,260 years of persecution experienced by the woman in Revelation 12:6,14.

Point 4

The world will follow the directives of Babylon, the dragonlike beast. Babylon will be most oppressive and all encompassing. The world has not seen anything like this beast before. Martial law and economic restrictions will be imposed everywhere due to the state of emergency caused by astounding devastation. Most freedoms will be taken away from the people overnight. Of course, these things will frighten many people. Resistance to these sweeping changes will appear to be futile. Most will agree, "You can't fight the beast. You can't win!" {13:4} Babylon rises out of the sea which confirms that it rises to power out of nations, multitudes and peoples. (Water represents multitudes of peoples, nations and languages. Revelation 17:15) The various parts of the beast that comprise Babylon—the lion, bear and leopard—represent remnant portions of ancient world empires. Compare Daniel 7:12 with Revelation 13:2.

When Babylon rises to power, one of the seven heads that had been fatally wounded is healed. This points forward to the restoration of papal power and dominion. Just as the Papacy ruled for 1,260 years before it was wounded by Napoleon, the Papacy will return to great power! Any observer of current affairs recognizes that in the last dozen years, the Papacy has reached a level of prominence in international policies not seen since its fall in 1798. The deadly wound is almost healed because the time is almost here!

Point 5

The great red dragon in Chapter 12 (having seven heads and 10 horns) is the power within the dragonlike beast, Babylon. This may be confusing for a moment. One way to understand this is to think of a person putting his hand in a hand puppet. The power of the puppet comes from the hand within the puppet. In a similar way, Satan's evil hand will control the religious and political bodies that make up Babylon and through them, he will lead powerful men to war upon the saints.

Satan's objective for Babylon is simple: gain control of the world so that when he appears upon earth, his coming will be received as the arrival of Almighty God. Satan's physical appearing is controlled by God. He physically appears during the fifth trumpet. (Revelation 9:1-12) Upon arriving, the devil will use his miracle-working powers to deceive millions of people into joining his efforts to establish a one-world government. But some will refuse to accept his offer. So, Satan leads his followers into the bloodiest of "holy wars." The sixth trumpet war unites the followers of the devil against those resisting his one-world order. By rallying those who believe he is God, the devil will take control of the world and persecute all who refuse his demands. Satan takes by force what he could not achieve through deception! The last resort of false religion is always force.

The reader needs to understand this brief sequence to understand what Chapter 13 is all about. The story in Chapter 13 is running parallel to the story of the trumpets and the three angel's messages. (See the apocalyptic chart in the appendix.) Also, the reader must know that Jesus controls the

timing of these events. Note the precision of the sixth trumpet: **"And the four angels who had been kept ready for this very hour and day and month and year were released to kill a third of mankind."** (Revelation 9:15)

Submit or else

Revelation 13:8 says, **"All inhabitants of the earth will worship the beast - all whose names have not been written in the book of life...."** The Greek word in Revelation 13:8 for worship means to obey, yield or be submissive. In fact, the meaning of the word is also associated with the idea of kissing. "To kiss" is an act of submission. Kissing as a gesture of humility and submission is seen in the Eastern cultures today. Political leaders in the Middle East often embrace one another with a kiss to signify mutual respect. In this light, the kiss of Judas betraying Jesus in the garden can be seen of as the height (or depth) of hypocrisy!

Notice that Revelation 12:17 and 13:8 simply puts everyone into one of two camps: All the inhabitants of the world will either submit to the laws of Babylon, or to the laws of God.

The rise of Babylon

The first four trumpets provide the catalyst for union of the religious systems of the world. While people are being lulled into a false sense of security with political developments of peace and safety on earth, Jesus quietly seals the 144,000. Since the world is busy with the endless round of things to do, the process of selecting the 144,000 goes unnoticed. As the call for global peace becomes loud, the trumpets will suddenly begin and the world will be literally shaken to pieces. During the months of panic that follow, the full gospel message will go throughout the earth announcing that the world is coming to an end, and that Jesus is coming. The 144,000 proclaim that salvation is still available because Jesus is still interceding in the heavenly sanctuary, but He won't remain there much longer.

Panic and fear will immediately displace feelings of security as the infrastructures of society collapse. Health insurance, social security, pensions and savings will simply disappear. People in every land will turn from political optimism to religious wonderment. They will rush to their clerics to understand the meaning of the devastation of the trumpets. They will want to know the meaning of these "acts of God."

"The cause is simple," religious leaders exclaim. "We have forgotten God. We have done wickedly; therefore, these judgments have come upon us. The pursuit of world peace is not enough. We must recognize God's authority to stay His anger. He is angry with our sinful ways. The only solution is to repent and obey God so that His judgments will stop." Ironically, a large number of politicians will be among the first to agree! Clerics will advance the notion that laws requiring righteousness should be quickly enacted. "Let punishment for wrong-doers be sudden and swift, lest we all perish." American clerics will quote Daniel saying, "...all this disaster has come upon us, yet we have not sought the favor of the Lord our God by turning from our sins and giving attention to (His) truth." (Daniel 9:13)

In various lands, laws requiring immediate reform will be imposed. Everyone must submit or suffer immediate punishment. What other options are there? Clergy from all religious bodies will unite and form a global organization so that God may be appeased *with the world* and the devastations stopped. But, the union of men will be caught in a conflict. How can the people of earth appease a universal God when their religious systems fundamentally disagree on what God requires? Now begins the great controversy.

Many people will speak out against the official plans to appease God. Some will argue that "righteous legislation" does not make saints! At first, people resisting the laws mandated by the global union will fall into two categories: refuseniks and saints. The refuseniks will be a large number of people who are opposed to restrictions of liberty by anyone. These aren't necessarily the saints, nor do they accept the gospel of Jesus. They simply refuse to go along with the implementation of "sin laws" on the basis of freedom of conscience. On the other hand, the saints will be opposed to a number of legislated reforms for two reasons. First, God does not accept "forced" righteousness. He is a God of love, and He only accepts worship from those who cheerfully choose to obey Him. The object of the trumpets is not to force the inhabitants of earth into righteous behavior. (If God had wanted to save the world in Noah's day, He could have closed the door *after* it began to rain. However, salvation either comes on God's terms, or it doesn't come at all.) Secondly, the saints will be very outspoken against the legislation of "righteous laws", because those dealing with the worship of God will clearly conflict with the Ten Commandments of Almighty God.

First among equals

As mentioned before, the world will try to appease God so that the judgments will stop. This coming global organization will rapidly develop under the aegis of universal brotherhood and suffering, and the pope will be found to be the only one qualified to serve as chief executive of such a diverse group. Since the judgments are global, and this is a global problem, all religious systems of earth will be represented. The pope has earned the right to be chief executive. For more than a dozen years he has traveled the globe seeking unity and he will seize the opportunity and lead the world in this confederation. The Papacy is uniquely qualified to conduct this work for it alone has diplomatic ties with every major religious and political power in the world! This recognition

is the basis for the healing of the deadly wound.

The term Babylon means confusion. Since the religious coalition will be comprised of the seven religious systems of the world, the reader can see that confusion is unavoidable. For example, the Moslems will see the solution to the wrath of God differently than Protestants. The Moslem concept of Jesus is quite different than the Christian concept of Jesus. But, differences will have to be overlooked. What will be urgently needed at this time will be solutions! Clerics and politicians will unite saying, "We must implore Almighty God to stop the judgments!"

Babylon's heads

Who makes up Babylon? What do the seven heads and 10 horns represent? John saw seven heads and 10 horns three times in Revelation. The first time is recorded in Chapter 12, the second time in Chapter 13, and the last time in Chapter 17. Revelation carefully maintains this repetitious identity of Satan so that the remnant might clearly understand the work and progression of the devil's activities. By having a clear picture of what's going on, God gives the saints an explanation of the enemy's disguise and war plans. Let's investigate the seven heads and discover who they represent. Remember, a correct identity of the heads requires that all specifications about the heads be satisfied. Notice the following details about the heads from Chapter 13:

- Each head has a blasphemous name. {v1}

- One of the heads had been wounded and healed. {v3}

- The beast was given a mouth to blaspheme God. {v5}

From chapter 17 we learn more about the 7 heads:

- The seven heads are seven mountains or hills. {v9}

- The seven heads are seven kings. {v9}

- Five have fallen. {v10}

- One is. {v10}

- One is yet to come. {v10}

- The beast that ascends out of the Abyss will be the eighth king and is a companion of the seven heads. {v8,11}

The specifications brought together

From Chapter 13 we see that each head has a blasphemous name. This indicates that each head is religious in nature, for each head assumes the prerogatives of God. We also find in Chapter 13 that one of the heads had been wounded, but is now healed! This head is without doubt the Papacy. The wound to this religious system was inflicted in 1798 by Napoleon. (Daniel 7:25) When this beast rises, that wound is healed. Incidently, if one head is the

Papacy, then the remaining heads must represent the same thing as the Papacy; namely, a religious system.

From Chapter 17 we notice that each head is a mountain or a hill (the Greek word 'oros means either). The symbolism of seven religious bodies as seven hills is not hard to understand from the Bible. Seven represents a complete number, a finished or full count. (There are seven colors in the rainbow, seven notes on the musical scale, seven continents, seven days in a week, etc.) Hills or mountains in John's day were reserved as places of worship or for the dwelling of deity. Ancient temples or shrines were placed in prominent places high above the terrain, because these holy places were believed to be the dwelling place of God. Even Israel is often referred to as "Mt. Zion," or "My holy hill."

To get the essence of this symbolism from John's perspective, a few examples are provided: **"O Lord, in keeping with all your righteous acts, turn away your anger and your wrath from Jerusalem, your city, your holy hill. Our sins and the iniquities of our fathers have made Jerusalem and your people an object of scorn to all those around us. While I was speaking and praying, confessing my sin and the sin of my people Israel and making my request to the Lord my God for his holy hill."** (Daniel 9:16,20)

"I have installed my King on Zion, my holy hill." (Psalms 2:6) **"...Lord, who may dwell in your sanctuary? Who may live on your holy hill?"** (Psalms 15:1) **"Who may ascend the hill of the Lord? Who may stand in his holy place?"** (Psalms 24:3)

"Blow the trumpet in Zion; sound the alarm on my holy hill. Let all who live in the land tremble, for the day of the Lord is coming. It is close at hand—" (Joel 2:1) "Then you will know that I, the Lord your God, dwell in Zion, my holy hill. Jerusalem will be holy; never again will foreigners invade her." (Joel 3:17)

"On that day you will not be put to shame for all the wrongs you have done to me, because I will remove from this city those who rejoice in their pride. Never again will you be haughty on my holy hill." (Zephaniah 3:11)

The people of the United States should easily understand the significance of the seven hills. We refer to the official building of the U.S. Congress as *Capitol Hill.* The seven religious systems of the world are symbolized as hills because people *look up to these religious systems for knowledge and understanding of God.*

These seven religious bodies are also seven kings, that is, they have dominion and subjects. People obey and follow their respective religious systems as a means of serving God. For example, Americans have been amazed at the religious zeal and loyalty of Moslems. Many Moslems have a commitment to Allah that most Protestants cannot understand. But perhaps the most conclusive issue connected with the identification of the heads is timing. John was told, "five are fallen, one is and one is yet to come." We ask *when* is this phrase to be applied? If we can locate the point in time when five are fallen, we should be able to determine

the identity of these seven heads with reasonable certainty. John's attending angel said, "This calls for a mind with wisdom... Five have fallen, one is, and the other has not yet come; but when he does come, he must remain for a little while." (Revelation 17:9,10)

To locate when the five heads are fallen, we need to determine when the conversation takes place between John and the angel. This writer believes the angel spoke to John in contemporary time. In other words, in A.D. 95, five heads had fallen. If this is true, a simple explanation can solve the mystery of the heads and meet all the specifications about the heads.

According to Webster, the term "fallen" does not only mean destroyed or collapsed; rather, in a larger sense it means "brought down" or demonstrated to be "false." (This point is confirmed in the second angel's message. Revelation 14:8) Looking at the end of the first century, we find a simple solution regarding five fallen religious systems. When Jesus became flesh and dwelt among men, five religious systems were "brought down" or exposed as false. The physical presence of Jesus upon earth unmasked the vain and foolish teachings of man.

Five religious systems exposed as false the day Jesus was born:

1. Heathenism
2. Atheism
3. Judaism
4. Eastern Mysticism
5. Islam*

*The term "Islam" refers to the Arabic faith. Although the title today includes the 6th century A.D. influence of Mohammed, the term Islam is used here to identify the ancient Arabic faith. Even though Mohammed is believed by many Christians to be the founder of Islam, it must be emphasized that Mohammed *did not* invent a new religion. Rather, he united, organized and expanded the beliefs of nomadic Arabians. Even though he is considered by the Moslems to be the last, and therefore the greatest of God's messengers, the Arabs trace the origin of their faith back to Ishmael and his 12 sons. Moslems regard Ishmael as the father of their faith and not Mohammed. See Genesis 21:13.

These five religious systems are anti-Christ and were proven false by the birth of Jesus for the following reasons:

1. Heathenism is religion apart from the knowledge of the true God of Heaven. In this system, man creates his own gods according to fantasy or whim.
2. Atheism denies the existence of the God of Heaven and His claims upon man.
3. Judaism rejects the claims of Jesus as the Messiah and seeks salvation through obedience and ceremonies.
4. Eastern Mysticism teaches that man can become God.

5. Islam denies that Jesus is the Son of God and as such, the Savior of the world.

There's more!

John was also told that one head "is," and that one "is yet to come." The *new* head or religious system that had begun in John's day was Christianity. What was called Christianity for a thousand years is now called Catholicism. John was a charter member of that new religious system and this is why the angel said "one is." We have already studied how Christianity rose and fell as Satan gained control of it. By 1798, the Reformation produced a newer head or religious system that would exist for "a little while." This system is known as Protestantism. Looking back over the landscape of history, Protestantism is a "new comer" to the religious world in terms of existence since it is only four centuries old. The other six religious systems are twenty or more centuries old.

In summary, the seven heads represent:

1. Heathenism
2. Atheism
3. Eastern Mysticism
4. Judaism
5. Islam
6. Catholicism
7. Protestantism

Review

Can you think of anyone on earth that is not included in this list of seven religious systems? Are all specifications about the heads satisfied with these conclusions? Have we followed the rules of interpretation? Rule 1 tells when the beast arises. Rule 2 tells where we are in the chronology. Rule 3 explains the meaning of the symbols. (The rules are found on page 4.) So, given the list above, please answer the following questions:

- Are all seven heads blasphemous? Do they teach things contrary to God's Word?

- One of the heads was wounded, but the deadly wound is healed when the dragonlike beast rises from the sea. Wasn't head number six, the Papacy, injured in 1798, but hasn't it been rapidly returning to power?

- Do people of the world look up to their religious system as speaking for God? Does the representation of seven hills fit in this context?

- Do people obey their religious system? Does this make each religious system a king with subjects?

- Were five religious systems exposed as false the day Jesus was born?

- Did John belong to the sixth religious system which later apostatized?

- Will Satan rule as God over the seven heads when he appears?

The eighth king

When Satan appears on earth claiming to be God, he will set himself above these seven kings and thus become the eighth and greatest king. (Revelation 17:11) According to 2 Thessalonians 2:4 and Daniel 11:36, he will set himself up over the seven heads and claim to be everyone's God.

The reason the devil is called the eighth king is interesting. Remember when the little horn rose in Daniel 7 and plucked up three horns by the roots? The little horn became the eighth horn and it ruled over the remaining seven horns with complete authority. The parallel here is identical. The devil will appear and rule over the seven heads with greater authority than all of them.

Many will dislike the devil's actions, but they will be powerless to stop him. Notice what Paul says, **"Don't let anyone deceive you in any way, for that day will not come until the rebellion occurs and the man of lawlessness is revealed, the man doomed to destruction. He will oppose and will exalt himself over everything that is called God or is worshiped, so that he sets himself up in God's temple, proclaiming himself to be God."** (2 Thessalonians 2:3,4)

The 10 horns

Horns in prophecy represent kings. Remember the horns on the ram and goat in Daniel 8? The 10 horns represent

10 kings (also symbolized by the 10 toes of Daniel 2) that will give their authority to Satan after he has conquered the world during the sixth trumpet war. Since the devil will be regarded as God by millions of people on earth, the seven religious systems will completely unite with Satan so that he can establish a one-world government. And the world will be divided up into 10 sectors. At that time, the devil will install his 10 kings over the political affairs of the world.

Today, several industrialized nations belong to an economic block that deals with global trade and financial issues. For many years this group was known as the G-7. It included Canada, Italy, West Germany, France, United States, Japan and Great Britain. Since the world has changed so drastically in the past three years, the members have changed but the purpose remains the same. The G-7 organization is a *type* of the coming union of the 10 kings. The Bible doesn't name these 10 kings that will appear during the sixth trumpet, and in fact, says very little about them. However, this author anticipates that the world will be divided by Satan himself during the great war of the sixth trumpet. Then the spoils will be divided and given to 10 kings. Satan will then set up these kings (actually his pawns) because they went along with his schemes of conquering the world. (Daniel 11:39) Regardless of just how the 10 are established, we shall soon see who they are!

For now, understand that Satan is going to take great advantage of the whirlwind changes that we are seeing all over the world. He is getting prepared to take over the world and wage war on the saints. He will align the world's religious systems and political powers into a giant confederation. He will gain complete control of the world. He will force people to obey him and his wrath will ultimately focus on any and all that resist him. He will be especially angry with the people of God who powerfully, plainly and scripturally demonstrate that he is not "The Lamb of God," but an imposter. In fact, the dragonlike beast of Chapter 13 has a strong ally. It is the "lamblike" beast that appears during the fifth trumpet. The devil will speak like a lamb at first, but he will end up speaking as a dragon.

Summary

The rise of the dragonlike beast is in response to the devastation of the first four trumpets. The seven heads of the dragonlike beast represent the seven false religious systems of the world. The Papacy will lead out in the establishment and union of this international organization. And, it will compel legislative assemblies to enact laws respecting God. This will be most confusing. However, the confusion will be greatly reduced when the devil arrives and he merges all seven systems into one great image. The end result is that the devil will control the world and thus be able to inflict a great deal of martyrdom upon the saints through false religions.

Notes

Chapter 20

The Four Beasts of Revelation Part III

Synthesis

Thus far, we have investigated the identities of the Lamb, the dragon and the dragonlike beasts. Now, we must investigate the identity and role of the last beast, the lamblike beast.

We have reached the following conclusions from our earlier study:

- The Lamb = Jesus

- The Dragon = The devil

- The Dragonlike = Babylon

- Seven Heads = Atheism, Heathenism, Eastern Mysticism, Judaism, Islam, Catholicism and Protestantism

- Ten Horns = Ten kings that will begin to rule over the earth during the sixth trumpet

The title belonging to the dragonlike beast, Babylon, fittingly describes this beast because cultural and religious diversities cannot be merged by human power. They can only be mixed — even if they live side by side for 3,000 years.

In other words, it is not humanly possible to combine the seven religious systems of the world into one global religion. What do Moslems have in common with Protestants?

But there is one who will achieve a merger of all religions! It is the devil. Through miracle- working powers he will deceive billions into thinking that he is the God of Heaven. He will proclaim that the kingdom of heaven is now among men and that he is here to usher in the seventh millennium of peace.

The devil appears

The fifth trumpet is the appearing of the devil. (Revelation 9:1-11) Because the world will be little more than a heap of ruins as a result of the first four trumpets, his appearing could not be better timed for what he intends to do. He will appear here, there and everywhere, claiming to be God. As such, he will claim to be the Savior of the world and millions of desperate people will receive him as God. After all, what do they have to lose?

The devil will be able, by means of the miracles and signs that he has power to do, to convince leaders the world over that he is what he claims to be; namely, God. Religious leaders will quickly endorse him and seek his favor. In this context, he will begin to merge the seven heads into one global confederation or one-world body. He will achieve a merger through very skillful manipulation and through demonstration of many signs and miracles. Hundreds of millions of people will believe he is God through miracles alone.

War

After the devil has gained many followers, he will manipulate religious and political leaders into believing there can be a one-world government with him reigning as God. At a prescribed moment, the devil will suddenly move to take control of the world. He will ignite a civil world war in every quadrant. Americans will be fighting Americans. Russians will be fighting Russians. The French will be fighting the French. At stake is the control of each government. This is the sixth trumpet world war.

The devil's plan is to first use deception, then force. During the sixth trumpet, Satan will set up a universal command and control center that will allow him to have control over all the people of earth. This coming one-god/one-religion/one-world union is identified in Revelation 13:14 as the "image of the beast" and in Revelation 17:1, the union is identified as "the great harlot."

The image

The consolidation of the world's religious systems is called an image to the dragonlike beast because it will be a copy of something that already exists. In other words, everyone on earth already belongs to one of the seven religious systems. After the devil appears, he will insist that the seven systems be merged together and he will take a little "doctrine" from each system and form a new one-world system. Thus, it is called an image to the first beast in Revelation 13. The Bible also says that the image is set up in *honor* of the first beast. In other words, the devil will lead the people of earth to think that this one-world union is the fulfillment and destiny of all seven religions of the world. World leaders will honor the religious systems that made the image possible by *borrowing* doctrines from each religious system. Thus, the image is a consolidation scheme which the devil will use to destroy the saints.

The image will exercise even greater rebellion against the gospel and war upon the saints more intensely than Babylon did before Satan arrived upon earth. So, the basic difference between the "image of Babylon" and Babylon itself is world-wide consolidation.

Babylon, in its initial state, will be diverse due to religious differences and cultural backgrounds whereas the image is consolidated and better united (at least temporarily). According to Revelation, the only difference between Babylon and its image is power. Both are rebellious toward God and are exceedingly corrupt. But, because the image is the final apostasy of the world on a global stage, it is a greater power than the diversity of Babylon.

As said earlier, the image is the one-world church/state the devil will set up. To satisfy the needs of diverse cultures and religions, he will take doctrines or policies from each and weave these together to form the image. It is important to know that the devil will establish Sunday as the universal day of worship. This action will be necessary because the world is divided on the day of worship. One billion Moslems worship on Friday, 25 million Jews worship on Saturday, and 1.6 billion Christians worship on Sunday. So, why will he choose Sunday as the day of worship? In honor of the most powerful religious system on earth, the Papacy. As a result of this papal doctrine, *more people on earth regard Sunday as the day of worship than any other day of the week.*

The whore

The dual identity of the image as a filthy woman in Revelation 17 reveals a good deal more about the character of the image. A whore is a woman who has exchanged her virtue and moral integrity for something of perceived value. A whore has no loyalty. She goes to the highest bidder. Whoredom is a deep pit. In it, all that matters is money, power, glory or fame. And what makes a whore detestable is that she exchanges her soul for these temporal prizes. A whore may be

outwardly beautiful and greatly desired, but her attraction is short in duration and when her lovers abandon her, they do so with disgust.

The image and the whore are the same entity. In Revelation 13, the word "image" is used so that we can understand that the devil's one-world religion will *look like* the false religious systems that he merges. In Revelation 17 and 18, the symbolism of a whore is used to describe the one-world union so that we can understand the willful exchange of religious values for the sake of survival. The point here is that religious and political leaders and billions of followers will abandon their sacred religious beliefs which they have claimed for centuries to represent the truth about God and willfully join themselves to the devil for the sake of power, money or survival. This sounds like a fairy tale, and were it not for the prophecy of Revelation, totally unbelievable. Nevertheless, this appears to be forthcoming.

Dragon / dragonlike

The reader should notice that the seven-headed, ten-horned beasts described in Revelation 12, 13 and 17 follow a decided progression. In Chapter 12, the dragon is the devil himself. In Chapter 13, the dragonlike beast, now having *earthly* beast features, is the devil's hand puppet, even though it is diverse. But in Chapter 17, the dragonlike beast is shown as the devil's final product. Here, the whore, the devil's church/state rides upon the religious and political leaders of the world. She controls or directs the dragonlike beast's activities because she is now in charge. Because Satan can disguise himself "as an angel of light" (2 Corinthians 11:14), God provides a way for us to correctly identify the progressive activities and works of Satan as end-time events unfold.

The lamblike beast

Now we come to the most important and most powerful beast in Revelation's study. Notice the following details taken from Revelation 13:

1. This beast arises out of the earth. It has two horns like the lamb, but speaks like the dragon. {v11}
2. At first, the lamblike beast uses his powerful influence on behalf of the dragonlike beast (Babylon) having seven heads and 10 horns. This means that upon his appearing, the lamblike beast supports the varied responses to appease God, mandated by the seven heads in their respective nations. When he is in Israel, he will encourage the Jews to obey their religious leaders. When in America, he will encourage the Americans to obey their leaders. By doing this, the lamblike beast gains the confidence and support of the leaders of each religious system. {v12} Later, the devil presses for a one-world church/state.

3. The lamblike beast performs great and miraculous signs, even causing fire to come down from heaven to earth in full view of men to convince them of his divinity. This miracle will convert thousands of agnostics in a split second. {v13}
4. The lamblike beast deceives millions and millions upon the earth by means of his miracles which he does on behalf of the dragonlike beast. {v14}
5. The war of the sixth trumpet is initiated when the lamblike beast *orders* the inhabitants of earth to set up an image in *honor* of Babylon. Note: It is customary to honor something or someone that has passed away. In setting up the image, the devil honors the false religious systems that made the image possible by incorporating a universal set of false doctrines. {v14}
6. The lamblike beast gives life to the image, causing it to speak and make laws whereby all who refuse to worship it are to be killed. {v15}
7. The lamblike beast forces everyone on earth to receive a mark on their right hand or forehead. {v16}
8. Those without the mark cannot buy or sell. {v17}
9. The mark contains the name or the number of the lamblike beast. {v17}
10. The number of the lamblike beast is a man's number. It is 666. {v18}

If the reader does not have a predisposition on the identity of the lamblike beast already, the name itself reveals who it is. Thirty times in Revelation Jesus is called the Lamb, and the lamblike beast is the arch rival of Jesus. Look at the following points and notice how they connect to reveal that the lamblike is none other than the devil masquerading as the Lamb of God upon earth.

Point 1

This is the only beast in either Daniel or Revelation that does not rise out of the sea. This beast does not rise out of people, multitudes, nations and languages, nor does it need them for power.

A fascinating issue must be raised. John gives no description of this beast other than it having two horns like *the* lamb. That's right. In the Greek, the noun for lamb in verse 11 has no article such as "a" or "the." In English, there is a big difference between saying *a* lamb and *the* lamb. Often the Greek language will omit the article if the noun is obviously known or previously identified. In other words, the Greek syntax supports the idea that John is really saying, "I saw a beast rise up out of the earth and it looked like *the lamb* of God, but it only had two horns, whereas the lamb of God had seven." (Compare with Revelation 5:6.)

Even if the readers disagrees with this grammatical point, consider this. Why would John ignore the entire appearance of this beast and just notice that its two horns look like a lamb? A literal translation of the Greek says, "And I saw another beast rising up out of the earth, and it had two horns like lamb, and it spoke as dragon." Again, notice the missing article before the word dragon.

This writer believes the contrast in Revelation 13:11 between Jesus, as "The Lamb," and this beast, having two horns like The Lamb, is obvious and intentional. Knowing that the devil is going to appear on earth claiming to be God, it is highly consistent to contrast the lamblike beast against The Lamb. When Satan appears on earth in his assumed role as God, the caricature of his being "lamblike" at first will be most appropriate.

John says this beast "looked lamblike, but spoke like a dragon!" Again, we see the contrast because John has already introduced and identified the dragon. Its harmless appearance and its dragonlike speech are direct opposites. The devil's appearance is designed to deceive, and his ability to speak indicates that he will make cruel laws to destroy the saints. Perhaps the reason John does not provide more detail about the appearance of this beast is that he immediately recognized who it was.

The abyss is in the earth

John was introduced to the appearing of the devil earlier in the story of Revelation as the angel from the Abyss. (Revelation 9:1-11) And he also knew that the beast from the Abyss would kill the Two Witnesses. (Revelation 11:7) So, we ask, who is the beast from the abyss?

Note the origin of the lamblike beast. John says the lamblike beast rises "out of the earth." Does John infer that rising out of the earth and coming out of the Abyss are similar? Yes. Here's why:

"**The beast, which you saw, once was (visible), now is not (visible), and will come up out of the Abyss (and be visible to the people on earth) and go to his destruction. The inhabitants of the earth whose names have not been written in the book of life from the creation of the world will be astonished when they see the beast, because he once was (visible), now is not (visible), and yet will (visibly appear before the people of earth).**" (Revelation 17:8)

Now, there are only four beasts in Revelation. The Lamb is in heaven. The dragon was cast into the earth. The dragonlike (Babylon) rises from the sea. And, the lamblike rises up out of the earth. Thus, the only beast that can come up out of the abyss is the lamblike. This point is made clear in this text: "**The great dragon was hurled down—that ancient serpent called the devil, or Satan, who leads the whole world astray. He was hurled *to* the earth, and his angels with him.**" (Revelation 12:9) The point here is that the devil was hurled *into* the earth and the lamblike beast comes up *out* of the earth! (The Greek word *eis* translated as "to the earth", primarily means "into the earth.")

Next, consider these two texts: "**The fifth angel sounded his trumpet, and I saw a star that had fallen from the sky to the earth. The star was given**

the key to the shaft of the Abyss. They had as king over them the angel of the Abyss, whose name in Hebrew is Abaddon, and in Greek, Apollyon." (Revelation 9:1,11) "**And I saw an angel coming down out of heaven, having the key to the Abyss and holding in his hand a great chain. He seized the dragon, that ancient serpent, who is the devil, or Satan, and bound him for a thousand years.**" (Revelation 20:1-2)

From these two texts, we find that an "angel king" is let out of the Abyss during the fifth trumpet and "the dragon" is returned to the Abyss after the second coming of Christ. In other words, the devil, who was once visible in John's vision was cast into the Abyss of earth and is now confined to invisibility. But, God is going to let him physically appear before the people of earth. (And most of the world will be astonished when they actually see this creature.) He is an evil and wicked destroyer even though he will appear to be a dazzling being of great glory. Then, after the second coming, the devil will be returned to the Abyss for 1,000 years.

Lastly, the lamblike beast does not rise out of any existing kingdom of earth — he just appears out of nowhere! This point is underscored by the fact that all the beasts in Daniel and the seven-headed, ten-horn beast of Revelation 13 rises out of water. We know that water represents people, multitudes and nations. But, the lamblike beast does not rise out of water *for he does not need people, multitudes and nations as the source of his strength.* He rises up out of the earth. And most of all, this beast is the arch-rival of Jesus in Revelation's story. The lamblike beast is more powerful and influential that the seven-headed, ten-horned dragonlike beast, Babylon.

The irony of the final conflict is that again, the two angel-kings, Michael the Lamb and Lucifer, the *lamblike*, will do battle. The wicked followers of Lucifer will war upon the saints of Michael. There will be much loss of life. And even though Satan may will win the battle for a season, he will lose in the end and his defeat will be complete.

Point 2

The lamblike beast has power exceeding the dragonlike beast, for it makes the earth and its inhabitants worship the dragonlike beast! This fact alone makes it impossible for the lamblike beast to be a particular nation on earth. According to Daniel 2, one nation will not rule the world again. One nation can never again be greater than the sum of all others.

In 1699, a number of prophetic expositors in Europe wondered if the lamblike beast could possibly be the emerging new world, the land of America. Their reasoning was built upon the idea that beasts in the book of Daniel were nations, so why shouldn't the lamblike beast of Revelation be an empire? As Protestants settled America, many brought this idea with them. Then, in the 1830's, Baptist evangelist, William

Miller, reached the conclusion that the end of the world was imminent. *That conclusion* necessitated the fulfillments of Daniel and Revelation. They reasoned that if the world was going to end about 1844, then Daniel and Revelation would have to be fulfilled before 1844. In this context, the pioneers searched the prophetic positions of reformaticn writers and even recent history to find things that could be used to satisfy the prophetic passages of Daniel and Revelation.

Reviewing the disappointment of 1844 is a lot like visiting a great convention hall after the convention has ended and the delegates have gone. All the fixtures are still present, but now that the party is over, the decorations and materials lying on the floor are worthless. So, after the 1844 disappointment, most Protestants abandoned their prophetic positions and went off in search of other matters. But God had a purpose for these things. As explained in the study on the seven seals, God designed that a special group of people would gather up the pieces and discover the importance of 1844. These people would carry the judgment-hour message of the third seal throughout the earth. And this work continues at this time.

But this isn't the end of the story. Much in the books of Daniel and Revelation still await fulfillment. In these final days of earth's history, the meaning of the prophecies of Daniel and Revelation are now opening up. For some, this requires unlearning a number of things so that greater truths can be learned. Now that the whole world is about to experience the great tribulation, God is revealing what is coming at His people from Daniel and Revelation so that they might prepare.

The point here is that in Revelation's story, none of the four beasts are nations. The dragonlike beast is made up of seven religious systems and 10 political powers, but the beast is the conglomerate, Babylon. While the USA may be the only superpower in the world today, America's day of humility is soon to come. We are going to experience a financial collapse that will make Russia's mild by comparison.

Knowing that the first beast represents the religious and political powers of the whole world, it is interesting to know that when Satan first arrives, he encourages the world to worship according to their respective religious systems. The Bible says that the devil acts on behalf of the first beast. In other words, to gain followers, Satan *uses* the fallen religious systems to his advantage. But, when the devil has gathered enough support, he will change the process and force the earth to set up a consolidated religious system. This is how Satan becomes the eighth king over earth.

Point 3

The lamblike beast will gain control of many people through his deceptive miracle-working powers. His most convincing miracle will be to command fire to come down out of heaven in full view of men.

Fire has been called from heaven on a few occasions. Once at Mt. Carmel, Elijah prayed that God would demonstrate that He was stronger than Baal by sending fire from heaven to burn up the sacrifice. (1 Kings 18) Again, fire came down from heaven at Elijah's request and consumed 100+ soldiers who refused to believe he was a prophet of God. (2 Kings 1) When Solomon prayed at the dedication of the temple, fire came from heaven and consumed the burnt offerings to signify the approval of God. (2 Chronicles 7) The power to call fire from heaven will be an overwhelming deception calculated to deceive those who know nothing about the Bible. Even worse, this ability will serve as confirmation that the devil is a god. People will fall prostrate at the feet of Satan saying, "Who can do such mighty works but God?"

Point 4

As mentioned before, Satan orders the inhabitants of the earth to set up an image to Babylon when he has gained enough power. And when the image is set up, Satan decrees that all who refuse to worship the image are to be killed. This image is the consolidation of Babylon's religious systems. Remember, Babylon has seven heads and 10 horns. Babylon is diverse and multi-national. Satan wants a *one-world* government. In other words, Satan sets up a universal coalition representing all religious and political powers of earth. This body shall create laws and inflict severe injury upon all refusing to obey its decrees. The image of Babylon is simply a global church/state and the devil will be its high priest and king.

Point 5

Most of the world will receive the mark of the lamblike beast in order to survive. Without the mark, no one, anywhere in the world, can buy or sell. How does Satan achieve this?

When Satan arrives on earth, the world will be suffering greatly from the effects of the first four trumpets. All infrastructures will have been devastated. The planet will be mortally wounded because of such great destruction. To stabilize what remains of the world economy, leaders of their respective nations will implement rationing. Satan only needs to deceive those controlling the laws of rationing to obtain control of the economic systems of the world. By using severe sanctions against weaker nations, Satan will achieve global control over the economy of the world. All governments will have to cooperate or there will be total ruin. Think of the horrific consequences of refusing to go along with the system! What if the Middle East couldn't sell its oil? What if Japan could not export its goods? What if America could not buy oil or Japanese products? What about the most critical product of all: food? The global economic dependence of the nations upon each other that exists right now is exactly what Satan needs.

People will not be able to buy or sell anywhere on earth unless they obey the laws set down by the devil. As people agree to cooperate, they will receive a permit to buy and sell. This permit will be imprinted on the hand or the forehead. This is the mark of the beast. Those refusing the permit will have no earthly means of support. Those standing for Jesus will not be able to pay their rent, buy food or meet even the barest necessities of life. This is the demonic plan of Satan. This is the test of faith that God wants, for He will provide for His children in the most wonderful ways.

What a time of wrath! The only way the remnant will survive is by faith in the promises of God. This condition literally pushes everyone into one of two camps: those obeying the devil for survival and those obeying God because they trust in Him.

Many who know what is right but are unwilling to live by faith, will join the camp of the enemy out of necessity. On the other hand, those who know what is right, even though they may have been hardened criminals, and are willing to live by faith will be saved. Thus, "the just shall live by faith." Jesus asked His disciples, **"...When the Son of Man comes, will he find faith on the earth?"** (Luke 18:8)

This is the final exam of earth. The one thing that will separate and polarize the people of earth is faith in God. Faith is easy to talk about, easy to define and easy to understand. However, living by faith and facing an insurmountable wall day after day is altogether another matter. Jesus is leading His children today in small steps. He tests us in small ways to see if we are willing to live by faith, so that when the final exam comes, we are prepared!

Point 6

The lamblike beast has a name. It is a man's name. The number of the name is 666.

Revelation doesn't reveal the name Satan takes when he appears. In fact, Revelation doesn't tell us the name Jesus takes when He appears! Notice, **"His eyes are like blazing fire, and on his head are many crowns. He has a name written on him that no one knows but he himself."** (Revelation 19:12) Angels call him Michael. Human beings call him Jesus. But, at the second coming, Jesus takes a new name that is unknown to us at this time. If Satan knew the name Jesus is going to use, he would steal it and use it to make his deception even more secure.

The devil's name will be associated with the number 666, for God has ordained this. Even though no one knows the name the devil will use, billions of people already know about the stigmatism of 666. Think about it. People will willingly receive this number on their foreheads or hands *knowing* that it is the mark of the Antichrist. Billions will do this for the sake of survival. Is this a prostitution of one's beliefs?

This writer is convinced that the mark on the forehead or hand is a visible tatoo. Tatoos are non-transferrable. Tatoos are simple to implement and they are universal. They will work as

well throughout the billions in China as in India. Tatoos also deface the body. From ancient times, tatoos have been used. (See Genesis 4:15 and Exodus 13:9,16.)

Some suggest the number will come from a derivative of Roman numerals for each letter in his name. Protestants took the Latin title of the pope, *Vicarious Filii Dei,* which means, "in place of the Son of God," to arrive at the number 666. Many Protestants still believe the pope is the Antichrist of Revelation 13. The problem though, is that there are many names that add up to 666. However, all specifications of a prophecy must be met in order to declare a fulfillment. (Remember rule 2 in the rules of interpretation?) The pope belongs to one of the seven heads. He cannot be the lamblike beast, neither can the Papacy be the dragonlike beast.

The number 666 is found in the Old Testament. Solomon received 666 talents of gold (about 25 tons) per year from his kingdom as a royalty. (2 Chronicles 9:13) I believe the number in Revelation is literal, not symbolic, and it will clearly reveal participation in the devil's coming one-world order. Soon, we'll know just how the details fit. So, this number, along with all the other specifications of Revelation 13:11-18 will be a positive indication that the world is really following the devil! Here's why:

When Satan is seen on earth, he will physically appear as a dazzling being. Paul says, **"And no wonder, for Satan himself masquerades as an angel of light. It is not surprising, then, if his servants masquerade as servants of** righteousness. **Their end will be what their actions deserve.**" (2 Corinthians 11:14,15) Few mortals have ever seen anything that compares with the glory that will surround Satan. His appearance is designed to deceive. His actions, at first, will appear generous and gracious. He will heal the sick and show concern for the poor. He will work wonderful and extravagant miracles. Billions will watch him on TV! He will deceive, if possible, the very elect! For all of his kindness and benevolence, there is a high price. He will make great demands. And as time passes, his demands upon people will become very hard, even dragonlike.

Satan, a man?

As Jesus became a *man* to save the world, the devil will become a *man* to destroy it. The future appearing of Satan as a man is clearly referred to in several places of the Bible! Speaking of Satan's destruction at the end of the millennium, Isaiah says, **"Those who see you stare at you, they ponder your fate: 'Is this *the man* who shook the earth and made kingdoms tremble, *the man* who made the world a desert, who overthrew its cities and would not let his captives go home?'** " (Isaiah 14:16,17)

Notice what Ezekiel says of Satan, **"In the pride of your heart you say, 'I am a god; I sit on the throne of a god in the heart of the seas.' But you are *a man* and not a god, though you think you are as wise as a god."** (Ezekiel 28:2)

The important point from these two verses is that the devil is regarded as a man even though he is more than a man. This concept should not be too hard to understand, for we think of Jesus as a man and He is much more than just a man.

Paul calls the devil the *man* of lawlessness. **"Don't let anyone deceive you in any way, for that day (the second coming) will not come until the rebellion occurs and the man of lawlessness is revealed, *the man* doomed to destruction. He will oppose and will exalt himself over everything that is called God or is worshiped, and will even set himself up in God's temple, proclaiming himself to be God... Then the lawless one will be revealed, whom the Lord Jesus will overthrow with the breath of his mouth and destroy by the splendor of his coming. The coming of the lawless one will be in accordance with the work of Satan displayed in all kinds of counterfeit miracles, signs and wonders, and in every sort of evil that deceives those who are perishing. They perish because they refused to love the truth and so be saved."** (2 Thessalonians 2:3,4,8-10) Three interesting points need to be made from Paul's comments: First, the second coming occurs *after* the man of lawlessness is exposed. Why Paul calls Satan the man of lawlessness will be seen shortly. The first point is that Satan opposes and exalts himself over all that is called God on the earth. This means he will be recognized by the people of the world as greater than the God of Islam, the God of Catholicism, the God of the Baptists, Methodists, etc.

Secondly, the coming of Satan will be accompanied by all kinds of counterfeit miracles, signs and wonders to deceive those who are perishing. It is tragic but true, that many people would rather base their faith on miracles than God's Word — the Bible. In other words, people would rather believe in one who can perform miracles than use their reasoning powers to understand the will of God. Through signs and wonders, Satan will gain control over the world. The only way he can be stopped is by intervention from Jesus. At the end, Lucifer and Michael will meet face to face at the second coming. At that time, Satan's glorious body (apparition) will be destroyed by the splendor of Christ's glory!

Lastly, Paul identifies the devil as the man of lawlessness because Satan will implement many cruel laws. This sounds strange that the lawless one would make many laws. But, the point is that his laws will be arbitrary and evil. Satan's laws will be like the laws of Hitler during World War II — without virtue or redeeming value. Don't be deceived. Just as Jesus was more than a man, the devil will be more than a man. But, the difference is vast. Satan, the man/god, the destroyer, the lawless one will bring death and suffering whereas Jesus brought life.

A temporary end

At the second coming, Satan's forces and great world system will be destroyed by Jesus. His freedom to appear upon earth in the form of a man will be removed, and the apparition that he used to appear as a man will be burned up in the lake of fire that destroys Babylon.

John tells us that the dragonlike beast and the false prophet are thrown alive into a lake of fire at the second coming! (Revelation 19:20) The dragonlike beast is Babylon which has seven heads and 10 horns, and the false prophet is its great spokes-partner, the lamblike beast. The false prophet is another description of the lamblike beast. Compare Revelation 19:20 with 13:13,14. The reason that the devil is identified as the false prophet at the second coming is that he will face God's 144,000 *true prophets* who fearlessly revealed his identity during their time of testimony.

It is ironic that the greatest demonstration of power used by Satan is the very means by which he will be destroyed. At the second coming, Jesus *calls down fire from heaven* to demonstrate His sovereign power and this fire will burn up Babylon and the false prophet! (Revelation 18:8) At that time, the destruction of Babylon will be complete and final. Those not destroyed in the lake of fire will be left to rot upon the face of the earth. (Revelation 19:21)

The finale

After the second coming, John saw an angel coming down from heaven with the key to the Abyss, and Satan was thrown into the Abyss and locked up for 1,000 years. With all the wicked slain, the righteous in heaven, Satan is confined to the spirit world again for 1,000 years. He is put back into the Abyss. Before Jesus executes final judgment upon Satan and the wicked, He wants the righteous to understand His judgment upon each person. Thus, the saints spend 1,000 years reviewing and confirming the decisions Jesus made about each person. John said, **"I saw thrones on which were seated those who had been given authority to judge. And I saw the souls of those who had been beheaded because of their testimony for Jesus and because of the word of God. They had not worshiped the beast or his image and had not received his mark on their foreheads or their hands. They came to life and reigned with Christ a thousand years."** (Revelation 20:4)

The saints will determine the amount of punishment due each of the wicked during this time-period. While thugs like Hitler may think they have escaped the punishment for their crimes, they have yet to face their victims and God's justice. God is going to arrange such a meeting. Every wrong done will be fully recognized and rewarded. Imagine the surprise of the wicked as they behold their evil deeds fully exposed before the hosts of heaven and earth!

At the end of the thousand years, Jesus returns to earth with the Holy City and the saints, and the wicked are resurrected. Every eye will behold the New Jerusalem. Then, Satan will be "loosed" from the spirit world for a short time and he will incite billions of wicked people to capture the Holy City. As the angry mob rushes upon the city, Jesus stops them in their tracks and shows each wicked person the plan of salvation as it relates to their life from a giant panoramic scene in the sky. At the end of the drama, every one acknowledges that God has been fair. Then, the seventh seal on the book of life is opened, and everyone sees that the devil's charges against God were false from the beginning. God does not manipulate His subjects. Everyone chose his destiny. As the wicked realize their loss, indescribable agony overtakes them and they turn upon each other with demonic rage. Jesus calls fire from heaven for the last time and burns up all angel and human sinners. Malachi says, **"'Surely the day is coming; it will burn like a furnace. All the arrogant and every evildoer will be stubble, and that day that is coming will set them on fire,' says the Lord Almighty. 'Not a root or a branch will be left to them.... Then you will trample down the wicked; they will be ashes under the soles of your feet on the day when I do these things,' says the Lord Almighty."** (Malachi 4:1-3)

Summary

This concludes our study on the beasts of Revelation. For review, we have seen: The lamb is Jesus. The dragon is the devil. The dragonlike is Babylon and the lamblike is the physical appearing of the devil for a short time. The seven heads are seven false religious systems of the world, and the 10 horns are 10 kings that shall rule over the earth beginning with the sixth trumpet.

The greatest drama of all ages is soon to begin. The opening of the fourth seal is about to take place. The wrath of God will be seen because the trumpets are about to blow. The four winds will be loosed. The 144,000 will be ready and most of the world will be caught by complete surprise.

One thing is certain, once the censer of Revelation 8:2-5 is cast down, an irreversible sequence of events will take us to the physical appearing of Jesus! May God help us to get ready, for ready or not, He comes.

Notes

Chapter 21

The Faith of Jesus

144,000 apostles

We have learned that the 144,000 are specially chosen people (like the first apostles) to whom the responsibility is given to proclaim the everlasting gospel. These people are extraordinary in many ways. They are God's finest representatives upon earth. Notice: **"Then I looked, and there before me was the Lamb, standing on Mount Zion, and with him 144,000 who had his name and his Father's name written on their foreheads.... And they sang a new song before the throne and before the four living creatures and the elders. No one could learn the song except the 144,000 who had been redeemed from the earth. These are those who did not defile themselves with women, for they kept themselves pure. They follow the Lamb wherever he goes. They were purchased from among men and offered as first fruits to God and the Lamb. No lie was found in their mouths; they are blameless."** (Revelation 14:1-5)

Two points about the 144,000

First, these have a unique experience. No one else can sing their song of experience, for upon these people Jesus placed the great responsibility of teaching the everlasting gospel. They speak truth – no lie was found in their mouths. They are pure in heart, they are not defiled with immoral behavior.

These suffer for the cause of Jesus in ways most people don't understand! For comparison, consider the difference between parents and children during World War II. Children suffered for the moment while parents suffered from a larger knowledge. Parents worried about the outcome of the war, about their children and the future. Parents having larger concerns suffered in proportion to their concerns. They simply had more to worry about!

In a similar way, the call to be an apostle, prophet, teacher or evangelist of the everlasting gospel is the most encompassing responsibility ever put upon a human being. The accountability that goes with the calling and selection is beyond the scope of most people's understanding. Jesus understood this responsibility. He said, **"The Spirit of the Lord is on me, because he has anointed me to preach good news to the poor. He has sent me to proclaim freedom for the prisoners and recovery of sight for the blind...."** (Luke 4:18) In a similar way, the apostle Paul said, **"Yet when I preach the gospel, I cannot boast, for I am compelled to preach.**

Woe to me if I do not preach the gospel!" (1 Corinthians 9:16)

The 144,000, like Jesus, have the Spirit of the Lord upon them and like Paul, are compelled to preach the everlasting gospel contained in the Scriptures. They are pure in heart (their actions spring from pure motives) and truthful in their speech. The power of the Two Witnesses (the Bible and Holy Spirit) resting upon the 144,000 demonstrate their calling!

The second point is that the 144,000 are first fruits of the harvest at the end of the world. Remember, the Feast of Tabernacles? This joyful feast happened at the end of the religious year. This feast celebrated the final harvest of the year. The first fruits of the harvest were given to the high priest. In the same fashion, the 144,000 are God's finest people at the time of earth's harvest. This does not imply He loves others less; rather, like a proud father at graduation, He beams to see 12,000 people from each tribe who have reached the same spiritual maturity that He had when upon earth. These overcame sin just as He overcame sin!

The great throng of the redeemed will not feel that Jesus is unfairly partial to this group of people. In fact, those living at the time of the great tribulation will recognize their indebtedness to one or more of the 144,000, for they heard or learned of the gospel through their efforts! Everyone will rejoice that the terrible struggle is over. Everyone will cry for joy unspeakable. The reward Jesus gives each person far exceeds any

suffering endured for Christ's sake. John saw the 144,000 sing a *new* song that caused heaven's arches to ring with happiness inexpressible.

Three messages

When the trumpets begin, the people of earth will be awakened to the sinfulness of their course. Into this bedlam, God sends 144,000 people especially endowed with a knowledge of Scripture and the power of the Holy Spirit. They have a message from God. The giving of this message was represented to John as an angel flying above the earth in midair. John says, **"Then I saw another angel flying in midair, and he had the eternal gospel to proclaim to those who live on the earth - to every nation, tribe, language and people. He said in a loud voice, 'Fear God and give him glory, because the hour of his judgment has come. Worship him who made the heavens, the earth, the sea and the springs of water.' "** (Revelation 14:6,7) We learn five important things from these verses:

1. The Greek word for angel also means messenger. In other words, John saw the everlasting gospel go to everyone that lives upon the earth via a messenger.

2. The everlasting gospel was represented to John as being "loud" for every person on earth must hear it!

3. People will be told to fear God because His judgment-hour has come. (This message will go

throughout the earth when the trumpets begin and people are fearful. The point here is that they are to fear Jesus and not Babylon!)
4. People are told to worship the Creator of heaven, earth, sea and springs of water. (This message is directly opposed to the laws of men mandating false worship to appease God.)
5. The first four trumpets affect the earth, the sea, the fountain of waters and the heavens—the very items mentioned in this message. The people of earth will be told to worship God, the Creator, for He has brought these events to pass that all may know who Jesus really is. The call to worship God will be in direct opposition to the laws of Babylon which demands false worship.

Then John saw another message for earth. He says, **"A second angel followed and said, 'Fallen!' 'Fallen is Babylon the Great, which made all the nations drink the maddening wine of her adulteries.' "** (Revelation 14:8) The 144,000 tell the world that Babylon the Great is fallen and thus brought down. The term fallen doesn't mean broken down or impotent. It means exposed as false. The confederation between religion and politics is inspired by Satan and does not appease God. In fact, it is called "adultery" in Revelation 17 because spiritual things belong to God and civil things belong to governments. The second angel's message warns that even though Babylon's influence is popular, imposing and all powerful, the premise behind the development of a global church/state is false and is exposed for what it really is: the handiwork of Satan.

Application

As you already know, the eternal gospel goes throughout the earth during the seven trumpets. People will be stirred and aroused to hear what the judgments are about. The eternal gospel will be presented so *loudly* that everyone, far and near will hear. With trumpets in one ear and the everlasting gospel in the other, how can any miss the meaning of the moment?

People will be told that the great day of judgment has come, for Jesus is concluding His work in the heavenly sanctuary and mercy is about to end. Great multitudes will be told that the trumpets are designed to warn the world of Christ's return and if they wish to receive salvation, they must now **worship** the Creator of heaven, earth, the sea and springs of water. The word worship means to submit or render obedience.

The irony of the matter is that people will be told that they must worship the Creator at a time when Babylon is *saying almost the same thing!* Remember, clerics of all faiths in different lands will be saying that God has sent these judgments and He must be appeased before they can stop. Babylon will legislate a number of ways to render obedience to God. The Moslem will look to the Koran for information on worship. The Jews will review the Talmud, the

Mishna and the Torah. Catholics will inquire of the pope for instruction on worship. But to what authority will Protestants appeal for information on worship? Tradition or the Bible?

A great mystery

Jesus has very clearly expressed in the Bible how His subjects are to worship Him. This is not a matter left to human design. Think about this. If humans can tell God how He is to be worshiped, then who has the greater authority? The problem that Babylon faces is that each religious system will be enacting laws to worship the same God in different ways! For example, Moslems regard Friday as a holy day, the Jews regard Saturday and Christians regard Sunday! Remember, Revelation 13:8 says, **"All inhabitants of the earth will worship the beast (Babylon, which has seven heads and ten horns) - all whose names have not been written in the book of life belonging to the Lamb that was slain...."** Is there a right way and a wrong way to worship God? Yes.

Cain and Abel demonstrated the difference. Both worshiped God. Abel worshiped God by bringing a lamb to the altar and sacrificing it according to God's instruction. Cain, on the other hand, feigned the worship of God because he did it on his terms. He didn't follow God's instruction. Cain didn't raise sheep. He didn't like the idea of killing animals. So he brought fruit from his garden. God was displeased with Cain and refused his worship but Abel's offering was

received. (Genesis 4:1-16) Cain became angry and slew his brother. Why? John warns, **"Do not be like Cain, who belonged to the evil one and murdered his brother. And why did he murder him? Because his own actions were evil and his brother's were righteous. Do not be surprised, my brothers, if the world hates you."** (1 John 3:12,13) John says Cain's act of worship was evil! Indeed, it was blasphemous. Cain took the prerogative of God. He decided how he would worship God.

The crux of the matter is this. God accepts our worship if we worship him in spirit and truth; that is, if we worship God according to all we know to be true. The eternal gospel that goes to every nation, kindred, tongue and people contains information about the worship of the true God that will be new to most people. The first angel's message of Revelation 14:7 says loudly, **"Fear God.... Worship the Creator."** The reason the first message begins in this manner is that most of the world does neither correctly! God knows about our darkness. This is why the light of the everlasting gospel will remove the darkness that Satan has placed around the subject of worship. Those honest in heart, who worship God according to all the truth they have, will rejoice to learn the full truth about worship!

Worship the Creator

How are we to worship our Creator? As said earlier, the worship of God has not been left to human invention. Jesus, our Creator, clearly explains in the Ten

Commandments, how He is to be worshiped. Carefully review the first four commandments. They are found in Exodus 20:3-11:

1. "You shall have no other gods before (other than) me."
2. "You shall not make for yourself an idol in the form of anything in heaven above or on the earth beneath or in the waters below. You shall not bow down to them or worship them; for I, the Lord your God, am a jealous God, punishing the children for the sin of the fathers to the third and fourth generation of those who hate me, but showing love to thousands who love me and keep my commandments."
3. "You shall not misuse the name of the Lord your God, for the Lord will not hold anyone guiltless who misuses his name."
4. "Remember the Sabbath day by keeping it holy. Six days you shall labor and do all your work, but the seventh day is the Sabbath to the Lord your God. On it you shall not do any work, neither you, nor your son or daughter, nor your manservant or maidservant, nor your animals, nor the alien within your gates. For in six days the Lord made the heavens and the earth, the sea, and all that is in them, but he rested on the seventh day. Therefore the Lord blessed the Sabbath day and made it holy."

The first four commandments are the basis of true worship. They clearly explain the reverence and respect due our Creator, Jesus. We are not to worship any other god. We are not to create an idol and bow down before it. We are not to use the name of God in a careless way. And we are to keep the seventh day holy as a memorial to our Creator and His creation.

The Ten Commandments are divided into two groups. The first four commandments deal with man's relationship to God and the last six commandments deal with man's relationship to his neighbor. Actually, the Ten Commandments define the two basic laws of life. Jesus said, "...love the Lord your God with all your heart and with all your soul and with all your mind. This is the first and greatest commandment. And the second is like it: Love your neighbor as yourself. All the Law and the Prophets (the Scriptures) hang on these two commandments." (Matthew 22:37-40)

Love is the basis of salvation. The two commandments Jesus spoke of in Matthew 22 are clearly spelled out in the Ten Commandments. The meaning of love is not left to human definition. In fact, the word "love" today commonly means sex, lust or passion. What a perversion! Jesus came from heaven to correct human misunderstanding on this point. According to Jesus, true love produces obedience! "Whoever has my commands and obeys them, he is the one who loves me. He who loves me will be loved by my Father, and I too will love him and show myself to him....

If anyone loves me, he will obey my teaching.... He who does not love me will not obey my teaching....” (John 14:21-24)

Satan has obscured the importance of the first four commandments from most of the world. He has especially cloaked the fourth commandment, which contains divine instruction on worship, in darkness. Satan's purpose for doing this is quite simple. If people forget their Creator, they will turn to other gods, for man needs a god of some kind. Man needs something to look up to — something to worship. We were created with this need. And if man forgets his Creator, he creates his own god(s).

Satan has had enormous success in displacing the Creator with man-made gods. The trumpets correct this. People all over the globe will be awakened to the knowledge of the true, living and omnipotent God! The everlasting gospel will contain a clarion call to **worship the Creator** on His holy day.

Review the fourth commandment on the preceding page and notice the following:

1.   The seventh day of the week is holy because Jesus rested on the seventh day to commemorate the creation of the world! He made the seventh day uniquely different from the other six at creation! (Genesis 2:2,3)
2.   The seventh day alone is holy. The other six days are for our use and work.

3.   Knowing that Satan would lead the world to forget the Sabbath, Jesus begins the fourth command-ment with, “Remember.”

But the law of God was nailed to the cross

If you ask most Christians about the Ten Commandments, they will admit that nine of the ten are valid and important. It's against God's law to steal, kill, commit adultery, curse God or worship idols. In fact, most of the Christian world is comfortable with nine of the Ten Commandments and readily acknowledge that they are the basis of morality. But ask most Christians about the fourth commandment and you'll suddenly hear that the Ten Commandments were nailed to the cross and are not binding.

It is the author's opinion that lawlessness abounds in America for this simple reason. For two hundred years Protestant clerics have taught that the Ten Commandments of God are not binding. If we would reason from cause to effect, we would recognize the hopeless state in which our society finds itself is due to the practice of this very doctrine. Where there is no law, there is no order, safety or harmony. The alternative is chaos, death, suffering and evil of every sort.

Many Christians can't reconcile the simultaneous harmony between law and grace. They, however, do exist and harmoniously relate. We need grace *because* there is a law. If there was no law, grace wouldn't be needed! In fact, if there is no law, there can be no sin! See Romans 4:15 and 1 John 3:4-6. And grace does not do away with the law either! (Romans 3:31) If the judge grants a speeder grace so that he does not have to pay a speeding fine, does this mean the speed limit is eliminated?

In practice, the harmony of law and grace is easy to understand if you are married. When two people are united in love, there are certain non-negotiable rules that must be followed. Faithfulness is one such rule. So it is with our Creator. If we love Him, we will abide by His non-negotiable rules. These are known as the Ten Commandments.

Different people

People may be grouped into a variety of categories concerning the Law of God.

a. There are people ignorant of the requirements of God's law. These have not had sufficient reason or opportunity to know and inquire about God's will.
b. There are people who are negligent or careless about God's law. These people know about God's law, but pursuit of earthly things makes religious interest and practice a low priority.
c. There are those who observe the law as a ritual necessary for salvation. These people think they keep the law and feel justified by their assumed righteousness. Being technically right is very important to these people.
d. There are people who believe there is no defined or implicit law. These people don't believe the Ten Commandments are necessary or binding today. Many Christians hold this to be true without realizing the consequence of what they believe. When pressed on this matter, most Christians admit that nine of the Ten Commandments should be lived by.
e. There are people who openly and defiantly rebel against God's law. These don't want to know God and don't care what He says.
f. There are people seeking to know God and sincerely want to live in harmony with the principles of God's law. These are willing to go, to be and do all that God asks.

This last group lives by faith. They realize that the law of God is based on two great principles: love to God and love to man. The first four commandments show our love to God and the last six reveal our love to man. These obey the commandments of Jesus *out of gratitude and love* for His salvation. They well know that obedience does not merit or bring salvation.

There is a two step process to harmonizing the life with the law of God. First, a person must realize that he cannot save himself through obedience to the law and that inherently, our nature is attracted to sin or lawlessness. This is why we need grace—for all have sinned. Secondly, those willing to live by faith recognize that Jesus alone can transform our sinful nature. By opening our minds and hearts to the sweet influence of the Holy Spirit, we receive power to be overcomers. Sinners become saints through this miraculous process! Using an analogy, it means we must be born again every day.

The final exam is a test of faith

Jesus has carefully designed the final exam of earth. By allowing Satan and his forces to gain control of the world for a short time, He will see who has the faith to be obedient!

Consider the issues carefully. Circumstances will be so desperate that obeying Jesus will be impossible except by faith! In other words, those who render obedience to Jesus will only be able to do so through faith in His promises. This is why John identified the remnant as follows, **"Then the dragon was enraged at the woman and went off to make war against the rest of her offspring - those who obey God's commandments and hold to the testimony of Jesus."** (Revelation 12:17)

The third angel

But, if you still have doubts that John was talking about the Ten Commandments when he described the remnant, look at the last message given to the world. John says, **"A third angel followed them (the first two angels) and said in a loud voice: 'If anyone worships the beast and his image and receives his mark on the forehead or on the hand, he, too, will drink of the wine of God's fury, which has been** poured full strength into the cup of his wrath. He will be tormented with burning sulfur in the presence of the holy angels and of the Lamb....' This calls for patient endurance on the part of the saints who obey God's commandments and remain faithful to Jesus."** (Revelation 14:9-12)

These verses contain the most solemn threat ever presented to the human race. The issue is worship! This message will sound when Satan appears on earth in person. This message is specifically focused on the lamb-like beast. Notice the following points:

1. If any man worships (submits to) the beast that sets up the image (the lamb-like beast), he will be tormented with burning sulfur in the presence of the Lamb of God!
2. If anyone receives the mark or permit or worships the image (the one-world confederation), he will receive God's wrath full strength!
3. Those refusing to worship Satan must be patient in their suffering. They are identified as obeying God's commandments and remaining faithful to Jesus.

Of the Ten Commandments, only one deals with worship in an external way. Satan knows this and for this reason he has led the world into worshiping on days other than the Lord's day. According to the Bible, the Lord's day is Saturday. Jesus said, **"...the Son of Man is Lord even of the Sabbath."** (Mark 2:28) Many Christians mistakenly think that Sunday is the Lord's day even though the Bible never says the first day of the week is the Lord's day.

Reasons to worship on Sunday?

There is no scriptural support for Sunday worship as Catholics and Protestants claim, neither is there support for Friday worship as Islam claims. When Protestant America makes and enforces laws regarding the sacredness of Sunday to appease God, America will quickly go from national apostasy to national ruin. During the trumpets, this nation will enact laws enforcing worship on Sunday, a day that is clearly and openly defiant to the law of God Almighty! At this time, clerics will use certain scriptures to deceive people into thinking that worship on Sunday is scriptural. Here are the texts they will use:

Some will refer to Acts 20 for evidence that Sunday worship was practiced by the apostles. Notice, **"On the first day of the week we came together to break bread, Paul spoke to the people and, because he intended to leave the next day, kept on talking until midnight."** (Acts 20:7)

Note: In the Bible, a day begins at evening and ends at evening. Since creation this has been an unchanging process. See Genesis 1:5. The Jews also regarded a day from evening to evening and kept the Sabbath from Friday sundown to Saturday sundown. See Luke 23:50-56 and Leviticus 23:32.

The timing described in Acts 20:7 is as follows: Paul stayed with the believers at Troas for seven days. (Acts 20:6) On the evening of the first day of the week, at supper time, the believers came together to eat supper with Paul and to say good-bye. The first day of the week in Paul's time began Saturday at sundown, or what we now call Saturday evening. Paul preached until midnight and then journeyed to Assos the following morning which was Sunday morning.

So Paul met with believers on Saturday night to eat supper and say good-bye. Does this change or abrogate the fourth commandment of God?

Some Christians argue that Paul insists that offerings for the poor be taken on the first day of the week. Notice: **"Now about the collection for God's people: Do what I told the Galatian churches to do. On the first day of every week, each one of you should set aside a sum of money in keeping with his income, saving it up, so that when I come no collections will have to be made. Then, when I arrive, I will give letters of introduction to the men you approve and send them with your gift to Jerusalem."** (1 Corinthians 16:1-3)

In Paul's day, money was not a common medium of exchange as it is today. Most trading was done with barter; i.e., a person traded a chicken or something for cloth or pottery. Paul instructed the church in Corinth to begin each week by setting aside a sum of money so that when he came to them, they would have money to send to the persecuted believers in Jerusalem. Paul would not be able to travel with roosters, goats, pottery and other things of value. Again, the question is asked, "Does Paul's instruction change or abrogate the fourth commandment of God?"

Some Christians suggest that worship on Sunday is proper because Jesus arose from the dead on Sunday morning, the first day of the week. Yes, the resurrection is important, and the Bible does provide a celebration of the resurrection! It's called baptism. Notice what Paul says, **"What shall we say, then? Shall we go on sinning so that grace may increase? By no means! We died to sin; how can we live in it any longer? Or don't you know that all of us who were baptized into Christ Jesus were baptized into his death? We were therefore buried with him through baptism into death in order that just as Christ was raised from the dead through the glory of the Father, we too may live a new life."** (Romans 6:1-4)

Does baptism change or abrogate the fourth commandment? Not at all. In fact, only eight texts in the New Testament mentions the first day of the week and not one of them says that the sacredness of the seventh day was transferred to Sunday!

What was nailed to the cross?

Many Christians argue that the Ten Commandments were nailed to the cross. Yet, this doesn't solve the problem. Whatever happens to the fourth commandment, happens to the other nine! So, what was nailed to the

cross? Only the ceremonies of the sanctuary services that were a shadow of the heavenly sanctuary were nailed to the cross. The key word here is "shadow." Notice what Paul said to the believers in Colosse, **"For in Christ all the fullness of the Deity lives in bodily form, and you have been given fullness in Christ, who is the head over every power and authority.... When you were dead in your sins and in the uncircumcision of your sinful nature, God made you alive with Christ. He forgave us all our sins, having canceled the written code, with its regulations, that was against us and that stood opposed to us; he took it away, nailing it to the cross.... Therefore, do not let anyone judge you by what you eat or drink, or with regard to a religious festival, a New Moon celebration or a Sabbath day. These are a shadow of the things that were to come; the reality, however, is found in Christ. Don't let anyone who delights in false humility and the worship of angels disqualify you for the prize...."** (Colossians 2:9-18)

If you'll look at these verses carefully, you'll see that Paul is talking about the regulations regarding *religious feasts, New Moon observances and Sabbath days.* The Sabbath days that Paul is talking about are not found in the Ten Commandments. Rather, the term Sabbath days here applies to Sabbath "feast" days such as the Passover or Day of Atonement. See Leviticus 16:31, 23:26-32. These feast days fell on different days of the week (like our birthday) because they occurred on the same date each year. When a feast day and the seventh day simultaneously occurred, it was a special holy day! The death of Jesus incidently, took place on such an occasion. The Passover in A.D. 30 occurred on the seventh-day Sabbath that year! See Mark 15:42-47 and John 19:14.

The Jews confused the law of God with the law of Moses much like we do today. Even though one set of laws was written by the finger of God, and the other, by the hand of a man, the Jews never did understand the relationship between the laws.

Note: The lesser law of Moses, containing the ceremonial rules, were kept in a pocket on the side of the ark, while the Ten Commandments were kept inside the ark. (Deuteronomy 10:1,2, 31:26) After a permanent temple was erected in Jerusalem, the law of Moses were not kept in the pocket on the ark and consequently, they were lost for awhile! (2 Kings 23:2)

The Jews loved to argue about the laws. An expert lawyer even challenged Jesus with a test to see which law was the greatest. (Matthew 22:34-40) As said before, the Jews misunderstood the purpose of the laws and as a result, spirituality degenerated into a great legal system of darkness. (Matthew 23:2-15)

When Paul began to explain the purposes behind the laws, and show distinction between them, you can understand the Jewish lawyers' intense hatred for him. When Paul claimed that ceremonial laws were now meaningless, this was too much! He was captured and eventually died in prison for his convictions. (Acts 21:27-36) Paul was very explicit. The laws that were nailed to the cross were *shadows* of the real thing. The ceremonial laws requiring the sacrifice of lambs were no longer necessary because the Lamb of God had died and the shadow was fulfilled. In other words, ceremonial laws were temporary until their meaning was fulfilled. Consider Paul's dilemma. How could he get the Jews to cease doing something they had been doing for 1,800 years? We have the same dilemma. How do we get Christians to worship on Saturday when Sunday observance has been going on for 1,800 years?

Paul is very clear in Hebrews 10 and Galatians 3 that the ceremonies never brought salvation in the first place; rather, they were temporary and were designed to teach us about salvation! Paul wrote the book of Hebrews about 33 years after Jesus returned to heaven and he is very clear that the seventh day Sabbath of the Ten Commandments is to be observed. Paul says, **"There remains, then, a Sabbath-rest for the people of God for anyone who enters God's rest also rests from his own work, just as God did from his."** (Hebrews 4:9,10) In fact, all through his life, Paul faithfully observed the seventh day Sabbath. (Acts 13:44, 16:13, 17:2, 18:4,11)

Can't break one commandment

If we take the position that Jesus nailed the fourth commandment to the cross, then He nailed nine others there too.

Whatever we do with the fourth commandment, we must do with the other nine. If we choose to ignore the fourth commandment, we must ignore the other nine. John wrote the epistle bearing his name (1 John) about 70 years after the ascension of Jesus. He didn't believe the Ten Commandments had been done away with. He says, **"We know that we have come to know him (Jesus) if we obey his commands. The man who says 'I know him,' but does not do what he commands is a liar, and the truth is not in him. But if anyone obeys his word, God's love is truly made complete in him. This is how we know we are in him. Whoever claims to live in him must walk as Jesus did."** (1 John 2:3-6)

James wrote, **"If you really keep the royal law found in Scripture, 'Love your neighbor as yourself,' you are doing right! But if you show favoritism, you sin and are convicted by the law as lawbreakers. For whoever keeps the whole law and yet stumbles at just one point is guilty of breaking all of it. For he who said, 'Do not commit adultery,' also said, 'Do not murder.' If you do not commit adultery but do commit murder, you have become a lawbreaker."** (James 2:8-11)

James brings us to an important and fundamental conclusion regarding the royal law, the Ten Commandments of God. He says we must obey all the commandments. If we break one, we're guilty of breaking them all because the King's law is only fulfilled by love. We must first love God with all our heart, mind and soul and then our fellowman as ourselves.

Keeping the Sabbath will not save anyone. This is why the final test is carefully designed to test faith. Will you have the faith to obey God and keep His Sabbath holy?

Summary

Solomon summed up the issues of life. He said, **"Now all has been heard: here is the conclusion of the matter; Fear God and keep his commandments, for this is the whole duty of man. For God will bring every deed into judgment, including every hidden thing, whether it is good or evil."** (Ecclesiastes 12:13,14)

So, here's the conclusion. Those who love Jesus will obey Him and keep His commandments even though Satan arrays the whole world in opposition. The observance of the seventh day Sabbath will be the object through which the supreme test of love and faith for Jesus will come. This test will expose those who love Jesus enough to live by faith. This test will separate the entire world into two camps: those worshiping the lamb-like beast and those worshiping The Lamb of God. Think about it. This test puts an entirely new meaning on the concept that eternal life comes by faith! Do you have enough faith in God to obey Him at any cost? Where will you stand?

Chapter 22

Four Global Announcements

Revelation not only predicts the coming manifestations of the wrath of God (and the response of the religious and political systems of earth), it also reveals four profound announcements that God shall send to every nation, kindred, tongue and people. These four announcements will be more widely known than AIDS.

Time has not arrived

As of this moment, these four messages are essentially dormant because the appointed time for these messages has not arrived. But, don't misunderstand, elements of all four messages are being proclaimed by Christians around the world. However, the four messages — occurring as a four-part sequence, require a specific progression of global events to be universally effective. And, when *universal* circumstances become appropriate, these four messages will penetrate every mind with the brilliance of sunlight. Even though they can be understood before their moment of glory, they have not yet received the power that is to accompany them.

There is nothing more powerful than a truth whose time has come. Like a runaway train, *timely* truth can penetrate any blockade — whether physical, mental or spiritual. The key word in the previous sentence is timely. Timing is everything. And the greater the resistance, the greater the exposure and power of *timely* truth. Just as heat is generated in an electrical circuit when there is more power than the circuit can bear, so these four messages will cause a great controversy among all peoples, nations and languages.

The four messages

What are these four messages? In abbreviated form they are:

1. Obey God
2. Disobey man's laws
3. Disobey the devil's demands
4. Do not receive the mark of the beast

See diagram on page 226 for a chronological placement of these messages. The first of these four messages will begin in a powerful way just before the censer in Revelation 8:2-5 is cast down. The global earthquake and attending phenomena that marks the judgment of the living serves as the starting gun for the world announcing the Great Tribulation. (Think about the significance of the earthquake as it relates to commerce. Can you imagine the consequences of thousands of collapsed bridges and freeway overpasses in the USA?) I believe there is a short interval of time between the global earthquake and the sounding of the first trumpet, perhaps no more than eight months. During this interval of time, the 144,000 will continue proclaiming the first of the four announcements — but comparatively few people will listen or give them due consideration. Then, when the first trumpet occurs, the world will behold a fulfillment of the first trumpet which the 144,000 predicted. It is important to know that the fulfillment of prophecy does not change the announcement of the 144,000; rather, the first announcement will receive much greater attention by the people of earth as a result of the first trumpet. As a result, more people will respond to the gospel call.

To appreciate the impact these announcements are going to have, one has to understand the events that surround each message because each message is given in opposition to what is actually taking place. For example, the first announcement (in abbreviated form) is "Obey God." While every born-again Christian already understands the importance of this statement, the implication of this message is that most people aren't obeying God even though they think they are! In other words, the reader must recognize that these four announcements have two dimensions.

The first dimension is the revealing of the will of God to all men. The second dimension is the revealing of the rebellion within man against the will of God. Thus, each announcement ignites a higher level of opposition as it is given until the people of earth are fully separated — as sheep or goats.

Right to the point

God uses few words. Speech is such a temporal and momentary means of communication. For example, over the course of your lifetime, how many sermons you have heard and forgotten? God prefers to be understood by His actions because man may learn much about the nature and character of God through the study of His behavior over millenniums of time. So, His words are few and far between, and everything the last generation needs to know about salvation has been written in the Bible. So, God is going to speak to the people of the world through His servant-prophets, the 144,000. These will present four compelling messages from the Bible that all will hear. Within the context of these four messages, men and women, boys and girls everywhere will hear the gospel invitation: *Receive Jesus Christ as Savior AND Lord so that you can be saved.* To receive Jesus as Savior is to recognize that one cannot save himself. Salvation is only possible through faith in Jesus. To receive Jesus as Lord is to recognize the authority of Jesus. If we accept Jesus as our Lord and Master, we voluntarily become subject to His commandments. But what brings the properties of salvation into sharpest focus is this: During the Great Tribulation, men will enact a number of laws that will stand in direct opposition to the laws of God. The result is that the subject of salvation will become simple to comprehend: One will not be able to obey God without great love for God and faith in His promises.

World response to the trumpets

I maintain that one cannot correctly understand Revelation's story, especially the four announcements of Revelation, without first understanding what the fourth seal and the seven trumpets are all about. (Time will soon reveal if my assertion is true or false.) The reason I maintain such a position is that one has to first comprehend something of the global holocaust caused by the first four trumpets to appreciate the panic and desperation that will galvanize the whole world into a confused but collective unit to appease an angry God. This collective unit of seven religious systems is called Babylon, and it will rapidly rise to a coalition having great power — once the Great Tribulation begins.

I am also convinced that the four angels holding back the four winds in Revelation 7:1-4 are the first four angels having the seven trumpets. Without going into much detail, here's why: The four angels holding back the four winds have power *to harm* the earth. Specifically, they have power to harm the land, sea and trees. After the 144,000 are selected and sealed, the four angels *will harm* the land, sea and trees. The only place in Revelation where the land, sea and trees are specifically harmed is found in Revelation 8:7-9. Here, the first two angels of the seven trumpets accomplish the harm that God wants them to do. I also find that the devil and his angels are not permitted to harm the land, plants and trees; rather, they can only hurt people who haven't received the seal of God. (Revelation 9:4) If the devil's angels could harm the land, plants and trees, all humanity would prematurely die. Thus, the devil could thwart the work of God to reach all people with the gospel. So, God prohibits the devil and his angels from harming the environment. (Incidently, trumpets five through seven are called curses or woes because they directly affect people.)

So, an understanding of the fourth seal and the seven trumpets is central to Revelation's story. The fourth seal contains four literal judgments from God: sword, famine, plague and wild beasts. These four judgments are the four winds that shall be loosed after the 144,000 are ready to do their work! And, the seven trumpets are the means by which the four judgments occur. And the coalition of the world's religious systems (the rise of the dragonlike beast out of the sea, Revelation 13:1) is man's *response* to the first four trumpets. This background information is imperative. It sets the stage for God's four announcements. And once the setting is properly understood, one can see why these four announcements are as volatile as dynamite.

Two Witnesses

To make the testimony of the 144,000 credible, Jesus will give them two assets: a clear grasp of five Bible doctrines and Holy Spirit power. The Two Witnesses will make the 144,000 servant-prophets a formidable group of people even though they are few and far between. Here is a mystery. The 144,000 will be largely disconnected from each other by geography and communication — but they are very similar in character and they bear *the same* four powerful announcements during the probationary period of the Great Tribulation.

God's purpose for empowering the 144,000 is this: The gospel is not only a proclamation of the love of God, it is a demonstration of God's love. The 144,000 will be a group of chosen people that have a love for the salvation of souls. They will be individuals who love God with all their hearts, mind and soul and their neighbors as themselves.

In Revelation, we find that the gift of prophecy is given to the 144,000. (Revelation 7:3; 10:7; 12:17) The gift of prophecy is called the "testimony of Jesus" because this phrase refers to a process that is most exciting to understand. In Revelation 1:9, we read, **"I, John, your brother and companion in the suffering and kingdom and patient endurance that are ours in Jesus, was on the island of Patmos because of the word of God and the testimony of Jesus."** Did you notice that John was suffering on the island

of Patmos because of the testimony of Jesus?

Notice what an angel told John the testimony of Jesus is: **"At this I fell at his feet to worship him. But he said to me, 'Do not do it! I am a fellow servant with you and with your brothers who hold to the testimony of Jesus. Worship God! For the testimony of Jesus is the spirit of prophecy.' "** (Revelation 19:10) What does the last sentence of this text mean?

Putting these two texts together, we find that John was on the isle of Patmos because of the spirit of prophecy! What is the spirit of prophecy? What is the spirit of St. Louis? What is the spirit of praise and thanksgiving? What is the spirit of the Olympics? Basically, the spirit of something is an attitude about that something. *The spirit of prophecy is an attitude of esteem for prophecy.*

Prophecy is a gift that comes directly from Jesus. Notice these two verses from Paul: **"Follow the way of love and eagerly desire spiritual gifts, especially the gift of prophecy. Tongues, then, are a sign, not for believers but for unbelievers; prophecy, however, is for believers, not for unbelievers."** (1 Corinthians 14:1,22) Paul makes an interesting point that prophecy is for believers — not unbelievers! Why would he say that? Because believers (should) have an eager attitude or spirit for prophecy, a desire to know the will, the plans and purposes of God. And, the gift of prophecy is to be especially desired among the people of God, for it is the most direct means of knowing the plans and will of Jesus. The testimony of Jesus can come through Bible prophecy (the book of Revelation is called the testimony of Jesus; Revelation 22:16) or through a prophet. Regardless of the method of delivery — prophecies from the Bible or through a prophet — the testimony of Jesus remains in constant agreement. In other words, a true prophet and a correct understanding of Bible prophecy will be found to be in agreement.

(This last concept needs a qualifying remark. No prophet has ever been shown everything about the times and dates set by God. (Acts 1:7) Paul says of prophets, "For we know in part and we prophesy in part." (1 Corinthians 13:9) The end result is that when Old or New Testament prophets were shown scenes concerning the end of the world, they all thought the end was imminent or near. However, their supposition about God's chronology has been proven wrong by nearly two millenniums. Keep in mind that God only unlocks His chronology when the time for fulfillment arrives. This means that the final generation can know they are the last generation because they alone are enabled to assemble all that the prophets were shown. (Daniel 12:9) The point here is that true prophets have been wrong about the timing of Christ's appearing. (See 1 Corinthians 7:29; 1 John 2:18; Hebrews 1:1; 9:26, 10:37, John 21:22,23, 1 Peter 1:20,4:7, Romans 13:11,12.) However, a correct understanding of Bible prophecy will be found to be in agreement with the content of the visions given to true prophets. (For more information on this matter, see Appendix B in my book, *18 End-Time Bible Prophecies.*)

Here's how the mechanics of the gift of prophecy works: First, Jesus says something in heaven. The Holy Spirit hears what Jesus says. Then, the Holy Spirit carries the information to the prophet(s). Read the following verse twice and notice the mechanics of this operation: **"But when he, the Spirit of truth, comes, he will guide you into all truth. He will not speak on his own; he will speak only what he hears, and he will tell you what is yet to come."** (John 16:13) The gift of prophecy is the vehicle through which the testimony of Jesus comes. The 144,000 are servant-prophets which will receive "the word of the Lord" (testimony) from Jesus via the Holy Spirit.

This matter nicely comes into focus when we read Revelation 12:17: **"Then the dragon was enraged at the woman and went off to make war against the rest of her offspring — those who obey God's commandments and hold to the testimony of Jesus."** In short, the last generation of God's people will be those obeying God's commandments (remember the first announcement?) and holding to the testimony of Jesus as communicated via the Holy Spirit to the 144,000. (Incidently, the devil in verse 17 goes off to make war against the remnant. The war is described in Revelation 13:7. Notice: **"He [Babylon, the dragonlike beast] was given power to make war against the saints and to conquer them. And he was given authority over every tribe, people, language and nation."**) During this coming war, the saints will be greatly encouraged by the close presence of Jesus!

Doctrine is important

Within the context of the four announcements that shall be given by the 144,000, five doctrinal truths will be revealed. They are:

1. The salvation of God
2. The worship of God
3. The sanctuary of God
4. The return of God
5. The conditions of man in life and death

These five doctrines converge and bring Revelation's story into clearest focus. For example, if one does not understand the worship of God, how can he understand the first announcement found in Revelation 14:7 which says, "Worship God?" If one does not understand the sanctuary of God, how can he understand the meaning of the throwing down of the censer in Revelation 8:2-5? If one does not understand the condition of man in death, how can he understand the purpose and importance of two resurrections? If one does not understand that the saints are going to experience the great tribulation and face martyrdom, how can he be prepared? I am not suggesting that every person on earth is going to receive the equivalent of a college education in these doctrines. On the

contrary, I am saying that every person on earth who wants to be saved will receive a *saving knowledge* of these five doctrines. The difference between a saving knowledge and years of study will be irrelevant. What will be relevant is knowledge sufficient for faith and a determination to stand firm for God and His truth.

A calendar of events

There is an important difference between doctrinal truths and apocalyptic prophecy, and many people do not understand the distinction. Perhaps the easiest way to understand the distinction is to think of apocalyptic prophecy as a calendar of events. Each element within a prophecy belongs to a specific moment in time. For example, the first trumpet in Revelation 8 happens at a specific moment in time. In fact, the Bible says that the sixth trumpet happens at a specific hour, day, month and year! (Revelation 9:15) So, every apocalyptic element has a date connected with it. Thus, apocalyptic prophecy is essentially a calendar of predicted events.

On the other hand, doctrinal truth is knowledge from God about His love and interest in man. Even more, doctrine reveals God's interest and ideals for man, and within these ideals we find God's purpose for man and our power of choice to determine our destiny. I am personally convinced of something that seems strange to most people. I believe that many people would knowingly and freely choose to forfeit heaven if they could see the conditions and type of life that all in heaven will live. Think about this concept a few times. Can you imagine a person living in heaven for eternity and not being able to get something he wanted? Suppose someone wanted to get a promotion, a better paying job, and God said, "No." How long could one live with this desire and God's refusal and remain happy? (I chose this illustration, for this is a repetition of Lucifer's fall.)

Most people don't search the Scriptures to better understand doctrine. Rather, most of us become satisfied with a few simplistic ideas about this or that and that's the end of searching the Bible for more truth. And Bible classes at Church are often discussions revealing the poverty of our knowledge rather than serious investigation into the infinite realms of God's Word. It's a lot like our high school days. Can you still work an algebraic problem, or have your mathematical skills decayed to the point that basic math is a challenge?

The point here is that apocalyptic prophecy and doctrine are brother and sister. Apocalyptic prophecy has to do with *when*. Doctrine has to do with *why*. Put them together and we discover wonderful things about God's purposes which were set in motion before the creation of the world!

The messengers

Now that these matters have been examined, let's examine the fullness of the four announcements that are soon

to be heard. The first announcement is this:

"Then I saw another angel flying in midair, and he had the eternal gospel to proclaim to those who live on the earth — to every nation, tribe, language and people. {7} He said in a loud voice, 'Fear God and give him glory, because the hour of his judgment has come. Worship him who made the heavens, the earth, the sea and the springs of water.' " (Revelation 14:6-8)

The delivery of the four announcements is represented to John as the work of angels — flying in midair. Will God's angel's deliver the four announcements to the inhabitants of earth? No, not directly. The 144,000 servant-prophets will bear that responsibility. The Greek word for angel is *aggelos* which simply means messenger. Notice how Jesus used the word *aggelos* in this text: **"Then what did you go out to see? A prophet? Yes, I tell you, and more than a prophet. {10} This is the one about whom it is written: 'I will send my messenger [aggelos] ahead of you, who will prepare your way before you.' {11} I tell you the truth: Among those born of women there has not risen anyone greater than John the Baptist; yet he who is least in the kingdom of heaven is greater than he."** (Matthew 11:9-12)

Clearly, the word *aggelos* in verse 10 applies to John the Baptist — a herald of the first advent, and in Revelation 14:6 the *aggelos* represents the 144,000 — heralds of the second advent.

What is the first announcement given to every person living on earth?

1.   Fear God
2.   Give Him glory, because the hour of His judgment has come
3.   Worship the Creator who made the heavens, earth, sea and fountain of waters.

Let's look at each element within the first message, "Fear God." The Greek word for fear is *phobeo* which means to cause fear or terrify. (The English word phobia is a derivative.) This command means exactly what it says. God is above any power or authority. He can speak worlds into — or out of — existence. He requires His subjects to hold reverent respect for His authority and His throne. No ruler, in heaven or on earth, can tolerate insolent subjects and maintain the dignity of His throne. Peter puts some perspective on this saying, **"For if God did not spare angels when they sinned, but sent them to hell, putting them into gloomy dungeons to be held for judgment; {5} if he did not spare the ancient world when he brought the flood on its ungodly people, but protected Noah, a preacher of righteousness, and seven others; {6} if he condemned the cities of Sodom and Gomorrah by burning them to ashes, and made them an example of what is going to happen to the ungodly.... This is especially true of those who follow the corrupt desire of the sinful nature and despise authority. Bold and arrogant, these men are not afraid to slander celestial beings."** (2 Peter 2:4-6,10)

Thus, the work of the 144,000 on behalf of the world begins after the global earthquake. They begin with a call to fear God as Supreme Ruler, having the authority of life and death over all the inhabitants of earth. As the reader might expect, this message flies in the face of the world's attitude about God. Like Pharaoh of old they scoff, "Who is *your* God that we should be so concerned?"

The second element within the first announcement contains more detail. It says, "Give Him glory, because the hour of His judgment has come." The Greek sense of giving glory is equivalent today as giving high honor or exalted recognition. We give great glory to Olympic athletes when we stand them on a podium and place a metal around their necks which recognizes their accomplishments. This glory is not imaginary. Often, it is converted into millions of dollars for product endorsements.

In God's case, we give God glory by recognizing that all His works and commands are faithful and true. We give God glory by exalting His laws and commands above anything else. We give God glory by putting Him first, above anything else. Indeed, this is the point of the first announcement because the hour of His judgment of earth has begun. In other words, when this message goes forth, God begins the judgment of the living. He begins sealing everyone in their decision for life eternal or for death eternal.

I need to make an important point here. God does not make a unilateral decision upon each person during the judgment of the living as He did upon the dead. Rather, during the judgment of the living, He seals people in their decision for faith or rebellion. He sends the gospel to every nation, kindred, tongue and people with great convincing power to see who will receive His truth and live by faith, and who will refuse His invitation and rebel against Him. Here's the mechanics of the process:

1. Each person on earth will hear the full gospel invitation.
2. As they hear, they will have to decide for or against the message. There will be no middle ground because desperate circumstances will require each person to accept the gospel as delivered by the 144,000 or reject it. (When survival itself is at stake, decisions aren't too complicated — they may be hard to make, but the issues are clear.)
3. Once a decision is made, God will test each person to see if he is solid in his decision. If he isn't, the testing become more intense until a solid decision is reached.
4. After the test reveals the final decision, that person is sealed in his decision of faith or rebellion. The sealing is final.

So, this element of the first announcement, *the hour of His judgment has come,* clearly reveals that test-day has arrived. The Great Tribulation has begun.

The last element within the first announcement logically follows the first two elements. Notice how they fit together:

1. Fear God. Have due respect for His authority.
2. Give Him glory because the hour of His judgment has come. Understand that His terrible judgments are the only means left to awaken the world to its sinful course, and He must take these drastic actions so that every person, regardless of religious background, might hear His truth and understand that He is now sealing each person's decision for eternity.
3. Worship the Creator who made the heavens, the earth, the sea and fountain of waters. This third command is a call to worship God. Strange as this might sound to some, God can only be worshiped on His terms. Think about this. If we can determine the time or manner for the worship of God, we would have greater authority than God. So, the call to worship God involves time and manner. The time is His holy Sabbath day, Saturday, the seventh-day of the week. (Exodus 20:8-11) As shown in Chapter 21, God's holy day is the seventh-day of the week. In addition, the Bible also reveals that God can only be worshiped in spirit and truth. (John 4:23) The point is that God will not make anyone worship Him on His holy day. However, those who love Him,

those who honor Him will choose to obey His commands. (John 14:15) In other words, the 144,000 will call the inhabitants of earth to worship God on Saturday, according to His fourth commandment. They will call the inhabitants of earth to worship God in a spirit of humility and in the joy of truth on His holy day.

Remember, these four announcements have two dimensions. The first is the revelation of the will of God. The second dimension is the revelation of the rebellion of man. The point here is that at the time the first announcement goes forth, men will scoff at God's commandment, "Remember the Sabbath day, to keep it holy." Thus, respect for the holiness of God will be revealed.

But, the story gets even more interesting. The call to worship the Creator who made the heavens, the earth, the sea and the fountain of waters is not a rhetorical phrase. Notice how the elements are to be affected by the first four trumpets:

Trumpet 1 Earth, trees and grass burned up
Trumpet 2 Sea creatures die, ships sink
Trumpet 3 Fountains of waters contaminated
Trumpet 4 Heavens turned dark

Now, the first announcement says, "Worship the Creator who made:"

1. The heavens
2. The earth
3. The sea
4. The fountains of waters

Is there a direct connection between the first four trumpets and the first message? Yes! Look compare the devastation of the four trumpets with the first announcement. But people will scoff at the first message because it begins shortly prior to the sounding of the first trumpet. But, when the trumpets begin, something revolutionary occurs. People will suddenly get very religious. There's a funny thing about fear.

Then, a second announcement joins the first. (The reader should understand that the four announcements join sequentially together and swell the gospel call so that in their unison they become fully heard by everyone.)

The second announcement begins

I believe the first four trumpets happen in rather quick succession. Perhaps the time period is about one month. Regardless of the time frame, the devastation of the first trumpet is powerfully convincing because the first trumpet will set many millions of acres on fire by flaming meteors. Then, ka-boom! A great asteroid hits the sea and the tidal wave does horrific damage to seaports all around that ocean. Then, ka-boom! A another great asteroid hits a continent and the resulting ground waves sheer water wells and septic systems. The result is contaminated water and millions die from the plague of typhus or typhoid. Then, a deep rumble occurs within the belly of the earth and volcanos belch tons of ejecta into the atmosphere. Whole islands disappear and darkness settles upon portions of the world.

The people of earth are stopped in their tracks. Truly, this will be a time when the people of earth stand still and behold something about the wrath of Almighty God. The first four trumpets are so overwhelming, so extensive, so horrific and so great that every knee will tremble before the wrath of God. Just as Mt. Sinai shook when Jesus descended upon it to speak His Ten Commandments, the whole world will tremble the day Jesus begins His judgments of the living and manifestations will continue until He has opened every mind and ear to hear what He has to say.

In response to the first four trumpets, religious leaders will do two things. First, they will quickly conclude that these judgments have come upon the world because the people of earth (not just one nation) have offended God. Christians will use texts like Daniel 9:13,14. Moslems, Jews, Eastern Mystics and heathen will reach the same conclusion by turning to their spiritual authorities. Almost spontaneously, religious leaders will call for a global conference to address the wrath of God. They will say things like, "The global union of mankind to appease a universal God can be diverse. Let us each do our part to

put away sin so that God will not destroy us." The end result of the conference will be a new world organization. It is identified as the dragonlike beast in Revelation 13:1-8.

As a result of the trumpet destructions, martial law and contingency constitutions will be implemented all over the world. Rationing will become the common means of controlling the supply and distribution of the necessities for life. Thus, the right to buy and sell will be curtailed. (Later, it will be even more restricted and controlled by the devil's forces.) In short, the world will receive a mortal blow and men will recoil for survival.

Then a most interesting response will occur. While the 144,000 were proclaiming, "Worship the Creator," men scoffed. But now every heart is filled with fear. As religious leaders call for laws compelling respect for God, politicans will be powerless to stop the surge of popular demand. And, given the circumstances, who can argue with the movement? Martial law will be installed in heavily damaged areas. And a national movement will begin in America to enforce Sunday laws. Sunday, religious leaders will say, is the Lord's day and it should be given due respect. It's a day for family, and *reverence for God has been an important family value that has been lost during this century.* Commercial businesses will be required to close on Sunday for reasons consistent with the times. The net effect is that Sunday will, at first, be exalted in America for business and family reasons. Later, as circumstances worsen, it will be declared as God's day of rest. (Friday will be similarly exalted in Moslem countries and Saturday will be exalted in Israel.)

The reader must understand this next point. The laws of man that cooperate with the laws of God are approved by God. (Romans 13:1) However, when the laws of man run contrary to the laws of God, God is not pleased, and eventually, He destroys those laws and lawmakers. (Daniel 4:25) The relationship that will exist between religious leaders and civil authorities will become unholy the moment civil authorities enact a law respecting the sacredness of Sunday, for Sunday has never been the Sabbath of God. In fact, the fourth commandment clearly says that the seventh-day is God's holy day. God's law clearly mandates worship on the seventh-day of the week. But, the religious coalition that shall be formed by leaders all over the world will pressure civil authorities to mandate the worship of God on the prevailing day of worship in that nation. What makes this action so vile is this: What body of men can tell God when He is to be worshiped? Even more, what body of men have the authority to tell others *when* they must worship the God of Heaven? Such an act is a violation of the first human right — the right to freedom of conscience in the worship of God.

So, in response to the actions of men, God sends a second announcement throughout the earth. It says, **"A second angel followed and said, 'Fallen! Fallen is Babylon the Great, which made all the nations drink the maddening wine of her adulteries.' "** (Revelation 14:8)

Babylon is fallen

We often limit the word fallen to mean a fall from power or a fall from a high place. However, the word fallen goes farther. It also means to be found corrupt or deceptive. For example, we can say that PTL Club's founder, Jim Bakker, is fallen. In reality, he fell in several ways. He fell from his post as president of an enterprising ministry, he fell from high visibility on TV, and he fell from respect when it was found that his actions were dishonest, intending to deceive. To say that Jim Bakker is a fallen man is a truth *now* self evident.

What initiates the second announcement of the 144,000 that Babylon is fallen? The answer is found in the verse, "[it] made all the nations drink." In short, when religious and political leaders of the world cross the line and *knowingly* enforce laws compelling false worship, they fall from God's grace and are exposed as false religion. Let me explain.

God has permitted the establishment of seven global religious systems. These seven are identified as Atheism, Heathenism, Judaism, Islam, Eastern Mysticism, Catholicism, and Protestantism. (These are the seven heads of Babylon found in Revelation 13.) During the Great Tribulation, God is going to clearly reveal to every person on earth that these religious systems are false. Even though they claim to speak for Him, none do. Even though they claim to have the truth about Him, none do.

And even though they claim to have the solution to appeasing God and stopping His judgments, none do.

Remember, after the global earthquake, the 144,000 will begin to proclaim with great power that the hour of God's judgment has begun. They also call everyone to the true worship of Jesus the Creator on His holy Sabbath, but few will listen and give heed. Then the trumpets sound and what do the religious systems of the world do? They influence politicians to make laws *requiring* the worship of God. The last resort of all false religions is the use of force. This is what the Bible means when it says, "[Babylon] *made* all nations drink the maddening wine of her adulteries." The idea here is that the people of all nations are forcibly required to obey Babylon. As a result, the religious systems that constitute Babylon are now exposed for what they really are: false.

The matter almost becomes comical because universal agreement on the appeasement of God is not possible. The Catholics and Protestants require the exaltation of Sunday and the Moslems and Jews want to exalt Friday and Saturday, respectively. Try to mentally surround the dilemma. There is *one* angry God. There is *one* devastated world. There are *seven* religions claiming to have the truth about *one* God that needs to be appeased. There can be no unanimity on the day of worship. In fact, it is this very dilemma from which the first

beast of Revelation 13 derives its name: Babylon.

The real point here is that God sends a second announcement to the world at just the right moment. As the world coalition of religious powers rise to authority for the purpose of appeasing God, God says through His servants, "Babylon is fallen, is fallen." They, the religious systems of the world, will be exposed as false. They do not know God's truth. And God hopes, of course, that people will choose to see His truth.

The third announcement is given

Timing is everything. Consequently, the third announcement is directly connected to the sounding of the fifth trumpet. (The fifth trumpet is the physical appearing of the devil.) One must understand that nothing has ever happened on earth (except Mt. Sinai) that can be compared to the physical appearing of the devil. Certainly, none among the living today have ever seen such a display of power, glory and beauty that shall attend the devil and his angels when they appear on earth.

Without going into detail, the primary work of the devil, once he is here in the flesh, is to take the world captive through deception. He will make a display all sorts of miracles and perform wonderful signs to convince people that he is Almighty God. His stated purpose will be the ushering in of a new age, where he, as God, rules the earth. Millions will receive him as God. Many Moslems will believe that he is Allah. Many Jews will believe that he is the promised Messiah. Many Catholics and Protestants will believe he is the long-awaited Jesus Christ. Atheists will have to admit this is a superior being. Heathen will acknowledge him as the Great Spirit of the ages and many Eastern Mystics will receive this being as the God of the New Age. In short, he will be able to satisfy millions of diverse people with his claims of being God.

Revelation identifies the physical appearing of the devil as a beast that appears to be "lamblike" or Christ-like, yet he speaks like the "dragon." (Revelation 13:11) But the speech of the devil will reveal his true identity because, after a pleasant season of gathering believers unto himself, he will begin to place very heavy demands upon his followers. Notice this text concerning the devil: **"He also forced everyone, small and great, rich and poor, free and slave, to receive a mark on his right hand or on his forehead."** (Revelation 13:16)

The work of the devil is divided into three phases. First, the deceptive phase. Secondly, the controlling phase and lastly, the destructive phase. So, the first thing he does is gather billions of believers unto himself. Then, he motivates them to take control of the world for the sake of establishing a new kingdom. (The war to take control of the world is the sixth trumpet.) And upon gaining control over the world, the devil will move his followers to destroy the people of God as thoroughly and quickly as possible (especially, the 144,000). The Bible

says, **"He [the devil] was given power to give breath to the image of the first beast, so that it could speak and cause all who refused to worship the image to be killed."** (Revelation 13:15)

In this setting, the third message is given. It says, **"A third angel followed them and said in a loud voice: 'If anyone worships the [lamblike] beast and his image and receives his mark on the forehead or on the hand, {10} he, too, will drink of the wine of God's fury, which has been poured full strength into the cup of his wrath. He will be tormented with burning sulfur in the presence of the holy angels and of the Lamb.' "** (Revelation 14:9-10)

The symbolism in both the second and third announcements out the drinking of wine is important. To drink wine that is maddening (second announcement) or to drink the wine of God's fury (third announcement) refers to internalizing some event or digesting some experience. For example, Jesus said to His disciples, **" 'You don't know what you are asking,' Jesus said to them. 'Can you drink the cup I am going to drink?' 'We can,' they answered. {23} Jesus said to them, 'You will indeed drink from my cup....' "** (Matthew 20:22-23) So, the third announcement is a direct warning against obeying and worshiping the devil. This announcement will really bring controversy. Consider the problem: Many will believe the devil is God. The 144,000 will be claiming that he is the devil. What will be the feelings of those on the devil's side toward the 144,000 and their followers?

The world will be caught in a great decision: Worship the devil and receive the promised wrath of God, or worship God and receive the immediate wrath of the devil. In this furnace of persecution, *only those who have strong faith* in God will be able to stand firm for truth's sake. Yes, here is the process that proves that salvation comes by faith. James says, "But someone will say, 'You have faith; I have deeds.' Show me your faith without deeds, and I will show you my faith by what I do. {24} You see that a person is justified by what he does and not by faith alone." (James 2:18,24)

The fourth announcement

The final announcement given by the 144,000 is a plea from the heart of God. At this time, the importance of this plea is only comprehended by God since no human has ever seen anything comparable to the seven last plagues. In some respects, the seven trumpets are samples. However, the fourth announcement occurs just before the seventh trumpet sounds. (The seventh trumpet marks the end of God's mercy and the beginning of the final woe, the seven *last* plagues.) John says of the seven last plagues, "I saw in heaven another great and marvelous sign: seven angels with the seven last plagues — last, because with them God's wrath is completed." (Revelation 15:1)

The fourth and final announcement to the world is this: "After this I saw another angel coming down from heaven. He had great authority, and the earth was illuminated by his splendor. {2} With a mighty voice he shouted: 'Fallen! Fallen is Babylon the Great! She has become a home for demons and a haunt for every evil spirit, a haunt for every unclean and detestable bird. {3} For all the nations have drunk the maddening wine of her adulteries. The kings of the earth committed adultery with her, and the merchants of the earth grew rich from her excessive luxuries.' {4} Then I heard another voice from heaven say: 'Come out of her, my people, so that you will not share in her sins, so that you will not receive any of her plagues; {5} for her sins are piled up to heaven, and God has remembered her crimes. {6} Give back to her as she has given; pay her back double for what she has done. Mix her a double portion from her own cup. {7} Give her as much torture and grief as the glory and luxury she gave herself. In her heart she boasts, 'I sit as queen; I am not a widow, and I will never mourn.' {8} Therefore in one day her plagues will overtake her: death, mourning and famine. She will be consumed by fire, for mighty is the Lord God who judges her.' " (Revelation 18:1-8)

The message is self-explanatory. However, there are four uses of Old Testament language in these verses that help make this announcement more encompassing and understandable. So, look up the references given below from your Bible and compare the fourth message with these scriptures. You will find this interesting. To help you get started, I've included a few remarks.

Jeremiah 5:26,27 talks about cages full of birds. So, what does Revelation 18:2 mean saying that Babylon is "a home for demons and a haunt for every evil spirit, a haunt for every unclean and detestable bird?" Jeremiah explains how wicked men are like those who set traps to snare birds. The trap works well because birds don't understand the trap nor their fate. In a similar way, this announcement is designed to unmask the fact that religious and political leaders of the world are leading people into a great trap where they shall receive the wrath of God without mercy. The tragedy is that millions refuse to admit the coming consequences of their doing.

Jeremiah 25:15-17 speaks of God sending Jeremiah through the land and making all nations drink of God's cup of wrath. The point here is that God is sovereign and He makes the nations drink of His cup of wrath if they drink the maddening wine of Babylon. See also Psalm 60:3.

Jeremiah 50:8-41 speaks of a parallel to flee ancient Babylon. Read the entire selection and see why God calls His people to come out of Babylon.

Lamentations 1:1-3 speaks of Israel's former greatness. How like a queen, she ruled over the land, and then after the wrath of God came upon her, she became helpless, like a widow. Compare this scenario with Babylon's great power until the time of the seven last plagues.

Summary

The purpose of the four announcements is the gathering of all saints into one fold. Salvation will be freely offered to any and all who will receive Jesus and Savior as Lord — no matter how bad or terrible the past life. These four announcements not only reveal the love of God to save to the utmost, they also reveal the will of our Creator. These four announcements will fully expose the rebellion of sin that contaminates the hearts of men and women.

Timing is everything. These messages will be borne by the 144,000, and they will be heard by every nation, kindred, tongue and people within a short time-period, perhaps 1,000 days in length. These four announcements occur at specific moments in the progression of end-time events. The final result of these four announcements will be a great harvest of souls at the second coming. John says, **"After this I looked and there before me was a great multitude that no one could count, from every nation, tribe, people and language, standing before the throne and in front of the Lamb. They were wearing white robes and were holding palm branches in their hands. {13} Then one of the elders asked me, 'These in white robes — who are they, and where did they come from?' {14} I answered, 'Sir, you know.' And he said, 'These are they who have come out of the great tribulation; they have washed their robes and made them white in the blood of the Lamb.' "** (Revelation 7:9,13,14)

Chapter 23

The Close of Probation

The promise of salvation

We have studied the Two Witnesses of Revelation 11. They are identified as the Bible and the Holy Spirit. These two powers work together for the salvation of man. The Bible is the testimony of God. The Holy Spirit is the power of God. Together, they testify of salvation and its requirements. Everyone on earth will hear their message before the end comes. The clarion message of salvation will cause a great controversy upon earth. The preaching of the gospel truth will cause great anger and resistance from those who love evil, for "those who love evil hate the light."

Every person on earth will be reached during the short time-period of the trumpets. The powerful struggle against the gospel will only give the gospel greater attention! Like a great forest fire, the gospel will first spread through populated cities and then to distant places of the world. Persecution will force people to flee for safety and as they flee, the gospel will be carried with them. This is how the gospel will go to every nation, kindred, tongue and people. The 144,000 expose Babylon's doctrine as lies and in return, Babylon seeks to destroy them and their followers.

There is a historical parallel to the scenario in the paragraph above. After Jesus ascended to heaven, the apostles preached the gospel of Jesus and the promise of His return with great power and 3,000 were baptized at Pentecost! The religious leaders and civil authorities could not tolerate such interest in the truth. So, the fires of persecution were kindled and as the saints scattered to the four corners of earth, they carried the gospel with them!

Jesus warned his disciples, **"There will be great earthquakes, famines and pestilences in various places, and fearful events and great signs from heaven. But before all this, they will lay hands on you and persecute you. They will deliver you to synagogues and prisons, and you will be brought before kings and governors, and all on account of my name. This will result in your being witnesses to them. But make up your mind not to worry beforehand how you will defend yourselves. For I will give you words and wisdom that none of your adversaries will be able to resist or contradict. You will be betrayed by parents, brothers, relatives and friends, and they will put some of you to death. All men will hate you because of me. But not a hair of your head will perish.**

By standing firm you will save yourselves." (Luke 21:11-19) Two points should be emphasized from these verses:

1.   Jesus has promised to give His followers the words to say when challenged for their faith!
2.   Even though the world will hate you, Jesus says, "You will save yourself by standing firm."

It must be emphasized that Jesus has promised to be with each one of His children during this time of trial. He said, **"...and surely I will be with you always, to the very end of the age."** (Matthew 28:20)

The Spirit of Prophecy

We have seen earlier that the remnant are identified as keeping the commandments of God and holding to the testimony of Jesus. (Revelation 12:17, 14:12) We know what the commandments are, but what is the testimony of Jesus?

Toward the end of John's vision, he was so grateful to his attending angel that he bowed at his feet to worship him. But the angel said, **"...Do not do it! I am a fellow servant with you and with your brothers who hold to the testimony of Jesus. Worship God! For the testimony of Jesus is the spirit of prophecy."** (Revelation 19:10)

The angel said the testimony of Jesus is the spirit of prophecy. What does this mean? It means that the remnant have prophetic understanding through the ministry of the Holy Spirit. In other words, they will understand what God is going to do and why. The remnant will anticipate the fulfillment of each event and be prepared for it! Daniel was told, **"Many (of the remnant) will be purified, made spotless and refined, but the wicked will continue to be wicked. None of the wicked will understand, but those who are wise will understand."** (Daniel 12:10)

The remnant will not be caught by surprise. They will be prepared through careful Bible study and prayer. Perhaps one of the clearest evidences of this point is found in Revelation 17:8. Notice, **"The beast, which you saw... will come up out of the Abyss and go to his destruction. The inhabitants of the earth whose names have not been written in the book of life from the creation of the world will be astonished when they see the beast...."** In other words, John says the world will be astonished when Satan appears, while those studying the prophecies will be prepared!

Three groups of remnant people

The apostles were a select group of men. They were given a special opportunity to learn about Jesus and the kingdom of heaven that others did not have. For three and a half years they walked with Jesus and learned from Him. He was preparing them for the great work they must do after He returned to the Father.

After the ascension of Jesus, the apostles received the power of the Holy Spirit. It was quite an experience. It happened at the Feast of Pentecost which was 50 days after the Passover. Attendance at the feast was required according to ceremonial law, so Jews from all over Asia were in Jerusalem at the time. To expedite the gospel, the Holy Spirit created a great noise—a sound like a violent wind came from heaven and what appeared to be tongues or flames of fire appeared on the heads of the apostles.

This interruption of the Pentecost service gained immediate attention, for those with flames of fire upon them began to speak in the native languages of the Jews present. The author of Acts says, **"Now there were staying in Jerusalem God-fearing Jews from every nation under heaven. When they heard this sound, a crowd came together in bewilderment, because each one heard them speaking in his own language. Utterly amazed, they asked; 'Are not all these men who are speaking Galileans? Then how is it that each of us hears them in his own native language? Parthians, Medes and Elamites; residents of Mesopotamia, Judea and Cappadocia, Pontus and Asia, Phrygia and Pamphylia, Egypt and the parts of Libya near Cyrene; visitors from Rome (both Jews and converts to Judaism); Cretans and Arabs - we hear them declaring the wonders of God in our own tongues!' "** (Acts 2:5-11) This demonstration by the Holy Spirit caused three things to happen:

1. The gospel immediately transcended the language barrier, for everyone heard the gospel in his own tongue!
2. The number of Jews receiving Jesus Christ and His gospel increased thirty-fold that day.
3. Those accepting the gospel carried their new-found faith to distant lands where the apostles would never be able to go.

Notice the process: Jesus started His ministry with only 12 disciples. When the Holy Spirit was given to them at the Pentecost ceremony, Jesus reached 3,000 more Jewish people! These new converts went home and told even more Jewish people about Jesus. About three and a half years later, Jesus sent the disciples to the Gentiles to gather an even larger harvest of believers! (Remember A.D. 34—the commission of Peter and the conversion of Saul?) This is how the gospel went throughout the world in ancient times and this is a sample of how the gospel will go throughout the world in our day.

In Revelation, we have a process almost identical to Pentecost. First, Jesus selects and seals 144,000 people as "spark plugs." These people know the testimony of the Bible. They have studied themselves full, thought themselves straight and prayed for power to give the message. Jesus then grants the request of these people for power by giving them the power of the Holy Spirit's "latter rain."

Note: The term latter rain refers to the second or large rain that fell in Palestine in the Autumn of each year just before harvest time. The first rain (a small or early rain) usually occurred in the Spring of the year and winter crops were harvested and presented before the Lord at the Feast of Pentecost. The analogy is that both rains brought the crops to maturity. The larger and more bountiful harvest occurred at the Feast of Tabernacles in the Autumn because the "latter rain" brought the summer crops to maturity. See Deuteronomy 11:14, Jeremiah 3:3, Joel 2:23 and Hosea 6:3.

God is now unfolding Revelation's mysterious story because the time of fulfillment has come. Jesus is selecting and preparing those who will constitute the 144,000 from among those who understand Revelation's story. These in turn, will explain to the world the actions of Jesus when He opens the fourth seal.

As people hear the gospel message, many will immediately see it's harmony and through faith, accept its truthfulness. Some will join the Revelation movement and become part of the first remnant. In effect, the first remnant is a support group for the 144,000. When the trumpets begin to sound, the combined army of the 144,000 and the first remnant are prepared for their work. They fearlessly march into Babylon to gather the rest of God's people who haven't heard the everlasting gospel! Jesus calls to those in Babylon, "...Come out of her, (Babylon) my people, so that you will not share in her sins, so that you will not receive any of her plagues; for her

sins are piled up to heaven, and God has remembered her crimes." (Revelation 18:4,5) The gathering of the final harvest consists of three steps:

1. The selection and sealing of the 144,000
2. The gathering of an early remnant to support the 144,000
3. The gathering of the latter remnant out of Babylon

The close of mercy

Jesus does not sneak up on people and close the door of mercy without warning. On the other hand, the devil delights to snuff out life and thus abruptly end their opportunity to receive salvation. The apostle Paul understood this quite clearly. He said, "...Today, if you hear his voice, do not harden your hearts!" (Hebrews 4:7) Jesus is tenderly calling. He is about to conclude His work in the heavenly sanctuary. Are you ready to live by faith? Are you obedient to His call? If you are, you can be one of the early remnant. This opportunity comes as a result of receiving the gospel!

The closing of mercy during the time-period of the trumpets consists of four steps. They are:

1. Each person on earth must hear the everlasting gospel.
2. Each person will be required to make a decision about the gospel.
3. Each person is tested on his decision.
4. Each person is sealed in his decision.

Mercy closes for an individual as the four steps occur. Since people in different lands hear the warning message of Revelation at different times during the trumpets, the sealing of some occurs before others during the judgment of the living. When all have heard the final invitation, made their decision and are sealed in their decision, probation is ended. The Ancient of Days then dismisses the court.

The proclamation

From our study on the trumpets, we learned that corporate probation ends with the throwing down of the censer. The sins of earth have reached the point of no return. The judgment review of the books in heaven is completed at this time and the judgment of the living is necessary. This means that each person will now be judged. In other words, the trumpet time period is the "hour of God's judgment." It is a time of judgment for the living and the seventh trumpet marks the end of the judgment process. Notice how John describes the close of mercy in Revelation 14:14-20: **"I looked, and there before me was a white cloud, and seated on the cloud was one 'like a son of man' with a crown of gold on his head and a sharp sickle in his hand. Then another angel came out of the temple and called in a loud voice to him who was sitting on the cloud, 'Take your sickle and reap, because the time to reap has come, for the harvest of the earth is ripe.' So he that was seated on the cloud swung his sickle over the earth, and the earth was harvested.**

Another angel came out of the temple in heaven, and he too had a sharp sickle. Still another angel, who had charge of the fire, came from the altar and called in a loud voice to him who had the sharp sickle, 'Take your sharp sickle and gather the clusters of grapes from the earth's vine, because its grapes are ripe.' The angel swung his sickle on the earth, gathered its grapes and threw them into the great winepress of God's wrath. They were trampled in the winepress outside the city, and blood flowed out of the press, rising as high as the horses' bridles for a distance of 1,600 stadia (180 miles)." Several points need to be made from these verses.

1. There are two gatherings.

Jesus, the Son of Man, is seated on the white cloud and is told by an angel coming from the temple that the time for harvest has come. The action of swinging the sickle over the earth symbolizes the gathering of God's children into safety. Everyone has made his decision, so the harvest *is ripe*, and mercy is ended.

Later, another angel comes from the temple with a sharp sickle and he is told to gather the wicked and put them into the winepress of God's wrath. This action symbolizes the gathering or bundling of the wicked to receive the wrath of God—the seven last plagues. (Note: John comments that the amount of wicked people (grapes) thrown into the winepress of God's wrath is incredible! Remember the third angel's message mentions the winepress.)

Compare these Revelation 14:14-20 with Matthew 13:24-43. In Matthew 13, Jesus told a parable of the man who sowed good seed in his field, but the man's enemy sowed weeds to ruin his crop. The man's servants asked if they should pull up the weeds, but the owner said, **"No. Because while you are pulling up the weeds, you may root up the wheat with them. Let both grow together until the harvest. At that time I will tell the harvesters: First collect the weeds and tie them in bundles to be burned, then gather the wheat and bring it into my barn."** (Matthew 13:29,30)

At first, the parable in Matthew may appear just opposite of John's account from Revelation because the wicked are first bundled together and then the wheat is gathered into the barn. The problem, though, is quite simple. The good and the bad grow together until the *time* of harvest. The wicked will be gathered together or bundled first. The confederation of Babylon happens first! The coalition or global union of the world literally happens before the wheat is gathered into "the barn" at the close of probation.

The Father holds the door of mercy open as long as there is one person who has not heard the invitation. Remember, Jesus came to save to the utmost. This is the mystery of God. No one will perish without first having an opportunity to be saved. The gospel offers salvation full and free to those willing to live by faith! It is because

everyone has made his decision that Jesus is told to swing His sickle over the earth. The harvest is ripe and ready for the picking. The wheat has been gathered in and the door of mercy is closed.

Then an angel gathers the wicked which have been bundled together by receiving the mark of the beast. These have refused the gospel invitation. Even worse, these have allied themselves with Satan to destroy God's people and this makes God angry. Therefore, He visits them in wrath without mercy to avenge the cruel suffering inflicted upon His innocent children.

2. Jesus doesn't know when probation is to close

Jesus is told *when* to close probation by the angel coming from the heavenly temple. The decision to close probation is not made by Jesus. The Father decides when enough is enough! Notice what Jesus said about this: **"No one knows about that day or hour, not even the angels in heaven, nor the Son, but only the Father. As it was in the days of Noah, so it will be at the coming of the Son of Man. For in the days before the flood, people were eating and drinking, marrying and giving in marriage, up to the day Noah entered the ark; and they knew nothing about what would happen until the flood came and took them all away. That is how it will be at the coming of the Son of Man. Two men will be in the field; one will be taken and the other left. Two women will be grinding with a hand mill;**

one will be taken and the other left."
(Matthew 24:36-41) These verses bring
out two points we must understand:

a. Only the Father knows when
   mercy ends. Some believe this
   verse applies to the second
   coming, but a close investigation
   shows this is not possible. The key
   to understanding these verses is
   found in a comparison with
   Noah's experience. Jesus said that
   in the days before the flood,
   people were eating, drinking and
   marrying. Nothing is inherently
   wrong with any of these things if
   we put God first in our lives. Noah
   preached of the coming flood for
   120 years and the people of earth
   were well aware of Noah and his
   message. They also saw the giant
   boat. What they didn't know about
   was the close of mercy! The day
   Noah entered the ark, the door
   was closed. The closing of the
   ark's door sealed eight people
   inside and a world outside. The
   closing of the door of mercy in
   heaven is the issue — this is the
   moment in time that matters most.

b. Matthew clearly points out that
   men and women can work side
   by side, yet when the door of
   mercy closes in heaven, one will
   be found safe inside and the other
   locked outside forever. The most
   serious moment in all of
   Revelation is found in Revelation
   14:14-16. This, as far as salvation
   is concerned, is the end. When
   Jesus comes in the clouds of glory,

He brings His reward with Him for
the eternal reward of each person
has already been decided!
(Revelation 22:12)

The seventh trumpet reviewed

It might be helpful to refresh our minds
with the contents of the seventh trumpet
to make sure all the elements of the
close of probation come into focus. At
this point in time, Satan is at maximum
power. He appeared on earth during the
fifth trumpet and deceived many, and
during the sixth trumpet, he took control
of the world through force. The
effectiveness of the Bible and the Holy
Spirit has been either destroyed by the
dazzling miracles of Satan or by the
threat of death, and everyone upon earth
has made their decision. John writes,
**"The seventh angel sounded his
trumpet, and there were loud voices in
heaven, which said: 'The kingdom of the
world has become the kingdom of our
Lord and of his Christ, and he will reign
for ever and ever.' And the twenty-four
elders, who were seated on their thrones
before God, fell on their faces and
worshiped God: saying, 'We give thanks
to you, Lord God Almighty, who is and
who was, because you have taken your
great power and have begun to reign.
The nations were angry; and your wrath
has come. The time has come for
judging the dead, and for rewarding
your servants the prophets and your
saints and those who reverence your
name, both small and great - and for
destroying those who destroy the earth.'

Then God's temple in heaven was
opened, and within his temple was seen**

the ark of his covenant. And there came flashes of lightning, rumblings, peals of thunder, an earthquake and a great hailstorm." (Revelation 11:15-19) These verses point out five important issues:

1. At the time of the seventh trumpet, Jesus is promoted again! At this time the kingdom of the world becomes the kingdom of Jesus. He has finished His priestly work of atonement. He now begins to rule as King of Kings and Lord of Lords. Just before taking His great power to rule, Jesus makes a final proclamation, **"Let him who does wrong continue to do wrong; let him who is vile continue to be vile; let him who does right continue to do right; and let him who is holy continue to be holy."** (Revelation 22:11)

2. Jesus is angry because, for the most part, the world has rejected His invitation to life eternal, and even worse, they killed many who carried the invitation to the great wedding banquet! John says, **"I saw the woman was drunk with the blood of the saints, the blood of those who bore testimony to Jesus."** (Revelation 17:6) (Compare this with the wedding parable in Matthew 22:1-14.)

3. The nations are angry (remember, this is a time of wrath). They are angry because of the outcome of the sixth trumpet. This trumpet describes the great war that Satan conducts to forcibly gain control of the world. What he can't get through deceit, he takes by sheer force.

4. The 24 elders who have observed the great work of Jesus since 1844, agree that time has come to do three things. They say:

a. "Time has come to judge the dead." The word, "judge," in this phrase means to avenge. In this scene the elders are saying that the time has come to *avenge* the death of God's people who died when the fifth seal was opened! Jesus avenges the shed blood of His children by sending the seven last plagues. After pouring out the third plague, the angel with the vial says, **"...You are just in these judgments, you who are and who were, the Holy One, because you have so judged; for they have shed the blood of your saints and prophets, and you have given them blood to drink as they deserve."** (Revelation 16:5,6)

b. "Time has come to reward your servants and the prophets." When probation closes, the death and destruction of God's people also ends! Daniel 12:1 says, **"At that time Michael, the great prince who protects your people, will arise. There will be a time of distress such as has not happened from the beginning of nations until then. But at that time your people - everyone whose name is found written in the book - will be delivered."** The saints, whose names are written in the book of life, will be delivered from death! Since probation is closed, the death of God's people would have no redemptive value, so King Jesus says, "Enough."

c. "The time has come to destroy those who destroy the earth." Satan, at the time of the seventh trumpet, has fully established his headquarters and operations on earth. Those refusing to cooperate with his evil government are to be destroyed. Such is the purpose of the sixth trumpet war. The use of nuclear arms during this war not only destroys the target or impacted area, it renders much of earth uninhabitable. The entire world will be convulsed with misery and agony. Even though Babylon finally rules the world, she will fall. Jesus personally undertakes the destruction of Babylon the Great — for she is the one destroying the earth. This destruction is fully described in Revelation 18!

5. The last point that we learn from the seventh trumpet is that God's temple in heaven is opened and the ark of the covenant is seen. The temple is opened or vacated because court is over. There is no more mercy. The gospel has gone to every nation, kindred, tongue and people. The gospel invitation is withdrawn. Every decision has been made.

It is the author's opinion that the people of earth will actually see the ark of the covenant that contains the Ten Commandments during the trumpets time-period. This very ark was constructed by Moses in the wilderness and the Ten Commandments, written by Jesus Himself, still rest inside the ark. When the king of Babylon overtook Jerusalem in 600 B.C., Jeremiah hid the ark in a cave and it remains safe and secure until the time of its discovery. It will be brought forth as a witness to the world that God's great law has not — and cannot be changed. When the seventh trumpet sounds, then the ark in heaven is seen too! The world will behold that indeed, the one on earth is a copy of the one in heaven.

The effect of both arks appearing during this time is ominous. First, everyone has heard the gospel call to "worship God" according to His law. Every person has made a decision — whether to obey or disobey. The remnant have faith enough to obey the fourth commandment. The rest of the world put their faith in Satan and receive the mark of the "lamb-like" beast. Secondly, when the wicked see the ark from heaven containing the Ten Commandments they will be terrified at the condemnation they have brought upon themselves by enforcing laws of worship contrary to the Great Lawgiver. John says, "...there is no rest day or night for those who worship the beast and his image, or for anyone who receives the mark of his name." (Revelation 14:11) Yet, in a rebellion that is unexplainable, the wicked only set their hearts and minds to destroy the people of God. Under Satan's cruel leadership, they agree to destroy all of God's people at a set time.

The final abomination

To rid the earth of God's people, Babylon will issue a universal decree. This decree will grant immunity to everyone wishing to kill the remnant at a certain point in time!

The wicked don't know that God's people can't be killed. And to frustrate their plan, Jesus distracts their rage with seven last plagues. The wicked receive all the suffering they have brought to the children of God. The Lord says, **"Vengeance is mine. I will repay."** (Hebrews 10:30) Read Esther 3-9 in your Bible and see how Satan was able to bring about a universal death decree against God's people. Also note how the captivity of God's people was turned. Esther's story is a close parallel of what will occur at the very end.

Daniel saw the universal death decree and was even told when it would occur! The angel said, **"From the time that the daily sacrifice is abolished and the abomination that causes desolation is set up, there will be 1,290 days. Blessed is the one who waits for and reaches the end of the 1,335 days."** (Daniel 12:11,12)

A proper understanding of these verses brings comfort. We already know that the throwing down of the censer in heaven at the beginning of the trumpets marks the conclusion of the daily service of corporate mediation in heaven. This verse says that the universal death decree will be 1,290 days later. (About 43 months.) The final abominable act of Satan will be to desolate the earth of God's people. Thus, it is called the abomination that makes or causes desolation.

But verse 12 says, **"Blessed is the one who waits for and reaches the end of the 1,335 days."** The entire time- period from the throwing down of the censer unto the second coming of Jesus is 1,335 days. From the throwing down of the censer until the death decree is 1,290 days. Daniel was told that those who wait for and reach the 1,335th day will be blessed! These are especially blessed because they have endured the great tribulation and will hear the words of Jesus, **"...Come, you who are blessed by my Father, take your inheritance, the kingdom prepared for you since the creation of the world!"** (Matthew 25:34)

May God prepare each of us with the experience we need to receive this glorious blessing!

Chapter 24

The Seven Last Plagues

Review a few things

The close of mercy will be like the closing of Noah's door. When the door of the ark was closed, those inside couldn't go outside and those outside, couldn't get inside. Every decision was forever sealed with the closing of the door. Jesus says of Himself, **"...These are the words of him who is holy and true, who holds the key of David. What he opens, no one can shut; and what he shuts, no one can open."** (Revelation 3:7) As it was in Noah's day—"so shall it be."

All inhabitants of the earth will receive the mark of the beast except those keeping the commandments of God and having the faith of Jesus. The mark will be necessary for survival. No one will be able to buy or sell except those having the mark. The remnant will be cut off from any and all earthly support. They can only live if they live by faith. What a time to be upon the earth!

The emotional distress during the time of wrath will be overwhelming for those who have not made it a practice to place their faith in Jesus. The coming tribulation will be greater than anything ever known upon earth, but Jesus has promised to provide the necessary grace we need to endure this awful time. No wonder Zephaniah said, **"...Listen! The cry on the day of the Lord will be bitter, the shouting of the warrior there. That day will be a day of wrath, a day of distress and anguish, a day of trouble and ruin, a day of darkness and gloom, a day of clouds and blackness, a day of trumpet and battle cry against the fortified cities.... Neither their silver nor their gold will be able to save them on the day of the Lord's wrath. In the fire of his jealousy the whole world will be consumed, for he will make a sudden end of all who live in the earth."** (Zephaniah 1:14-18)

Luke adds to Zephaniah's description of the last days saying, **"There will be signs in the sun, moon and stars. On the earth, nations will be in anguish and perplexity at the roaring and tossing of the sea. Men will faint from terror, apprehensive of what is coming on the world, for the heavenly bodies will be shaken."** (Luke 21:25,26)

Don't be overwhelmed! Paul says, **"...And God is faithful; he will not let you be tempted beyond what you can bear. But when you are tempted, he will also provide a way out so that you can stand up under it."** (1 Corinthians 10:13)

Joel, speaking of the great testing time at the end of the world, said, "Multitudes, multitudes in the valley of decision! For the day of the Lord is near in the valley of decision. The sun and moon will be darkened, and the stars no longer shine. The Lord will roar from Zion and thunder from Jerusalem; the earth and the sky will tremble. But the Lord will be a refuge for his people, a stronghold for the people of Israel." (Joel 3:14-16)

Babylon's reward

Just as we cannot understand the depth of God's mercy, we cannot understand the severity of God's wrath contained in the seven last plagues. To understand why Jesus is so angry with Babylon and those who receive the mark of the beast, we turn to Revelation. Notice:

"He (the seven-headed, ten-horned beast, Babylon) was given power to make war against the saints and to conquer them. And he was given authority over every tribe, people, language and nation. All inhabitants of the earth will worship the beast - all whose names have not been written in the book of life belonging to the Lamb...." (Revelation 13:7,8)

"...He (Satan, the lamb-like beast) ordered them (the people of earth) to set up an image in honor of the beast who was wounded by the sword and yet lived. He was given power to give breath to the image of the first beast, so that it could speak and cause all who refused to worship the image to be killed." (Revelation 13:14,15)

"I saw that the woman was drunk with the blood of the saints, the blood of those who bore testimony to Jesus...." (Revelation 17:6)

"They (the leaders of Babylon) will make war against the Lamb, but the Lamb will overcome them because He is Lord of Lords and King of Kings and with him will be his called, chosen and faithful followers." (Revelation 17:14)

"In her (the harlot, the one-world congress) was found the blood of prophets and of the saints, and of all who have been killed on the earth." (Revelation 18:24)

These verses contain a great deal more information than you would casually notice. On the surface, these verses describe a one-sided conflict between people. The saints don't kill people! However, the larger issue in these verses focus on the cumulative effects of sin and rebellion within the human race. These verses describe an open, willful and explicit rebellion against God, His gospel and His messengers.

Psychologists and social scientists have written extensively on the cumulative nature of behavior. For example, the abused child often becomes a child abuser. The child of an alcoholic often adopts the attitudes of his parents and in adulthood either becomes drug dependent or manifests a co-dependent attitude about life. In simple terms, the effect of sin upon succeeding generations is degenerative.

The second commandment addresses this very point! Jesus says, "**You shall not make for yourself an idol in the form of anything... for I, the Lord your God, am a jealous God, punishing the children for the sin of the fathers to the third and fourth generation of those who hate me, but showing love to thousands who love me and keep my commandments.**" (Exodus 20:4-6) Two important points must be made from the commandment:

1. Jesus is a jealous God. He is jealous for our happiness and well being. He is jealous for our sakes and not His. Human jealousy means burning with selfish interest, but in God's case, as in any loving parent's heart, He is jealous for the benefit of His children. Just as a loving parent deeply wants his or her child to succeed and be happy, Jesus wants no less for His children.

2. Does Jesus punish the children of sinful parents because their parents are evil? A surface look at the second commandment would so indicate. But look again at the commandment. Jesus does not unjustly punish the descendants of sinful parents. Rather, this commandment affirms that our Creator grants the power of choice. Because human beings have reasoning powers, we can make choices that lead to destruction and choices that lead to life. Jesus allows the inheritance of sin to continue within a family or society until it self destructs. However, when the world in a corporate sense reaches this point, He steps in.

We see these two points demonstrated before the flood. "**The Lord saw how great man's wickedness on the earth had become, and that every inclination of the thoughts of his heart was only evil all the time. The Lord was grieved that he had made man on the earth, and his heart was filled with pain. So the Lord said, 'I will wipe mankind, whom I have created, from the face of the earth - men and animals, and creatures... for I am grieved that I have made them.**" (Genesis 6:5-7)

Entertainment tonight?

Today, we shudder at the thought of lions eating Christians in ancient Roman amphitheaters in the name of entertainment. We call gladiators fighting to death before a blood-thirsty crowd "barbaric." But are we any different than the ancient pagans when it comes to entertainment each evening?

In the past forty years, TV has played an enormous role in destroying our social values. Generations of children have grown up watching violence, murder, theft, rape, lying, cheating, deception and illicit sex. Is there any wonder that we have become corrupted by beholding these values? Take sin out of television programs and who would watch them? What would be entertaining?

Ask most young people why they are attending school and the usual answer will tell of materialistic goals rather than service for others. This generation is the "me generation" and it is more self-centered than the preceding one. Parents can't blame their offspring for having these values either. The older generation bears a great responsibility for the present condition. Today, most of America's children are reared in human farms we call "day-care centers" while both parents work to possess the material things of life. The family unit has disintegrated because we deem the things of this life more important than our children! The most important things in life aren't things! Think about tomorrow. What will be the cumulative effects of our sins?

The root problem is that we have broken all Ten Commandments, especially the first four commands which tell us how we should love our Creator. When we forget God, we forget our neighbor. We become self-centered. By neglecting the first four commandments, we have made void the last six commandments. The royal commandments have been set aside. We now love ourselves as we should love our neighbors!

Jesus, talking about the last days, said, **"Because of the increase of wickedness, the love of most will grow cold."** (Matthew 24:12) Paul, talking about the last days, said, **"But mark this: There will be terrible times in the last days. People will be lovers of themselves, lovers of money, boastful, proud, abusive, disobedient to their parents,** **ungrateful, unholy, without love, unforgiving, slanderous, without self-control, brutal, not lovers of the good, treacherous, rash, conceited, lovers of pleasure rather than lovers of God - having a form of godliness but denying its power. Have nothing to do with them."** (2 Timothy 3:1-5)

Consolidation

The socio-political changes happening around our world appear positive at the moment. Reduction in armament, increased trade among countries and open dialogue seems in vogue. But a dangerous process is taking place. World control is being consolidated into the hands of fewer and fewer people. For example, in this country, 5% of our population owns more than the remaining 95%! The rich are getting richer and the poor are getting more numerous. In just a matter of time, the wealthy and the politically elite will form a global economic body to control the world.

What does this have to do with Revelation? Revelation indicates there will be a global consolidation of wealth and power. Notice that when Babylon collapses, it is the merchants and the kings of the earth that are crying! **"When the kings of the earth who committed adultery with her and shared her luxury see the smoke of her burning, they will weep and mourn over her. Terrified at her torment, they will stand far off and cry: 'Woe! Woe, O great city, O Babylon, city of power! In one hour your doom has come!' The merchants of the earth** will weep and mourn over her because no one buys their cargoes any more...." (Revelation 18:9-11)

When the trumpets begin, the current leadership of the world will be able to respond quickly through the various communication links established through trade. The first four trumpets bring horrific destruction and each government will quickly implement contingency laws to deal with the state of emergency. In this setting, freedoms all around the world will be restricted in the name of survival.

Since the trumpets will be duly recognized as acts of God, religious leaders will become very powerful because they will have direct influence upon law makers. Law makers will cooperate with the suggestions of clerics because they know that in a state of emergency, people are spiritually inclined. "Appease God," the clerics cry. And lawmakers respond with a flurry of laws requiring righteous behavior. As nations all over the world attempt to deal with the multitude of problems associated with the trumpets, they quickly turn to legislation for economic stability. The laws will appear reasonable to the majority of people and penalties for civil disobedience will be severe.

In America

Laws establishing reverence for Sunday will be enforced in America. (Most states already have laws regarding the sanctity of Sunday observance on their legislative books. However, these laws are not uniformly enforced at this time.) At first, Sunday laws will be defended in the name of economic necessity, but as time progresses, the cry, "We have forgotten God," will be loudly proclaimed as the reason for the trumpets. The irony of this matter is that man's solution to the trumpets will be opposite to the gospel invitation! At the very time the gospel is proclaiming, "Worship the Creator on His holy day," men will be making laws respecting a day of worship contrary to God's law! Because the majority of people in America think Sunday is the Lord's Day, laws will be respecting the sacredness of Sunday. Thus, reverence for Sunday will appear to be a reasonable solution to the problem. It is interesting to note that today, very few people actually feel Sunday is all that sacred and thus keep the day holy. The trumpets will change this attitude overnight!

The centerpiece of Revelation's story for America is that Sunday is not, nor has it ever been, the Lord's Day. There is no support for the sacredness of Sunday, Monday, Tuesday or any other day in the Bible except the seventh day. Even more, there is no commandment explaining how another day is to be kept if it is indeed a day of worship.

When laws are made respecting Sunday as a day of worship, a number of dissidents will arise. Some will argue the loss of "constitutional rights" and others will intellectually argue for "freedom of worship." However, neither of these groups will be able to hold back the tide of religious zeal.

Another group will argue that the trumpets have a specific purpose. That purpose is to call attention to the worship of the Creator of earth on His holy Sabbath, the seventh day of the week. The resulting controversy that attends the issue of worship will totally eclipse all other controversies in America such as abortion, human rights and environmental problems. (These current controversies are nothing compared to the coming controversy surrounding the gospel!) As a result of the trumpets, America will experience economic, religious and civil anarchy. Under the guise of patriotism, America will repudiate its Bill of Rights!

As the controversy matures, the issues become clearly stated. By the time the fourth trumpet occurs, survival will be the all consuming issue before every mind. All over the world, the story of Revelation will be told. Americans will hear why the seven first plagues are falling and why they should obey the Law of God. They will hear the first angel's message which says, "Worship the Creator according to His holy law." All will be invited to receive the everlasting gospel and live by faith. The clarity of Revelation's story and the power of the Holy Spirit will attend these presentations. The Bible and the Holy Spirit will witness to every man, woman and child. The gospel will reach 260 million Americans in a very short period of time.

America chooses the lamblike beast

In spite of the unmistakable evidence provided from scripture and the power attending the first angel's message, America will continue her downward course. She will make more laws regarding the sanctity of Sunday and increase the penalties for disobedience. Satan personally arrives upon earth during the fifth trumpet claiming to be God. Most Americans (and the world) will ultimately accept this villain of mankind as the true God. The great American motto, "In God we Trust," will be dedicated to the lamblike beast.

Satan knows all about Revelation's story. His greatest thrill will be to deceive people at a time when truth was never so clear. His goal is simple. He wants to destroy the world before Jesus returns. Over a hundred years ago, a great author summed up the devil's plans saying, "The first day will be extolled, and the Protestant world will receive this spurious sabbath as genuine. Through the nonobservance of the Sabbath that God instituted, I will bring His law into contempt.... Thus the world will become mine. I will be the ruler of the earth, the prince of the world. I will so control the minds under my power that God's Sabbath shall be a special object of contempt. A sign? I will make the observance of the seventh day a sign of disloyalty to the authorities of earth. Human laws will be made so stringent that men and women will not dare to observe the seventh day Sabbath. For fear of wanting food and clothing, they will join with the world in transgressing God's law. The earth will be wholly under my dominion." Ellen G. White, *Prophets and Kings,* page 184.

The wrath of God - full strength

By the time probation closes, every person on earth will have heard the arguments of the everlasting gospel and made a decision. The people of earth will stand in two camps: those obeying Jesus and those obeying Satan. Those obeying Satan have put their faith in him, and they will join with Satan in warring upon those that refuse to go along. Those receiving the mark of the beast rejected the clearest presentations of Bible truth. These will turn their backs upon God's mercy. Even worse, these people will passionately work to destroy the saints and covet the commendation of the devil!

Even though Satan and Babylon conquer the world (Revelation 13:7), John saw the victory of the saints over Satan and his followers. **"And I saw what looked like a sea of glass mixed with fire and, standing beside the sea, those who had been victorious over the beast and his image and over the number of his name. They held harps given them by God and sang the song of Moses the servant of God and the song of the Lamb...."** (Revelation 15:2,3) In losing, they win! Jesus said, **"Whoever finds his life will lose it, and whoever loses his life for my sake will find it."** (Matthew 10:39)

The seven last plagues

The seven last plagues fall upon all who receive the mark of the beast. The seven last plagues will be a horrible reward for the wicked. They will be rewarded for their cruelty to God's people. The seven last plagues, contain the wrath of God — full strength. In brief, the plagues are:

1. Terrible sores
2. Sea turns to blood
3. Springs of waters turn to blood
4. Sun scorches people with fire
5. Satan's kingdom plunged into darkness
6. Armageddon
7. Second coming / Great fiery hail stones

These plagues do not affect God's people. **"A thousand may fall at your side, ten thousand at your right hand, but it will not come near you. You will only observe with your eyes the punishment of the wicked."** (Psalm 91:7,8) These plagues are beyond the comprehension of man for the world has never seen the wrath of God — full strength! In fact, Daniel says it will be a time of trouble as never before! (Daniel 12:1)

Interesting points

Three points need to be made:

1. Many of the seven last plagues parallel the destruction caused by the seven trumpets. As the first four trumpets affected one-third of the

earth, the seven last plagues affect the entire world!

2. Notice this parallel. The fifth trumpet marks the arrival of Satan and the fifth plague marks the "unmasking" of Satan! Satan, prior to the fifth plague, blames the trumpets and the first four last-plagues upon the saints and their "rebellious" behavior. When Jesus pours out the fifth plague, the world sees that this creature claiming to be God, isn't God—for God would not destroy His own throne! See Revelation 16:10,11. The light of truth shines. The religious and political leaders of the world recognize they have been following a demon. This realization starts a domino-like collapse of Babylon. John says, **"The beast (Babylon) and the ten horns you saw will hate the prostitute (World Congress). They will bring her to ruin and leave her naked; they will eat her flesh and burn her with fire."** (Revelation 17:16)

3. To maintain control of what is left, Satan rallies the world one last time by sending his evil angels throughout the earth in a great deceptive ploy to destroy the saints, who allegedly "put the curse upon his throne." Satan entices the kings of the earth to unite in a universal death decree. John says of Satan's represent-atives, **"They are the spirits of demons performing miraculous signs, and they go out to the kings of the whole world, to gather them**
for the battle on the great day of God Almighty.... Then they gathered the kings together to the place that in Hebrew is called Armageddon." (Revelation 16:14, 16)

Armageddon

The battle called Armageddon is the sixth plague. John warns us that Satan's demons will deceive the world into unity for the final desolation of the saints through a universal death decree. Daniel also saw the intended destruction of the saints. (Daniel 12:11) The kings of the earth agree on the simultaneous destruction of those worshiping on Saturday and gather to the place that in Hebrew is called, "Armageddon."

Remember, in Revelation 9 the name of the angel king from the Abyss meant "destroyer" both in Greek and Hebrew. See Revelation 9:11. Just as this title describes Satan, the Greek equivalent of Armageddon describes a place or a state the world reaches. The word Armageddon comes from two words, "har megido" and are translated— Armageddon. These two words mean "the mountain of God", or "the place of God."

The world under Satan's leadership reaches the height of rebellion against God and His saints during the fifth plague, for the entire world is agreed upon the simultaneous destruction of the very people Jesus is coming to save. This is the final straw. Now the wrath of Jesus knows no restriction. The world is planning to destroy the "apple of His eye." Rebellion has brought the world to "the mountain of God." Now the world will know, as in Elijah's day on Mount Carmel, who is the true God. The world will see Him and face His wrath. John says, **"The seventh angel poured out his bowl into the air, and out of the temple came a loud voice from the throne saying, 'It is done.' Then there came flashes of lightning, rumblings, peals of thunder and a severe earthquake. No earthquake like it has ever occurred since man has been on earth, so tremendous was the quake. The great city split into three parts, and the cities of the nations collapsed. God remembered Babylon the Great and gave her the cup filled with the wine of the fury of his wrath. Every island fled away and the mountains could not be found. From the sky huge hailstones of about a hundred pounds each fell upon men. And they cursed God on account of the plague of hail, because the plague was so terrible."** (Revelation 16:17-21)

John also says that the people of earth cry out: **"They called ...to the mountains and the rocks, 'Fall on us and hide us from the face of him who sits on the throne and from the wrath of the Lamb! For the great day of their wrath has come, and who can stand?' "** (Revelation 6:16,17)

Paul tells us the splendor of Christ's coming destroys all the living. **"And then the lawless one (the man of sin) will be revealed, whom the Lord Jesus will overthrow with the breath of his mouth and destroy by the splendor of his coming."** (2 Thessalonians 2:8)

Zephaniah says, **"Neither their silver nor their gold will be able to save them on the day of the Lord's wrath. In the fire of his jealousy the whole world will be consumed, for he will make a sudden end of all who live in the earth."** (Zephaniah 1:18)

The earth is left desolate

The hail that falls upon the earth at the second coming is like the fiery hailstones that fell upon the earth during the first trumpet. The basic difference between them is size and the amount of devastation. The hail of the first trumpet burns up 1/3 of the earth (grass, trees, etc.) while the hail of the seventh plague burns Babylon up. John says that the beast (Babylon, having seven heads and 10 horns) and the False Prophet (Babylon's eighth king, its lamblike leader – the devil) are destroyed by this fire at the second coming. **"...The two of them were thrown alive into the fiery lake of burning sulfur. The rest of them were killed with the sword that comes out of the mouth of the rider on the horse, and all the birds gorged themselves on their flesh."** (Revelation 19:20,21)

The rider on the horse is King Jesus. John says, **"I saw heaven standing open and there before me was a white horse, whose rider is called Faithful and True. With justice he judges and makes war. His eyes are like blazing fire, and on his head are many crowns.... On his robe and on his thigh he has this name** written: **King of Kings and Lord of Lords."** (Revelation 19:11-16) At this time, the conquering which Jesus set out to do with the opening of the first seal is finally completed!

The saints taken to heaven

The second coming will be a scene beyond expression. As Jesus draws near the earth, the righteous dead are resurrected to behold Jesus. Paul says, **"For the Lord himself will come down from heaven, with a loud command, with the voice of the archangel and with the trumpet call of God, and the dead in Christ will rise first. After that, we who are still alive and are left will be caught up with them in the clouds to meet the Lord in the air...."** (1 Thessalonians 4:16,17)

It is important to note that Jesus does not stand upon the earth at the second coming. The saints meet Him in the air! They return with Jesus to heaven for one thousand years. John says of the righteous dead, **"They came to life and reigned with Christ a thousand years. The rest of the dead did not come to life until the thousand years were ended."** (Revelation 20:4,5)

What do the saints do for a thousand years? John says, **"I saw thrones on which were seated those who had been given authority to judge... they will be priests of God and of Christ and will reign with him a thousand years."** (Revelation 20:4,6)

For one thousand years the saints will open the books and review the judgment process of God. They will be fully satisfied with the eternal decision of each person. No doubts will remain as to the fairness and judgment of Jesus for each person. Meanwhile, the earth is desolate. The wicked are dead and Satan and his angels are put back into the Abyss where they wait for divine justice.

Satan lives on

If Satan is the False Prophet mentioned in Revelation 19, and the False Prophet is burned up at the second coming, how can he remain alive during the millennium? The answer is that Satan (like Jesus) is not *limited* to the body of a man. Remember, Satan was allowed out of the Abyss (or spirit world) during the fifth trumpet. He takes the form of a man, but Satan is still an angel. At the second coming, Satan's apparition of a man claiming to be God is destroyed, but the evil angel king and his demons remain alive until the end of the thousand years. At the time of the second coming, John says, **"And I saw an angel coming down out of heaven, having the key to the Abyss and holding in his hand a great chain. He seized the dragon, that ancient serpent, who is the devil, or Satan, and bound him for a thousand years. He threw him into the Abyss, and locked and sealed it over him, to keep him from deceiving the nations any more until the thousand years were ended. After that, he must be set free for a short time."** (Revelation 20:1-3)

The saints returned to earth

When the thousand years of research into God's character are finished, the New Jerusalem and the saints return to earth with Jesus. The second resurrection now takes place. The first resurrection took place at the second coming, and the second resurrection occurs a thousand years later. Jesus said, "Blessed and holy are those who have part in the first resurrection. The second death has no power over them...." (Revelation 20:6)

The Bible is very clear that there are two resurrections: one to eternal life and one to eternal death. Jesus said, "Do not be amazed at this, for a time is coming when all who are in their graves will hear his voice and come out - those who have done good will rise to live, and those who have done evil will rise to be condemned." (John 5:28,29)

After the wicked are resurrected at the end of the thousand years, Satan is released from the Abyss (spirit world) for a short time. He immediately stirs the vast multitude into rebellion. He convinces the numberless crowd that Jesus intends to do them great harm. He incites a dramatic uprising to destroy the New Jerusalem and the saints which have come down to earth. (Revelation 20:7-10)

As the wicked rush with rage upon the holy city, Jesus speaks. The multitude stop in their tracks. Silence falls upon the breathless mob for about half an hour. (Revelation 8:1) Jesus, as King of Kings and Lord of Lords,

speaks. The anger and rebellion of the numberless mob dissipates. As lightning pierces darkness, the wicked realize they stand before their Maker. He is not a tyrant. He is not angry. He speaks with great authority.

Jesus explains the plan of salvation to the waiting multitude. As the wicked behold the love of God, each person understands the economy of salvation. Each person's life is presented from the open books of record. The wicked see their deeds just as God saw their deeds. There is no room for excuses or self-justification. There is no place to run. He who sees the hearts and reads the motives presents each life record of sin and rebellion for what it really is with unvarnished clarity. The wicked know why they are condemned. They now know who Jesus is, why He died on Calvary and why they cannot be saved. The wicked clearly see that they are outside the gates of the holy city because they chose evil rather than righteousness.

At the end of this revelation, every knee bows before Jesus with deepest emotion. The wicked bow before the justice of Jesus and the righteous bow before the mercy of Jesus. Jesus said, "Before me every knee will bow; by me every tongue will swear. They will say of me, 'In the Lord alone are righteousness and strength.' All who have raged against him will come to him and be put to shame. But in the Lord all the descendants of Israel will be found righteous and will exult." (Isaiah 45:23-25)

Every knee will bow before Jesus. Those who bow in faith before the close of probation will be saved. Those who bow after the close of probation will be lost. In both cases, all creatures will recognize that, **"In the Lord alone are righteousness and strength."**

Notes

Chapter 25

The Gift of Prophecy

Coming to terms

The remnant are identified in Revelation as keeping the commandments of God and having the testimony of Jesus. (Revelation 12:17) In Revelation 19:10 we learn that the testimony of Jesus is the spirit of prophecy. What is the "spirit of prophecy?" Knowing that Satan has obscured the law of God, should we be surprised to learn that he has also counterfeited the spirit of prophecy?

For the sake of definition, the "gift of prophecy" or the "spirit of prophecy" is the gift of knowing the unknown. Webster says prophecy is "a prediction made under divine influence and direction, or a discourse made or delivered by a prophet under divine direction."

The Bible interchanges the idea of prophesying under divine influence and the gift or ability to prophesy. King Saul, for example, received the ability to prophesy even though he was not considered a prophet. **"When they arrived at Gibeah, a procession of prophets met him (King Saul); the Spirit of God came upon him in power,** and he joined in their prophesying. When all those who had formerly known him saw him prophesying with the prophets, they asked each other, 'What is this that has happened to the son of Kish? Is Saul also among the prophets?' "** (1 Samuel 10:10,11)

A few good questions

Is the gift of prophecy in all churches today? Is this gift prevalent throughout the world? Is it limited to Christianity? What characteristics distinguish those who speak in God's behalf? How can we tell if someone is truly giving a revelation that came from God? What distinguishes a "prophetic revelation" from a "sanctified or educated guess?" These issues must be studied carefully, for there is a growing interest in manifestations of supernatural power.

Paul speaks about spiritual gifts

The most eloquent writer in the Bible on the gifts of the Spirit is the Apostle Paul. Perhaps his position on the subject is appropriately encompassing because, of all writers in the Bible, he is one of the wealthiest recipients of spiritual gifts. Few would contest that Paul stands head and shoulders above his contemporaries due to his combination of natural ability and spiritual gifts. He influenced the theology of Christianity more than any of his peers.

Paul points out there are several different gifts of the Spirit. These include wisdom, knowledge, faith, healing, miraculous powers, discernment of spirits, speaking in tongues, interpretation of tongues and prophesying. He stresses that the gifts have a direct purpose. They bring growth and harmony to the Church instead of chaos. Notice some of his comments:

1.   Paul says the gift of prophecy is for believers. This is in direct contrast to the gift of tongues which is for unbelievers. (1 Corinthians 14:22) Paul also points out that there may be an ecstatic experience of joy in the Lord, where a person may speak in a language beyond words; however, he emphasizes such experiences are to be private and not public. (1 Corinthians 14:2,9-17)

2.   Paul says that the manifestation of spiritual gifts is given for the common good of all. (1 Corinthians 12:7) This text does not imply that every believer receives the manifestation of some spiritual gift. Rather, the *manifestation* of spiritual gifts occurs for the common good of all mankind — believers and non-believers alike. Paul recognized the value of spiritual gifts and clearly encouraged the church to seek for them, especially the gift of prophecy. (1 Corinthians 14:1) But, desiring a gift does not mandate the receipt of the gift.

3.   Paul clearly says the Holy Spirit determines what gift (if any) a person receives. (1 Corinthians 12:11) He goes to great lengths in Chapter 12 to point out that the body is made up of many parts. Since the body of Christ has many members, we all benefit in the administration of the gifts to those upon whom the gifts have been granted. (1 Corinthians 12:27-30) He clearly points out that God **has not** appointed everyone to be an apostle, prophet, miracle worker, teacher, etc.

4.   Paul stresses there is something more important than the gifts of the Spirit. It is the grace of the Spirit. Paul says, "desire the greater gifts ...faith, hope and love...." (1 Corinthians 12:31, 13:13) The gifts are temporal, while the graces of the Spirit are eternal.

Paul points out that if we speak with the tongues of gifted men or even angels and have not love, it is nothing. {13:1} If we have the gift of prophecy and the gift of faith and have no love, it is nothing. {13:2} If we give all we have to the poor and die a martyr's death and have no love, it is nothing. {13:3} Love, agape love (love that is God like), is more important than all other gifts. In fact, the gifts of tongues, knowledge and prophecy will pass away {13:8-10} but love will never cease. {13:8}

A brief survey on the gift of prophecy

The Bible does not provide a crisp definition of what it takes to become a prophet. A job description is also missing. Apparently, the post or job of being a prophet is an "appointment" rather than the achievement of a sanctified state. And each appointment within the Scriptures appears to be unique to the circumstances of time and place. For example, the boy Samuel was called to be a prophet during the time of the judges of Israel. The physician Luke was called to be a prophet during the time of Christ. Anna and the four daughters of Philip were also called to be prophets too! (Luke 2:36; Acts 21:9) Prophets are human beings and have failings too. Remember Jonah and the whale? Did you ever hear about the infamous Balaam? (Numbers 22,23) Notice the following points about the office of prophet:

Point 1

Abraham, the venerable father of Israel, was not perfect even though he was a prophet! In fact, the first mention of the term prophet in the Bible is in Genesis and it applies to Abraham. **"Now Abraham moved on from there into the region of the Negev and lived between Kadesh and Shur... and there Abraham said of his wife Sarah, 'She is my sister.' Then Abimelech king of Gerar sent for Sarah and took her. But God came to Abimelech in a dream one night and said to him, 'You are as good as dead because of the woman you have taken; she is a married woman.' Now Abimelech had not gone near her, so he said, 'Lord, will you destroy an innocent nation? Did he not say to me, 'She is my sister,' and didn't she also say, 'He is my brother'? I have done this with a clear conscience and clean hands.' Then God said to him in the dream, 'Yes, I know you did this with a clear conscience, and so I have kept you from sinning against me. That is why I did not let you touch her. Now return the man's wife, for he is a prophet, and he will pray for you and you will live. But if you do not return her, you may be sure that you and all yours will die.' "** (Genesis 20:1-7)

Abraham is called a prophet because God directly communicated through him. Abraham prayed for Abimelech and God spared his life. Jesus spoke to Abraham from time to time and the relationship between them was recognized by those who came to know Abraham. (This scripture reveals the fact that prophets can make serious mistakes. Even though Sarah was Abraham's half sister, she was his wife. The prophet intentionally mislead Abimelech on this matter for fear that Abimelech would kill him and take his beautiful wife.)

Point 2

The Bible treats the office of prophet as a divine appointment. When God has a spokesman, He speaks through that person. **"He (the Lord) said, 'Listen to my words: When a prophet of the LORD is among you, I reveal myself to him in visions, I speak to him in dreams.' "** (Numbers 12:6)

Point 3

God warned Israel that no one should imitate the office of prophet. If anyone claimed to be a prophet and in reality, he had not been appointed as such, the consequences were to be fatal. Even more, if the testimony of a former prophet lead people to stray from the commands of God, he was to be put to death. Jesus said, **"If a prophet, or one who foretells by dreams, appears among you and announces to you a miraculous sign or wonder, and if the sign or wonder of which he has spoken takes place, and he says, 'Let us follow other gods' (gods you have not known) 'and let us worship them,' you must not listen to the words of that prophet or dreamer. The Lord your God is testing you to find out whether you love him with all your heart and with all your soul. It is the Lord your God you must follow, and him you must revere. Keep his commands and obey him; serve him and hold fast to him. That prophet or dreamer must be put to death, because he preached rebellion against the Lord your God, who brought you out of Egypt and redeemed you from the land of slavery;**

he has tried to turn you from the way the Lord your God commanded you to follow. You must purge the evil from among you." (Deuteronomy 13:1-5)

Point 4

When God speaks through a prophet, the situation is unavoidably difficult for two reasons. First, if a person rejects the words of a prophet, God will hold the person accountable. Secondly, and more importantly, if the prophet has spoken presumptuously, he must be put to death. The litmus test of a prophet is accuracy in prediction. **"...If anyone does not listen to my words that the prophet speaks in my name, I myself will call him to account. But a prophet who presumes to speak in my name anything I have not commanded him to say, or a prophet who speaks in the name of other gods, must be put to death! You may say to yourselves, 'How can we know when a message has not been spoken by the Lord?' If what a prophet proclaims in the name of the Lord does not take place or come true, that is a message the Lord has not spoken. That prophet has spoken presumptuously. Do not be afraid of him."** (Deuteronomy 18:19-22)

Point 5

When God gives someone the ability to prophesy, people recognize the power of God is uniquely upon that person. Remember the text about King Saul? Notice this one about Samuel: **"And all Israel from Dan to Beersheba** recognized that Samuel was attested as a prophet of the Lord." (1 Samuel 3:20)

Point 6

A prophet cannot obey the words of another prophet if they are contrary to what he has been told. Read the story found in 1 Kings 13:11-30. You'll be very surprised.

Point 7

The prophet cannot of his own power prove his divine appointment as spokesman for God. Only God can confirm or demonstrate the appointment. Notice how this happened to Elijah. "At the time of sacrifice, the prophet Elijah stepped forward and prayed: 'O Lord, God of Abraham, Isaac and Israel, let it be known today that you are God in Israel and that I am your servant and have done all these things at your command.' " (1 Kings 18:36)

Point 8

The decision to become a prophet is not made by man, neither is the office hereditary. God chooses or appoints prophets. He told Elijah, "Also, anoint Jehu son of Nimshi king over Israel, and anoint Elisha son of Shaphat from Abel Meholah to succeed you as prophet." (1 Kings 19:16)

Point 9

When people refuse to heed the words of God's prophets, God Himself sends them a delusion that they might be damned. (2 Thessalonians 2:11,12) Read a most incredible story in the Old Testament from which Paul took special insight. (1 Kings 22:5-23)

Point 10

God is very protective about the way His name is honored or dishonored by prophets. God will not tolerate the defamation of His name. (Ezekiel 36:22,23) The story of Naaman and greedy Gehazi confirms this point. (2 Kings 5:19-27)

Intermediate summary

The office and work of a prophet is very serious business. God does not trifle with the responsibilities of this office. Prophets of God are held to the highest standards of accountability. Those who presume to speak for God when God has not spoken to them are evil impostors. Those who assume the authority or office of a prophet when God has not spoken to them will be severely punished. This is among the gravest offenses a mortal can commit.

The 10 points above bring us to three conclusions:

1. First, the prophet must carefully and fearlessly represent what God has said or revealed to him. In

many scriptures, the prophets indicate that the word of God comes to them in an audible or visionary process leaving no doubt in their minds that God has clearly revealed something.

2. Secondly, 1,500 years of Old Testament history indicate that those called to be prophets usually have few friends. See also Matthew 23:37.

3. Lastly, false prophets often exist as contemporaries of true prophets. It seems strange but true that where there are no true prophets, there are few false prophets. Can it be possible that when God appoints prophets that Satan is allowed the same privilege or vice versa? This question leads us to the second identifying mark of the remnant in Revelation. The gift of prophecy is not only one of the identifying marks of the remnant, the gift of prophecy stands in direct opposition to false prophets having similar powers! This point brings us face to face with the ultimate question: How can we tell if a prophet is speaking for God?

Testing the Prophet

Testing or proving the validity of a spiritual claim is difficult at best. If someone claims to have the gift of knowledge or discernment, how should the claim be tested to see if it is true or false? If someone claims to have the gift of healing, how should the claim be tested to see if it is true or false? If someone has the gift of faith, how should that be tested? Why would we want to test the gifts anyway?

The core issue behind the manifestation of gifts is credibility. Who represents God? Who speaks for God? Who speaks truth and what is the truth? All claims of spiritual gifts have to be tested. Here's why. Paul said, **"The Spirit clearly says that in later times some will abandon the faith and follow deceiving spirits and things taught by demons."** (1 Timothy 4:1) John also warned, **"Dear friends, do not believe every spirit, but test the spirits to see whether they are from God, because many false prophets have gone out into the world."** (1 John 4:1)

Satan's purpose

Satan has two reasons for deceiving people. First, he wants to lead them into rebellion against God, and secondly, he wants them to destroy God's people. Revelation clearly demonstrates this process and predicts that Satan and his demons will be quite successful on both counts.

"And he (Satan) performed great and miraculous signs, even causing fire to come down from heaven to earth in full view of men. Because of the signs he was given power to do on behalf of the first beast, he deceived the inhabitants of the earth. He ordered them to set up an image in honor of the beast who

was wounded by the sword and yet lived. He was given power to give breath to the image of the first beast, so that it could speak and cause all who refused to worship the image to be killed." (Revelation 13:13-15)

Recognizing that Satan and his demons seek to deceive the world, understanding that his lies are very close to the truth and wanting to know if someone speaks on behalf of God through the gift of prophecy, we ask: How should we test the validity of a person claiming to have received a message from God?

Five tests

There are at least five tests mentioned in Scripture to test a person claiming to be a prophet of God to see if he is a true prophet or a false prophet.

1. Fruit inspection

Jesus, knowing the last days would be filled with false prophets, said we should measure a prophet by his lifestyle. "Watch out for false prophets. They come to you in sheep's clothing, but inwardly they are ferocious wolves. By their fruit you will recognize them. Do people pick grapes from thornbushes, or figs from thistles? Likewise every good tree bears good fruit, but a bad tree bears bad fruit. A good tree cannot bear bad fruit, and a bad tree cannot bear good fruit. Every tree that does not bear good fruit is cut down and thrown into the

fire. Thus, by their fruit you will recognize them." (Matthew 7:15-20)

Even more, Jesus, knowing that false prophets can heal the sick, cast out demons and work wonderful miracles, goes on to say that miracles are not to be received as evidence or credibility. "Not everyone who says to me, 'Lord, Lord,' will enter the kingdom of heaven, but only he who does the will of my Father who is in heaven. Many will say to me on that day, 'Lord, Lord, did we not prophesy in your name, and in your name drive out demons and perform many miracles?' Then I will tell them plainly, 'I never knew you. Away from me, you evildoers!' " (Matthew 7:21-23) Imagine the surprise many people will have when they are told that their wonderful miracles, done in the name of Jesus, occurred through the power of Satan!

2. Be skeptical of any prophet working miracles

Jesus warned that many would come in His name at the end of the world and deceive many people with great signs and miracles. "At that time if anyone says to you, 'Look, here is the Christ!' or, 'There he is!' do not believe it. For false Christs and false prophets will appear and perform great signs and miracles to deceive even the elect — if that were possible. See, I have told you ahead of time." (Matthew 24:23-25)

By leading the world to believe that people are currently in heaven or hell, Satan has carefully set the stage for a series of demonstrations that will capture the attention of the world. Many of these miracles will involve direct and open communication with those who have died! By having apparitions appear in various places, Satan will confirm his deceptions by having these dead people say that false doctrines are truth! The masses will receive these delusions with enthusiasm because they don't know what the Bible says. In reality, this is nothing less than the work of demons. Now you can see why the power granted to the Two Witnesses, the Bible and Holy Spirit, is so great. They not only combat the demons from the Abyss, they must overcome great ignorance!

Isaiah saw the great danger of people turning to these exciting and mysterious events. He warned, **"When men tell you to consult mediums and spiritists, who whisper and mutter, should not a people inquire of their God? Why consult the dead on behalf of the living? To the law and to the testimony! If they do not speak according to this word, they have no light of dawn."** (Isaiah 8:19-20)

The term "law" used by Isaiah refers to the first five books of the Bible, a phrase we often see in Scripture. The term, "testimony" refers to the Ten Commandments of God. The ark which contained the tables of stone is often called the "ark of the testimony." (Exodus 25:21,22) Isaiah is saying that if a prophet's words do not agree with the Scriptures and the law of God, the prophet is full of darkness. And in truth, the false teaching of the immortality of the soul has become

almost universally accepted and predisposes most of the world to accept the teachings of false prophets.

3. Does the prophet obey the commandments of God?

John places a great deal of weight on the importance of the law of God. Persons that lead people to rebel against God's commandments cannot have the true gift of prophecy. In Revelation, the remnant are not only identified as having the gift of prophecy, they "obey the commandments of God."

Throughout his writings, John stresses the importance of obedience to God—not as a means of salvation, but as a result of their love for God. **"Whoever has my commands and obeys them, he is the one who loves me. He who loves me will be loved by my Father, and I too will love him and show myself to him."** (John 14:21)

Jesus, our Creator, has the right to ask human beings for obedience. He not only created us, He created all the laws by which we live. Neither natural nor moral laws can be violated without serious consequence. Jesus gives us the choice of whether we will obey Him and worship Him. He will not force us.

A person having the true gift of prophecy must be in compliance with the truths that God has revealed. John says, **"The man who says, 'I know him,' but does not do what He commands is a liar, and the truth is not in him. But if anyone obeys his word, God's love is truly made complete in him. This is** how we know we are in him: Whoever claims to live in him must walk as Jesus did." (1 John 2:4-6)

Since the seventh day Sabbath of the fourth commandment will be the object of special attention during the trumpets, the importance of this test is critical.

4. Does the prophet strengthen the work of the gospel?

Paul says, "But everyone who prophesies speaks to men for their strengthening, encouragement and comfort." (1 Corinthians 14:3) The person having the gift of prophecy must edify or strengthen the believers. As said earlier, a prophet's life must also demonstrate the fruit of piety. The messages of true prophets bring men and women to repentance. Paul said, "But if an unbeliever or someone who does not understand comes in while everybody is prophesying, he will be convinced by all that he is a sinner and will be judged by all, and the secrets of his heart will be laid bare. So he will fall down and worship God, exclaiming, 'God is really among you!' " (1 Corinthians 14:24,25)

5. Correct interpretation of Bible prophecy essential

Jesus is omniscient. Therefore, He knows every detail about the future. He has revealed the future in the Bible and His servants, the prophets, won't miss the mark. They will neither add to the record written in Revelation nor will they take away from it. This simple point cannot be stressed hard enough.

Summary

The gift of prophecy is a deep subject. Most of the world is ignorant of the demonic forces that would lead them astray. Our age is peculiarly cursed with insight into technology while at the same time having great blindness to spiritual things.

The gifts of the Holy Spirit have been bestowed at various times and in various ways to help God's people accomplish the commission of carrying the everlasting gospel to every nation, kindred, tongue and people. Here is a fundamental point: The gifts and graces of the Holy Spirit combine to accomplish the gospel commission, not to draw attention to themselves.

An evil and wicked generation seeks signs as proof of credibility. (Matthew 12:39) God is not challenged by demands for signs for the devil can turn sticks into snakes too. (Exodus 7:11) The devil can heal the sick, cast out demons, speak wonderful truths and he can appear very righteous and beneficial — all to accomplish his deceitful ends.

Revelation predicts the gift of prophecy will be an identifying mark of the obedient remnant. The difference between Satan's miracles and the miracles worked by God's servants is this: Satan's miracles give credibility to rebellion against the Word of God while God's miracles give credibility to the truths contained in Scripture. This is the

bottom line. This separates true from
false prophets.

Notes

Chapter 26

The Making of the Remnant

Our last chapter contains a review and an invitation. A review of the gospel is necessary because the gospel propels us to a decision. In due time, we either accept or reject the gospel because of basic internal needs to resolve conflicts. Some people try to avoid difficult decisions by putting them far into the background of consciousness. They say, "I'll think about this tomorrow." Postponement, though, is really a decision, too. It is a mild rejection. Suppose you asked someone to marry you. Any answer other than "yes" is actually rejection, isn't it? The danger with postponement is that it easily leads to greater rejection until we are firmly decided. In the case of the gospel, we must listen to the Holy Spirit. The more we reject His promptings, the more difficult to respond.

This lesson also contains an invitation to attend this seminar again. If the Holy Spirit has impressed you that this message is important, you need to read it again for two reasons. First, your understanding of the gospel will increase 100% the second time you study it. Details will become much clearer and more meaningful. Secondly, knowing what Revelation is about, you need to find an interested friend and share this message with him. **"The Spirit and the bride say, 'Come!' And let him who hears say, 'Come!' Whoever is thirsty, let him come; and whoever wishes, let him take the free gift of the water of life."** (Revelation 22:17)

The proclamation of the gospel

The full gospel must reach every person before Jesus comes. John said, **"Then I saw another angel flying in midair, and he had the eternal gospel to proclaim to those who live on the earth - to every nation, tribe, language and people."** (Revelation 14:6) Jesus said, **"And this gospel of the kingdom will be preached in the whole world as a testimony to all nations, and then the end will come."** (Matthew 24:14) The question is, "Who will help spread the gospel?" We know that the 144,000 will lead the way during the shaking and the trumpets, but they can't do the work alone. They need the help and support of the remnant!

What is the gospel?

Would a counterfeiter print a $9 bill? No. People would immediately recognize the folly. A $9 bill couldn't be a counterfeit since real $9 bills don't exist.

Thus, a counterfeit has to be an imitation of something that exists.

The devil has counterfeited the gospel and his imitations are in every land. In America, the devil's counterfeit of the gospel is *almost* indistinguishable from the real thing.

Many people honestly believe Satan's counterfeit gospel. Jesus understands. He looks down upon the earth with love at those living up to all they believe to be true. In His great mercy, He accepts those who do not know the truths of the gospel. Jesus does not hold a person responsible for truth he doesn't know. On the contrary. James tells us that sin is held against us **when** we know better and **then** refuse to do it! **"Anyone, then, who knows the good he ought to do and doesn't do it, sins."** (James 4:17)

The Lord loves the people of earth with a love beyond human understanding. Those living up to all they know to be right glorify God, and He is pleased. Peter says, **"For the eyes of the Lord are on the righteous and his ears are attentive to their prayer, but the face of the Lord is against those who do evil."** (1 Peter 3:12) Because truth has been obscured from most people by Satan's devices, Jesus is going to enlighten the entire world with the gospel in the near future. Those who are sincere in heart will receive the full gospel and the remnant will be made up. Those who recognize the confirmation of the Holy Spirit will move forward and receive the gospel truth as it reaches every nation, kindred, tongue and people! Thus, the remnant will be gathered into one body. Jesus said, **"I have other sheep that are not of this sheep pen. I must bring them also. They too will listen to my voice, and there shall be one flock and one shepherd."** (John 10:16)

The net effect of the gospel will be to unify those who hear the voice of Jesus into one large group called the remnant. This will finally be accomplished during the trumpets. People will either receive the gospel and by faith, obey the commandments of Jesus as the first angel's message commands or they will reject the gospel and receive the mark of the beast. There will be no middle ground. The rapid sequence of events coupled with rigorous laws requiring Sunday observance in America will push everyone to a rapid decision.

What is the gospel and its counterfeit?

In a sentence, the gospel is the complete story of salvation. The gospel explains the role of our Creator, the nature of man, the sinless life of Jesus on behalf of man, the work of Jesus in the heavenly sanctuary as our mediator and the second coming. If you look closely at the previous sentence, you will observe God's great love expressed through the five fundamental teachings of the gospel. They are easy to remember when you begin them with the letter "S":

1. Salvation by faith

2. Sanctuary in heaven

3. State of the dead

4. Second coming of Jesus

5. Sabbath worship

The devil has distorted and ruined each of these elements as far as possible. We will briefly survey each of the counterfeit elements of the gospel within the Christian world:

Counterfeit 1

One of Satan's most powerful counterfeits is that salvation either comes by obedience to God or by intellectual assent to what is true. Satan's trickery on this subject is very subtle. He can actually deceive an evil person into thinking he is righteous! For example, Satan led the Pharisees to think they were righteous even though they were far away from the kingdom. Jesus said, **"...on the outside you appear to people as righteous but on the inside you are full of hypocrisy and wickedness."** (Matthew 23:28)

Asking a person what he believes is not enough. The Pharisees thought they were righteous. So, to see what a person actually believes, we have to do some fruit inspection. Jesus said, **"...every good tree bears good fruit, but a bad tree bears bad fruit, and a bad tree cannot bear good fruit."** (Matthew 7:17) The problem is that what people say and what people do may not be consistent. Notice two extreme examples. The first example describes a religious type we will call "workers."

A worker can say, "I'm saved by faith," while at the same time, be working his way to heaven. People having this problem are usually identified by zealous and/or rigorous obedience to the teachings or ideals of their denomination. Workers tend to see sin as acts of commission, i.e., sins or wrongful deeds acted out. Living by the rules is very important to these people. In their hearts, they have confidence that they are saved because they are obedient to the rules. They look at themselves and see very little wrong. Workers, in day to day living, regard obedience as the *primary process* through which salvation occurs even though they say, "Salvation comes by faith!"

The Jewish religion at the time of Christ typifies this great deception. The sin that blinds these people is pride. They can't see why they don't have salvation! After all, they don't see anything wrong with themselves! These people tend to criticize those breaking the rules but rarely speak about the greater sins of omission. Here is a paradox. Workers tend to see the violation of rules as great sins while disregarding the spiritual or physical needs of those around them. Jesus said to the Pharisees, **"...Woe to you Pharisees, because you give God a tenth of your mint, rue and all other kinds of garden herbs, but you neglect justice and the love of God. You should have practiced the latter without leaving the former undone. ...And you experts in the law, woe to you, because you load people down with burdens they can hardly carry, and you yourselves will not lift one finger to help them."** (Luke 11:42,46)

The coming exam will overtake these people. Workers will not be able to obey God, for civil laws will become so strict that obedience will be impossible! (Remember how Hitler threatened the Germans if they should help an enemy of the reich?) To avoid suffering and possibly death, the workers will have no option but to worship the beast! When the great religious organizations of the world merge as a result of the great destruction of the trumpets, whose rules will the workers follow?

The tragic point with this deception of Satan is that he makes obedience of greater importance than the purpose of obedience! Jesus said of the Jews, **"They worship me in vain; their teachings are but rules taught by men. You have let go of the commands of God and are holding on to the traditions of men."** (Mark 7:7,8)

On the other end of the scale, Satan has another counterfeit about salvation that is equally dangerous and perhaps more widely received in America than the worker concept. In brief, this counterfeit holds that if you believe you're saved—you're saved! In general terms, this doctrine teaches that obedience to the Ten Commandments is unnecessary, even more, an insult to God's salvation. The Christian is under grace, not under the law, and his primary duty is to love his neighbor as himself. By simply assenting to the fact that Jesus died on Calvary, one may have salvation, full and free!

We will call these people "thinkers." Thinkers tend to enjoy their religion more than workers because their religion is people-oriented. Whereas, workers are quite critical in nature, thinkers are generous and casual about behavior. The thinker's gospel has very few limitations. Righteousness that comes with intellectual assent is simply a gift from God, so take it, and join the church. The heart of the thinker's gospel is the golden rule, "Do unto your neighbor as you would have him do to you."

The thinker's gospel sounds good. This is why it is so popular in America. The thinker's gospel has transcended mainline denominations and has become the dominant theme of 20th century Protestantism. This point is proven by asking, "What theological differences exist in day to day living between Methodists, Lutherans, Baptists, Presbyterians and all others in America?"

Certain characteristics of thinkers and workers have been presented in the extreme to demonstrate the kind of people such theological processes produce. What we do reflects what we believe! Old Testament history clearly tells us that Israel vacillated between these two poles. The reason Israel was so unsteady is that they forgot that salvation comes through a love - faith relationship with God. Loving Jesus for all that He has done comes first. Having faith in Jesus means doing, going and being as He directs. The faith relationship requires prayer and study each day to know His will, and Satan offers a million diversions to prevent us from spending time in either.

Satan has cleverly counterfeited the gospel of the workers and thinkers by using *partial* truth in each case! Don't be fooled. Either doctrine is deadly. The simple truth about salvation is this: Salvation by faith means a complete surrender of the will to Jesus. It means to be, to do, and to go as Jesus directs your life. True salvation produces a life of action. Obedience comes as a result of salvation—not salvation as a result of obedience! Look closely at Hebrews 11 and you will observe that each of the great men and women in this Hall of Faith was obedient to God's commands! Paul says of Abraham, **"By faith Abraham, when God tested him, offered Isaac as a sacrifice. He who had received the promises was about to sacrifice his one and only son, even though God had said to him, 'It is through Isaac that your offspring will be reckoned.' Abraham reasoned that God could raise the dead, and figuratively speaking, he did receive Isaac back from death."** (Hebrews 11:17-19)

The old gospel favorite by James Sammis and Daniel Towner, "Trust and Obey," sums up the gospel very well:

"When we walk with the Lord

In the light of His Word,

What a glory He sheds on our way!

While we do His good will,

He abides with us still,

And with all who will trust and obey.

Trust and obey,

For there's no other way

To be happy in Jesus,

But to trust and obey."

Counterfeit 2

Knowing that Jesus, our High Priest, is conducting a very special service in heaven is crucial to understanding what is going on in heaven at this time. This wonderful truth has almost been totally obscured by Satan. He has led most Christians to ignore the Old Testament sanctuary services by causing them to believe the ceremonies were only for the Jews. For this reason, most Christians never investigate this subject. Since the rituals and ceremonies attached to the earthly sanctuary are not part of Catholic/Protestant heritage, most Christians are unsure why Paul directs us to the heavenly sanctuary in the book of Hebrews. Paul clearly says, **"The point of what we are saying is this: We do have such a high priest, who sat down at the right hand of the throne of the Majesty in heaven, and who serves in the sanctuary, the true tabernacle set up by the Lord, not by man."** (Hebrews 8:1,2) Since the sanctuary in the wilderness was a model of the real one in heaven, shouldn't we understand what the services meant? Since Jesus is our High Priest, shouldn't we understand why we need one in the heavenly sanctuary?

Satan doesn't want us to know about the sanctuary in heaven, for if we don't know about the true tabernacle in heaven, we don't need to understand the importance of 1844. If we don't know about 1844, we won't know when the "appointed time of the end" began. If we don't know when the appointed time of the end began, we won't suspect the coming time of wrath that occurs when Jesus opens the fourth seal. Neither will we suspect the rapid and climactic culmination of earth's events that occurs during the trumpets. If we don't understand the Old Testament trumpets that warned of the approaching Day of Atonement, we can't understand the purpose of Revelation's trumpets. Even worse, Revelation's story makes no sense apart from the work of Jesus in the heavenly sanctuary! Satan has led Protestantism to believe that the law of God and the law of Moses were nailed to the cross. By doing away with both, the purpose of both has been forgotten.

Counterfeit 3

The third truth that Satan has counterfeited is the truth about death. Satan has led most of Christendom to believe that when a person dies, he really doesn't die! On the surface, this counterfeit may not seem too bad. If you have ever lost a loved one or close friend, there may be some consolation in the idea that they are better off in heaven. On the other hand, if you have lost an enemy, there also may be some consolation in the idea that he is worse off than before!

But the issue of consolation is not the essence of the matter. Two elements

stand at the heart of this matter. First, Satan has caused many people to distrust God, even to the point of hatred, by leading them to believe in the doctrine of eternal torment. By misrepresenting the character of God before the human race, Satan has blinded many to the loving character of God. (Remember, he deceived one third of the angels too!) Secondly, the idea that people go to heaven (or hell) immediately after death gives credence to spiritism, psychic powers and so-called "metaphysics." Through mysterious supernatural manifestations, Satan is already deceiving a large number of people. But his best demonstrations are yet to come! He will cause apparitions of deceased people to appear on earth! These apparitions will be nothing less than demons in the form of human beings sent throughout the earth to deceive people into believing that Satan is God. John saw these apparitions and said, **"They are spirits of demons performing miraculous signs, and they go out to the kings of the whole world, to gather them for the battle on the great day of God Almighty."** (Revelation 16:14)

Again the point must be made. Satan has strategically set the stage for his final deceptions. Since most people would rather depend upon their senses than trust their knowledge of the Word of God, they will be easy prey. When these demons appear, they will be an overpowering deception. If possible, the remnant could be deceived, too! When they come, these counterfeits will appear to be just as real as your own Mom or Dad. How can you argue that the dead know nothing when the form of a dead person stands "in the flesh" before you? The Bible is clear that the dead are dead. **"For the living know that they will die, but the dead know nothing...."** (Ecclesiastes 9:5) Jesus said that when He comes, **"those in the graves will hear his voice."** (See John 5:28 and 1 Thessalonians 4:15-17.) You can anticipate that the devil will use the lying testimony of many apparitions to disprove the Word of God.

Counterfeit 4

The fourth deception of the gospel that Satan has given the Christian world is the truth about the second coming of Jesus. He has many Christians either believing that there is a "secret rapture" or that the second coming is in the distant future. Both of these counterfeit doctrines have the same effect. Most Christians are either unaware of the coming tribulation or they believe they will be spared the awful agony of the testing time that is coming upon the whole world.

The secret rapture counterfeit holds two fatal flaws. First, this doctrine eliminates the urgent need to understand Revelation and the timely preparation for the things coming upon the earth. Since many Christians believe the rapture occurs before the second coming, they are lulled into false security by thinking they have nothing to prepare for. Secondly, and even worse, is that when Satan comes, this group will likely receive him as "the Christ" because the second

coming hasn't taken place! The net effect of this deception is that when the trumpets begin, these people will be immediately overwhelmed, and in great panic they will go along with the idea of appeasing God through legislative action.

In the other camp, many Christians scoff at the suggestion that the Lord is about to return. They see no reason for all the excitement. They say, "All things continue as usual - why all the fuss?" These people are content in their spiritual poverty. They have no idea of the things coming upon the earth, and even worse, they don't want to hear about it! They like spiritual programs that feature talented singers and gifted speakers with clever ideas. They don't want to hear about the coming wrath of Jesus.

So, Satan has the Christian world convinced that they are either safe from the tribulation, due to the rapture, or that life continues as usual—no worry. Unfortunately, his deceptions are widely accepted.

Those receiving the everlasting gospel are not focused on gloom or doom. These people are focused on the greatest and most awesome event in earth's history: the revelation of Jesus at the second coming. These know that the testing time precedes the second coming, they know about the future rise of Babylon and the appearing of Satan claiming to be God. They know that their faith will be fully tested—yet they are positive about their relationship with Jesus and they have peace in their hearts, for they claim the promises of

God. They are committed to being "overcomers" because they "have ears to hear what the Spirit is saying to them." They walk by faith and they will be prepared for a mighty work when the trumpets sound.

Counterfeit 5

Satan has led most of the world to deny the importance of the seventh-day Sabbath. Friday is the day of worship for more than one billion Moslems. About fifteen million Jews recognize Saturday as God's holy day, and one and a half billion Christians (all Christian faiths combined—Catholics, Protestants, Greek Orthodox, Anglican, etc.) believe in the sacredness of Sunday. Nearly three billion people have no regard for the sacredness of any day of the week.

It should be very clear that worshiping on Saturday does not now, nor can it ever bring salvation to a person. If an illegal alien sneaks into America and keeps all the laws, he does not become an American by obeying the laws. Rather, an alien becomes an American by submitting to the immigration process of becoming an American. Part of the process involves an oath stating that he will be loyal and obedient to the laws of America! Salvation, in a similar way, comes when we submit our lives to Jesus. This means we are willing to go, to be and to do as He directs. The doing part of the process involves obedience to all Ten Commandments. Thus, the remnant are identified as

"keeping the commandments of God and having the faith of Jesus."

The change

The history of the change from Sabbath to Sunday worship by early Christians is important reading for anyone wanting to understand the everlasting gospel. Each person should look into this matter and understand from a historical perspective how it came to be. A few paragraphs follow to briefly explain how it happened.

Since Christianity was born in the cradle of Judaism, Roman rulers did not see much difference between Christians and Jews. Consequently, Romans persecuted Christians just as they did the hated Jews. Even more, early Christians were soon forced to disassociate themselves from the Jews because the Jews persecuted them too!

When Rome destroyed Jerusalem in A.D. 70, the Christian Church was dispersed. Christian theology was in its formative stages at this time and as Christians scattered all over the world, they took with them "partial knowledge" about the gospel. The Apostles wrote a number of letters over a period of 50 years to establish the Christian faith. However, it was inevitable that Christian leaders would arrive at different theological conclusions. Without the benefit of communication, Christians in Alexandria, Egypt arrived at doctrines that were different than Christians in Rome. As a result of time and distance, arguments broke out between Christians over various doctrines.

When Paul was imprisoned at Rome, he established the Christian faith there. Since Rome was the capital of the world, it was only natural that the new Christian Church in Rome should gain more power and influence with Roman leaders than other Christian churches that were geographically far away from the hub of civilization. It is also a well known historical fact that Christians in Rome soon compromised their beliefs to avoid the fierce anger of Caesar. Christians in remote areas however, remained less affected.

After 300 years, the undisputed center of Christianity was Rome. Constantine became the first Christian emperor (he saw that Christianity offered an expedient way to unite the disintegrating Roman empire), and he is distinguished historically for implementing the first Sunday laws in March, A.D. 321.

An early church writer, Socrates, tells us that Christians in Rome were "feasting" on Sunday (the weekly holiday of the Romans honoring the Sun-god) by the fourth century while the rest of the Christian world still worshiped on Saturday. Socrates, *Ecclesiastical History, Book V, Chap 22, Ante-Nicean Christian Library, Vol II,* (Boston, 1887), p. 132.

As time passed, the primacy of the head officer of the Church (the pope) became even greater. Eventually he engineered the destruction of the Heruli, Ostrogoths and Vandals. These three tribes, followers of Arius of Alexandria, believed that Christ was not eternal God but a created being.

When they were finally destroyed, the authority of the pope became universal. (Remember the three horns that were plucked up by their roots in Daniel 7?)

Sunday observance

Early Christians in Rome did not understand the importance of God's law. To gain wider acceptance and increase the number of converts among the Romans, they adapted a philosophical approach to worship that reflected Roman practices. Thus, Sunday, the "holiday," became Sunday, the "holy-day." Historically, Sunday was transmitted throughout the Christian world without any biblical support! It is important to note that neither history or Roman Catholicism offers any scriptural support for Sunday worship or sacredness. The following statement, given at the Council of Trent, appropriately places the authority for the change in the day of worship with the "Roman Church," not with the Scriptures. (The Council of Trent, Italy, was held from 1545 to 1563 to deal with outrageous charges by Protestants that the Church was disobeying the plain teachings of Scripture.) On January 18, 1562, the Archbishop of Reggio made a speech in which he openly declared that tradition stood above Scripture: "The authority of the church could therefore not be bound to the authority of the Scripture because the Church had changed Sabbath into Sunday, not by the command of Christ, but by its own authority." (*Canon and Tradition*, Dr. J.H. Holtzman, p. 263.)

In the late 19th century, Dr. Edward T. Hiscox, author of the *Baptist Manual,* said: "There was and is a command to keep holy the Sabbath Day, but that Sabbath day was not Sunday. It will be said however, and with some show of triumph, that the Sabbath was transferred from the seventh to the first day of the week, with all its duties, privileges, and sanctions.

Earnestly desiring information on the subject, which I have studied for many years, I ask, where can the record of such a transaction be found? Not in the New Testament, absolutely not. There is no scriptural evidence of the change on the Sabbath institution from the seventh to the first day of the week. I wish to say that this Sabbath question, in this aspect of it, is the gravest and most perplexing question connected with Christian institutions which at the present claims attention from Christian people; and the only reason that it is not a more disturbing element in Christian thought and in religious discussions, is because the Christian world has settled down content on the conviction that somehow a transference has taken place at the beginning of Christian history." (A paper read before a New York Ministers Conference, Nov. 13, 1893).

By denying the requirements of God's Ten Commandments, Americans have reaped a harvest of lawlessness. Yes, most people will casually agree with the validity and importance of nine of the commandments. But question the validity of the fourth commandment and the response will likely be that all Ten Commandments were nailed to the cross.

It is clear that the ceremonial laws were nailed to the cross when Jesus, the Passover Lamb, died. It is also true that civil laws which related to Israel's legal economy in ancient times are not applicable today. (However, many of the principles found in our civil laws today are the taken from the Jewish civil laws of the Old Testament.)

But, Israel received several types of laws from God:

1.   Moral (Ten Commandments)
2.   Ceremonial (pertaining to divine services)
3.   Civil (pertaining to the theocratic government)
4.   Health / Lifestyle

Satan has led Christians to erroneously combine these four groups of laws into one group and then nail them to the cross! The cunning and sophistry of Satan is unbelievable! By leading the human race to abandon the health and lifestyle laws, we see unrestricted use of injurious foods, alcohol, tobacco, marijuana, crack, heroin and drugs. Some say that the drug problem is America's greatest problem. But is it? Could our greatest problem be lawlessness?

We see homosexuality and other gross sexual practices overtaking our society. America has become polluted with every vile and imaginable sin because we have received counterfeit teachings from

Satan. We have put our faith in the doctrines of the devil!

The road to self-destruction doesn't end with the abandonment of health and lifestyle laws. By leading America to abandon the great code of moral behavior, Satan has gained control of this country. Our great printing presses roll out billions of evil magazines offering the bodies of young men and women to those having an appetite for sexual immorality. Those having an insatiable thirst for money and possessions have plenty to feed their appetite on in this form of idolatry. People interested in gossip and slander find food for their depraved souls in the supermarket checkout line — food suitable to their warped senses. Some interested in these awful pleasures have a hard time deciding what to read, for there is more available than any perverted mind can possibly absorb. The printing industry of America has been taken over by Satan and he feeds Americans with soul-destroying garbage!

How ironic! The printing press was invented for the express purpose of printing the Bible! Radio and TV development in America exceeds any other nation on earth and Satan has gained control. These great and extensive powers promote evil on every channel by the minute. We may talk about environmental pollution, but it is far behind the pollution of our hearts and minds. The very airwaves have become polluted!

Satan has almost succeeded

The devil has counterfeited every truth in the gospel! This is why the trumpets must sound and the 144,000 appear. Jesus will gather His remnant through a proclamation of the gospel. Do you want to be part of the gospel movement?

The gospel is called "eternal" or in the King James Version, "everlasting," because it has always existed! It has not changed, for God has not changed. What is changing is our understanding. We now see and understand more of God's holy word — the Bible!

Your turn

Just as surely as knowledge has dramatically increased during the past century, our knowledge of the gospel has also increased. If you believe this seminar has treated the Scriptures fairly and if you see the reasonableness of the gospel message presented here, you need to do three things:

First, completely dedicate (or re-dedicate) yourself to Jesus. This simply means that you are willing to be what He wants you to be, willing to do what He wants you to do and lastly, willing to go wherever He sends you. This is what the life of faith is all about.

Secondly, you need to read this book again. You'll pick up many things that you missed the first time through.

Lastly, find a friend who is open to this material and share this message with him.

Your active support, influence and dedication to the gospel will cause heaven's choir of billions of angels to rejoice. The angels are anxious to come and retrieve us from this planet. Jesus is anxious to deliver us. Since the only thing we can take with us to heaven is our friends, let's win as many as we can! Come, be a part of the remnant while there is still mercy!

"...The hour has come for you to wake up from your slumber, because our salvation is nearer now than when we first believed. The night is nearly over; the day is almost here...." (Romans 13:11,12)

Notes

Appendix A

Jubilee cycles explain a year for a day

The purpose and beauty of the ancient Jubilee calendar is now beginning to unfold. Its purpose has been shrouded in mystery for centuries, but now the secrets of the Jubilee calendar are becoming known. Dating back to the days of the Exodus, this time mechanism was given to Moses for some very interesting reasons.

A rest for the land

Upon entering the Promised Land, God had Joshua divide the land of Canaan into twelve "parcels." Each tribe was given a parcel according to its size, and the families within a tribe were given a tract of land. All were free to use the land as they saw fit. They could even sell the land to fellow Hebrews in other tribes, but when the Year of Jubilee arrived, the land had to revert back, at no charge, to the original tribe and family that received it from Joshua. The exception to this rule was city property. (Joshua 14, Leviticus 25:10,29)

The Year of Jubilee was celebrated at the end of each Jubilee cycle. Study the chart on the next page and notice that each day of the week represents a year. (A full sized chart showing 70 Jubilee cycles can be obtained for $2

by calling our office (513) 848-3322.) Notice that at the end of each week, the seventh year is a sabbatical year for the land. Understand that the sabbatical year *was not a sabbatical year for the people,* but for the land. (Leviticus 25:2) After seven weeks of 49 years had fully ended, the Year of Jubilee commenced. You will notice that the 50th year celebration occurs during the first year of the next cycle of 49 years (See 1388 B.C.). At first, this confuses many people. How can the 50th year of celebration also be the first year of the next cycle? Consider the mechanism: The Jews marked off 49 days (seven weeks) from the Feast of Unleavened Bread to observe Pentecost. If Passover occurred on a seventh-day Sabbath, then seven Sabbaths and one day later, the 50th day, the Day of Pentecost fully arrived. (Leviticus 23:15,16) Understand that in this case, the 50th day, the day of Pentecost, is also the first day of the week. The point here is that God's Jubilee calendar is based on recurring cycles of seven weeks. And, the 50th year of the old cycle falls at the same time as the first year of the new cycle. (For those who are thinking ahead, this is the only way that the 70 weeks of Daniel 9 can equal 490 years.)

The first two Jubilee cycles

W	Day	Yr	Jubilee Cycle 1	Jubilee Cycle 2
			The Exodus 1437 B.C.	1st 50th Yr 1388 B.C.
	Sun	1	1437 B.C.	1388 B.C.
	Mon	2	1436	
	Tue	3	1435	
	Wed	4	1434	
	Thu	5	1433	
	Fri	6	1432	
1	Sat	7	1431	1382
	Sun	8		
	Mon	9		
	Tue	10		
	Wed	11		
	Thu	12		
	Fri	13		
2	Sat	14	1424	1375
	Sun	15		
	Mon	16		
	Tue	17		
	Wed	18		
	Thu	19		
	Fri	20		
3	Sat	21	1417	1368
	Sun	22		
	Mon	23		
	Tue	24		
	Wed	25		
	Thu	26		
	Fri	27		
4	Sat	28	1410	1361

(chart continues with fifth week)

W	Day	Yr	Jubilee Cycle 1	Jubilee Cycle 2
	Sun	29		
	Mon	30		
	Tue	31		
	Wed	32		
	Thu	33		
	Fri	34		
5	Sat	35	1403	1354
	Sun	36		
	Mon	37		
	Tue	38		
	Wed	39		
	Thu	40	Canaan!	
	Fri	41		
6	Sat	42	1396	1347
	Sun	43		
	Mon	44		
	Tue	45		
	Wed	46		
	Thu	47		
	Fri	48		
7	Sat	49	1389	1340

1 Jubilee cycle = 7 weeks = 49 years

Not man's calendar

The Jubilee calendar was given to Israel for two wonderful reasons. First, God made Israel His time-keepers for mankind. They were the only people to receive the perpetual responsibility of marking the passage of time as God sees time. And, to prevent Israel from guessing at time, God synchronized His eternal calendar on two occasions. First, He told Moses *when* to start counting. (Exodus 12:2) Then, for 40 years, He constantly verified the days of the week in the minds of His people by doubling the amount of manna that fell on the sixth day and withholding manna on the seventh day of the week. (Exodus 16:26)

In addition to synchronizing His people with His calendar, God required the perpetual observance of the seventh-day Sabbath to mark the passage of the weekly cycle. This observance would distinguish His people from others. God declared that His seventh-day Sabbath would be a sign between Him and His people. (Exodus 31:17) But keeping up with the weekly cycle was only part of His larger purpose. God also required the observance of new moons to mark the passage of monthly cycles. (2 Chronicles 2:4) He required the observance of the Passover on the 15th day of the new year to mark their yearly anniversary of deliverance. He required the observance of each seventh-year sabbatical to mark seven year cycles within the Jubilee. And God required the observance of the Year of Jubilee to mark the completion of each 49 year cycle. (Leviticus 26:14-44)

Not observed now

Because Jubilee cycles aren't observed today, many people depreciate the importance of these timing cycles. When Jesus died on Calvary, the observances of feast days and ceremonies became unnecessary (Colossians 2:11-16, Galatians 4:9-11), but the time-periods they marked remain with us. As far as God is concerned, the weekly cycle, the monthly cycle, the yearly cycle, the week of years and the Jubilee cycle are still intact. (This assertion will be demonstrated later.) The point here is that when Jesus died, the ceremonial services that occurred at these specific times became unnecessary, but the cycles of time remain. In fact, the cleansing of the heavenly sanctuary is directly connected to 2,300 day/years which have their origin in the Jubilee calendar!

A starting point

A day in the Jubilee calendar represents a year. Verify this point by looking at the chart on page 328. The Jubilee calendar marks the passage of time by counting "weeks of years." That is, a week of seven days represents seven years. This may sound complicated, but remember, the Jews did not have a fixed date by which to mark their calendars like we do today. When we say 1992, what are we referring to? We are saying that there have been 1,992 years since the birth of Jesus (actually, 1,992 years is incorrect but this is beside the point). Because our calendar dates from an event that is recognized by all nations, we can keep track of the years quite easily. But suppose the Japanese did not base their calendar on the birth of Jesus, what year Honda would they be selling in the U.S.A. right now?

The weekly cycle is a template

God foreknew the problems of keeping track of time, so He created a calendar *based on the template* of the weekly cycle. Many people understand the importance of the cycle of the week, but few understand the importance of the other cycles. We'll investigate two.

The sabbatical

God declared that a sabbatical year *for the land* must occur every seventh year. (Leviticus 25:3-7) Every seventh year, the land was not to be planted or harvested. In His divine wisdom, God accomplished two important things with the seventh-year sabbatical. First, the land itself received a much needed rest. Secondly and more importantly, He wanted to test Israel's faith every seventh year. He wanted to see if they would trust Him enough to provide for their needs. Think about this, would it take considerable faith for an agricultural nation to let the land lay fallow for a whole year? So, God declared that years 7, 14, 21, 28, 35, 42 and 49 were perpetual Sabbatical years. The land was to receive its rest.

The Year of Jubilee

The 49th year was the last sabbatical of a Jubilee cycle. It was considered a high year because it was the seventh sabbatical. And the high sabbatical of the 49th year was followed by the once-per-generation Year of Jubilee. Again, the immediate purpose of the Year of Jubilee was the test of faith. God wanted His people to realize that the land they enjoyed was a gift from Him. He wanted them to know that they did not work for it, earn it, nor deserve it. Therefore, it was to be given back to its original owner every 50 years with the same cheerful spirit that He gave it to them because the land was not theirs to own. He wanted them to know that they were only stewards of it. And, if they were faithful, they could remain upon the land. If they were unfaithful to Him, He promised to throw them out. (Joshua 24:13, Leviticus 18:24-28; 25:23 and Jeremiah 2:7) He also required that they were not to plant or harvest their fields during the Year of Jubilee, for it was a holy year. (Leviticus 25:11,12)

The harmony of time

The observance of the seventh-day Sabbath kept the weekly cycle intact. The observance of new moons kept the monthly cycle intact. The observance of the Passover kept the yearly cycle intact. The observance of seventh-year sabbaticals kept the week of years intact. And, the observance of the Jubilee cycle was to keep the land in the hands of its original owner as well as mark the passage of time.

Note: In all but the first Jubilee *cycle* of 49 years, there were eight sabbatical years per Jubilee cycle. These include the Year of Jubilee (year 1) plus seven sabbaticals (years 7, 14, 21, 28, 35, 42, 49). See chart on page 328.

Warning

When God gave Israel the Jubilee calendar, He made clear their responsibility. He warned, **"But if you will not listen to me and carry out all these commands... then I will do this to you: I will bring upon you sudden terror, wasting diseases and fever that will destroy your sight and drain away your life.... Your land will be laid waste, and your cities will lie in ruins. Then the land will enjoy its sabbath years all the time that it lies desolate and you are in the country of your enemies; then the land will rest and enjoy its sabbaths. All the time that it lies desolate, the land will have the rest it did not have during the sabbaths you lived in it."** (Leviticus 26:14-35)

If we look carefully at the penalty for violating the sabbatical years we may correctly estimate their value in God's sight. *The penalty for violating the sabbatical years was severe because God wanted Israel to live by faith. He also wanted Israel to perpetuate His calendar.* Since the Jubilee calendar was initiated at the time of the Exodus (Exodus 12:2), God designed that Israel should never forget their deliverance, their

benevolent Creator and God. He required them to observe His sabbatical years. Anything God calls holy has an important lesson in it. He does not declare something holy to tempt man with disobedience.

The Bible almost silent

The silence regarding sabbatical or Jubilee celebrations in the Bible leads me to conclude that Israel didn't often measure up to God's ideal. In fact, only one Year of Jubilee is mentioned in all the Bible: Isaiah 37:30 and 2 Kings 19:29. Here we find that the 49th sabbatical year and the Year of Jubilee occurred during the 14th and 15th years of Hezekiah's reign (2 Kings 18:13, Isaiah 36:1) which could have fallen on 703/702 B.C. This small point will become important when we try to identify the year of origin for the Jubilee cycle.

God's patience = 70 units

God's patience with Israel's backsliding is beyond human understanding. For centuries He tried to get Israel to shape up and accomplish all that He had in mind. But they refused. Eventually, Israel filled up their cup of iniquity. God's patience expired when Israel violated a total of 70 sabbatical years.

When the number 70 was fully reached, Israel was expelled from Jerusalem and hauled off to Babylon by King Nebuchadnezzar. They had to remain in Babylon for 70 years because the land had gone without 70 sabbaticals of rest! Remember God's warning? **"All the time** that it lies desolate, the land will have the rest it did not have during the sabbaths you lived in it." (Leviticus 26:35) It appears that God's patience with Israel reached its limit with 70 years of sabbatical violations and He had them evicted from the land. Notice what the Bible says about their captivity, "The land enjoyed its sabbath rests; all the time of its desolation it rested, until the seventy years were completed in fulfillment of the word of the Lord spoken by Jeremiah." (2 Chronicles 36:21)

How are 70 sabbaticals counted?

How do we know that Israel was placed in captivity because they had violated 70 sabbatical years? "Now, son of man, take a clay tablet, put it in front of you and draw the city of Jerusalem on it. Then lay siege to it.... You are to bear their sin for the number of days you lie on your side. I have assigned you the same number of days as the years of their sin. So for 390 days you will bear the sin of the house of Israel. After you have finished this, lie down again, this time on your right side, and bear the sin of the house of Judah. I have assigned you 40 days, a day for each year." (Ezekiel 4:1-6)

Notice how the math works. If we add the 390 years of Israel's sin to the 40 years of Judah's sin, we obtain a sum of 430 years of sinful living. This is why Ezekiel had to lay on his right and left sides for a total of 430 days — a day for each year. In 430 years, there are eight Jubilee cycles plus a

partial cycle (the 9th) which contains 38 years. The point is that 430 years contain exactly 70 sabbaticals! (Keep in mind that there are 8 sabbaticals in a Jubilee cycle of 49 years.) Here's how the total of 70 sabbaticals is found:

Jubilee Cycle	Years	Sabbaticals
1	49	8
2	49	8
3	49	8
4	49	8
5	49	8
6	49	8
7	49	8
8	49	8
9	38	6
Total	430	70

Day/Year again

While in Babylonian captivity, God spoke to the prophet Daniel and told him that He was going to give Israel another chance. This opportunity would also have a limit of 70 units. However, instead of granting Israel 70 sabbaticals of time, God used the next larger unit within the calendar. He granted Israel 70 sevens (70 weeks of years). (Daniel 9:24) This, God hoped, would be enough time for Israel to become all that He wanted. Note the progression within the Jubilee calendar. God moved from 70 sabbaticals of patience to 70 weeks of patience. Seventy weeks in the Jubilee calendar contain 490 literal years, and 490 literal years equals 10 Jubilee cycles.

According to Daniel 9, the 70 weeks were to begin with the decree to restore and rebuild Jerusalem. In the Spring of 457 B.C., Artaxerxes, the world monarch of the Persian empire, issued a decree granting the Jews complete sovereignty as a nation. The decree was issued on or about the 1st day of the 1st month (Ezra 7:9) for Nehemiah and company left for Jerusalem on the 12th day of the 1st month. (Ezra 8:31) He carried the decree to the Jews in Jerusalem. He arrived in Jerusalem on the first day of the fifth month (late July, the month of Ab) where he read the declaration of the Jews after resting three days. (Ezra 8:36) Two things appear highly symbolic about the timing of these events. First, the decree was issued in the Spring, *right on time,* because God's calendar of weeks runs from Spring to Spring. (Exodus 12:1-3) So, the timing of the issuance of the decree fully complies with the beginning of a new week in God's calendar of weeks. Secondly, 457 B.C. is a Jubilee Year. The significance here is that God returned the land to the Jews in His Jubilee year by moving upon the heart of Artaxerxes. Are these matters of no consequence? I don't think so, especially after reading Ezra 1:1.

Note: For a careful explanation of the 70 weeks and how the appearing of Jesus Himself confirmed the synchronisms of the weeks of years, the reader is referred to chapter 9 in this book.

When A.D. 33 arrived, the 70 weeks expired. The Jews had not progressed as God desired. Israel had greatly rebelled against the Holy One of Israel Himself. So, in A.D. 70, God sent the Romans upon Jerusalem and it was completely destroyed again.

7 x 10 = 70

Have you begun to notice that God's patience may be measured in units of 70? Consider this: When Israel violated 70 sabbaticals, God had them removed from the land by Babylonian King Nebuchadnezzar so that the land might receive its rest. When Israel violated the 70 weeks, God had Jerusalem destroyed by Rome's army in A.D 70. Again, the land got its rest.

If you are a student of the Old Testament, you know that judgment day, the most important day of the sanctuary service, was the Day of Atonement. It occurred on the tenth day of the seventh month. The month and day of this service combine to form 70. It may be that seven represents the fullness of God's patience and ten represents the limit of His mercy. One thing is certain, 70 units seem to indicate a time for judgment. You may have already considered the possibility that the total existence of sin will be 7,000 years, which just happens to be 70 centuries. And, the length of life itself is often called threescore and ten which of course, is 70 years. (Psalms 90:10) Are these instances of 70 units coincidental? I'm not saying that numerology (the study of numbers) is a dependable key. I am saying that these things should cause us to be on our toes.

Kindness has a limit, too

The first use of 70 sevens is found in Genesis 4:24. But, the finest explanation is found in the New Testament. **"Then Peter came to Jesus and asked, 'Lord, how many times shall I forgive my brother when he sins against me? Up to seven times?' Jesus answered, 'I tell you not seven times, but seventy-seven times.' "** (Matthew 18:21,22) The NIV and other translations of this verse seem to say 77 times. Actually, Jesus didn't say 77 times. Rather, He turned to Peter and said, "seventy-sevens." Peter immediately understood the phrase. Just as Israel had been forgiven by God and granted seventy-sevens (490 years) of redemptive opportunity, Peter was to forgive his brother and grant him the same redemptive grace.

Prophetic time periods

It is beyond the scope of this article to examine all the prophetic time periods in the Bible. However, this point can be made: *All apocalyptic time periods occurring within the operation of Jubilee cycles are to be interpreted in Jubilee units of time. Under this system, a day represents a literal year.* This also means that prophetic time periods outside of Jubilee cycles are to be interpreted as they are given, i.e., literal units of time. This concept becomes very interesting when we consider the possibility that there may be a finite number of Jubilee cycles. That number could be 70.

Notice how the Jubilee principle works with respect to prophetic time periods. Before Jubilee cycles were given, prophetic time periods were literal. Therefore, Noah's 120 years of warning (Genesis 6:3) were 120 literal years because they happened *before* Jubilee cycles began. The 1,260 days of Daniel 7:25 and Revelation 12:6,14 are to be interpreted using Jubilee units. Therefore, they represent a 1,260 year time period. The 1,000 years of the seventh millennium will be literal years because they occur *after* the expiration of Jubilee cycles.

One other point. Some ask why the 70 years prophesied by Jeremiah were literal since they occur during Jubilee cycles. Answer: The 70 years of Babylonian captivity were payment-in-kind for violating the 70 seventh-day sabbaticals. So, Israel spent a year in captivity for each seventh-day sabbatical violation. The seventy years of captivity is a repetition and enlargement of the day/year principle that went into effect at the time of the Exodus. For example, Israel served a year for each *day* the spies were in the promised land. (Numbers 14:34) Then, God went to the next level of magnitude. Israel served 70 literal years in Babylon for violating 70 sabbatical *years*.

Consider this twice

Suppose there is a week of millenniums; that is, each day of creation stands for a period of 1,000 years. Suppose that the millennium of Revelation 20 is not a random number, but actually the seventh millennium or sabbatical millennium for earth. The idea here is that the whole earth gets its rest for 1,000 years because the wicked are dead and the saints are in heaven. Suppose that the second coming of Jesus is on or about the 6,000th year. If the reader will consider this possibility, this simple concept will clear up several problems regarding time periods in Daniel and Revelation.

A most interesting possibility develops. Assume there are 70 Jubilees of time. The 70th Year of Jubilee would be 1994. Add to this date, the 1,335 literal days of Daniel and something very interesting happens: Now, the Jubilee calendar and the millennial calendar reach to 1998 which can be reasonably shown to be the 6,000th year!

The real point here is that after the Jubilee expires, prophetic time becomes literal. This simple mechanism explains why some time periods are day/year and others are literal time.

God reckons Jubilees after A.D. 33

Two prophecies confirm the perpetuity of Jubilee cycles long after the demise of ancient Israel in A.D 70. The first prophecy is found in Daniel 7:25. Here the Bible foretells that the little horn power would persecute the saints of God for a time, times and dividing of time. This time period of 1,260 day/years began in A.D. 538 and ended in 1798. History clearly confirms the duration of this time period and even more, verifies the presence and operation of the day/year principle. But even more, the fulfillment of this prophecy confirms the continued operation of the Jubilee Calendar, for without it there is no hermeneutical reason to apply the day/year mechanism to this verse. In other words, the operation of the Jubilee calendar is clearly confirmed by historical events.

Some argue that in symbolic prophecy, a day *always* equals a year. This is not a true rule. Look at Daniel 4:16. Seven times are sentenced upon king Nebuchadnezzar who is *symbolized* as a tree in this prophecy. Furthermore, the Hebrew word *'iddan* in Daniel 4:16 is identical with Daniel 7:25 and Daniel 12:7. The word is translated as "time." I believe it refers to the geometric equivalent of one revolution of the Sun about earth much like Native-Americans use "one moon" to represent one month. And, one revolution (or circle) mathematically contains 360 degrees. Thus, a time equals one year of 360 mathematical days — not actual days. I am unaware of any ancient calendar having a 360 day solar cycle.

As far as I know, only Jehovah Witnesses consistently apply the day/year principle to Daniel 4:16 and Daniel 7:25 and Daniel 12:7. But, the reader should require some principle or method of calculation to determine when time is literal and when time is day/year. To me, the answer is quite simple. If the time period is part of apocalyptic prophecy *and* it occurs during the operation of the Jubilee calendar, the time period must be interpreted as Jubilee units, i.e., day/years.

The second prophecy that confirms the perpetuity of the Jubilee cycle long after the demise of ancient Israel is found in Daniel 8:14. Whatever question may have existed about the use of day/years within the Jubilee Calendar is eliminated by the fulfillment of this prophecy. Because this prophecy begins in 457 B.C. and reaches down to A.D. 1844. Here, two impressive points must be recognized. First, the day/year principle is clearly at work because the time (70 sevens = 490 literal years = 10 Jubilee cycles) granted to Israel is "cut off" from this larger prophecy. (Hebrew: *chathak* means to snip off from a larger piece) In other words, if the 70 sevens are reckoned in Jubilee units of weeks, then the 2,300 days of Daniel 8:14 must also be reckoned in Jubilee units of day/years because the 70 sevens are cut off from the 2,300 days. Secondly, and maybe even more importantly, this prophecy clearly points out that Jesus Himself, the One who created the prophecy, connected His ministry in the heavenly sanctuary to the timing mechanism established by Jubilee cycles. If Jesus reckons the operation of the Jubilee calendar to be important, shouldn't we?

Exodus dating

Often the first question raised by the Jubilee chart is its beginning date. Debate on the date of the Exodus from Egypt has gone on for centuries and considerable diversity of opinion exists. So, can the date of the Exodus be determined?

First, no one has proven with absolute certainty the date of the Exodus. And neither have I. Given the lack of solid evidence, most scholars will grant a small variance to whatever date they settle on. For this reason, 1437 B.C. is not an extraordinary date. But, it is a *calculated* date using well respected events whose dating has been verified outside the Bible.

Secondly, 1437 B.C. is not only historically plausible, it is the *only* date that compliments the weekly cycle of years without insurmountable difficulty. If the reader can tolerate the idea that the Jubilee cycle serve a greater purpose than marking the passage of time, the end result will be a new appreciation for the intricate workings and plans of God.

Ultimate purpose

The Jubilee calendar offers a simple solution to the problem of which prophecies are day/year and which are not. In essence, the calendar operates like this: if a prophetic time period falls within the time period of 70 Jubilees and that prophecy belongs to the family of 18 apocalyptic prophecies found in Daniel and Revelation, it must be interpreted by the day/year principle. After the expiration of the Jubilee calendar, all prophetic time periods are to be interpreted as literal time. Thus the 1,000 years of the millennium are literal years and not 1,000 years of day/years.

As said before, if we add 1,335 literal days to the end of 70 Jubilee cycles, we reach into 1998 which can be reasonably demonstrated from genealogies recorded in the Bible to be on or about the 6,000th year. As a bonus, it can be easily shown that all time periods in Daniel and Revelation will harmoniously fit together if Jubilee units are applied to those time periods that fall within the Jubilee calendar rule. Further, the literal units of time mentioned in Daniel and Revelation complement the expiration of the Jubilee calendar so that 6,000 years is reasonably demonstrated.

How 1437 B.C. is calculated

The calculation of 1437 B.C. is not complicated. Basically, the process requires assembling known dates with one uncertain time period. After placing them on a time-line, we then impose the Jubilee scheme upon them. For the sake of brevity, assume the Spring of 1437 is a possible starting date. It is a Sunday year and it is the first year in a Jubilee cycle if one accepts the dating of the 70th week to be A.D. 27 - 33.

Some argue that Jubilee cycles were not observed until after the Jews entered Canaan. I don't think this was God's plan for three reasons. First, He gave the calendar to Moses on Mt. Sinai. (Leviticus 26:46) I believe Mt. Sinai occurred about 18 months after the Exodus. Secondly, about six months after Mt. Sinai, the spies were sent into Canaan. Then, God applied the day/year principle which had just been

revealed. And, I contend that the day/year principle is only found under the operation of the Jubilee calendar. Lastly, when God began counting the 40 years of wilderness sentence, He began counting from the Exodus – not the return of the spies from Canaan. Total time in the wilderness was 40 years. This shows that God reckoned time, specifically, the operation of day/years which demonstrates the presence of the Jubilee calendar from the Exodus. But most important of all, if the Exodus does not mark the beginning of the Jubilee calendar, then the weekly cycles of years cannot be determined.

The mathematical process for calculation is as follows:

- 1 Kings 6:1 says that the temple of Solomon was begun during the 480th year after the Exodus. So, 1437 - 480 = 957 B.C.

- 457 B.C. marks the beginning of the 70 weeks. It also confirms the synchronism of the day/years within Jubilee calendar. Thus, 457 B.C. has to be a Sunday year. Total time between 957 B.C. and 457 B.C. = 500 years.

- A Jubilee year occurred during the 14th year of Hezekiah's reign. (Isaiah 36:1, 37:30) This can easily be demonstrated to occur during 702 B.C. Total time between 957 B.C. and 702 B.C. = 255 years.

- It can be shown that from Solomon (957 B.C.) to Hezekiah, (702 B.C.) 13 kings ruled in Judah over a period of 256 years inclusively if one allows for coregent reigns. According to the Bible, the total number of years that all kings ruled is about 304. However, this count includes several coregent reigns. A coregent reign is where a new king begins to rule while the old king is still ruling. This common practice insured a stable transition from one king to another.

● The seventy years of captivity in Babylon have been confirmed outside of the Bible as 605 B.C. to 536 B.C. Also, the third destruction of Jerusalem (compare 2 Kings 25:8,9 with Jeremiah 52:5; 32:1,2) during Nebuchadnezzar's 19th year has been confirmed as August, 586 B.C. from sources outside the Bible. The point here is that Israel was taken captive in a 49th year so that the land began to enjoy its Sabbath rest as a new Jubilee cycle began in 604 B.C.

● The beginning of the 70 weeks found in Daniel 9 occurs in 457 B.C. during the seventh year of the reign of Artaxerxes. This means that the 70th week of years occurred between A.D. 27 (the Sunday year) and A.D. 33 (the Sabbath year). Jesus Himself confirmed the timing of this prophecy by appearing and dying in the middle of the week, A.D. 30. (See Galatians 4:4, Daniel 9:27.) The death and ministry of Jesus confirms the synchronisms of the Jubilee calendar.

● The 70 weeks predicted in Daniel 9 are synchronous with the weeks of the existing Jubilee calendar from which they are taken. In fact, the 457 B.C. decree of Artaxerxes is the only decree of four decrees made, which occurs at the beginning a Jubilee year. Given the purpose of the Jubilee year and the condition of Israel at the time, this is particularly significant. Thus, the 70 weeks of years (490 years) are synchronous with the Jubilee cycles that were already operating at the time.

● The 1,260 day/years of persecution found in Daniel 7:25 ended in February, 1798, when Berthier captured the pope and sent him into exile as a prisoner. The time allotted for this persecution began in A.D. 538 and ended in 1798. This specific time period is also mentioned two more times in the Bible: Revelation 12:6 and 12:14. Because this time period is not connected to the 70 week prophecy of Daniel 9, and because this time period begins five centuries after the fall of Jerusalem, the historical fulfillment of this prophecy demonstrates the continued operation of the Jubilee calendar. Please note that February 1798 marks the end of a Jubilee year because the Jubilee calendar begins in March/April. 1798 was to Protestants what A.D. 34 was to Christians: a Jubilee year!

The larger scheme

Consider the years 1437, 457, 34, 1798 and 1994. All of the these are the first year of Jubilee cycles. Is it just a coincidence that each of these five dates marks the beginning of a new trusteeship of God's truth? When God called Israel out of the bondage of Egypt in 1437 B.C., He made them trustees of His everlasting gospel. They were to be a light on a hill, the salt of the earth, BUT, they failed. God then turned to Christians. In A.D. 34 the trusteeship of the everlasting gospel was transferred and God marked the transition, by converting Saul into an apostle to the Gentiles (Acts 9) and by sending Peter to the home of a Gentile (Acts 10). *These things happened in the Jubilee Year of A.D. 34.*

After while, the Christians repeated the same mistakes as their Jewish forefathers. The persecuted became the persecutor. And in February, 1798, according to divine decree (Daniel 7:25), the rule of the Catholic Church was broken when General Berthier took the pope captive. *This happened in the Jubilee year of 1798!* From this time, Protestantism has had unrestricted freedom to accomplish the task of carrying the everlasting gospel to all the world.

But, the Protestants have lost their mission and purpose. They have fallen away from the truths of the everlasting gospel just as their forefathers did and their trusteeship is about to be taken from them and given to the final generation: the remnant. This could happen in the upcoming Jubilee year of 1994!

If we add up the trusteeships in units of Jubilee cycles, we find an interesting balance. The Jews received 30 full Jubilees of opportunity. Christians received 36 full Jubilees of opportunity. Protestants, I believe, will receive four full Jubilees of opportunity and finally, the 144,000 will achieve in a mere 1,260 days what the others failed to do. Could this be a Gideon-like miracle?

The $6.40 question

When all of the data is added together, we are still left with some uncertainty because the length of coregent reign of kings cannot be firmly established.

Many scholars have painstakingly reviewed the biblical list of 40 kings in Judah and Israel ending with Zedekiah, They have also taken into account the known reign of contemporary kings in Babylon, Egypt and Assyria. They generally concur that the Exodus has to fall within the window of 1470 - 1430 B.C. So, the 1437 B.C. date easily falls within many dating schemes for the Exodus. However, only 1437 B.C. compliments the synchronous operation of the weekly cycles of seven years with important dates like 604, and 457 B.C. If we accept the presence and operation of the Jubilee calendar, we have a simple but profound explanation for why some prophecies use the day/year mechanism and others do not. This little key opens up a new world of discovery about the literal timing of end-time events.

Summary

It is impossible to prove that 1437 B.C. is the dating of the Exodus. The matter has to remain in the category of "plausible." If this point is true of things in the past, the future is even worse. No one can prove something that has not happened. Neither does God ask us to believe something without first giving us substantial evidence upon which to build our faith. Therefore, we have a wonderful opportunity to study these things and see if they are of any value. In spite of all that has been said, this point is true: 1994 will soon be here. We'll soon know if this date marks the end of God's patience with human beings and the beginning of the seven trumpets of Revelation! Be watching and waiting!.

Notes

Appendix B

Quick Reference Data

Apocalyptic Rules of Interpretation

1. Apocalyptic prophecy is defined in this volume as prophecy that predicts a chronological sequence of events. Apocalyptic prophecy has a beginning and ending point in time. Elements within the prophecy mark progression towards fulfillment or completion. Consequently, elements within apocalyptic prophecy do not occur more than once and they chronologically occur as predicted.
2. Other types of prophecies are subordinate to apocalyptic structures. A fulfillment of an element or a prophecy occurs when both the specifications and the chronological sequence are met.
3. If a prophecy contains symbolic language, the Bible must explain the meaning of the symbol with relevant scripture.

The 18 Apocalyptic Prophecies of Daniel and Revelation listed by text. For the placement of the elements within each prophecy, see apocalyptic chart on the next page.

1. Daniel 2:31-35 Image of a man
2. Daniel 7:1-11 Terrible monster
3. Daniel 8:1-12 Ram vs goat
4. Daniel 9:24-27 Israel's probation
5. Daniel 11:2-35 Israel's future
6. Daniel 11:36-12:2 King of the North
7. Rev 4:1-6:17 Seven seals
8. Rev 7:1-8:1 144,000/multitude
9. Rev 8:2-9:21 Seven trumpets
10. Rev 10:1-11:13 Two witnesses
11. Rev 11:14-11:19 Seventh trumpet
12. Rev 12:1-14:5 Christ vs Satan
13. Rev 14:6-15:4 Warning messages
14. Rev 15:5-16:21 Seven last plagues
15. Rev 18:1-8 Last call
16. Rev 19:1-20:6 Babylon / Devil
17. Rev 20:7-21:1 Final destruction
18. Rev 21:2-22:5 New Earth

(Revelation 17:1-18 - Discussion)

(Revelation 22:6-21 - Epilogue)

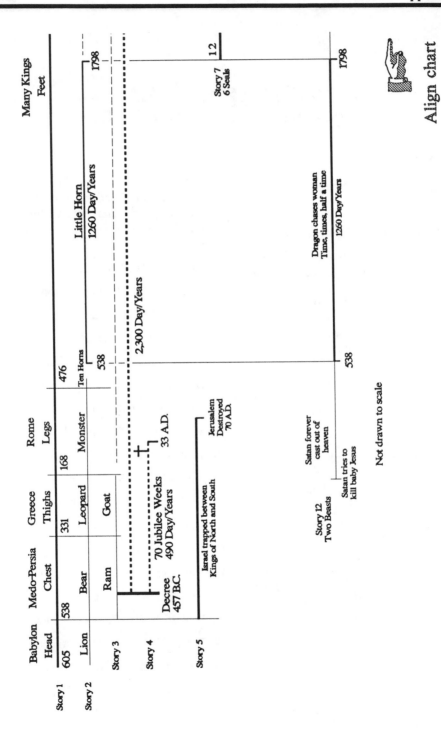

Align chart

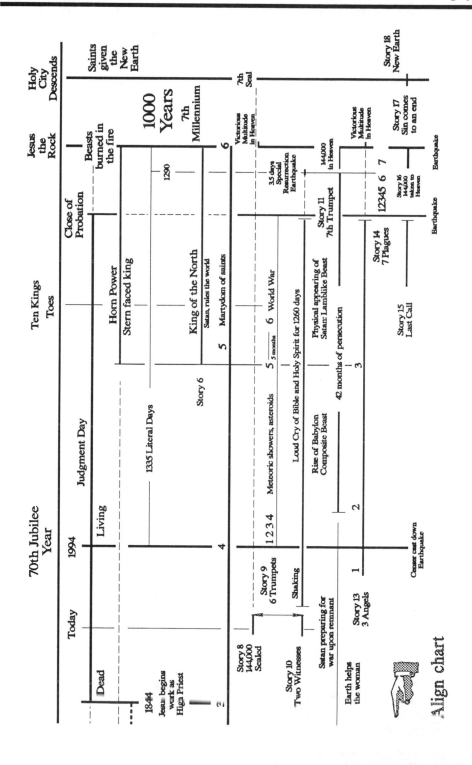

Align chart

Supplemental Bible Study Helps

Bible Study Helps - Audio/Video Tapes

Revelation Tapes The following is a list of current seminar studies on Revelation given by author Larry Wilson. Video tapes may be purchased separately or the entire set of 21 tapes may be purchased at a reduced price. Keep in mind that each tape is a building block; therefore, no presentation is complete within itself. For best results, they should be viewed or heard in the order listed below.

1. The wrath of God and the full cup principle

2. The purpose and process of Bible prophecy

3. Who is Jesus? Why did He die for man?

4. Michael and Lucifer, the origin of sin

5. The Plan of Salvation - 2 tapes

6. The wonderful prophecies of Daniel - 3 tapes

7. Judgment day is almost here - 2 tapes

8. Introduction to Revelation / Rules of Interpretation

9. The seven seals - 2 tapes

10. The seven trumpets - 2 tapes

11. The beasts of Revelation - 3 tapes

12. The man of sin and the 144,000

13. The Two Witnesses

14. The mark of the beast and God's everlasting covenant

continued on next page

Other Bible Study Helps by Larry Wilson

1.   *18 End-Time Bible Prophecies* This book is a verse by verse explanation of the 18 prophecies found in Daniel and Revelation. It is written in a style as though God spoke to Daniel and John in our day. The book offers a parallel reading with the NIV so actual Bible texts are easy to reference. Highly recommended as a companion to this volume. Approximately 275 pages.

2.   **Day Star Newsletter** Monthly issues. The newsletter usually contains one or two Bible studies on topics that relate to current issues and/or the prophetic stories found in Daniel and Revelation. Some remaining back issues are available.

3.   *Warning! Revelation is about to be fulfilled* This 175 page book describes coming events in a story-like format. It is a must for anyone interested in a quick survey of coming events. A very handy book for sharing with friends and family. For quantity pricing on this or other books, give us a call. (Spanish version also available.)

Wake Up America Seminars, Inc.
P.O. Box 273
22 North Main St.
Bellbrook, Ohio 45305
(513) 848-3322

Call between 9 am and 4 pm Eastern Time, Monday - Thursday, for prices and availability. For immediate shipment, Discover, Visa and Mastercard is accepted.